NEXT
GENERATION
MANUFACTURING

NEXT
GENERATION
MANUFACTURING

METHODS AND TECHNIQUES

JAMES A. JORDAN, JR.
FREDERICK J. MICHEL

JOHN WILEY & SONS, INC.

New York • Chichester • Weinheim • Brisbane • Singapore • Toronto

This book is printed on acid-free paper. ∞

Copyright © 2000 by NGM Knowledge Systems. All rights reserved.

Published by John Wiley & Sons, Inc.

Published simultaneously in Canada.

This publication is designed to provide accurate and authoritative information in regard to the subject matter covered. It is sold with the understanding that the publisher is not engaged in rendering professional services. If professional advice or other expert assistance is required, the services of a competent professional person should be sought.

Library of Congress Cataloging-in-Publication Data:
Jordan, James A., 1936–
   Next generation manufacturing : methods and techniques / James A. Jordan, Jr. and Frederick J. Michel.
     p. cm. — (National Association of Manufacturers series)
   Includes bibliographical references and index.
   ISBN 0-471-36006-6 (alk. paper)
     1. Manufacturing industries—Management.   2. Manufacturing industries—Economic aspects.   3. Management.   4. Production planning.   I. Michel, Frederick J.
   II. Title   III. Series.
   HD9720.5 J67 2000
   658'.023—dc21   99-053198

Printed in the United States of America.

10 9 8 7 6 5 4 3 2 1

To our wives, Joan and Lucille,
for their constant encouragement throughout our careers and
for their patience and support during the writing of this book

Preface

In the decade of the 1990s, two significant initiatives provided a baseline for defining the future of the successful manufacturing enterprise—the U.S.-based Next Generation Manufacturing (NGM) Project[1] and the international Intelligent Manufacturing Systems (IMS) program.[2] Together, the two initiatives provide a consistent, worldwide vision for global manufacturing. In this book, we discuss the vision primarily as the NGM Project portrayed it.

The NGM Project was undertaken to identify the steps manufacturing companies should undertake to become globally competitive between now and 2010. The NGM Project resulted in both a *vision* for the future of manufacturing and a *framework for action*. The actions, if undertaken by industry, government, and academe, should ensure global manufacturing competitiveness.

The NGM Project was led by U.S. industry with support from the U.S. National Science Foundation (NSF). Nearly 500 experts, most from industry, participated. The Leaders for Manufacturing (LFM) Program at MIT, Lockheed Martin Energy Systems' Oak Ridge Centers for Manufacturing Technology, and the Agility Forum provided the leadership. An Industry Steering Committee, made up of the leaders of 10 major manufacturing industry associations and professional societies, made sure that the Project was grounded in the realities faced by today's companies. They recruited volunteers from their member companies to staff the Project. About 100 people served on six working groups that focused on the important areas of a manufacturing enterprise. These working groups developed 10 white papers on the issues that will be key for companies to achieve success in the twenty-first century. The work of the Project was validated by a committee of more than 50 manufacturing executives chaired by Thomas J. Murrin, dean of the A.J. Palumbo School of Business Administration of Duquesne University and formerly president of the Energy and Advanced Technology Group of the Westinghouse Electric Corporation and subsequently Deputy Secretary of Commerce.

Executives from leading manufacturing companies defined some of the pragmatic *dilemmas* they face. Starting with this base, the NGM Project described the key competitive *drivers* shaping the future competitive environment, identified the *attributes* of a successful competitor in that environment, and characterized the capabilities, termed *imperatives,* required to meet the drivers and to thrive. See Figure P.1. The imperatives were grouped into four *operational strategies:*

1. Building a strong workforce.
2. Developing and implementing advanced knowledge processes.
3. Using advanced manufacturing systems, processes, equipment, and technology.
4. Integrating competitive strengths.

The NGM Project resulted in a set of recommendations for each of the imperatives. Many can be implemented now. Some suggest changes in management and workforce practices, some applying new standards for systems and equipment, some using simpler manufacturing processes, and some tying everything together. Other recommendations suggest cooperative efforts to change business practices, government regulations, and the establishment of an industrywide manufacturing infrastructure.

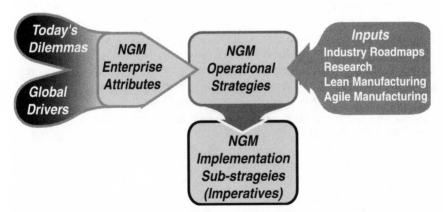

Figure P.1 Flow of the Next Generation Manufacturing (NGM) Project

Two notable movements contributed heavily to the NGM Project. Lean Manufacturing, epitomized by the Toyota Production System and described in the seminal 1990 book, *The Machine That Changed the World*.[3] It emphasizes the elimination of waste—waste of time, waste of people, waste of money—in manufacturing operations. A second major influence was Agile Manufacturing. It places emphasis on structuring an enterprise for a quick and effective response to a broad spectrum of foreseeable and unforeseen changes. The agility movement started in 1991 with the two-volume report, *21st Century Manufacturing Enterprise Strategy: An Industry-Led View*,[4] and the formation of an industry-government partnership, the Agility Forum.

U.S. industrial policy is based on a strong industry-led manufacturing sector capable of contributing to the national economy while supporting, affordably, the country's national security needs. To that end, the National Science and Technology Council (NSTC) has served as a catalyst for the private and public sector to focus on advancing manufacturing science, technology, practice, and the enterprise concept. This policy also served as a background to the NGM Project.

The manufacturing enterprise is continuing to advance and we have augmented the results of the NGM Project with some of the most recent advances. Since the end of the NGM Project, electronic commerce and its impact on manufacturing enterprise have come rapidly to an unexpected level of maturity. Recognition is given to the increasing importance of the use of e-commerce, networking, and information technology for achieving productivity improvements across the product lifecycle.

We have also extended the work of the NGM Project by developing ways to link NGM with corporate strategic goals for achieving and sustaining profitability. We have expanded the concepts of NGM by addressing management issues and financial issues not fully addressed heretofore. The idea of a Balanced Scorecard for strategic corporate objectives, developed by Robert S. Kaplan and David P. Norton,[5] has proven useful for creating a competitive structure and measuring performance of a manufacturing company.

■ THE PLAN OF THE BOOK

This book explores Next Generation Manufacturing in three ways:

1. Through the eyes and thoughts of the fictional CEO of the fictional Big Aircraft, Inc. (BAI) as the CEO prepares for a periodic strategy planning meeting with BAI's management team.

2. Through an exposition of Next Generation Manufacturing as BAI's CEO sorts through all the issues the management team must consider.

3. Through your eyes as you work through the exercises found at the ends of many of the chapters. The exercises are phrased as if you were a senior manager in a manufacturing company. Even though you may not have such a position, you should imagine yourself in such a position in your favorite company.

■ NOTES

1. NGM Project, *Next Generation Manufacturing: Framework for Action* (Bethlehem, PA: Agility Forum, 1997). The report is available for download from www.dp.doe.gov/ngm/default/htm

2. See the IMS Program's web site at www.imsorg.org for an introduction to the IMS Program.

3. James P. Womack, Daniel T. Jones, and Daniel Roos, *The Machine That Changed the World* (New York: Rawson Associates, 1990).

4. Roger N. Nagel, Rick Dove, et al., *21st Century Manufacturing Enterprise Strategy: An Industry-Led View,* Steven L. Goldman and Kenneth Preiss (Eds.) (Bethlehem, PA: Iacocca Institute, 1991).

5. Robert S. Kaplan and David P. Norton, *The Balanced Scorecard: Translating Strategy into Action* (Boston: Harvard Business School Press, 1996).

JAMES A. JORDAN, JR.
FREDERICK J. MICHEL

December 1999

Acknowledgments

The careers of the authors had a beginning that was poles apart, but both started in technical fields. Over the years, we held positions in research, design, manufacturing, support operations, marketing, and program management. During these assignments, we also gained substantial experience in other countries. We taught at universities, worked in the private sector on commercially sold products and on projects for the U.S. government. Throughout our careers, we were fortunate enough to have assignments that kept us on the cutting edge of technology, a pleasure that is not granted everyone working in the field of technology. We had the good fortune to be working for managers who gave us these opportunities, but are too numerous to mention individually. And that fortunate state took place during a time period when technology changed at a pace greater than ever.

In 1995, the National Science Foundation initiated the *Next Generation Manufacturing Project*. The objective was to develop a *framework for action* that U.S. manufacturers could use as a guide to chart a course for success in an increasingly complex and competitive global business environment. Individuals from 100 companies, industry associations, professional societies, government agencies, and academic institutions worked together to develop a broadly accepted framework for next-generation manufacturing enterprises. We want to thank Dr. Joseph Bordogna, Deputy Director of the National Science Foundation for making this project come to reality. Three organizations provided leadership to the project, the Agility Forum at Lehigh University, the Leaders for Manufacturing (LFM) program at MIT, and the Department of Energy's Technologies Enabling Agile Manufacturing (TEAM) project at Oak Ridge, Tennessee.

Because of our extensive backgrounds and broad experience in technology and management, the authors were asked to participate in the project, becoming members of the Advanced Manufacturing Systems and Operations taskforce, one of six taskforces populated by about 100 people. Our taskforce developed two significant products, the NGM Project's descriptions of Rapid Product and Process Realization (RPPR) and of Enterprise Integration (EI). These experiences provided us with the foundation for this book. The others in the taskforce taught us a great deal. We are particularly indebted to Dick Hartke formerly of NCAT, Dick Engwall of Engwall Associates, Hector Gallegos of the Leaders for Manufacturing program, Merrill Hessel formerly of NIST, Keith Jesson of Rockwell CDAG, Alec Lengyel of the Agility Forum, Gene Meieran of Intel, Steve Rickets of NCMS, Sal Scaringella of AMEF, MaryJo Scheldrup of Rockwell CDAG, Tom Shaw of Andersen Consulting, and Tom Young formerly of Sandia National Lab. The insights provided by these team members were invaluable.

One of us—Jim Jordan—worked closely with the Consortium for Advanced Manufacturing-International (CAM-I) in the early years of the Next Generation Manufacturing Systems (NGMS) project, conducted within the international Intelligent Manufacturing Systems (IMS) program, and with the Agility Forum's Agile Virtual Enterprise (AVE) Focus Group. Our colleagues in CAM-I, the IMS program, and the Agility Forum contributed much to our views. For example, the ideas on the lifecycle of the networked extended enterprise in Chapter 11 were first developed in the AVE Focus Group.

The concept of the Balanced Scorecard developed by Robert Kaplan and David Norton provided us with an important way to link the results of the NGM project with the strategic interests of corporate executives.

We are particularly indebted to our editor, Jeanne Glasser, and to the editorial staff of John Wiley & Sons for their guidance and support in leading the authors through the shoals of the publishing business, an entirely new experience. The authors also want to thank Dan Johnston for providing information on the Volvo experience at the Kalmar facility, Kang Lee of NIST for information on his work leading to the establishment of a standard for interfacing sensors and transducers, and Al Inselberg of Tel Aviv University for information on techniques that combine visualization and data mining.

One other name must be mentioned, Tom Murrin, dean of the A.J. Palumbo School of Business Administration of Duquesne University, for his support of the Next Generation Manufacturing Project and his encouragement of the authors to write this book.

J.A.J.
F.J.M.

Contents

xiii

NEXT
GENERATION
MANUFACTURING

Chapter 1

Manufacturing Excitement!

It's Sunday evening and you and your spouse are flying home after celebrating the wedding of your college roommate's daughter. It has been a delightful weekend, renewing old friendships, revisiting old haunts, enjoying a happy young couple who have a bright future, relaxing, a great break before next week.

You shift gears and get a familiar rush of energy as you think of the week ahead. You reach into your briefcase for the express mail package, delivered to your hotel this morning, from your executive assistant, Alexia. In addition to the latest version of next week's calendar, she included a few short papers that could aid your preparations for the week.

The Executive Leadership Team (ELT) of Big Aircraft Incorporated (BAI) is meeting on Thursday and Friday to set strategy for the next year. The meeting won't be easy. Big challenges threaten today's bottom line and could impact BAI's future for the next decade or more. You have to facilitate the meeting, guiding it so that by Friday afternoon, the whole committee will have agreed to a high-level action plan.

The ELT is a strong group—individuals who didn't get where they are by being shy. They have a lot of ideas about how to solve BAI's problems. Each has his or her own special responsibilities and competencies so their solutions tend to be "rifle shots." Part of your job will be to ensure that BAI's strategies and action plans address all the important issues.

BAI is an important manufacturer of four families (very large, large, medium-sized, and commuter) of commercial aircraft. The company is well recognized and respected. Since its founding 60 years ago, BAI has become a success, but there is significant, aggressive, global competition—Boeing and Airbus, but also emerging competitors from Canada, Europe, Brazil, the former Soviet Union, Japan, and China.

You want BAI to continue its success and to grow its position, something it can do only if it remains strong and profitable. Some of the questions facing the ELT are:

➤ Will BAI lose orders if it has to stretch deliveries? Or should BAI increase the size of the assembly operations? Are there enough skilled people available to staff the assembly facility if BAI expands it? Should BAI hire and train additional people?

➤ Is the supplier base capable of handling additional orders—while maintaining the quality BAI needs? Are they willing to expand? Can they find the skilled people they will need?

➤ Does BAI have a sound basis for its make/buy decisions? What about co-production—are BAI's co-producers capable of meeting schedule requirements and quality standards?

➤ Is BAI navigating the maze of cultural and language differences among its suppliers and co-producers? Is BAI being smart about currency fluctuations? Can BAI absorb the costs of supply bottlenecks, especially since many assembly operations are performed serially?

➤ Is there enough design and engineering talent available to undertake development of a new very large aircraft? Would there be partners available who would not only make capability and capacity available, but also be willing to share the risk? What about the competition: Do they have the will and the capability to compete with us?

➤ Does BAI's ELT really know what's going on? Are we getting the right information? Are our people getting the information they need? Does our information system have the required capacity and transparency? Are our systems internally compatible? Are they compatible with those of our suppliers? Have we adequately addressed lifecycle costs including an efficient service support system?

➤ Does BAI have enough capital to finance both a new development program and a ramp-up in production? What strategy should we follow in dealing with security analysts?

How are you going to keep the discussions balanced? As you think about this question, you consider tomorrow's key meetings.

First, the weekly highlights meeting with the ELT will provide a dose of reality. You'll hear about today's problems and the team's plans for solving them.

Then, the market forecasters will present their views of the market—next year and in the next decade. BAI is a global company. Although based in the United States, since 1990, 63 percent of BAI's sales have been outside the United States. The expansion of the global economy in the early and mid-1990s resulted in a considerable expansion of air travel for business and for recreation. The rate of increase outside the United States and of intercontinental flights was greater than that within North America. This led to a stronger increase in the demand for commercial aircraft than predicted by BAI's market forecasts. Orders came in rapidly and backlog grew, especially for the medium-sized aircraft that are used for intracontinental flights.

Some airports seem to be reaching saturation and regulatory authorities are seeking to reduce congestion of the airspace. For a while airlines saw an insatiable demand for additional seating capacity on intercontinental flights and there appeared to be growing interest in even larger aircraft.

Then came the so-called Asian crisis, a shock to the global economy that rippled around the world, resulting in a dip in demand, even some planes sitting in storage because the customers could not pay for them. For a few months, it looked like recession was just around the corner, but then things stabilized. You are sure this won't be the last glitch in the economy before you retire.

You speculate about what the forecasters will say. They will give detailed forecasts for the next six months based on what the marketeers think their customers are already committed to do, but as the forecasters look further out, they will use lots of qualifiers: "As long as China's economy continues to grow. . . . If there is no blowup in the Middle East. . . . If consumer confidence stays high. . . . If there are no more surprises in the credit industry. . . . If. . . . If. . . . "

What is it going to take to compete in a world like that?

Tomorrow afternoon after your lunch with your old friend, the CEO of ABC/Flightways, you are meeting with a group tasked to rethink the *product and process realization process,* with the idea of reducing the time to income while minimizing lifecycle costs. BAI essentially is a designer and assembler. The company depends to a great extent on an extensive supplier base. BAI is the integrator of the entire aircraft and therefore is responsible for its performance and for customer satisfaction. BAI actually manufactures some of the structural parts and some of the avionics. A number of subsystems and components come from suppliers who specialize in the design and manufacture of these products, and who are also suppliers to competitors.

Later in the afternoon, you are meeting with the BAI supplier council, a group of first-tier suppliers with whom you want to strengthen relationships—you realize you cannot make major improvements in product realization without having them on board.

First thing Tuesday is a meeting with BAI's senior vice presidents for human resources and knowledge management and the vice president for labor relations. They have lined up a series of presentations on what they call the knowledge processes—innovation, change, and knowledge supply. BAI has survived a competition that has seen the collapse of a half dozen competitors in the past 20 years, and the emergence of a half dozen new competitors outside the United States. You think BAI has survived because BAI has been smarter than the others, but smarts are subtle and elusive. BAI has operated through several economic cycles, with times of great demand followed by times in which the order rate was very low. In response to the increased demand, the company has sometimes hired additional people only to lay them off shortly thereafter. The past hiring-and-firing policy has affected the morale of the labor force and the reputation of the company in the community—and sometimes BAI lost some smart people it didn't want to lose. Now you have to partner with the unions to find the right combination of people, knowledge, and technology so you can sustain BAI's competitive advantages.

After lunch, you'll follow up on the implications of the proposed processes for product realization for BAI's workforce. You know knowledge and human resources are closely coupled. You also know that it is getting harder and harder to attract and keep the people BAI needs, that you are going to have to grow the workforce with the right policies and training.

In the late afternoon, you have a meeting with the Community Leadership Council. Lately the Council has focused on education. Everyone has gotten the idea that you, and the rest of industry, need educated workers. But nobody quite knows how to sort out the roles and responsibilities industry and education share in developing and supporting a productive twenty-first-century workforce.

Wednesday morning, the information systems guys, who report to the VP-Knowledge Management, are going to give you a *roadmap,* their best guess on what BAI will have to do to use technology for competitive advantage.

That afternoon, you'll meet with a consultant from the local university whose methodology for relating operational investments to corporate business measures is attractive. The ELT is going to have to sort through many attractive, but potentially costly, alternatives.

The final presentation will be a wrap-up to make sure that all the pieces fit into context. You'll then have a few hours for final prep—and you will be ready for the ELT meetings on Thursday and Friday.

With the week's calendar as backdrop, you turn to some of the readings your administrative assistant provided. The first is a survey of challenges CEOs are facing. Done by the Baldrige Award people, the survey results came out in July 1998. A quick glance lets you know that BAI is not alone. The Baldrige Foundation's 1998 survey of chief executive officers elicited the following list of challenges as the most important ones they were currently facing:

➤ Globalization.

➤ Improving knowledge management.

➤ Cost and cycle time reduction.

➤ Improving supply chains globally.

➤ Manufacturing at multiple locations in many countries.

➤ Managing the use of part-time, temporary, and contract workers.

That looks a lot like a list of the things you have been worrying about. A second list gave the next tier of concerns:

➤ Developing employee relationships based on performance.

➤ Improving human resources management.

➤ Improving the execution of strategic plans.

➤ Ongoing measurement and analysis of organizational processes.

➤ Developing a consistent global corporate culture.

➤ Outsourcing of manufacturing.

➤ Creating a learning organization.

Those looked familiar, too. They seem to be some universal signs of the times.

The next article talks about four operational strategies for creating a so-called Next Generation Manufacturing (NGM) company. This piece argues that over time all companies will need to pursue all four strategies:

1. *Integrate the Enterprise.* The NGM Company will respond quickly to market opportunities using many different people, systems, and technologies. The workforce will be organized as teams and there will be teaming in extended enterprises.

Rapidly responsive teaming, getting the right things done at the right time, will require a high level of integration of people, systems, processes, and equipment.

2. *Use Human Resources Intelligently.* People will be the essential knowledge assets in a knowledge-competitive world. Having the right people, highly motivated and able to use their skills, when and where the company needs them will be crucial.

3. *Develop, Manage, and Employ Knowledge.* The NGM Company will need a steady supply of new knowledge to maintain its advantage—and the processes to ensure that the new knowledge will be put to its best use quickly. Once knowledge is put in practice, the company will have to manage the subsequent changes. ,

4. *Employ NGM Processes, Equipment, and Technology.* Processes, equipment, and technology will become obsolete rapidly if they are not designed and selected to accommodate growth and change. While the specifics of change may be unpredictable, the need is to design, build, or acquire multiuse equipment and processes.

Hmmm. This might be a way to organize your thinking for the Management Committee meeting.

Another article in the same series talks about 10 implementation substrategies that define essential sets of actions companies should take. It's carrying the operational strategies a step forward, pointing to the actions that are important to make the operational strategies real. It looks like a good way to connect so-called "Big M" manufacturing, the work of the whole enterprise, with the "Little M" of shop floor operations.

Maybe this is a way to continue shaping the thought process. This looks like the raw material for an action plan. The problem is to weave the right matrix of actions for BAI.

What else do you need to make this into a workable strategic process?

You begin sketching. You start with the "vision thing":

➤ If you have a pretty good idea of the competition and the competitive markets, you should be able to describe how BAI should "look" to compete effectively.

➤ If you know how BAI should look, you should be able to put measurements on goals that, if you reach them, will achieve that "look."

Next is the "how to":

> ➤ You need a strategy that gets you and keeps you "looking" the way you want to. You'll use the four NGM operational strategies for this.

> ➤ Then you need to identify the actions that fit the strategy. The NGM implementation substrategies suggest a set that looks comprehensive.

Finally, you need to know you are doing the right things right:

> ➤ You need to have measurements to help decide the investments you'll make and then show that your actions are "on track."

When you have finished doodling, you have the sketch shown in Figure 1.1, a simple plan for attacking some big-time issues.

Hey! This is pretty clever. It is a simple way to look at the big picture and help us understand what we need to do. Bet someone could write a great book about NGM if they could put some meat on these bones, and still keep it readable.

■ CHALLENGES AND REWARDS FOR LEADERS OF MANUFACTURING

That is the authors' goal: a book to assist those of you who want to lead your companies successfully into an uncertain future. Some of you are in the generation of leaders setting today's directions. Others

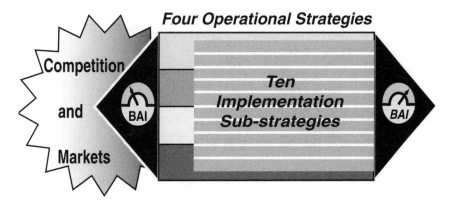

Figure 1.1 A Back-of-the-Envelope Strategic Planning Process

are in tomorrow's generation, already immersed in industry. Still others are just setting out on the path of excitement, adventure, and contribution, of risk and reward, of hard work and satisfaction, that will be the next generation of manufacturing.

You face greater challenges than any previous generation of leaders. The world is riskier now than ever before. Everything is changing explosively: the global economy, markets, competition, people, technology. Much is happening all at once. Time is the most valuable dimension, and because time is so precious, the margins for error are getting slimmer and slimmer. There is a sort of Heisenberg Uncertainty Principle at work here: The slimmer the margins for error, the bigger the challenge to leadership and ingenuity.

If you face greater challenges than your predecessors did, those of you who are successful can expect to reap rewards greater than most of them received. You can have greater worldwide impact for the good of society, the economy, and the industry. You have more freedom to listen to the entrepreneurial spirit, to innovate, and to create new products, new processes, new markets, new ways of doing business. The important contributors will receive commensurate financial rewards, but the biggest rewards will come from the fun of thriving in a tough world.

■ THE MAJOR THEMES

The tough world of manufacturing will be dominated by the five themes illustrated in Figure 1.2.

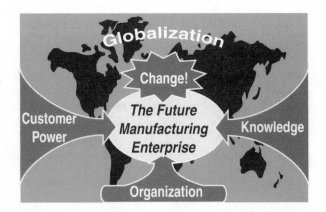

Figure 1.2 Five Themes for the Future of Manufacturing

➤ Customer Power

There have been times when manufacturers had the power to force their products on customers. No more! Customers now demand choice, or to put it more accurately, they demand what they want, not what the manufacturer chooses to sell. And now there is little difference in the standards set by markets anywhere in the world.

Everywhere in the world, customers demand high-quality products that meet their requirements and fit their pocketbooks. And they want those products when they want them—not before, not after. Competitors from every country fight for the customer's attention. It is true in every industry sector.

In the automotive sector, Henry Ford told his customers 80 years ago that they could order any color Model T they wanted—as long as it was black and had a 20 hp, four-cylinder engine—but they could have an optional electric starter. There was no viable choice if customers wanted an affordable and reliable automobile.

Today, the Thai banker who drives a red V-6 518i coupe between Bangkok and the beach at Hua Hin on the Gulf of Siam, is demanding—not just about color, but also about handling, acceleration, braking, and reliability—in her selection process, just as demanding as the American engineer who drives a gold V-8 Grand Cherokee between Silicon Valley and the beach at Pajaro Dunes on Monterey Bay.

The effects are remarkable.

Once the auto industry could design for model runs of a million or more vehicles spread over several years; now a market for 50,000 vehicles of a given model is considered to be substantial. Once it was okay for a new model to take 5 to 10 years to go into production; now GM has an 18-month target because the customers' attention spans aren't much longer.

The old, lean production paradigm was easy when the same basic product was being churned out year after year—one could continuously improve the design and the manufacturing processes to squeeze out any excess costs. The new paradigm of mass customization means that at the same time lean principles are applied to the base platform, low-cost ways of adapting the platform to new uses must be developed.

➤ Time and Change

Everything is changing—now! Today's common wisdom is right for today, but it is wrong for tomorrow.

Demand is based on what customers need and on what they want. These are often not the same, depending on the product's relative fad factor (RFF):

$$RFF = Price \times Number\ of\ weeks\ of\ customer\ interest$$

Changes in demand may be fashion statements, or they may be the results of changes in basic attitudes (say, regarding specific environmental protections), of consumer confidence levels (especially in conservative countries like Japan), of interest rates, of the emergence of conceptually competitive products, or simply changes in what customers need as lifestyles change.

The workforce changes, too. Some of the changes are simple and obvious, driven by gender and racial equality. Some are more subtle as, for example in the United States, where ethnic cultures are blended into companies by recent immigrants. The global availability of well-educated people places less educated workforces at a disadvantage. Changes in demographics (for example, longer lifespans) are reflected in the aging workforce.

The role of labor is changing, as automation and machines replace manual labor, but as the complexity of decisions and the skills and judgment required in the workforce increase.

Shareholders are more sophisticated in their demands. Shareholder interests vary between patience with the accretion of long-term value and a desire for short-term gains, with shifting emphases on fluid societal goals, with optimism over growth scenarios and pessimism when things look gloomy.

Some change is the result of natural phenomena. An earthquake in Japan or heavy snows in Europe can exacerbate regional economic woes and disrupt the supply of manufactured parts to plants throughout the world. A hurricane in Central America can wipe out developing markets.

The chaos theorists talk of the possible connection between a butterfly fluttering in the rain forests of Brazil and global climate change. While some may find this farfetched, flutters in the Brazilian economy, caused by a threat of nonpayment of debt, do reverberate throughout the global economy, influencing a myriad of individual buy/don't buy decisions.

Geopolitical changes can affect businesses. A change in government can open up a country as a market, or conversely, can severely limit market opportunities. Conflicts between countries and within countries can cause scarcities of natural resources. When geopolitical change is compounded by radical religious and cultural reform, the demand profile can change dramatically.

Once the time constant for global competition could be measured in the months, even years, it took sailing ships to cross oceans. Then in the days or weeks of steamships. Then the minutes and hours of intercontinental telephones and air flight. Ancient history as far removed from our reality as King Arthur's roundtable. Our reality is that within seconds of the birth of new knowledge or the creation of new data it is accessible anywhere in the world. The Internet and cellphones mean that new design techniques or real-time shop floor data are instantly available on Mt. Everest, in Antarctica, or in the Gobi Desert, let alone in Toronto or Milan, or Novosibirsk.

Finally, there is change in manufacturing itself. New materials. New technologies. New processes. Some are incremental, say a shift from milled metal parts to injection-molded plastic ones. Others are more dramatic, such as General Motor's shift from steel toward aluminum, or Boeing's move to digital prototypes. Some new concepts, like designer materials formulated for specific product applications, or fabrication at dimensions measured in nanometers, promise fundamental structural change for major enterprises.

All this means that the decision makers in a manufacturing enterprise are faced, every day, with changes that can affect profit and loss, perhaps even the life or death, of the enterprise. The changes come from all directions. They are major and minor. They are recognizable and subtle. They come with years' warning and they come with no warning at all.

The profound truth that lies under this pile-on scrum of changes is that nothing is stable about a manufacturing enterprise. It is always in flux. No static model can describe the enterprise. The mathematicians would say that no set of boundary conditions will remain fixed long enough for a company to settle into a stable state.

Time is an explicit variable. It instills a sense of urgency, a need for quick, crisp decisions. For the market-oriented, the significant question is: How long will the window of market opportunity be open? For the technologist, the question of interest becomes: How soon will it be that today's materials and technology are made obsolete? For the operations person, the question is: How soon before a better process is found? For the financially-oriented, the question of import is: Will we be able to recover our investment before the next change hits us?

➤ Knowledge-Based Competition

Companies used to compete on energy. Now they compete with knowledge.

The success of the industrial revolution lay in harnessing *energy*. Henry Ford succeeded because his mass production paradigm provided an efficient way to organize the energy of manual laborers. Ford supplemented manual energy with the energy from steam engines or electricity generators to drive lathes and mills, replacing the energy of craftsmen and laborers.

As the industrial revolution matured, companies used energy in more sophisticated ways. Some chose to compete with automation that reduced the manpower content to almost nothing. Others chose to use the energy of transportation to build efficient distribution systems, competing with fast container ships, MD-11 freighters, and optimized delivery vehicle scheduling.

Success in the information age will lie in effective use of knowledge.

Knowledge is data and information, but data and information that can be combined with human thought processes for useful decisions. The more refined knowledge is, the closer it is to *wisdom,* the capacity of judging soundly and dealing broadly with facts and knowledge. As used, the term implies depth of insight or ripeness of experience.

We have already seen profound changes as we make the transition from the industrial age to the information age. The electronic file transfer technologies of the 1970s and 1980s enabled the corporate restructuring and business processing re-engineering of the 1980s and 1990s. Business practices continue to change as we gain confidence with electronic commerce.

We are getting better and better at acquiring data. Our digital hardware and software for organizing and storing information are excellent. We can transport digital information from any point on earth to any other in seconds.

Yet, the transition to the mature information age is not yet complete. The lingering challenge is that of making useful knowledge out of information and data. Companies are finding, though, that they can better meet the challenges of *time* if they know what they know (and what they do not know) and then apply their knowledge effectively.

The shift to knowledge-based competition is already symbolized in the term *knowledge worker.* Originally, knowledge work was identified with so-called white-collar workers, the people who kept track of the company's business and administration. The term has spread to nearly all occupations; what used to be the blue-collar workforce now spends more time acquiring and manipulating data, turning it into knowledge, and subsequently making operational decisions, than they spend on manual activity.

➤ **Organizing for the Best Decisions**

Under the pressures of time- and knowledge-based competition, companies use *organization* to direct human intelligence to the actions needed to meet the company's objectives—now. Ultimately, the work of knowledge workers is decision making. Decision making is the processing of knowledge that leads to action.

Most decisions are interdisciplinary—they require inputs of several kinds of knowledge, the stuff we call *core competencies*. The design of an automobile, for example, requires visual artists; materials scientists; mechanical, electrical, chemical, and manufacturing engineers; and aerodynamicists, interacting among themselves and with accountants, logisticians, market forecasters, even customers.

The best decisions are made by those with the most information and expertise (core competencies) in the "decision space"—usually those closest to the object of the decision. A heavy equipment manufacturer may have a general knowledge of hydraulic pump design, but may lack the deep, most up-to-date, and detailed knowledge that a pump supplier has.

Peter Drucker, in his book *Management Challenges for the 21st Century,*[1] tells us that there is no one best way to organize a next generation company. The best organization for a company is the one that works best now and can grow into the one that works best tomorrow.

Companies are experimenting with organizational structures that focus the best competencies where they can best be used. In many companies, a *free market* model has been adopted, a model that assumes that a flux of competition and cooperation among the groups working in an enterprise will result in the most efficient use of resources in achieving a common goal.

Combining knowledge competition with time pressures has led to an international consensus that the enterprise of the future will be organized, at least in part, as teams of people each of whom embodies one or more core competencies, and so that the teams themselves possess definable core competencies.

Increasingly, companies find themselves without all the core competencies they need to complete a timely, competitive product. These companies team with others that possess the needed complementary core competencies.

Teams generally will not have time to wait for someone to tell them what to do. They will have to work autonomously, linking with other teams when they need to acquire or exchange information or to pass on results.

The work the teams do has to align with the enterprise's goals and their task objectives. They have to have a framework that both limits their autonomy and provides direction for it. This places a significant leadership, communications, and coordination burden on the company's leaders.

This "free-form" organizational approach is not intended to be one of anarchy, but requires a management philosophy and style that differs greatly from that commonly practiced in the past and still prevailing today, basically a rigid structure not too different from that of a military organization. This organization is essentially horizontal and based on the ideas of collaboration, open architecture, and free flow of information. It requires that people at all levels fully understand the minimum expected of them, accept responsibility for their job, and perform at the level and beyond that expected of them, working in an environment of trust.

➤ The Challenges of Globalization

Looming as the backdrop for customer power, knowledge, change, and organization is *globalization*. All of the top challenges found in the Baldrige Foundation survey involve globalization in one way or another.

Globalization is multifaceted. It is not just a question of competing in markets all over the world with products that appeal to different groups of people with differing needs and values. Today, it is a question of developing products with people all over the world. It is a question of manufacturing high quality products in different locations, with different cost structures, and with different cultures. It is a question of developing supply chains that, on the one hand, can service local content needs locally, but that on the other hand may be called on to provide components used in "global" products. It is a question of managing those supply chains so that they can meet ever more demanding requirements. It is a question of having the right knowledge at the right place anywhere on the globe, at the right time, accessible in a form that the people who need the knowledge can use it.

Look at the automotive industry—from the perspective of Detroit's Big Three: Ford, General Motors, and Chrysler. In the major automotive markets—the United States, Canada, Europe, and Japan—national companies have dominated. They have developed products whose regional character made them uniquely different from products made outside the region.

Ford and General Motors long ago developed a strong presence in the European countries. They developed, manufactured, and marketed specific products for Europe, or even for individual countries, just as they have done in Australia. The European activities were separate from the North American ones. Chrysler made abortive efforts at European importing and manufacturing operations or joint ventures that, with the recent exception of the Jeep SUV products, failed to capture market share or profit.

None of the Big Three formed entirely satisfactory alliances to serve Asian markets, although each developed strategic alliances, even with equity relationships, in Japan, Korea, and some other Asian countries. The European companies did better in penetrating niche markets, although the large volume markets were served by Japanese companies.

For many years, the Big Three treated the less-developed world as distinctly down-market, selling older models and models without many of the options demanded in the developed world. They often had to build for rugged road conditions and for ease of repair.

Supply chains tended to be captive within regions, although some suppliers with desirable core competencies developed a global presence.

Today, there is active consolidation in the global automotive industry. Among U.S. companies, Ford has taken the lead in developing "world cars," basic platforms for products, like the Mondero/Contour/Mystique, that can be marketed anywhere in the world. Ford has also purchased niche manufacturers, like Jaguar and Volvo, whose product lines and branding are complementary to its existing products. GM has begun experimenting with globalization of product lines.

The Japanese invaded the Big Three's home market, creating North American operations that compete fiercely on design, manufacturing, and marketing with operations that maintain tight links with the Japanese parent companies' engineering and management.

Chrysler took the radically different path of merging with Daimler-Benz and its very strong Mercedes-Benz brand, creating a company whose national (or international) flavor is not yet fixed. Through the merger, Chrysler instantaneously gained credibility in Europe and better access to worldwide markets.

As of this writing, the end is not in sight. After years of being King of the Hill, some Japanese manufacturers have fallen on hard times. There is some breakdown of the insularity that has characterized the Japanese companies. Renault has gained much control through its equity investment in Nissan and there is an expectation that other strategic alliances, equity participation, or even mergers, are coming.

What is going on in the automotive companies is mirrored in the supply chains. Suppliers are merging or forming alliances for two reasons: (1) to be able to serve their global customers better and (2) to assume greater responsibility for specific automotive subsystems.

The automotive industry example is replicated in industry after industry. Globalization starts with the world's financial institutions. Mergers in the United States are being extended to include major European partners and are beginning to include partnerships with Japanese institutions. Globalization is supported by the relentless financial flows resulting from instant communication among the world's stock exchanges.

■ INTO THE WEEK

In the next ten days, you will be grappling with the future of BAI. It will be a time of exciting decisions, choosing the right risks to take. If you get them right, BAI will be a competitive winner—and you will be rewarded. If not, . . .

This book will look over your shoulder, watching as you and your colleagues analyze the competitive environment, reaffirm BAI's strategic goals, refine operational strategies, and prioritize your action plans.

■ NOTE

1. Peter F. Drucker, *Management Challenges for the 21st Century* (New York: HarperBusiness, 1999).

Chapter 2

The New Competition

MONDAY, 8:00 AM: TODAY'S CHALLENGES AND DILEMMAS

The Executive Leadership Team's Weekly Highlights Meeting can be pretty contentious. "Highlights" is a euphemism. You want to know the good things BAI can expect in the next week, especially if you can use them to motivate your customers, employees, and stockholders, but you are more concerned about the problems—the negatives BAI will have to put right. You never want to fall into the trap of kidding yourself about problems. Your leadership team is a good one, trained to give objective assessments and to suggest action plans. They are forceful advocates for action based on facts and figures.

The problem is that you constantly have to balance so many issues at once. The list of dilemmas is a microcosm of the questions and the issues with which BAI lives.

Today, Janet, the VP-HR, will propose an education and training program that she wants to couple to incentive compensation, all with the motivation of retaining BAI's qualified employees. At the same time, Diane, the VP-Operations, will describe her staffing plan to meet her cost targets in the relatively soft times before orders pick up again. She says she must lay off some of the same employees Janet wants to educate.

Diane and Adolfo, the VP-Engineering, will present the case for a $153.5 million large-scale composites forming facility. The facility will use new, cost-saving technology to reduce the weight and increase the strength of wing structures, advantages that will give BAI a strong competitive advantage. Maria, the CFO, worries forcefully that the investment won't be depreciated before this wonder technology is made obsolete by the next one.

17

Tony, the VP-Knowledge, will report on the value of BAI's intellectual property (IP). He will argue that while it is impossible to put a dollar value on BAI's knowledge base, it is a big differentiater between BAI and your competitors. As soon as he ends his case for tight control over BAI's IP, Kuo-chin, the VP-Partnering, will present a draft knowledge-sharing agreement with AeroParts, a major supplier to you and to your competitors, that he thinks is necessary for you to gain access to the knowledge BAI needs to complete its next big projects.

Part of the reason for the knowledge-sharing agreement is to lock in a long-term relationship with AeroParts, even though yesterday's business reports said that the supplier was "in play" and might merge with another supplier. There was even a rumor that one of BAI's competitors was trying to buy AeroParts! The discussion about Flightpath International's request for a deep discount on their next order of jet freighters is eerily similar. How can you have a long-term relationship with a customer who is being romanced by competitors with better delivery positions and financing arrangements—and who might merge tomorrow with your competition's captive customer?

BAI can't do everything, of course. You know you are good at a lot of things, but you can't afford to be the world's experts at everything that goes into a complicated product. On the other hand, you can't afford not to have access to all the competencies you need, when you need them. Jose, the COO, is going to propose a strategic planning study to identify the processes that are, or should be, BAI's core competencies and to develop a plan for acquiring other competencies on an "as needed" basis.

In the background there is the continuing dilemma of simultaneously satisfying your customers, your employees, your stockholders, the governments of the countries and localities in which BAI does business, and the people in the communities where BAI operates.

Tough dilemmas. The answers from today's meeting are your team's best solutions—for today. Tomorrow will be different, and maybe the answers will be, too. What's next? What's around the corner?

BAI's dilemmas aren't unique. The NGM Report[1] summarized the results of an industry survey (see Figure 2.1) as a very similar set.

MONDAY, 9:00 AM: THE MARKET FORECAST

The marketeers didn't disappoint you. The short-term forecast was presented with the usual precision. The staff had scrubbed the regional forecasts, compensating for Bjornstad's typical over-optimism about the northern European market and for Rodriguez' doleful

Figure 2.1   Some of Today's Dilemmas

predictions about Latin America. The short-term forecasts had been correct seven out of the last ten quarters—the three bad predictions were related to the bursting of the Asian bubble, to unexpectedly aggressive financing packages being offered by the competition, and to the ripple effects of BAI's production delays.

The longer term forecasts drifted off into the mists of uncertainty. All one could say for sure was that some people were going to keep buying airplanes and that each order was going to be a battle. The last 15 minutes of the presentation was interesting, though. Some bright people (you'd usually say "guys" but half those sharp folks were women) had characterized the drivers that are shaping the competition.

■ GLOBAL DRIVERS OF THE FUTURE

Not only do companies have to deal with the dilemmas of today; they also have to prepare for a future that is a juggernaut looming down on them. The NGM project identified seven closely coupled forces that are shaping the future. These are:

1. Rapidly rising customer expectations.
2. Globalization of markets and competition.

3. Information that is available ubiquitously and globally.

4. The pace of technology change.

5. Global access to advanced technology.

6. Global skill-based competition.

7. Environmental responsibilities and resource constraints.

➤ Rapidly Rising Customer Expectations

Levi Strauss invented jeans and was the premier supplier for millions of us—it seemed they would hold that position forever. They were one of the most respected companies based in California, successful, with good relationships with the workforce, and seemingly with an unending franchise on ubiquitous blue denim pants. Yet in early 1999, they had to close many of their U.S. plants, victim of their customers' expectations for different styles, for different fabrics, for trendier brands of equal quality, and always for lower prices.

Daimler/Chrysler's 2000 Neon is still an entry-level car. But it has as standard equipment features that were optional only a decade ago, and did not exist 25 years ago. Many mid-priced cars come with service features—such as 24-hour/day roadside assistance—that had been the province of luxury cars. GM's OnStar™ technology provides access to central help facility as an option on most of its vehicles. Cadillac is developing a night vision system, demilitarized technology for seeing well beyond the reach of today's headlights. All this is transforming the car into a sophisticated information appliance, with each new feature appealing to the customers' divergent demands for drive-ability, comfort, safety, and panache.

End-users are quite intolerant of inadequate functionality, late delivery, or shoddy quality. They are an "instant gratification" generation, having grown up expecting near-perfection at an affordable price.

The successful people who sell products to end-users are aware of the need for customer satisfaction. They know that if they sell an inadequate product, they won't get a second chance with that customer, and may be tainted by rapidly spread word-of-mouth or a blunt Internet chat room discussion. They know that if they sell a poor quality product, their customers will hound them continuously. And they know that if they can't deliver the goods, someone else will.

As the end users grow more demanding, so too do the retailers and distributors who sell to them. They know that there is no pipeline, no shelf space, no mind share, for inadequate or over-priced products.

And as manufacturers respond to these higher expectations, it is inevitable that they in turn will put pressure on the supply chain. The supplier of imperfect parts that go into the product, or the supplier of poor quality post-sales maintenance of the product will quickly reflect negatively on the manufacturer.

➤ Globalization of Markets and Competition

The story of the automotive industry is repeated in industry after industry. The boombox is a global product. The rice cooker is a global product. Designer jeans are global products. Whatever you make, it's a global product, too. You may never know how it got there. You may never know where your supplier's suppliers are. Your product is everywhere, so you are, too (see Figure 2.2).

There is profitable demand for high-quality manufactured goods in nearly every country. Even in countries with high poverty rates, there is capital formation and there are growing numbers of people with middle-class desires and middle-class incomes. Furthermore, knowledge of products and their use for wealth generation in more affluent countries drives demand even in the face of punitive fiscal restraints.

The trick is to find the right way to reach into each of these regional and national markets, profitably and without blundering into cultural or legal restraints.

Figure 2.2 You May Think You Are in Illinois, but Really You Are in the Whole World

If markets have become globalized, so too have competitors. Your competitor for the electronic instrumentation market in Bangalore may be Hewlett-Packard's spin-off, Agilent Technologies, or a little company from Boston's Route 128, or an indigenous division of Tata Industries, or a start-up from Taiwan or Israel. Tomorrow, it may be a company from Bandung or Riga. You will never have a market anywhere in the world sewn up for long before a competitor tries to eat your lunch.

Yes, there are profits to be made all over the world. But when you compete all over the world, you also take on risks. The global competition is sure to be buffeted by unforeseen shocks in the global economy. Globalization, in the large, is proceeding inexorably. On a country-by-country basis, however, local economies suffer normal cycles. They suffer from nationalist egos, bureaucratic mismanagement, currency imbalances, and natural disasters. Minute by minute, day by day, though, it is a dance in which there are two steps backward for every three steps forward.

➤ Information That Is Available Ubiquitously and Globally

Information—about ideas, technologies, and business ventures—is available ubiquitously and globally. Internet access is eliminating artificial restrictions on the flow of information. The companies that can convert this sea of information into useful knowledge faster than their competitors will gain competitive advantage.

The Internet was born of an open culture, intended to facilitate the sharing of knowledge. That was the motivation of the pioneers, led by Doug Engelbart, who in the 1960s and 1970s developed the technologies for today's PC windows systems and for surfing the World Wide Web. The vision of communities that flourish through shared knowledge remains a motivator for much of the best development of Internet technology.

That vision of a community thriving by sharing knowledge shows up in the many *listserves* and *chat rooms* where people with a common interest exchange information. A lot of it is hobbyist information, but much of it is professional. Bioengineers discuss the best way to design computer interfaces for the disabled. Consultants trade specialist knowledge of contracts and intellectual property. An earnest engineer in Pakistan asks a question. Within a few hours he—and everyone else on the listserve—gets 10 or 20 answers that in combination give him a better solution than any you could have developed alone in days.

For an additional modest investment, you can gain expert knowledge on nearly any subject imaginable through subscription repositories. Trade and professional journals, handbooks, and other repositories of knowledge are easily accessible from any PC attached to the Internet. With the ubiquitous availability of cellular and satellite telephony, there are very few places on earth where someone with a laptop cannot reach into these sources.

To be sure, there is much information that is proprietary and kept more or less in confidence. But as anyone who surfs the Internet knows, there are incredible amounts of specialized knowledge available to anyone with patience and persistence. Knowledge can be found, if you are clever enough, with a simple search engine. If you are really clever, you can build an intelligent agent capable of searching public sites all over the world for specific information. Basic research results are widely circulated.

And for the really specialized knowledge, a well-crafted search will identify the company with the best process or the best technology or the best measurement system, so that you can deal directly with the best source for the knowledge you need. You may have to pay for it, but you gain advantage just in knowing how and where to get what you need without wasting large amounts of time searching for it.

There's no need for trial-and-error in isolation, for mastering baby steps before moving incrementally to advanced production techniques. You can learn—your upstart competitors in Uzbekistan can learn—from the big boys almost overnight and then start improving on their processes. Just as the Japanese did after World War II, but with time compressed from years to weeks.

➤ **The Pace of Technology Change**

Transistors replaced tubes in computers. Integrated circuits replaced discrete transistors. Microprocessors replaced multichip processors. Each time the cost/performance curves changed dramatically. Surface mount technology reduced costs. Linewidths etched on semiconductors go from two microns to one, from one to a half micron, from a half-micron to 0.18 micron, and each time there is a ripple effect in cost/performance ratios. There is no let-up in the pace of technology change. New technologies make it possible to build all the electronic circuitry needed for a powerful PC on a single chip. These new technologies are coming to maturity and supplanting old ones on an ever-reduced cycle. Companies that build and companies that use computers must adapt to this continuous torrent of technology change.

Changes in technology are most evident in computing and communications. The impact of some new technologies is incredibly swift, witness the proliferation of cell phones in Southeast Asia that is overcoming the difficulties of inadequate wire-based phones.

The changes in other industry sectors may not seem to come quite so fast, yet the level of innovation in the automotive industry, in the pharmaceutical industry, and in many other industries is higher than it has ever been.

For the manufacturing enterprise, the issue is not whether to adopt a new technology, the issue is when to adopt it or whether to skip over it by adopting its successor technology.

The pace of change must be managed. IBM talks about technology lifetimes in terms of "Webmonths," three chronological months. We are all familiar with PC "upgrade paralysis"—should I replace my PC now or wait a Webmonth for a PC which includes, at no additional cost to me, the next technology upgrades? Companies may not have to deal with technology advances in Webmonths, but the issues are similar: When should the company make a multimillion dollar advanced technology investment, and when should it commit to the generation of technology beyond?

➤ Global Access to Advanced Technology

To repeat: Everyone, globally, has access to advanced technology. The Internet and other improved communications technologies have made that possible.

This is a time when anyone with a passport can go from their workstation to any of the three largest cities in more than 150 countries in 36 hours. Upon reaching those cities, there will be people who went to the same university system; who worked in the same company, or a respected competitor; who will be a peer as a world citizen. Loose networks of entrepreneurs span the world; advanced technology flows across those networks.

Some of the new competition is as technologically advanced as the traditional competitors. Taiwan has developed new cities, cities built around R&D resources to mimic Silicon Valley and Route 128. Many of the technology leaders in these new cities timeshare, spending as much time in Austin or Santa Clara or Framingham as they do in Taiwan.

Technologically advanced competitors can spring up anywhere— even in traditionally poorly developed countries.

➤ Global Skill-Based Competition

Geopolitical and geoeconomic forces are flooding the world with skilled people at a time when high-value skills need not be co-located in the enterprise. All countries are seeking to upgrade the skills of their citizens, so there is more intense competition at all skill levels. For example, in 1980 the government of Singapore initiated a training and education program to increase by tenfold the numbers of people who could work in the information technology industries, a goal that they achieved within a decade. Singapore has continued to build on this base as it has moved away from low-value assembly jobs to higher value software and systems integration work.

In other countries, literate and numerate populations are finding ways to compete in the global skill markets. This is especially true as more of the value of manufactured goods lies in the software contained in the products and in the software that shapes and controls the manufacturing processes. India is a country of nearly one billion people, many of whom are well-educated, underutilized, and ambitious to better their conditions. India is using this strongly motivated talent pool to build a strong software export industry. It is no surprise that one of Hewlett-Packard's top software development groups, as evaluated by the Software Engineering Institute, is in India.

The opening of China to free markets since the accession of Deng Xiaoping has introduced even more educated workers onto the global labor market. Other countries, like Sri Lanka and the Philippines, are trying to mobilize educated populations. Still other countries, such as Myramar and Cuba, with higher literacy rates than the United States, have populations who will become significant in their regions when artificial, government-imposed, constraints are relaxed.

The breakdown of the Soviet bloc led to a free market for large numbers of highly skilled people. Other areas of the world have well-educated, but underutilized, populations. The new reality is that these people can and do compete in the world market. Companies like Asea Brown Boveri (ABB) expanded their operations in the mid-1990s primarily by opening facilities in Eastern Europe and Asia. Others from the former Soviet Union have emigrated to Europe and North America, competing for jobs with their technical skills.

➤ Environmental Responsibilities and Resource Constraints

As demand builds and more and more countries industrialize, environmental responsibilities and resource constraints will be increasingly important factors.

There is a continual tension among competing needs—the need to improve the living conditions of the world's less affluent people, the need to sustain the living conditions of the rest of us, and the need to maintain or improve the natural environment for the benefit of all. The result is a focus now on sustainable development, the development of a manufacturing industry that brings benefits to the greatest number of people while having a neutral, or even a positive, impact on the environment.

The intelligent use of energy reduces energy costs and improves profits. The intelligent re-use of water reduces water costs and improves profits. Co-location of facilities that use each other's wastes as raw materials reduces transportation costs and improves profits.

Other forces, usually imposed by government, push manufacturing companies to reduce adverse environmental effects.

■ EXERCISE

What is driving your company's future?

➤ Think about the major problems your company has had that have been caused by people and events outside your company.

➤ How would you characterize them?

➤ Compare your characterization with that of this chapter.

■ NOTE

1. NGM Project, *Next Generation Manufacturing: Framework for Action,* vol. 1 (Bethlehem, PA: Agility Forum, 1997). This four-volume report served as the most important source document for this book. Throughout the book, we refer to it as the *NGM Report.*

Chapter 3

Meeting Balanced Corporate Goals

MONDAY, 10:00 AM: BUILDING A VISION

After the marketeers left, your executive assistant, Alexia, came in to review preparations for Thursday's Strategy Retreat. You had asked her to put together some charts that could be used to frame the discussion. It is so easy to think of strategy strictly in financial terms. You can't overlook the centrality of making a profit, but you knew that BAI would have to act from a position of balance if it was going to be responsive to sudden changes in markets, technologies, and competitors. The successful manufacturing company will embrace corporate strategies that are multi-dimensional so that the company can sustain its balance.

Alexia's draft chart to summarize the balance issue is shown in Figure 3.1. She got a lot on the chart while trying to push BAI toward an improved, sustained performance. She had tried to include:

➤ The baseline health of the company—today's returns and today's operations must be sustained and grown into the future.

➤ That will require satisfying the market, building and retaining a customer base for the company's core competencies, recognizing that market requirements are dynamic and the core competencies needed to meet them will change.

➤ Operations that are lean enough to be profitable and agile enough to respond to change.

➤ To do this, BAI will need skillful and knowledgeable employees, working in a culture that will promote continued success as

Figure 3.1   BAI's Strategic Balance

knowledge, the global competition, and technology become increasingly complex and important.

➤ BAI's future health demands having the right people, processes, technologies, and a culture that can respond to changes. The changes will come from known trends and unpredicted events.

➤ The outcome is a balance, satisfying the interests of all stakeholders, including shareholders, customers, employees, suppliers, communities, and even the nations in which the company operates.

■ GOALS AND STRATEGIES FOR NEXT GENERATION MANUFACTURING

➤ Strategic Goals

Robert Kaplan and David Norton, in their book, *The Balanced Scorecard*[1] provide a convenient way to think about balanced strategic goals. They write about "perspectives" (see Figure 3.2) and use them to focus management attention on four kinds of goals for the business:

➤ *The customary financial goals that every company seeks to achieve.* The twenty-first-century company will be a restless entity, confronting and perhaps even forcing continual change. Without a stable customer or technology base, it will often take

Figure 3.2 Six Perspectives for Strategic Goals

on the characteristics of start-up and growth companies, making investments in the face of market and technology uncertainties. Increasingly, it will operate with a preponderance of noncapital assets, such as knowledge assets. Only rarely will the company enjoy a steady revenue stream from a "cash cow" without continually refreshing the base product family to meet evolving needs.

However, this same company will also need to show sustained profitability and shareholder value. Internet-based companies are showing great verve and flexibility, losing money as only flashy start-ups can, while building for the future. The future must come, however. At some point, there must be profits that can sustain further growth and provide shareholders with a real return on their investment. The survivors in the Internet world will be the companies with solid business plans that will yield profits before the next wave of change makes them as anachronistic as the early twentieth-century machine shops that built custom-made automobiles.

➤ *Goals related to the way customers see the company.* The NGM company cannot exist without customers. Its customers' current and future needs for and acceptance of the company's products and services will drive the company. Customers have many choices offered to them. The NGM company must be so attractive to its customers that it is the provider of choice.

The goals must relate both to the business results from any customer relationship—can the company make a profit, explicitly or implicitly, by serving a customer's needs—as well as to relationships that, from the customers point of view, are desirable. A company may choose not to serve certain customers or markets, but it should not be rejected by a customer or forced out of a market through customer dissatisfaction. Indeed, a decision not to serve a market should include a respectful treatment of the customers the company chooses not to serve. Who knows when the company will want to re-enter the market?

➤ *Goals relating to the efficiency and effectiveness of the company's operations.* The lessons of lean and agile manufacturing continue to be a primer for the NGM company. The NGM company's operations will optimize the time, quality, and cost factors. Process re-engineering should lead to less waste, but also to the ability to respond quickly to changes in markets and technology. Every operation will be expected to contribute directly to realization of the company's strategic goals and profitability.

➤ *Goals relating to the ways in which the company and its people prepare for the future through learning and growth.* Much is written about the "learning company," a company in which people continually learn. They learn to do today's job better. They learn to do tomorrow's job. They learn so that they will not lose value as the company changes and so that their careers will not stall.

Companies learn and grow, too. Johnson Controls and Lear have grown from being suppliers of seats to Detroit's Big Three automotive companies to designers and integrators of "cockpit subsystems," of complete automobile interiors. In the process, they have become expert not only in the manufacture of car seats, but in the ergonomics and design of seats, instruments, and other interior features.

All these are important goals. Jordan and Michel[2] have looked specifically at goals for a next generation manufacturing enterprise and say that to respond to the new competition, a company needs to have goals in two additional perspectives, called the *Globalization Perspective* and the *Innovation Perspective*. (Kaplan and Norton consider *Innovation* within their *Growth and Learning Perspective*.)

➤ *Goals that relate to the company's capabilities to compete and operate globally.* Globalization includes three important components: the globalization of markets, the globalization of products, and the globalization of production. Companies will need the ability to compete, if they choose, in any market anywhere. They will need to develop their products so that, ideally, they could be sold anywhere or, more realistically, so that they can be customized for specific markets with minimal incremental cost. For a host of market and economic reasons, companies, will need the ability to manage manufacturing operations anywhere.

➤ *Goals that relate to the company's abilities to develop and profitably implement new technologies, products, processes, product uses, and business and organization relationships.* The NGM company will live by the timely and competitive use of the best available knowledge, employed in new and creative ways. It will need to develop a culture, incentives, and rewards for innovation. The Innovation Perspective recognizes this all-important quality explicitly.

Given strategic goals in each of these perspectives, the company can define metrics. Measurements (see Figure 3.2) will show whether the company is making progress toward the goals and if the measurements in any set of goals lag behind, the company has warning that it is going out of balance.

Once the metrics are chosen, they can be used to guide investments in operational strategies and implementation sub-strategies. The objective is prioritizing the many possible actions to achieve a balanced improvement in the company's measurements. A specific prioritization strategy might, for instance, give precedence to actions that provide improvement in several perspectives. We will return to the metrics appropriate to strategic goals in Chapter 18.

➤ Attributes of the NGM Company

What should a company look like if it is to achieve a balanced set of corporate goals? One pervasive quality is responsiveness to change happening at an ever-increasing pace in all dimensions of manufacturing. Systems that have been thought of as being static, fixed in time for several years, will have to be more dynamic, responding to significant changes in a matter of weeks or months, even days in some industries. Time becomes an explicit variable in the business calculus.

According to the NGM Project, the attributes that a successful manufacturing company will need are:

➤ Customer responsiveness.

➤ Physical plant and equipment responsiveness.

➤ Human resource responsiveness.

➤ Global market responsiveness.

➤ Teaming as a core competency.

➤ Responsive practices and cultures.

Customer Responsiveness

The new products and services that succeed are the ones that meet a specific need when the customer has the need. The challenge is to know what the customer needs, or better yet, will need and then to provide what is needed. The company must develop such close relationships with customers that the customers perceive the company as a partner, a partner so interested in the customers' well being as to anticipate needs.

If Chrysler learns that customers want a four-door mini-van and provides them, while GM offers only two-door mini-vans, the result is predictable—Chrysler wins. If the customer wants a luxury SUV, can a manufacturer afford to wait for two years after Lincoln, Mercedes Benz, and Lexus have hustled to fill the niche? Can a computer workstation vendor afford to wait for months to offer the Linux operating system when it is already being offered by competitors like IBM and Hewlett-Packard? If Wal-Mart wants lavender dishtowels as part of a Spring promotion, can a vendor afford not to have the capability to provide whatever color is needed?

Customers live, breathe, are contrary and change their minds. Just when you think cassette tapes offer a stable market, CDs come along. Then DVD. Then ???? Sony needed to know its customers well enough to know that the CD Walkman was a necessary extension to its product line if it was going to maintain its Walkman brand franchise.

Customer psychology is a peculiar mix of herd instinct and individuality, of fadism and the desire for solid, affordable functionality. Fadism means that today's discretionary purchase sits on tomorrow's shelves and that the manufacturer who cannot participate in the fad will rapidly lose market share. Solid, affordable functionality means one thing when gas costs $1.01/gallon. It means something different when supplies are depleted and the cost climbs to $2.01/gallon.

Companies will succeed if they listen to—and hear—what the customer is saying. Companies will succeed if they watch trends, if they are aware of environmental, economic, and demographic changes, and if they use this knowledge to anticipate customer needs. The devaluation of the Brazilian real may mean your customer cannot export to hot, wet Brazil as many pumps that include your parts, but you may see a market for your customer's pumps in Saudi Arabia if you modify your parts for a hot, dry climate.

Physical Plant and Equipment Responsiveness

If you are going to respond to customer needs, and if those needs change rapidly and take on many variations, you are moving toward "quantity-of-one" manufacturing, or at least to the mid-ground of mass customization.

If you are going to manufacture a new product line, you know that you will enlarge the basic product for some customers, you'll shrink it for others. Some customers will want it in blue, others in green. Some will want it two-tone. You can be sure that as customers use the product for its intended purpose, they will want new, improved models with predictable features. A few will want a stripped down model with fewer features. And the adventuresome will find a use that you never thought of and will ask you to add wildly unpredictable features.

This is not a new phenomenon. Henry Ford knew about it. He added various body types to his Model T line, but eventually lost market share because he didn't have the flexibility to paint those bodies any color but black. Henry had years of glory because no one else could compete with him on cost and reliability, the two essential factors in the industry for two decades.

In today's world, Henry wouldn't last more than three months. Suppose people wanted many different colors. First, three guys in a garage would hire a paint shop to repaint Ford's products any of 50 different colors and then sell them online at a premium. Then they would contract with another supplier for unpainted vehicles at a discount, take online orders for cars of any color that could be mixed, have the paint shop paint them to order, and gain more profit. Then maybe they would buy unbranded and unpainted cars from several suppliers, giving them both a paint job and a proprietary brand, and so forth, and so forth . . .

To return to the point: If you are going to respond to wide varieties of customer need, you are going to have to have a chameleon-like factory, one that can shift from one product to another without added overhead. That means the factory will have to have reconfigurable, scalable, cost-effective manufacturing processes and equipment that adapt rapidly to specific production needs.

Rather than static production lines with unchanging tooling that can churn out millions of widgets, you need manufacturing cells where many different products can be produced using tooling that can be programmed, where the set up for the next production run can be done automatically as the current run is completed. You need factories with many cells that can be easily switched from one product family to another, and where the logistics are just as flexible, delivering parts and subassemblies where needed, as needed, and when needed.

Above all, you need factories where there is no waste of time in changing from one product to another or in expanding or contracting the capacity for a given product.

Human Resource Responsiveness

The company will need its entire workforce to be highly capable and motivated knowledge workers who can work in a flexible work environment, with substantial independent decision making.

The company will live by its wits. It will be confronted by change all the time. Each change will be a problem-solving exercise—sometimes in corporate headquarters, sometimes in the operations offices, often in the factory and on the shop floor. Yes, automation will take care of much of the simple, repetitive problem solving that can be written down in a well-defined algorithm. And using artificial intelligence may solve some of the less well-defined problems. But people will make the really important decisions in an NGM company.

Whatever they are doing, the people will have to make decisions under conditions of continual change. The pump part manufacturer's expert on the design of seals for high temperature and high humidity, may have to make quick decisions if the company diverts its next run of pumps to Saudi Arabia. The janitor can't have a set pattern for sweeping the factory floor if cells are reconfigured daily.

Everyone in the company will have to respond quickly and effectively. Given the reluctance to change that is characteristic of so many of us, the company will have to prepare itself and its people to be responsive, to welcome change—or at least not fight it—to quickly evaluate the new situations, and then to do whatever is necessary to meet the need.

Global Market Responsiveness

The NGM company's strategy will be to anticipate and respond to the continuously changing markets of the world, evaluating the possible markets for existing products and the new products or modifications to the existing one that might open new opportunities.

The NGM company's strategy will also be to conduct operations anywhere in the world where the business proposition supports the operation. The operation may involve purchasing supplies in Chile or Viet Nam. It may involve joint venturing in Hong Kong or the Czech Republic. It may involve setting up wholly owned facilities in Brisbane or Sao Paolo. The company will respond to the developments of new technologies in Zurich, to the developments of new products in Riga, to the availability of skills in Haifa, to any of a number of constantly shifting global variables.

Teaming as a Core Competency

There's no help for it. Teaming will be even more pervasive in manufacturing. Products will be produced by teams of organizations. Jobs will get done by teams of people.

Few companies will be able to do everything well. Vertical integration of the value chain will carry too high an overhead and impose too difficult a management burden, to be fully responsive. The company will routinely team within and outside the company to acquire and focus needed knowledge and capabilities to develop, deliver, and support their products and services.

So companies will team. Teams may be called *strategic alliances, managed supply chains,* or *even virtual enterprises.*

Ford's River Rouge plant was the ultimate in vertical integration. It embodied a business model that was very effective in its day, and Ford was by far the most successful automobile company. Today's most profitable automotive companies are the ones that outsource, that use other companies' selective expertise and more competitively priced parts rather than make the huge investment to develop the complete spectrum of expertise its products need.

Companies need to know how to team, whether they are assembling the final product, integrating the expertise of others, or whether they are supplying their expertise to the final assembler.

The need to respond quickly and the need to apply the very best knowledge to solve manufacturing problems converge on the need to combine knowledge and skills quickly and fluidly. That translates into teams of people, the ones with the best knowledge, doing problem solving and making decisions close to where actions must be taken.

Teaming is a learned skill. We learn how to do sports teaming when we play football or basketball. We learn how to team for combat if we are in an infantry squad. Teaming for manufacturing is a learned skill, too, and the NGM company will be populated by people who know how to team for manufacturing.

Responsive Practices and Cultures

A company may have the best people and the best equipment, it may have a presence throughout the world, and it may know its customers well. But the company will lose if it has a rigid culture, fixed in its understandings of today's markets, that dictates the way people are organized and work today and uses business practices rooted in the past. Tomorrow's successful company will have its roots in the values that yielded success in the past, reinterpreted for the future.

The history of business is littered with the dead bodies of once successful companies, companies that failed to understand that they needed to change.

For example, the core values of IBM were defined by Thomas J. Watson as:

➤ Respect for the individual.

➤ Service to the customer.

➤ Excellence in all undertakings.

These values are as valid today as they were 60 years ago, but IBM went through a painful time when the culture that it built to express those values failed. It failed because the culture was too rigid and did not respond to change in the marketplace, change in technology, and change in people. The culture had to be reinterpreted for the 1990s. Fortunately for IBM, the reinterpretation has been successful.

The challenge for companies like IBM is to reinterpret their core values continually in the light of change, avoiding the massive discontinuities that can destroy a company.

It is not just the Fortune 100 companies that must avoid rigidity. The culture of the Silicon Valley start-up, with an entrepreneurial vision and driven by technological excitement, cannot survive without change as its products, competitors, and customers mature.

The NGM company will nurture a fluid culture, seeking the right response to the latest changes, girded by underlying values, but not enslaved to an outdated vision of their application.

■ THE ROADMAP: FOUR OPERATIONAL STRATEGIES

The NGM approach says that four operational strategies (see Figure 3.3) are basic for the successful NGM company. Three relate to building important components of the company—the people, the smarts,

Figure 3.3 Linking Corporate Goals and Operational Strategies

and the processes and equipment for product realization. Underlying these is a strategy for integration. Integration is the second pervasive quality of an NGM company. Integration is what will allow the fruits of the other strategies to be spread over geography and time zones, working together efficiently and effectively. While companies may need to emphasize one or the other of these strategies, over time all companies will need to pursue all of them.

Having the Right People . . . Doing the Right Things

The first strategy is all about *people*. The manufacturing enterprise cannot function without people. "Lights out" factories are a wonderful dream. But the reality is that for the next generation at least, people will design them, build them, and run them. Sure, there may be fewer people on the shop floor. There may be more automation. A lot of the routine steps between design and production may be computerized. But there has to be a balance—until the blue-sky folks make perfect automated factories, let alone perfect automated enterprises.

The model of the "lights out" factory might have made sense for very high volume mass production. Today, there are too many decisions that have to be made, decisions with a level of complexity that just can't be programmed.

It's not just a question of decision making in the factory. Decisions anywhere in the enterprise can affect operations almost anywhere else. A decision taken deep in the supply chain may ripple through factory operations, maintenance planning, reliability and life cycle cost analysis, and so forth.

The decisions may be very practical—how to keep a manufacturing cell running at full capacity when a machine shows signs of failure or there's a glitch in the feedstock for one type of product. Or the decisions may be more far-reaching—making the compromises between initial cost and recyclability, between manufacturability and maintainability.

The point is that for a long time—maybe forever—people will be your company's essential knowledge assets in a knowledge-competitive world. So we cannot think of people as a commodity. We have to think of them as suppliers of the individual pieces that fit into a jigsaw puzzle of knowledge. We'll get the picture right if we have the right individuals in the right place at the right time, having the right-shaped skills, and interlocked with the right other people.

Knowing What You Need . . . Knowing What You Need to Know

The NGM company is going to compete by having more *knowledge*—and using it better—than the next company: knowledge of the market and the end user, knowledge of business processes and alternatives, knowledge about materials, design knowledge, manufacturing knowledge, knowledge, knowledge, knowledge. The value of people lies in their ability to use knowledge to make decisions. If the people don't have the right knowledge, the decisions they make are going to be faulty.

Knowledge is more than data, more than information. It's the stuff that people use when they are in the process of solving problems, the coupling between a database, a problem begging for a solution, and a committed act.

Knowledge is generated every day in your company and every other manufacturing company—and stored away in people's brains. Many companies learned that the hard way when they restructured and found that a lot of knowledge walked out in the heads of the people who took early retirement. They had generated that knowledge in the years they worked for their companies, but the knowledge was never written down or passed on in a way that someone else could use it. And some companies paid a lot of consulting fees to get the knowledge back.

We have to think about knowledge as if it were a tangible asset. The NGM Project speaks of the "knowledge supply chain," and says we should learn to manage our supply of knowledge. Knowledge is generated in the traditional R&D activities: universities do basic research, research labs do applied research, development labs make usable technologies out of applied research. Sometimes they even think about the best ways to use the technologies.

Knowledge is generated by our competitors. Companies that don't compete with us, but do things that complement what we do generate other knowledge.

Knowledge is generated every day by our customers—knowledge about what is good about our products and knowledge about what isn't so good, knowledge about how our product really gets used and knowledge about how they might be used, if only. . . .

So there is a sea of knowledge out there. It is dynamic. It is always in motion, always being refreshed. Your challenge is to have the processes in place to make sure that your company's people have the right knowledge at the right time.

Using the Right Processes, Equipment, and Technology

If a company is going to make the next generation of customerized products—products that meet very specific customer needs, needs that are different from those of the next customer—then the processes, equipment, and technology the company uses will have to be "next generation," too.

While the specifics of change may be unpredictable, the need is to design, build, or acquire multiuse equipment and processes. Companies will need processes and equipment that are agile. That means reconfigurable manufacturing cells, tooling that can be changed nearly instantaneously, machines that can be changed quickly from one use to the next, control systems that are programmable.

Processes and equipment will become obsolete rapidly if they are not designed and selected to accommodate growth and change in step with the progression of customer needs. A failing company will use $5 milion and 16 months to automate an assembly line specifically for a $300 specialty consumer electronics product for which there is a market forecast of only 50,000 units in an 18-month window of opportunity. A winner will have the flexibility to produce the product after spending three months and $100,000 designing and implementing the modifications needed to assemble the product on an existing line. The champion will be the company that can reprogram its processes and equipment in a day and a half.

Integrating the Enterprise

The dominant word among the attributes of an NGM company was *responsive*. How can an enterprise made up of dozens of teams of many different people, using a variety of systems, processes, and technologies, and that is spread across the world be responsive? Rapidly responsive teaming will require a high level of *integration* of people, systems, processes, and equipment.

The enterprise will have to be designed and built to operate as a unified, integrated enterprise. It takes a lot for a company that is distributed functionally and geographically to operate as an integrated unit. Companies will have to have so-called intelligent manufacturing systems, systems built to adapt to new conditions without outside intervention. Sometimes the adaptation will be done automatically by the equipment itself, but more often by the people who are working as part of the system.

It takes a robust information technology (IT) infrastructure to acquire and deliver the right knowledge to the right people, working with the right equipment. The architecture needs, on a grand scale, to be similar to that of the more recent PCs with plug-and-play capability. If the enterprise has to change continuously to stay on top of— or ahead of—the markets, it has to be able to add functions, work units, or new equipment with little or no overhead costs. It has to be able to change control algorithms, keep consistent enterprisewide versions of the product and process data models.

It takes interfaces between machines and people that help the people do their jobs better, that don't require the people to spend a lot of time thinking about computer technology, or about filtering out information they don't need, or translating from somebody else's jargon.

It takes more than technology to build a cohesive, unified enterprise. It takes a culture where people share the enterprise's goals and values. It takes a culture where everyone interprets verbal and non-verbal directions in a similar way, where everyone uses the same "language," even if it is represented in English, Persian, and Bahasa. It takes a culture where everyone feels that he or she is a member of the same team. It takes a culture where everyone can trust the other person to do his or her job—and takes pride in being trustworthy themselves.

Finally it takes business systems that bind the enterprise together, that account for and reward contributions fairly.

■ EXERCISE

Use the following checklist to assess your company's strategy.

A Strategic Checklist for the NGM Company

Questions	Your Company's Answers	Written Yes/No	Known throughout Company Yes/No
What are your financial goals this year? Next three years?			
What are your customer goals this year? Next three years?			
What are your internal operations goals this year? Next three years?			
What are your globalization goals this year? Next three years?			
What are your innovation goals this year? Next three years?			
What are your goals for learning and growth this year? Next three years?			
How responsive are you to existing customers? To new customers?			
What kinds of change can your plants and equipment respond to?			
How do your people respond to change?			
How well can you respond to global market opportunities?			
Are you good at multi-company teaming? Do your people team well?			
Does your company's culture encourage responses to changing conditions?			
Do you have the right people?			
Do you have the knowledge we need?			
Do you have the right equipment?			
Can your company act as a single unit?			

■ NOTES

1. Robert S. Kaplan and David P. Norton, *The Balanced Scorecard: Translating Strategy into Action* (Boston: Harvard Business School Press, 1996).
2. J. Jordan and F. Michel, *Competitive Next Generation Manufacturing Enterprise: Investing in the Future,* SME Technical Paper MM98-287 (Dearborn, MI: Society of Manufacturing Engineers, 1998).

Chapter 4

From Operational Strategies to Implementation Substrategies

MONDAY, 11:00 AM: BUILDING A STRUCTURE FOR CHOICE

As you handle a couple of pressing phone calls and sign some routine correspondence before lunch with your best customer and an intense afternoon, you think about all there is to work on to make sure BAI thrives. So many things to work on. You need to structure the choices so that you are convinced your strategies are covered.

■ THE NGM FRAMEWORK FOR ACTION

The NGM Project identified 10 *Imperatives*. We have chosen to call them *Implementation Substrategies* to emphasize the link between the four operational strategies and the strategies for implementing them. The Implementation Substrategies provide the guidelines for the projects a company will undertake in order to achieve its goals.

Companies will undertake many, many initiatives to achieve their short-term and long-term goals. The NGM Framework for Action (Figure 4.1) provides guidelines for companies seeking to position themselves for the next decade's competition. It is comprehensive in that it includes the initiatives throughout the manufacturing enterprise that, on balance, should receive priority.

43

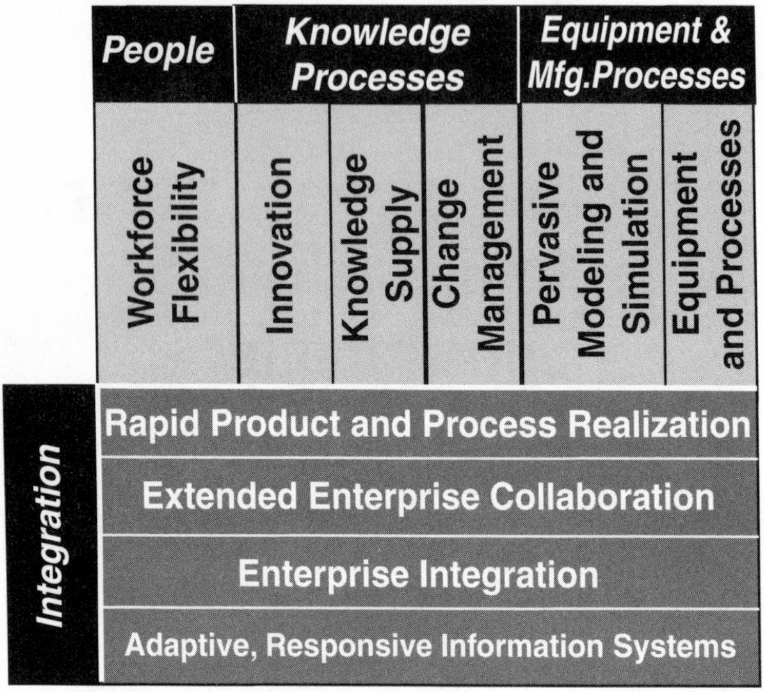

People	Knowledge Processes			Equipment & Mfg. Processes		
Workforce Flexibility	Innovation	Knowledge Supply	Change Management	Pervasive Modeling and Simulation	Equipment and Processes	
Integration	Rapid Product and Process Realization					
	Extended Enterprise Collaboration					
	Enterprise Integration					
	Adaptive, Responsive Information Systems					

Figure 4.1 The NGM Framework for Action

There are other initiatives that companies may find to be of higher priority. Common sense says that if a process is so broken that it threatens the survivability of a company, then that process must be fixed before the company can look to the future. For example, a company must respond quickly if one of its essential processes is found to yield toxic wastes whose effects were heretofore not understood. *The NGM Framework should be understood as a strategic framework, not a tactical plan.*

Every company will have to pick its way—just as Drucker says that there is no best organization for all companies, we say that there is no prescriptive formula for the transition to next generation manufacturing. The company will benefit, however, if it chooses its tactical initiatives in a way that supports its strategic initiatives.

It is worth noting that the Implementation Substrategies do not talk explicitly about two sets of underlying issues:

1. Quality and explicit quality initiatives, such as Quality Circles, Quality Function Deployment (QFD), Statistical Process

Control (SPC), and Six Sigma, are assumed. That is, there is overwhelming acceptance of quality as being an essential requirement for customer satisfaction and for economic operations. No company can survive for long if it does not deliver a product that meets the customers' standards or use processes that deliver high-quality results. Many of the actions recommended in NGM's Framework for Action will improve quality explicitly; all will improve the quality of some aspect or another of the company.

2. The NGM Project chose to weave environmental issues into many of the implementation substrategies, rather than separate out a specific substrategy for the environment and conservation of resources. As we will note in Chapter 20, studies with a longer term horizon expect environmental and resource issues to be a dominant force for manufacturing by the mid-twenty-first century.

➤ People: Having the Right People . . . Doing the Right Things

A company is a companionship of people who have melded together to pursue a common goal, namely a level of corporate business success that allows them to satisfy their individual goals. Operating a company is a balancing act: the company must succeed in a way that provides the rewards sought by the individual members of the company.

We adopt the notion that everyone working in a company is a *worker.* There is differentiation in roles, of course. Some workers have roles as executives or managers, others as leaders or facilitators, others as machine operators, or as accountants, or as customer service representatives.

As the company confronts changing markets, operating conditions, and competitions, it must flex in response. And the workforce must flex, too.

Workforce Flexibility

Workforce flexibility is defined in the NGM Report as the "set of practices, policies, processes and culture that enables the employee to feel a sense of security and ownership while enabling a company to capitalize on the creativity, commitment and discretionary efforts of its employees." There are two basic ways of looking at Workforce Flexibility: from the company's point of view and from the worker's.

➤ *The Company's View of Workforce Flexibility.* The company needs to have the best decisions made in the most affordable way. This means that right now the company needs the person or team who can best get the jobs done that need doing now. Tomorrow it needs the person or team who can best get the jobs done that need doing tomorrow. The person who does today's job may not have the knowledge or skills to do tomorrow's job. Today's job may require a team with 25 members. Tomorrow's job may require a team of 15 or one of 35. Today's manager may be best used for his or her technical contributions tomorrow. Tomorrow's job may need today's manufacturing cell operator to use her or his skills as a team leader.

The company, ideally, would like to see a workforce that fluidly fits itself to the job to be done, always with the right knowledge and skills, never with inadequate or unused knowledge or skills.

➤ *The Worker's View of Workforce Flexibility.* For many workers, at all levels in company hierarchies, worker flexibility is an oxymoron, a concept more to be feared as a threat to personal, financial and emotional comfort than to be embraced as a process yielding greater personal satisfaction and longer term stability.

Workforce flexibility comes with workers who can flex confidently with change. That means that workers:

➤ Have the ability and confidence to learn quickly to do tomorrow's job,

➤ Can work within teams whose members frequently change roles and who come and go, and

➤ Who are prepared to leave the company if need be with the assurance that they can find productive employment elsewhere.

Achieving workforce flexibility is therefore a responsibility shared between the company and the workforce.

➤ **Knowledge: Knowing What You Need to Know . . .**
Using What You Know

In an information age the company with the most *knowledge* wins. Knowledge is information in a form such that it can be used. In a world of ubiquitous information access and flows where there is a balanced supply of knowledge, competitive advantage is a matter of knowledge arbitrage. The strongest competitor at any given time is the one whose supply of knowledge and ability to use it is marginally better than anyone else's.

Data → Information → Knowledge → Wisdom

As industry has used automation to improve business processes, there has been an evolution in understanding just what it is that the business needs. That evolution is symbolized in the progression of buzzwords. First, we talked about data acquisition, databases, data management. Next, we began to talk about information, generally as the result of automated analyses of data, and about information management. Then we started talking about knowledge bases, knowledge management, and knowledge delivery. The implication of the term knowledge was that information was used in a form that was closer to the structures that humans use in cognitive processes—things like the rule bases of expert systems.

Recently, the term wisdom is creeping into consciousness as a mature, pro-active, response of a system to new conditions. Wisdom comes when all of the company's experience base, all of its explicit knowledge, and all of its tacit knowledge are processed with intuition and insight.

The NGM Report identified three processes that we group together as *Knowledge Processes* (see Figure 4.2). Markets, either existing or potential, stimulate the knowledge processes by presenting challenges. "We'd open up the PC market by 20 million units/year if only we could sell a PC for the cost of a VCR." "How are we going to meet the market

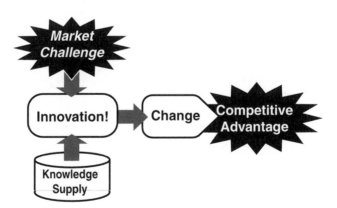

Figure 4.2 The Knowledge Processes Respond to Markets and Yield Competitive Advantage

requirements that California is imposing on our fleet mix?" "If only we had the fuel cell technology . . . " "If only we could deliver product in two days instead of two weeks . . . " "Since the availability of water is going to be the next resource inhibitor; if only we had a cheap desalination process. . . . " "If only we had a solution to. . . . "

"If only . . ." poses the challenge. The response is innovation—putting together new and old knowledge to come up with a solution. Innovation depends on knowledge. "Ah ha!" doesn't occur in a vacuum; it occurs in a complex pattern recognition when all the right pieces of knowledge jump into place. So there needs to be a supply of the right knowledge. Finally, any new solution, be it a product that forces the company to approach the market in a different way or a process that affects the company's internal operations will result in change. Unmanaged change can lead to destructive results.

Innovation

Innovation is the set of processes for creating solutions. Innovation includes both the initial creativity that crafts the solutions and the successful implementation of the solutions. Today, companies use innovation processes to improve everything from organizational structure and business practices to the technology used to develop and deliver products and services, and to the development of products and services themselves.

There is growing appreciation of innovation because it is seen as the way companies can keep ahead of, or at least differentiate themselves from, their competitors. Dell's use of the Internet for direct sales, beginning in 1996, shows the power of a well-executed implementation of a succession of novel ideas. Dell's competitors in 1999 were struggling to catch up with Dell's business model and achieve equally impressive results. Meanwhile, Dell is expanding its model to provide direct on-line support for large customers, to link with related Internet-based businesses such as Amazon.com, and to provide customers with non-Dell branded products. Even when the most successful followers of the Dell model, for example Apple, have been able to achieve process efficiencies said to be better than Dell's, Dell is viewed as the stronger competitor because Dell got there first.

The lead that a well-executed innovation gives a company can be squandered. The introduction in 1981 of the first IBM Personal Computer was a revolutionary success born not only of an innovative product design, but also of an innovative—for IBM in the 1970s and 1980s—outsourcing strategy, and especially of innovative business processes symbolized by the creation of a business unit that was outside many of IBM's normal bureaucratic procedures. IBM's response to the PC's astounding success was to forsake the imperatives to maintain an innovative technological advantage and to build on the innovative business unit. Instead, IBM delayed the introduction of a more advanced successor to the PC and folded the independent business unit into a traditional divisional structure.

Harvard Business School's Clayton Christopher[1] has documented the difficulties innovation can cause competitors. Christopher suggests that the most threatening innovations are the ones from non-traditional competitors. These are the least expected innovations and cause the greatest disruptions in established business plans. There is a direct correlation between the growth of online booksellers and the demise of several independent bookstores in the Silicon Valley.

These examples suggest that managing innovation is not something to be left to serendipity. Instead, the company should structure its innovation processes to yield exploitable serendipitous results.

Knowledge Supply

Innovation cannot happen unless there is an adequate supply of knowledge—knowledge of the market opportunity, knowledge of product design, of materials, and of manufacturing processes, knowledge of business processes, knowledge of customers, of partners, and of suppliers. This sea of knowledge must be filtered for just the right knowledge the individual decision maker needs to create a solution to a market opportunity, a technical difficulty, or a business issue.

Knowledge Supply is a new concept introduced in the NGM Report. The concept borrows from the concepts of supply chain management and applies them to the relationships among industry, universities, schools, and associations. The goal is to rapidly provide and continuously update the knowledge and talent needed to run businesses in a timely and cost-effective manner. Knowledge Supply is a pull process, whose goal is the just-in-time delivery of the knowledge just before it is needed to solve problems.

The concept of knowledge supply provides for the generation of new knowledge that should focus on specific needs; that is, it accelerates the use of basic and applied research in the innovative solutions to real tasks. Another goal is to develop the educational instruments by which new and existing knowledge can be taught in a fashion that helps workers use the knowledge quickly. Finally, a goal is to have in place the storage, the filtering tools, and the mechanisms that can deliver knowledge from any source in the enterprise to any worker who needs it.

Change Management

We call the impact of innovations and new conditions *change*. Innovation means that something new is created: a new product, a new process, a new technology. And because something is changed, there are likely to be ripples felt across the entire enterprise. An enterprise can nurture change or it can stifle it, depending on how the company manages, or mismanages, it.

Changing conditions require a response, usually one that means the person or company does something differently. Doing things differently demands some level of creativity and problem solving. *A wise company recognizes and manages the inevitability of change; an unwise one depends on luck to match change with solution.*

Change resonates with deep insecurities in the human psyche. Organizations can be badly hurt by unplanned and thoughtless changes, by changes that have been mismanaged, and even by well-planned, well-managed changes that have had unexpected side effects.

Organizations have two kinds of challenges regarding change:

1. They must develop a culture in which change is a state of being, placed in a context that reduces the sense of threat to the workforce. Part of change management is the process of continually applying deliberate change to the current state of the company in order to be prepared to deal effectively with continuous change.

2. They must manage each change initiative carefully to maximize benefits and reduce destructive effects. Communication and measurement processes need to be in place to ensure that those who need to know, do know of the change and understand its significance, and that the effects of the change initiative is as intended.

The NGM Report claims, "The ability to spark innovation into continuous positive change may be the true competitive advantage for the NGM Company of the future."

► NGM Processes and Equipment: The Right Tools for the Right Jobs

The Next Generation Manufacturing company will be characterized by its use of modeling and simulation, often coupled with agile and flexible manufacturing processes and equipment. These are two of the essentials required for competitive response to the market.

Pervasive Modeling and Simulation

Modeling and Simulation will become pervasive throughout the enterprise as a new way of doing business. The modern manufacturing enterprise is the sum of the large and small decisions made by people and so-called intelligent machines. Responsiveness ultimately depends on the speed and accuracy of the decisions people make, decisions that are then turned into effective action.

The decision vocabulary of the NGM company will be the vocabulary of models and simulations. They will ask "Does the model say we can build the function into the product?" or "Did you simulate the effects of changing the factory layout?" or under the best of circumstances, "What is the optimum organization of the extended enterprise to produce this product?" Companies will make countless decisions guided by the answers.

The first goal of modeling and simulation is to reduce the time before a decision is made—to use the speed of the computer to test alternative design concepts rather than build physical prototypes, to find the glitches in processes on a computer graphics display, not during the testing phase of implementation. Boeing's pioneering success in reducing the development time a full year by digitally prototyping the 777 demonstrates the value of this approach.

A second goal is to improve the quality of the decisions. Modeling and simulation is in transition, from the esoteric backroom application of the mathematical and computational sciences to poorly understood descriptions of reality, to dependable representations on which decisions can be based reliably.

In the case of the Boeing 777, one can argue that customer satisfaction with the resultant product shows that the masses of decisions made through models were the right ones.

Boeing invested greatly in developing the tools and the data to ensure that the models were accurate representations of reality. The potential returns justified the investment.

Lockheed Martin, together with a group of vendors and the U.S. Air Force, has built the Simulation Assessment and Validation Environment (SAVE), a modeling and simulation facility to support integrated product and process development (IPPD). This is a step toward virtual factories, in which all design and production decisions can be checked out before any physical effort is expended.

Over time in the NGM company, as models and simulations become more accurate, they will be extended to more and more areas of the business. They will make virtual production a reality even for lower value products. More and more production decisions will be based on modeling and simulation methods, rather than on build-and-test methods. Modeling and simulation tools will move from being the domain of technologists, to being tools for all involved in the product realization, production and business practices.

Equipment and Next Generation Manufacturing Processes

Once the decision to act has been made, quickly by knowledgeable people supported by accurate models and simulations, effective and responsive action must follow. That action will depend on *Equipment and Processes* matched to the needs of an ever-changing manufacturing environment.

Customers will ask plants to provide very large lots simultaneously with small lots, many standardized products simultaneously with customized products. Plant layouts will have to change as workloads and product mixes change. Product lines and manufacturing cells will need the built-in flexibility to accommodate changing processes on the fly.

Much of the needed flexibility will come in reconfigurable, scalable, and cost-effective manufacturing processes and equipment. Machines with static control systems designed for a limited scope of application will be replaced with machines with programmable controllers that will open the scope of applications more to unpredicted demands. Some existing machines will be retrofitted with controllers to do jobs never envisioned when the machines were first built years, even decades ago.

Similarly, tooling is being designed and built to be changed easily and quickly to accommodate changes in configuration of the parts in the manufacture of which the tooling is to be used. Computers control the re-setting, providing the capability for changing the configuration in real time.

Manufacturing execution systems will support flexible processes, processes in which the controllers of a variety of machines, perhaps in several manufacturing cells, may be simultaneously programmed for specific product runs. (See Figure 4.3.)

One lesson of the Toyota Production System and other lean manufacturing initiatives is that it costs less—in time and money—to do things right the first time. It costs less to make sure each step in a process gives a high quality result so that there is little need for inspection and rework at the end of the process. Getting things right requires in-process measurement, analysis, and corrective action. More equipment is being built to include in-process measurement capabilities and feedback loops for continually adjusting and readjusting

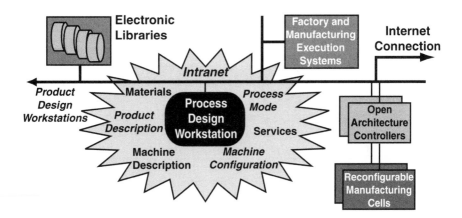

Figure 4.3   The Integrated Process Design and Execution Environment

machine settings. Analysis requires either human intervention (is the measurement shown on the dial out of tolerance?) or a control system to be able to make comparisons against the measurements predicted by models. In most cases of discrete manufacturing, people take the corrective actions, but in some cases, as in continuous process manufacturing, adaptive machines make the needed changes to bring processes back in tolerance.

In time, as models and simulations become more accurate, they will be used to guide real-time changes in processes. Data from real processes will be merged with data generated by models to simulate modified processes, ensuring their quality before they are implemented. Once implemented, the models and simulations will form the standard for control actions.

Six Sigma quality standards are being accepted at an increasing rate. The standard reduces scrap rate nearly to zero and optimizes the interchangeability of parts.

➤ Integrating the Extended Enterprise

The need to view the manufacturing company as an integrated enterprise was a major motivation for the CASA/SME New Manufacturing Enterprise Wheel.[2] The current Wheel is a graphical model that is the third generation of a progression that moved from a systems approach to Computer-Aided Manufacturing (CAM) to the factory automation of Computer Integrated Manufacturing (CIM) and now to an integrated view of the whole enterprise. The initial step in this progression was the recognition that computers could be used to control machine tools. Soon came the realization that computers could also be used to transfer information needed on the shop floor. The idea of integrating the information required by scheduling, purchasing, inventory control, and manufacturing engineers was the next step and the systems approach to manufacturing was born. The next logical step in the sequence of these events was to define formally the manufacturing system and infrastructure.

The New Manufacturing Enterprise Wheel augmented the understanding gained from the previous CIM Enterprise Wheel. The older version looked primarily at automation and integration inside the enterprise. The new Wheel looked outside as well and describes six fundamental elements for competitive manufacturing:

1. The central role of the customer and evolving customer need.

2. The role of people and teamwork in the organization.

3. The revolutionary impact of a shared knowledge and systems to support people and processes.

4. Key processes from product definition through manufacturing and customer support.

5. Enterprise resources (inputs) and responsibilities (outputs).

6. The manufacturing infrastructure which includes customers and their needs, suppliers, competitors, prospective workers, distributors, natural resources, financial markets, governments, and educational and research institutions.

In many respects, the CASA Wheel paved the way for Next Generation Manufacturing. The strategy and alignment of a manufacturing enterprise as represented in Figure 4.4 by the triangle integrating people, business practices, and technology brings a sharper focus to the interrelationship of the elements of the manufacturing enterprise and its relationship with the outside world.

In the NGM Framework, four Implementation Substrategies tie people, knowledge, equipment, and processes together into a viable, competitive company. The first, Rapid Product and Process Realization, is a mega-process that spans the product lifecycle. RPPR requires the second substrategy, Extended Enterprise Collaboration. In turn, effective collaboration requires the third substrategy, Enterprise Integration, supported by the fourth substrategy, Adaptive, Responsive Information Systems. (See Figure 4.5.)

The information systems and technology that enable enterprise integration are described in the Implementation Substrategy for Adaptive, Responsive Information Systems.

Figure 4.4 Aligning Goals and Operational Strategies Using Integration

Rapid Product and Process Realization

A manufacturing company makes a profit by supplying goods, or combinations of goods and services, that the customer wants strongly enough to be willing to pay prices high enough to include a satisfactory profit margin. *Rapid Product and Process Realization (RPPR)* is the collective name for the processes that result from the integration of

Figure 4.5 Integrating the Extended Enterprise

customer needs and wants, a systematic Integrated Product and Process Development (IPPD) methodology, cross-functional integrated product teams, and a computer integrated environment. Getting RPPR right is a pervasive theme of this book.

In recent years, there has been a strong emphasis on Integrated Product and Process Development (IPPD), the concurrent development of a product and the processes needed to manufacture the product. RPPR (see Figure 4.6) is a superset of IPPD that begins with the market conceptualization of a product and extends usually to the delivery of the product to the market and beyond that through the period of ownership and final disposal. There is an emerging understanding that the delivery of the product does not end the manufacturing enterprise's involvement, but that the enterprise has responsibilities, costs, and opportunities for profit that extend through final disposal of the product at the end of its useful life. The result is another superset, a mega-process we call Product and Process *Lifecycle* Management (PPLM). The emphasis of the NGM Project was on RPPR. We will discuss PPLM in Chapter 20, where we look further into manufacturing's future.

RPPR is accomplished by including all stakeholders, from concept development through planning for product disposition, in the design, development, and manufacturing processes, in a highly concurrent manner.

Enterprise Integration Using Adaptive, Responsive Information Systems

Enterprise Integration is defined as connecting and combining the people, processes, systems, and technologies of the extended enterprise to assure that the right information is available at the right location, with

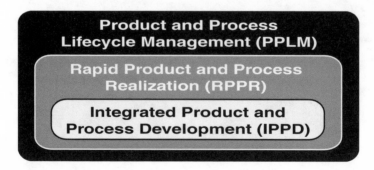

Figure 4.6   Positioning RPPR

the right resources, at the right time. It comprises all the activities necessary to ensure that, whether operating as an independent unit or as a part of an extended enterprise, the Next Generation Manufacturing (NGM) company can execute RPPR as a coordinated whole.

There are two important aspects of Enterprise Integration. One focuses on the technological issues of information acquisition, transport, storage, and delivery. *Adaptive, Responsive Information Systems* are information systems of Next Generation Manufacturing. Existing technologies that support the Internet and other networked systems will be the basis for systems that can be reshaped dynamically. New elements can be added, others replaced, and modules can be changed that are connected to redirect data flows through the total system.

Nirvana is "plug-and-play." Interoperability. My scheduler can be plugged into your Manufacturing Execution System. We can use Denise's product models, Ted's process models, parts availability from Danny's ERP system, and the data from Charlene's cell controller to interrupt the current production schedule with a high priority, high profit, job. No problem—everything and everyone talks to everything and everyone else, in the same language. We're not to Nirvana yet, but there are examples of companies moving toward this idyllic state.

The second important aspect of Enterprise Integration is the integration of people—those wonderful, unique, idiosyncratic mixes of brain cells, neurons, and muscles—within the enterprise's systems. This is deeper than just bits and bytes integration, or even the integration afforded when the semantic definitions are the same in everyone's computer application. This is the integration that comes when people understand common purposes, have tacitly understood and trustworthy behavior toward one another, and use all of their intellectual powers to achieve the enterprise's objectives. The effects of what a worker does in Dacca may ripple across oceans and result in the failure of a crucial decision made by a plant manager in Milan. A decision made in Terre Haute, couched in terms of a U.S. company's culture, may lead to disaster if it is misinterpreted by a peer manager in the Ukrainian culture of a plant in Kharkov. Enterprise Integration is the tricky business of getting people to trust one another, understand one another, and work together under the stresses and pressures of a common competitive goal.

Extended Enterprise Collaboration

Manufacturing is a complex endeavor. Although the production of a commodity part like a screw may look simple, the enterprise that assembles that screw and dozens, hundred, maybe even thousands of parts into something usable can be very complicated. Many different kinds of knowledge and skill must be combined in the RPPR process.

Few companies can afford the cost or time to build and maintain all the knowledge and all the skills they need to produce, distribute, and service even a moderately complicated product to serve global markets—say, cell phones including advanced materials, microelectronics, mechanical actuators in rugged packaging. Instead, companies seek alliances of one form or another to partner with or to procure from companies that have specialized expertise. The result is a formal or informal *collaborative extended enterprise.*

One common form of the extended enterprise is the managed *supply chain,* a form that has gained prominence through the efforts of major manufacturers to establish dependable relationships with groups of companies who can be relied upon to contribute expertise and to deliver high quality products and services on time.

The responsiveness of the extended enterprise depends on the quality of the collaboration among the partners. Extended Enterprise Collaboration is the seamless integration of a group of stakeholders who create and support a timely and cost-effective service or product. The stakeholders typically include the customer, both as the arbiter of market demand and as the end-user; partnering companies, including suppliers and service providers; and the internal and external investors who finance the development and purchase of the product. The stakeholders may include the education community as a resource for applied research and as a medium of knowledge delivery. The stakeholders may also include governmental agencies such as the National Institute of Standards and Technology (NIST) that provide new technology, the Environmental Protection Agency (EPA) that impose regulatory constraints, or the Securities and Exchange Commission (SEC) that impose regulation on technology reports that can affect share price.

In the extended enterprise, one company's systems must integrate with the partnering company's systems. The systems Wal-Mart and Wal-Mart's suppliers use wouldn't keep the store shelves stocked if there wasn't some level of systems compatibility among them. If the extended enterprise includes shared production tasks, say a basic assembly process in a factory in China and a finishing process in Belgium, then there must be compatibility of manufacturing systems. A company's systems are inevitably a reflection of the company's culture, so that at a minimum each company in an extended enterprise must have a rudimentary understanding of the other companies' cultures. Just as inevitably, the extended enterprise will develop its own unique culture, and culture that may reflect, for good or ill, back into the partners.

■ SUMMARY

There is no single prescription for next generation manufacturing. The attributes of an NGM company won't magically appear with one or two transformative action plans. The company's management has no "silver bullet" it can use, but it can lead the company in the right direction by instilling in the company a culture that accepts the challenges of the new, global, competitive environment with enthusiasm and confidence.

Within the framework of the four essential operational strategies—people, knowledge, processes and equipment, and integration—the company needs to act in a balanced way along all 10 of the implementation substrategies.

■ EXERCISE

Consider your company in terms of the implementation substrategies introduced in this chapter. Use the table below to assess its strengths and weaknesses.

Substrategies	Company Strengths	Company Weaknesses
Workforce flexibility		
Innovation		
Change management		
Knowledge supply		
Modeling and simulation		
Processes and equipment		
Product and process realization		
Enterprise integration		
Responsive information systems		
Extended enterprise collaboration		

■ NOTES

1. Clayton M. Christensen, *The Innovator's Dilemma: When New Technologies Cause Great Firms to Fail* (Boston: Harvard Business School Press, 1997).
2. Computer and Automated Systems Association of the Society of Manufacturing Engineers, *CASA/SME New Manufacturing Enterprise Wheel* (Dearborn, MI: Society of Manufacturing Engineers, 1993).

Chapter 5

Organizing the Company for Next Generation Manufacturing

The goal is for each NGM company to have the right organizational structure as it operates to meet each of its market opportunities. Organizational structures will have to:

➤ Be responsive and rapidly adaptable to new circumstances.

➤ Enable rapid and accurate decision making using the most appropriate combinations of human and machine intelligence.

➤ Accommodate the proliferation of machine intelligence capabilities in finer and finer grained manufacturing systems (in so-called "smart parts" and "brilliant machines," parts and machines with embedded computing hardware and software enabling floor-level decisions that are adapted to real-time conditions).

➤ Support distributed teams that mix human and machine intelligence and that operate semi-autonomously within widely varying cultural backgrounds.

Organizational structure provides and organizes the resources of an enterprise such that they can be best used to accomplish the enterprise's objectives. In the NGM company, the primary purpose of organization is to direct human intelligence to the actions needed to meet the company's objectives. Most decisions are interdisciplinary—they require inputs of several experts. The best decisions are made by those with the most information and expertise in the "decision space." These people are often those closest to the object of the decision.

The right organization for a company now is the one that works best for the company—now. The right organization for the company tomorrow is likely to be somewhat different. So the solution to the "right organization" question, as Drucker[1] reminds us, is a dynamic one with no single right answer.

Most enterprises are still structured in traditional hierarchical organizations. The hierarchies are decomposed in one or a combination of three basic models:

1. Functional decomposition into so-called silos or stovepipes (e.g., research, development, manufacturing, marketing, and so forth).

2. Geographical decomposition (e.g., eastern region, western region, international region). In the case of suppliers, geographic decomposition may result from co-location with major customers.

3. More recently, decomposition by brand or product family.

Matrixed organizations, in which personnel from different functional hierarchies are brought together to form a project team, provide one hybrid example of the traditional structures.

In hierarchically organized companies, the management systems often are just channels through which the upper levels of management try to direct and control the activities of the enterprise. This is true although in many hierarchically managed companies, important operational decisions are often made *sub rosa* within the informal networks of workers that exist at operational levels. Command-and-control is the prevailing management style in small- and medium-sized companies, and is often the style in larger companies. It is also true of most extended enterprises, in which one entity takes responsibility for command and control of the enterprise.

State-of-the-art thinking asserts that an enterprise's organization should promote more rapid decision making, should encourage flexibility, and should utilize the practical knowledge of the workforce. In response, many companies are:

➤ Reducing the numbers of levels in their hierarchies. There are instances where as many as seven levels have been replaced by as few as three. Many of the control functions of middle management are being replaced by electronic reporting of near real-time data analyzed with decision support tools.

➤ Replacing the traditional "the foreman gives the orders, the worker does what he or she is told" paradigm with a team-based one. When taken to its natural limit, the team is self-directed and even self-organizing.

➤ Developing multidisciplinary teams that take on responsibility for the accomplishment of large-grained tasks, often combining processes from several different functions.

➤ Beginning to use fluid organizational forms and virtual co-location to achieve transitory objectives.

There is an international consensus, as evidenced in the NGM Report and in the international Intelligent Manufacturing Systems (IMS) program, that an organizational building block of NGM companies will be teams of people each of whom embodies one or more core competencies. The teams will possess definable core competencies, which in turn will define the core competencies of the company. The company will team with other companies possessing

THREE EXAMPLES OF INNOVATIVE ORGANIZATION

In response to competitive pressures, Chrysler Corporation developed a focused organization, the platform team, to develop the LH series of cars. This team integrated many of the marketing, design and engineering, and manufacturing functions, using IT to support the integrated function. This organization was successful in significantly reducing the development time and has since been replicated successfully in the industry.

Texas Instruments' military products group has developed a team structure in which teams are certified as to the level of responsibility the team can take on—with success. In this structure, the best (Level 5) teams are self-directed after having been assigned high-level goals.

In 1992, IBM established a virtual enterprise, PowerParallel Systems, within its existing organization, to quickly develop, bring to market, and deliver the world's most powerful parallel processing computer. PowerParallel Systems merged core competencies in microprocessor development and production, in the applications of and production of mainframe computers, in market development, and in computer science research. The goal was achieved in late 1993.

complementary core competencies. The consensus is that NGM companies will look more and more like networks of globally distributed teams working together to achieve operational and strategic goals. (See Figure 5.1.)

Teams will help direct, energize, and, working with other teams, integrate the enterprise. They will set performance aspirations, intensify focus and commitment, energize workforces, build core skills, and spread knowledge to those who need it.

The teams often will not have time to wait for someone to tell them what to do. They will have to understand the big picture and their role within it well enough to make their decisions, to take their actions, autonomously, linking with other teams when they need to acquire or exchange information or results.

The teams cannot be completely autonomous. Their work has to align with the company's and the extended enterprise's goals. They must work within a framework that both limits their autonomy and provides direction for it—the management process Warnecke[2] calls *navigation,* providing a compass so every team steers in the right direction. The framework will include a set of imperatives, behaviors each team can expect from all the others—standards that can help determine when to make an independent decision, when to consult with neighboring teams in the network, when to seek consensus throughout the network, when to seek management direction. The framework also includes the rules for communication—how much and what

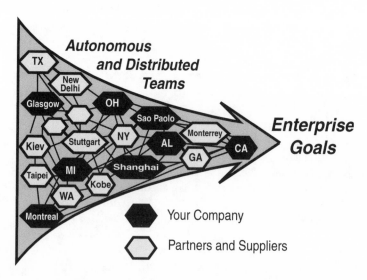

Figure 5.1 Organizing the NGM Company

kind of information is automatically pushed to other teams, what information is made available to be pulled as needed by other teams.

Change will continue to happen. The emerging picture is one of company organizations that fluidly shape themselves to provide the right competencies at the right time, with a minimal waste of resources. As teams respond to change it may be that the only way to get the new job done, in a timely way, may be to change the organization. Adaptive self-organization—given a culture of autonomy and a set of corporate guidelines for self-organization—is the way teams will respond to the new demands. There just won't be time to wait for headquarters to give them a new organization chart.

As the shaping process goes on, some teams or some team members, will have competencies that are no longer needed. One of the organizational issues NGM companies will face is the effect on people as they go through the metamorphosis from one organizational structure to the next.

■ COMPLEXITY THEORY AND NGM COMPANY ORGANIZATION

Many in the United States and abroad have used complexity theory to provide a theoretical explanation for the emerging trends in the organization of manufacturing enterprises. The basic unit to which complexity theory is applied is the individual who embodies a competency, or ability to get a job done, and a work ethic, a set of predictable behaviors, for doing the job. Individuals are aggregated into a team, a small group of people sharing their individual competencies to achieve a team goal.

This has led to the description of enterprises made up of teams that work autonomously, but cooperatively, in the achievement of enterprise objectives. In fact, many companies are implementing teams and team-based structures empirically. For example, Johnson Controls has a dynamic team-based structure.

The Fractal company concept promoted by Hans-Juergen Warneke, president of Germany's Fraunhofer Society, is an application of complexity theory. In this case, manual systems have replicated the ideas of the *fractals* of mathematics. Every team or work unit, at every level of the enterprise, is imprinted with the same work ethic resulting in all being self-similar and self-organizing. A key aspect of the Fractal Company is the process called *navigation*, the interpretation of the enterprise's goals by the fractal in terms of what the fractal itself can do and the alignment of the fractal's

In seven years, Skoda, the old-time Czech manufacturer now 70 percent owned by Volkswagen (VW), has been turned from being a nationalized underperforming operation producing out-of-date cars of dubious quality to a modern company at the industry's cutting edge.

The key to Skoda's achievement lies in reducing costs (and improving quality) by using a customer-focused, extended enterprise organized on Fractal Factory concepts. Skoda wraps VW-sourced parts in a body that Skoda designed for the practical Czech customer. The new Octavia is built on the same platform as the VW Golf but, "Everything you can see, touch and smell is Skoda," says Dirk van Braeckel, Skoda's design chief.

As a result, Skoda has become, along with Audi, the most profitable company in the Volkswagen Group. Increased production and sales led to sufficient cash flow to finance all the company's capital investments for 1998. Profit for that year was up 53 percent over the previous year.

Skoda's cars are built using VW's latest production techniques. VW has invested about $1 billion in a new, greenfield production facility that Skoda calls a fractal factory. Suppliers produce completed subassemblies on site, just in time to be installed in the Octavias as they pass slowly down the line. The line passes on either side of a central spine of glass offices, intended to keep production workers and white-collar staff in close and informal communication.

The complexity of the Skoda plant is decomposed into a number of subproduction lines—Skoda calls them fractals—where components and subsystems such as seats and completed dashboards are assembled, not by Skoda employees but by employees of suppliers including Rockwell, Siemens, and Johnson Controls. The system not only brings the suppliers closer to a project—and at an earlier stage—but also speeds up communication and encourages better quality. There are also significant benefits from having suppliers onsite to find problems before they arise.

---

*Matthew Carter, "Skoda: the Rebirth of a Driving Force," *The European*, vol. 3, (July 6, 1998) p. 8.

activities with the enterprise goals. A second essential activity comes with adaptive reorganization of the fractals in the face of changed conditions. The Fraunhofer Society's Institutes in Stuttgart and Magdeburg have piloted Fractal Factory concepts in several tens of small and medium sized companies, often with excellent results.

Similar work to apply complexity theory in manufacturing is being done by groups loosely associated with the Santa Fe Institute, a focal point in the United States for complex systems. The Agility movement[3] has drawn on the analogies developed by these groups, without incorporating the mathematics for analysis. The Next Generation Manufacturing Systems (NGMS) project,[4] being conducted within the international Intelligent Manufacturing Systems (IMS) Program, is exploring the emergent behavior of autonomous, distributed manufacturing systems and so-called *biological manufacturing systems* with the intent of automating concepts very similar to fractals. The Holonics project,[5] also part of the IMS Program, has also explored the development of organizations based on *holons,* atomic organizational units not unlike fractals.

■ LEADERSHIP AND MANAGEMENT

Flexible organizations will place great stress on our concepts of management. Directive management systems, in which all work is undertaken according to a grand plan handed down through the hierarchy, clearly won't work very well in the face of complexity and time pressures. As more power is delegated, NGM companies will depend even more on the leadership skills of its management.

Leadership is the set of behaviors that causes others to achieve results. The leadership may be directive, even threatening—"Take that hill, or else!" Or it may be exemplative—"Follow me and we'll take that hill." Or it may be facilitative—"I'll dig a trench here, give you covering fire there, and you can take the hill." Or it may be inspirational—"The country will be forever grateful if you take that hill." It can even take the form of benign expectation—"You have all the tools you need to take the hill, so I have every confidence that you will."

The best organization is one that works now. So too with leadership. Leadership is a very human thing, varying with the individuals involved and varying, too, with the situation. Leadership is relational. It depends on the relationship between those who choose to lead and those who decide to follow. The relationship is situation-dependent. It occurs in the context of a specific need and involves unique individuals, who have some common and some differing goals.

The competence called *management* is changing. A decade ago, Peter Vaill wrote:

> *The modern leader/manager is required to be able to reflect and philosophize to a degree that sometimes astonishes (and infuriates) the down-to-earth, no-nonsense, let's-get-on-with-it sorts of men and women who have traditionally held these jobs. The job has become more intellectual and scholarly, in the best sense of these words. It requires an ability to work with theory, interpret research results, identify and reconsider underlying assumptions, communicate at length with others both inside and outside the organization (as opposed to just being "briefed"), read critically, and write forcefully and concisely. All this is a direct though not often mentioned expression of the information age.*[6]

Executive leadership is often directive, but there is another thrust today—the thrust for executives to accomplish their goals through influence, facilitation, and coaching. This thrust is toward the model of *servant leadership*—the leader who empowers others and who fills the gaps. An aspect of corporate leadership lies in projecting a vision and strategy in ways that are compelling and which motivate the workforce.

As more power is delegated, more people—down to the individuals and teams who make operational processes work—will have to lead. The NGM company will be a network of core competencies that are embodied in individuals and small teams. The NGM company will be one in which the entire workforce is expected to possess and use leadership skills—it will have a culture of leadership. In a knowledge-based competition, these people and teams are the legitimate leaders for their competencies. The company will expect and defer to their leadership. Management may be the particular competence contributed by one team member, but leadership will be shared by everyone in the team.

McGill and Slocum, in an attempt to demystify leadership, think of leadership not in grand management visions, but in the everyday activities in which people going about their work assume a leadership position—what they call "little-leadership."[7] They point out that,

> *A critical factor for little-leadership acts to be effective is trust. Trust results from the perception of the leader's ability, beneficence, and integrity. The trust and respect afforded leaders are results not only of what they do but how they do things. If a leader has been unable to establish trust with others or if the leader's actions have destroyed trust in the past, the willingness of others to comply with the leader's wishes*

will be greatly diminished. The relationship between a leader's actions, however small, and followers, speaks more loudly than words.

Adapting from McGill and Slocum four behaviors for valid leadership:

1. Leadership demands knowledge. You need a trustworthy command of the problematic situation as it is and as it may develop—if you are a leader involved with technology, you need an understanding of the fundamental issues posed by the technology. Then you must use that knowledge to influence the situation so that it develops in the way you want. You need to know your core competence, but also understand how your competence fits with those that others possess to build a complete solution.

2. Action legitimizes leadership. In any leadership endeavor, there must be a demonstrable relationship between what you say and what you do. If you behave in ways that are consistent with the company' s common purposes, you will create a climate for others to do the same. A corollary to this is that you establish trust by building on "little wins"—you establish your leadership credentials by demonstrating the results of everyday acts.

3. Since leadership is based on the relationship between leader and follower, two-way communication is essential. For leaders, this means active listening—and then acting consistently with what they have heard—that creates involvement, commitment, and more trust.

4. Leaders ask followers to make choices. But first, they must create a context for those choices. Leaders need to know the sphere of legitimate leadership within which they and their teams operate—the choices they can make and the constraints within which they must make them. In turn, the leader needs to give followers the bounds, constraints, and priorities for their choices.

The complement of leadership is followership. The successful NGM company will need both great leadership and great followership. Followership is the skill of choosing the right leader to follow, the skill of recognizing and following the leader for specific competencies, and then shifting to follow the leader for other competencies. The team leader, the supervisor, the manager, will be a follower of the person or team with the specialized competence that is important at the moment. The next moment, leadership will shift to another team member.

Leadership and followership will flow dynamically within a team, a company, or an enterprise—at its best always seeking the best decisions, the most effective actions, with the smallest overheads. The entire NGM workforce will have to embody these qualities. The entire workforce—including executives and managers—will have to become comfortable with the transitory and reciprocal nature of their power and influence.

➤ Leadership and Change

The NGM company will compete based on the knowledge content of its products and processes. It will be dynamic, always changing. Much of the company's leadership will have to do with the use of knowledge within a context of change. A prerequisite for a successful knowledge process—innovation, change management, and knowledge supply—is management leadership and support. The leadership for these processes must start with a courageous and farsighted board of directors and executive team that demands innovation, is comfortable with change, and values knowledge.

Innovation and change are steps into the unknown. To be successful, both require creativity, experimentation, and discovery—and both carry some risk of failure. As you explore the unknown, you take risks, a risk of wasting your time, a risk of wasting company resources, a risk of failure. The leadership's view of risk-taking is crucial. Responsible risk-taking should be encouraged and continually reaffirmed. Mistakes should not necessarily be condoned but at least treated as a learning experience. The leadership needs to take the fear out of presenting unconventional ideas.

Your company's management has to lead the transformation to the NGM state, projecting a trustworthy vision of the transformed company. A clear vision is a necessary prerequisite for the robust, continuous change processes required. The transformation will require most of its workforce to perform their many daily duties differently from the way they have been. These different ways will rarely be defined in specific detail in procedures or manuals. The guiding force for these people is their understanding of the company's goals and objectives—as projected by the leadership—and the picture of the future that they carry in their mind. If a consistent, clear picture of the future state toward which the company is driving does not exist in each person's mind, the daily decisions will not help move toward the vision.

■ THE NGM COMPANY WITHIN THE COMMUNITY

Every nation, region, and community has an industrial policy that guides the way it thinks about manufacturing. That policy is manifested by the laws and regulations it enacts—or doesn't enact. Investments in knowledge lead to one sort of manufacturing over others, to one set of technologies over another, to one model for the manufacturing enterprise over others. The policy can be a protective and adversarial one in which the community assumes it must defend itself against industry. The policy can be dictated by companies on terms that leave many in the community feeling deprived and frustrated. Or the policy can be a collaborative one.

Companies have always lived as part of the community. They have attracted investment from the community. They have consumed the community's natural resources. They have sought out knowledge, skills, and labor from the community. In the best of situations, the community and the company have had a symbiotic, win-win relationship.

The model of next generation manufacturing is a collaborative one, and a collaborative industrial policy fits the model. The assumption is, like the extended enterprises and knowledge enterprises we will discuss in Chapters 11 and 15, respectively, that the economic well being of the community can best be achieved when companies, governments, and educational institutions collaborate. Collaboration implies that each brings a core competency to the table and that together they work out the best division of roles and responsibilities that will achieve the community's socioeconomic goals.

One effect of next generation manufacturing is that no one company can make long-term commitments to its employees. This is not a matter of cruel exploitation. It is simply a statement that the pace of competition and change is so great that no company can afford a "full employment" policy nor can a company provide all the social and career support companies did in the mid-twentieth century.

Given the less stable nature of employment, the community will have to be a more active partner in nurturing the lives of individuals, taking on some of the tasks that heretofore fell to companies. The individual will be in a continuing state of churn, forced to augment or replace the competencies that fed him or her, and his or her family, yesterday with new competencies with which to pay tomorrow's bills.

Often the individual will have to learn these competencies from sources outside the company—the company won't have the resources to invest in and teach the knowledge.

The community known colloquially as Silicon Valley is a prototype collaborative community, one in which the collaboration has happened more by accident than by design. The community is knowledge-rich, fed by two premier universities, Stanford and the University of California at Berkeley, augmented by two other University of California campuses, four second-tier California State University campuses, and several private colleges. Silicon Valley's entrepreneurial spirit grew from academic roots—notably the efforts of Hewlett and Packard before World War II and the many research institutes and companies that grew out of federally-funded research after World War II. The community that grew up valued innovation as an intrinsic good, as well as the foundation for wealth. Many of the practices of next generation manufacturing—especially those that promote fast-paced extended enterprises—have been modeled in Silicon Valley, and sometimes taken to extremes.

Silicon Valley has found that individuals, even companies, can't go it alone. There needs to be a community infrastructure that supports people who participate in transitory extended enterprises. Many of the tough problems of sustaining regional economic well-being come from the needs of next generation manufacturing for people who are productive and reasonably comfortable with the added responsibilities of being team members and knowledge workers. A first responsibility of the community infrastructure is education, the kind of education that prepares people to manage their careers and be lifelong learners. A second responsibility is to provide the commercial, communications, and regulatory infrastructure that can sustain extended enterprises.

The knowledge content of a manufacturing economy is a joint responsibility. Education has, or should have, as its core competencies the academic disciplines and the techniques and methodologies of formal learning. Manufacturing has, or can specify, the knowledge and skills needed by manufacturing people. Together, education and industry can use their core competencies to teach the knowledge and skills needed by the workforce. We need to build ways to ensure that education meets or leads the community's needs, rather than lags them. The problem isn't one to be solved just by educators. Industry must play a role in determining the end goals for education. So should government. And so should everyone who benefits from the social and economic activities of the whole community.

Education is only one issue for collaborative solutions. There is need for a collaborative regulatory environment—one that involves collaboration with customers, too. There is need for community collaboration on environmental, natural resource, and land use issues. There is just as much need for companies to invest in community as there is for communities to invest in the services they provide to companies.

■ GLOBALIZATION OF COMMUNITY

We write as if the company is fixed in one community. But it is not. It may be headquartered in one community, even to the point of drawing its dominant corporate culture from that community. But the "community" within which any global enterprise operates is a network of regional and local communities hosting its productive units. Just as there is no one-size-fits-all answer to organization or to leadership, there's no one-size-fits-all for industry/community collaboration. The complexity of this is well symbolized by the title of Thomas Friedman's book, *The Lexus and the Olive Tree,* where the robotics-built Lexus represents global high-tech extended enterprise and the centuries-old olive tree represents deep cultural roots.[8] In a sense, modern corporations "share" assets and corporate culture with all of the communities within which they operate leading to a blended culture for all.

It is essential to understand the importance of this facet of community as one thinks about the NGM workforce. The outputs of any manufacturing enterprise spring from not only the physical, mental, and organizational production, but also from the deeper infrastructure of the community. This includes the values, technological base, organizational structure, and communication norms of the population from which the company's workforce is recruited. Success in coming years will depend on unprecedented levels of cooperation, understanding, and trust across a globally defined culture.

■ EXERCISE

How would you characterize your company's organization?

➤ Is it well suited to the product line with which you are most closely associated?

➤ Does the organization facilitate communications and accurate decision making?

What do you think have been your company's five most significant decisions related to the product line?

➤ Who made them?

➤ How would you rate the quality of the decisions?

➤ Did the company's organization help or inhibit good decision making?

➤ How would you characterize leadership in your company?

    ➤ At the executive level? At the operational or floor level?

    ➤ What are the strengths? What are the weaknesses?

To what extent is your company a collaborator with the other companies, government, and education in your community?

■ NOTES

1. Peter F. Drucker, *Management Challenges for the 21st Century* (New York: HarperBusiness, 1999).
2. H-J. Warnecke, *The Fractal Company* (Berlin: Springer Verlag, 1993).
3. See Steven L. Goldman, Roger N. Nagel, and Kenneth Preiss, *Agile Competitors and Virtual Organizations: Strategies for Enriching the Customer* (New York: Van Nostrand Reinhold, 1995) and Kenneth Preiss, Steven L. Goldman, and Roger N. Nagel, *Cooperate to Compete: Building Agile Business Relationships Customer* (New York: Van Nostrand Reinhold, 1996).
4. The Consortium for Advanced Manufacturing—International (CAM-I) maintains a web page, www.cam-i.org/ngms.html, which provides access to the NGMS Project.
5. The University of Hanover maintains a web page, www. hms.ifw.uni-hannover.de/ for the Holonics Project.
6. Peter Vaill, *Managing as a Performing Art: New Ideas for a World of Chaotic Change* (San Francisco: Josey-Bass, 1989), pp. 21–22.
7. Michael E. McGill and John W. Slocum, Jr., "A Little Leadership, Please?" *Organizational Dynamics*, vol. 26 (January 1, 1998).
8. Thomas L. Friedman, *The Lexus and the Olive Tree* (New York: Farrar, Strauss, and Giroux, 1999).

Chapter

The Voice of the Customer—Again

11:30 AM: LUNCH WITH HAWK

Hawk Brewster. Josiah Jerimiah Brewster IV, but everyone has called him Hawk since he was a jet jockey flying A-4s. CEO of ABC/Flightways. Across Broad Continents was one of BAI's first customers, a loyal customer ever since the transition to jets in the early 1960s. You got to know Hawk nearly 20 years ago when he was ABC's director of fleet planning and you had just emerged from an assistant plant manager's job and were getting your marketing stripes. You've been good personal friends ever since.

Much in common, and you are both anachronisms—parallel careers, culminating as CEOs of the companies where you've lived your entire careers. You grew up in your companies and have been together a lot in the past two decades. You wonder how many of your successors will say that—or even want to say that—in an age where few companies and fewer careers have that sort of stability built into them.

You were pretty sure you knew why Hawk called you about lunch today. Sure, you are old friends, and he was coming to town to kick off the nonstop service to New Delhi. But ABC/Flightways has started a new bid cycle and it was a sure thing Hawk would talk about that.

You were right. One of the reasons you like Hawk is that he's an absolute straight arrow, tell-it-like-it-is, sort of guy. Trustworthy and open. But tough. His love of flying and of airplanes and of building the airline doesn't mask his Wharton MBA and the green eyeshade of his time in Finance.

So when Hawk started talking about the on-going effects of deregulation and competition, of the unforeseen incompatibilities brought by the merger with Flightways, of the hard won labor peace of three years ago that was now being buffeted at the start of talks about the next contracts, it was pretty clear where the discussion was leading.

When you are dealing with the alligators in your own swamp, it's easy to lose sight of the alligators that your customers are fighting off. BAI doesn't make a profit unless ABC/Flightways buys your planes. ABC/Flightways can't buy your planes unless they sell a bunch of seat miles.

ABC/Flightways can't buy your planes unless their product is better than the next airline's. For them, "better" is in the eye of the airline passenger. Since there is no "standard passenger" with a standard definition of "better," ABC/Flightways is constantly seeking the best compromise. Low fares. Better cabin service. No excess labor costs. Strategies to retain good employees. Frequent departures. Routes that blanket the world. Routes that each make a profit. Trying to make each passenger feel like the airline was there just to meet her or his needs. Trying to make the employees feel like they work for the best airline. Trying to make the shareholders feel that they have made the best investment in the industry.

Hawk's problems aren't unique. They mirror yours or those of anyone trying to build and sustain a profitable enterprise.

At lunch, Hawk was candid. Your competition was offering attractive deals. Selling ABC/Flightways this year was no sure thing. The nearly exclusive relationship with BAI was worth something to ABC. Since Flightway's fleet included your competitors' recent models, they have an improved access to the merged airline's decision makers and fewer training and maintenance hurdles to overcome.

The combined board of ABC/Flightways includes people who've overseen quite satisfactory relationships with those competitors. The board has made it very clear that the next deal for new aircraft will have to be absolutely the best deal for ABC/Flightways shareholders. It's a black-and-white imperative forced onto a complicated multi-attribute decision involving a plethora of shades of gray. So the first thing you understand is that however you structure your bid, it has to be structured in a way that helps Hawk show the board that it really is the best deal.

Then Hawk ticked off his, and the board's, concerns:

➤ The FAA determined that one of the BAI models bought 12 years ago has a design flaw. Fixing the flaw has cost BAI, but it has also cost ABC/Flightways a bundle. They want protection from that sort of problem with the new planes.

➤ ABC/Flightways planners have an aggressive schedule for fleet expansion. Can BAI meet the schedule? Missing deliveries by only a few months could cost the airline market share or new markets.

➤ On the other hand, Flightways overbought just before the recession of 1990 and their board members want to protect the airline if the economy suffers a similar downturn. How flexible can BAI be?

➤ ABC/Flightways planners see gaps in BAI's product line. Can BAI stretch the Egret or scale down the Eagle in time to meet the airline's needs? What about the SuperEagle?

➤ ABC/Flightways wants to get into the same-day express mail business. They need specially designed cargo handling equipment and cargo holds that can be converted from express mail to conventional cargo.

➤ ABC/Flightways is aggressively expanding in less developed markets. BAI will have to provide service in unfamiliar places. And they need multimedia training and operations manuals in a wide variety of languages—they can find or train skilled people, but those people may not be fluent in English.

➤ They need aircraft that can fly in and out of poorly maintained, high altitude, airports with wide temperature variations. Some countries, or even cities, seem almost paranoid on environmental issues. ABC/Flightways planes have to be environmentally "clean."

➤ As the airline expands globally, it has to show the countries in which it operates that it is a "good citizen." It would help if they could point to BAI's investments in manufacturing and support facilities.

It goes without saying that the cost/seat mile for any BAI model would have to equal or be better than the competing models.

Hawk never asks you many questions. He puts his cards on the table and expects you to be as open with him. So you told him about the strategy review leading up to your meetings on Thursday and Friday. You told him about your concerns, too:

➤ Your board was pushing you on margins. They were pushing you on revenues, too. Whatever deal you came up with was going to have to be a winner for BAI.

➤ ABC/Flightways wasn't your only customer with unique needs. And some of the other airlines' needs were crossways to theirs.

➤ You needed additional launch airlines before you could launch a new variation of Egret or Eagle.

➤ You were trying to understand the industry's signals on the desirability of a class of aircraft substantially larger than the Eagle. You felt its time would come, but when?

➤ Rapidly fluctuating demands lead to higher costs for you and the airlines, so you needed to build as much stability into your operations as you could.

➤ Many countries put demands on BAI for investment. It was a balancing act to keep costs in line, product on schedule, and quality in the Six Sigma range—and satisfy the Ministries of Industry and Development, or whatever the title that was used.

➤ You appreciated Hawk assigning some of his experienced flight and maintenance personnel to work on the recently introduced models. You felt that some of BAI's people ought to get experience working inside the airline to see how BAI's products really were used.

At the end of the lunch, Hawk left to send off his latest Eagle to New Delhi and you pondered. No more low fruit. Every bid, even with old friends, needed creativity and hard work. You had to prove your planes and your relationship were so valuable to ABC/Flightways that they just could not turn your bid down. Tall order. No time to waste. No margins for schedule or cost overruns. Lots of room for innovation, though—better designs, better manufacturing, better business processes, more and better service. There was urgency there—you had to get everyone on your team feeling that urgency. It had to show in the ABC/Flightways bid, and every other bid BAI tendered.

■ EXERCISE

Think about your three best customers:

What is happening with your customers' customers?

Are their numbers growing? Or shrinking? Are they, on average, older? Or younger?

How are their needs changing?

Is your product helping your customers keep their customers satisfied?

Are your customers as responsive to their customers as they need to be to maintain their competitiveness?

Are your products or business processes inhibiting your customers' responsiveness?

How can your customers use your products or services to improve their responsiveness?

Do your customers have the right people, with the right knowledge, in place to respond to their customers' needs?

Do you have the pipeline in place to provide your customers' people with the knowledge of your products, services, and processes that they need?

Are there services you can provide, profitably, to help your customers' people be more responsive?

How is globalization affecting your customers?

➤ Is your position as a supplier threatened by global competition?

➤ How can your customers use your products as they reach for global markets?

➤ Are your customers good team members?

➤ How can you help them team better with you?

➤ How can you help them team better with their customers?

➤ In what ways are your customers' corporate cultures like yours? In what ways do they differ?

Chapter 7

Product Realization

MONDAY, 1:05 PM: FACING A CHANGING MARKET

At 1:05, you hung up from the last of the calls that required immediate attention and joined the Cycle Time Reduction Task Force in the ELT Conference Room. The first chart of the presentation (Figure 7.1) was already displayed.

You and your COO, Jose Herrara commissioned the Task Force three months ago. You had watched as your customers changed. When the airline industry was regulated, there had been long-term stability. All the major airlines had established franchises. Everyone knew his place and fleet planning was less complicated. Aircraft were simpler,

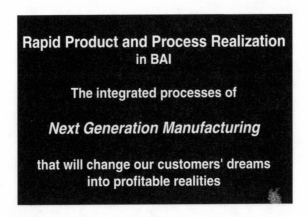

Figure 7.1 The BAI Product Realization Task Force Report

operations were simpler, and you could map out long-term product strategies with little regard for changes in the market structure.

Since the worldwide shift to airline deregulation started in the late 1970s, you had watched two phenomena. The explosive growth in passenger miles was good for BAI. But the constant churn of airlines, merging, starting up, dying off, was a constant challenge for BAI's market development. It had become difficult to predict when demand for a particular product would make it profitable to produce. Take the SuperEagle—you believed deep in your gut that its time would come, but you couldn't predict when; you couldn't invest much in it now if it's time was still 10 years off. But what if the market for 750-seat aircraft took shape in three years? Then there was ABC/Flightways' need for a plane intermediate between Egret and Eagle—you knew if you were going to build it, you would have to respond faster than ever before.

BAI wasn't unique. The recurrent themes at informal gatherings of CEO's were economic and governmental trends, managing investors, finding good people, getting product to market in time. It didn't seem to matter what the product was, everyone was feeling strong pressures to reduce the time to design, develop, and manufacture products. Time scales differed, of course. The personal computer (PC) people had to cope with the insatiable demand for "faster, better, cheaper" PCs, made possible by an almost continuous flow of faster, better, cheaper components and technology. Their time scales were measured in days and weeks. And now people are even talking about replacing PC's with smart telephones connected by Internet services. You had longer time scales—months and years—to work with. Your products are a lot more complicated than PCs, but the problems of change and growing complexity are universal. The automotive folks had intermediate time scales. But whatever the industry, the time you have to realize a new product profitably is a quarter of the time you had twenty years ago, and you shouldn't expect that pressure to change anytime soon.

You had been making strides. Applying concurrent engineering to products and manufacturing processes had helped a lot. So had the improved emphasis on quality that led to less rework. But you and Jose realized that the progress BAI had made was not enough. Your competitors were getting better faster than you were and your customers were coming to you with requests you'd have branded as outrageous a few years ago. BAI was going to have to get smarter.

Diane Wozinski and Adolfo Horgen, respectively Jose's vice-presidents for operations and engineering, took executive responsibility. They named a small team of management and technical leaders and chartered them to look at everything it takes to get a product from the "what I really need is . . ." or "wonder if we could make a profit on a product like . . ." stage to the point where you've delivered it to customers who are pleased with the value you've given them—and continue to be pleased even after delivery.

You didn't want just a description of how BAI did things now, with suggestions for incremental improvements. You wanted the task force to take the best ideas out there—for example, lessons from lean manufacturing, lessons from agile manufacturing, concepts from all the advanced manufacturing roadmaps and put them together for BAI the way the NGM Project did it for all of manufacturing. The task force had responded with a detailed white paper that included many specific recommendations.

■ CHARACTERISTICS OF RAPID PRODUCT AND PROCESS REALIZATION (RPPR)

The process for product realization in the NGM Framework for Action is called *Rapid Product and Process Realization (RPPR)*. RPPR includes all the processes to design, build, and maintain products through their expected life and final disposal. The name recognizes the fact that the processes of product realization are as important as the product characteristics themselves. Rapid Product and Process Realization addresses both the front-end (product conceptualization and design) and back-end (product production, maintenance, and recycling) efforts associated with the lifecycle of a product. The front-end effort involves the identification of market requirements, computer-aided design, functional modeling, virtual or actual prototyping, manufacturing process selection, and virtual manufacturing or factory simulation. The back-end effort addresses design for assembly, testing, disassembly, disposal and/or reuse, and other environmental issues. RPPR has some important characteristics that guide its implementation (see Figure 7.2).

The more a process, even a complicated process like RPPR, can be structured, the more it can be assimilated into a company's culture. As part of the reliable and stable culture of the company, the structure can reduce the communications overhead by providing a basis for common expectations and assumptions. The structure ensures that the essentials get done. If the structure is right, then the essentials are done efficiently and on time.

In reality, RPPR is a mega-process that includes many processes spread across many, many functions, across several geographic regions, and, unless the enterprise is one of the very few fully vertically

Figure 7.2 Characteristics of RPPR

integrated enterprises still extant, across diverse companies. Given the complexity of RPPR for all but the simplest of products, it is important that RPPR be integrated across functions and across geographic and company boundaries. There is a time factor to integration, too. There is a need for the integrated results to be available simultaneously for the many functions involved—and a need for integration so that work can follow the sun across time zones.

The goal is to develop products that are "right the first time"—with the right functions, with quality that meets or exceeds customer expectations. The goal is products that are viewed by customers as being of good value and that are available to the customer when and where he or she needs them. "Right the first time" also means a Six-Sigma design, one requiring little or no rework after the commitment to production. (*Six-Sigma* is a buzzword for "as perfect as humanly possible," derived from the statistical concept that all results falling within six standard deviations of a mean value should be within the specified tolerances for the process.) Finally, "right the first time" means Six-Sigma production processes, so that the chances of a product not meeting specifications when it comes out of each process is miniscule. "Right the first time" avoids the financial and time costs of rework. The NGM "right-the-first-time" Product Cycle gives you a big advantage over the old ways (see Figure 7.3).

Yes, RPPR should be a structured process, but RPPR should not be a rigid process. First, RPPR has to accommodate the myriad demands of the marketplace—now economy is important, tomorrow safety, and the next day style . . . *here. There,* the market has other priorities. Today's product is obsolete tomorrow, so RPPR needs to switch rapidly to a different product, or maybe to enhancements of today's. Mix.

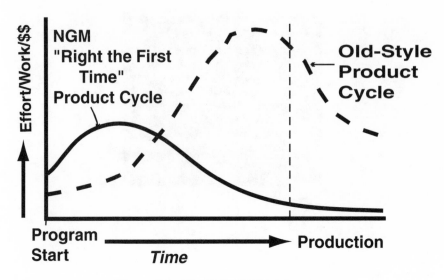

Figure 7.3 The NGM RPPR Advantage

Match. Mass customization. So not only should products be right the first time, they should be "right-all-the-time products." You want never to produce a wrong product or if you do, you want to be able to discontinue its production quickly and cheaply.

RPPR is a structure for a dynamic, nearly life-like, set of evolving processes. No wonder there is such fascination with the mathematics of complexity theory and emergent systems as a language to describe manufacturing systems!

In the past decade, it has become common to speak of *lean manufacturing* and of *agile manufacturing,* even to speak of movements or crusades for leanness or for agility. RPPR incorporates the important lessons of both movements. The lesson of lean manufacturing is that RPPR should include a continuing quest for eliminating processes and activities that do not add value to the product, for replacing necessary processes with ones that achieve the same or a better result for less cost, and for constantly improving the processes left in place. The great stress of agility is readiness to respond to change, ultimately even to respond to change that is not predicted or foreseen. The old adage, "If it ain't broke, don't fix it" may work for awhile, but when new competitors pass you in the dust, you may find it no longer holds.

RPPR consists of four essential elements (Figure 7.4):

1. A systematic Integrated Product and Process Development (IPPD) methodology that makes much use of modeling and simulation.
2. Innovative, educated, and skilled people able to work in geographically distributed multidisciplinary, multilingual Integrated Product Teams (IPTs).
3. Unit processes and equipment that are flexible and modular, even programmable by the process engineer.
4. An (extended) enterprisewide computing environment including interoperable and transparent, integrated business, design, manufacturing, and maintenance systems and tools.

RPPR is a superset of IPPD. RPPR starts when a company perceives a market opportunity because customers have said so or because the company in its creativity can conceive of a product whose value will become apparent to customers. RPPR includes all the processes leading to the delivery of the product into the customers' hands. It may also extend all the way to the end of the useful product

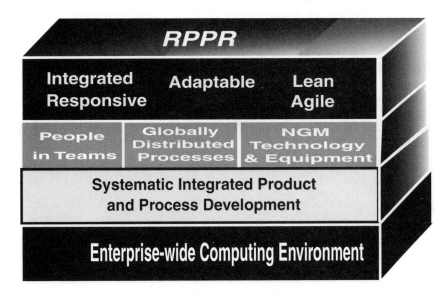

Figure 7.4 The Elements of RPPR

life, especially if the product is one that can be up-graded or reconfigured for additional functionality.

RPPR must consider the *entire* product lifecycle. It must do so first
because of the increasing numbers of customers who make purchase
decisions based on lifecycle cost, with a significant weighting on cumulative operating costs. Second, in many countries the delivery of
the product does not end the manufacturing enterprise's responsibility, especially if final disposal of the used product can degrade the
environment.

Nowhere are the lessons of RPPR more apparent than they are in
the personal computer industry, whose 25-year history is littered with
products that were unresponsive to the customers' evolving needs. The
late release of new products (for example, IBM's PS/2) cost market
share. Product shortages (e.g., IBM's ThinkPad™) have meant some
companies couldn't seize lucrative opportunities. On the other hand,
some inventories of quickly outdated products have depressed profits
at Apple, Compaq, and other companies. The unremitting price competition has forced companies to squeeze the costs out of their products—or die. The competition won by providing the functionality and
technology that customers want and use—available to them when they
want it. The pressures have forced the continual creation of new business models and new business processes, each tweaking the performance of its predecessors while reducing costs.

In the next five chapters, we will explore RPPR. Chapter 8 looks at
Integrated Product and Process Development (IPPD). Chapter 9 describes the impact of modeling and simulation on product and process
realization. Chapter 10 discusses the equipment and manufacturing
processes NGM company will use. Chapter 11 depicts the extended enterprises that will have to be formed by NGM companies to operate the
RPPR process. Finally, Chapter 12 surveys the systems support companies use today for product realization—these systems will gradually
assume the leanness and agility that next generation manufacturing
demands.

■ EXERCISE

Think about the way your company puts products in the hands of
your customers:

> ➤ How structured a process do you use? Is the process docu-
> mented? Do all the people who ought to know about it actually
> follow the process?

➤   How integrated is your product realization process?

➤   How much rework does your company have to do on accepted designs? How much rework is there when you are setting up production processes? How large is your inventory that requires rework (not the work-in-progress of good parts)? How much rework has to be done to "finished" products? How much rework has to be done after the product is delivery to the customer?

Think about the last major shifts in your industry. Was your company able to stay ahead of the pack in making the needed changes in the product realization process?

Chapter 8

Integrated Product and Process Development (IPPD)

The NGM Report places Integrated Product and Process Development (IPPD) at the heart of Rapid Product and Process Realization (RPPR). IPPD is the concurrent, coordinated development of the product and the processes to make the product. IPPD, as used here, is a generic term not meant to provide a specific recipe, but to convey the basic processes of product realization. Different terms are used by different industries to describe the various phases of product development. Over the years, many terms for this highly concurrent, interactive environment have evolved. Much has been written on similar concepts under other names; for example, *concurrent engineering, integrated product development, simultaneous engineering,* and *design build teams.* We do not endorse any one methodology or any one particular implementation of IPPD concepts over another. Each has the desirable objective of avoiding costly redesign, unanticipated problems in production, or compromises that degrade the final product. The key is to put in place the right processes. The interactions within the design process are *rapid, highly concurrent, highly interactive,* and *iterative,* and involve the customer and the entire supplier base with their appropriate counterparts.

The IPPD management strategy is the foundation for the relationships that lead to successful products, relationships within the company, and across the extended enterprise including customers, partners, and the supply chain. The IPPD strategy your company adopts sets the tone and style for the multiple activities necessary to create the quality processes, capabilities, and competencies you need. The strategy will have to support a meaningful and empowered environment.

IPPD is inherently team-based. The teams consist of the required core and support competencies, whether they are contained within your company or are supplemented by the core competencies of partners or by experts from the supplier chain. IPPD teams include all disciplines that could have an impact on the design—at any time in the product lifecycle, including disposition at the end of its useful life. The team should include anyone who is affected by the design in carrying out their own function, be it tooling, fabrication, test equipment, product support, field service, training, environmental disposition, or whatever. Corporate strategy based on IPPD depends on knowing the core competencies of the internal organization and, where they do not exist within the company, having the means to rapidly find and partner with needed external competencies.

In the NGM paradigm for IPPD, most, if not all team members, *simultaneously* participate in multiple product developments. Their core competencies will be so valuable that they will not normally be attached to a single team, unless they have a lead role. The introduction of the entire supply chain into the team at the earliest appropriate time is essential.

The distribution of the enterprise over space and time zones means that it will be harder to co-locate team members. Part of the motivation for well-structured IPPD is the facilitation of work by teams that are co-located virtually, teams in which physical, face-to-face, communication is replaced by electronic communication. Depending on the quality of multimedia support, though, face-to-face meetings may still be needed.

■ IPPD—A STRUCTURED PROCESS

IPPD is the vehicle to structure the cross-functional communications, the decision making, and the action required to minimize the time and effort needed to bring a product to market and to ensure its lifetime success. IPPD is also a vehicle to facilitate parallel product and process development to bring about an overall product solution faster than with the use of the traditional "design it, then figure out how to build it" approach. The goal is to make the best decisions, take the best actions, in the most timely way—throughout the development cycle.

There are many ways to structure IPPD. The key is to make the best decisions in a timely way, with transparency so that all can understand why the decisions were made, and with accountability. Accountability is needed:

> ➤ For the commitment implied when decisions are made within a group.

> ➤ To reward the decisions and actions that contribute to the success of a product.

> ➤ To create an audit trail to encourage learning from failure.

The structure should include defined prerequisites for commitment on product development, major product and process design decisions, and for entry into production. The structure should provide for capturing the design experience in ways that can be translated into useful knowledge repositories. This may be accomplished through traditional documentation or by using automated multimedia techniques for knowledge acquisition. The intent is to use design knowledge as the basis not only for the production processes, but also for maintenance and for user documentation and knowledge delivery.

The structure should provide for iteration, so that as decisions are made on matters of greater and greater detail, decisions that are likely to affect other parts of the IPPD process are surfaced and reviewed.

■ USING QFD TO STRUCTURE COMMUNICATION IN IPPD

We will use the tools of Quality Function Deployment (QFD) (see Figure 8.1) to illustrate one way to structure IPPD communication.[1] QFD is a popular technique to force the customer's view of quality into product and process design. QFD uses a sequence of matrices to ensure that what the customer thinks is important gets translated into design and manufacturing processes. The rows of the matrix are the "what's"—the intended results. The columns are the "how's"—the ways to achieve the intended results. At the intersections of the rows and columns is an assessment of the degree of influence a "how" has in achieving a specific "what."

For example, the first matrix in the QFD sequence relates the customer's requirements of the product, usually stated in qualitative, user-oriented terms, to its quantitative technical characteristics. The qualitative statement, "I want good, maybe not great, performance in my next car," gets translated into "0 to 60 mph in 9.5 seconds." "I do a lot of passing on two lane roads" becomes "45 to 65 mph in 4 seconds."

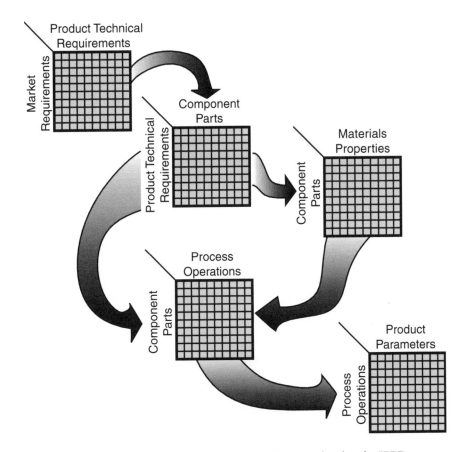

Figure 8.1 Using QFD to Structure Communication in IPPD

Auxiliary information—the customer thinks the finish on the car's door handle is very important, but the ease of using the door lock isn't since she or he expects to use a remote key most of the time; a stamped handle may cost 15 cents, a cast and plated one 60 cents. This information can be carried in rows and used as inputs on the prioritization of the customers' wishes, the technologies and materials to be used and in the production processes.

Figure 8.2 provides an example. In this case, there are seven market requirements to be fulfilled. The product has nine major technical attributes that are thought to contribute to meeting the requirements. The numerical entries in the matrix are weightings (9 = a very important contribution, 3 = an important contribution, 1 = some contribution, blank = no contribution). The weights are subjective. Arriving at

Product Technical Attributes	Attribute 1	Attribute 2	Attribute 3	Attribute 4	Attribute 5	Attribute 6	Attribute 7	Attribute 8	Attribute 9	Importance
Requirement A	3									5
Requirement B	3				1	9				10
Requirement C		9					3			5
Requirement D		1			3			9		2
Requirement E			9	3		9				7
Requirement F	1	9		9		1				2
Requirement G			3				1	1		2
Cost	10	50	5	50	5	80	20	5	60	
Our Quality	5	5	1	5	1	10	1	5	10	
Competitors' Quality	1	10	5	10	1	5	10	5	1	

(Rows labeled at left: Market Requirements)

Figure 8.2 Communicating Market Requirements to Product Engineers

the weights should be a team effort, involving customers as well as product developers.

Additional information can be displayed in the supplementary rows and columns. In Figure 8.2, we display, subjectively, the importance attributed by the customer to each of the market requirements. We also show the relative cost associated with each of the product technical attributes, the quality of execution of the product attributes and the quality in the competitors' products. The point of a matrix like this one is to help define the attributes on which the product developer should put emphasis and to raise questions (such as, "Attribute 9 is costing a lot, but not helping us satisfy a customer requirement. Should we put some of that money into Attribute 2, which has a big influence on customer satisfaction?").

Other matrices relate the technical characteristics with the attributes of particular components. Still other matrices relate the attributes to specific manufacturing processes.

Some companies use the QFD process simply as a check to ensure that adequate communication as all aspects of product and process development are considered. Other companies use QFD to drive decisions by using procedures based on the correlations of the information that particularly lend themselves to be displayed by the matrices.

One of the most influential examples of the use of QFD is that at Xerox Corporation, documented in an important *Harvard Business Review* article by Hauser and Clausing.[2] The "House of Quality" is the first of the QFD matrices relating the "Voice of the Customer" to the Product Technical Attributes. The "roof" of the house is a triangle in which the relationships among the Attributes can be shown.

The structured dialog with customers mediated by the House of Quality is credited with providing the impetus that transformed Xerox

QUALITY FUNCTION DEPLOYMENT (QFD) AT KIMBERLY-CLARK

Kimberly-Clark Corporation used QFD to help specify the manufacturing processes in the mill for the Surpass brand facial tissue. They started by listening to their customers, who told them qualitatively what they wanted. Their wants led to 16 essential product attributes. Kimberly-Clark found that the attributes were influenced by 72 process parameters, which in turn dictated equipment requirements. The customers' "want" expressed, say, as a "soft" towel, was translated into specific actions by operators on particular pieces of equipment.

Kimberly-Clark used QFD's series of "what/how" matrixes to organize, relate, and make judgments about the interactions, conflicts, and synergies among customer wants, product attributes, and process parameters. QFD converts customer-satisfaction measures into factual, actionable business and engineering measures. The first matrix translates customer desires, expressed in their own words, into engineering requirements that help satisfy those "wants." The engineering requirements then became the inputs matrixed with process characteristics. The process characteristics then were matrixed against actual process operations. This provided an audit trail from the real expressions of need given by the customer all the way to the equipment operator.

In addition to infusing the voice of the customer throughout product and process development, the use of QFD improved Kimberly-Clark's time-to-market. Diane Scheurell, a Kimberly-Clark research manager, is quoted as saying, "We declared production start-up one month early, we initiated product rollout two weeks early, and process redesign was nonexistent."[3]

from a stodgy 1970s company out of touch with customer needs to a strong, competitive 1990s company. Xerox' history provides an excellent example of the need for innovative companies to "re-invent" themselves time after time as new competitive realities unfold.

■ ESSENTIAL ELEMENTS OF IPPD

Within the structure of IPPD (see Figure 8.3), there are the essential elements of:

➤ An accurate comprehension of the customers' needs and requirements, validated with the customers' key operating units and staff, and with the customers' financial backers.

➤ An up-to-date knowledge of the relevant technologies—their state of readiness, their costs, their special requirements.

➤ Re-use of successful designs that are easily reconfigurable for new applications. The goal is to develop families of designs that can be quickly modified for custom needs.

➤ Prototyping of products, processes, and systems, with emphasis on "virtual" prototypes constructed through computer modeling and simulation, augmented by rapid prototyping technology.

➤ In-process verification, both of IPPD and of the developed processes, so that quality defects can be detected before fixing them becomes a costly and time-consuming exercise.

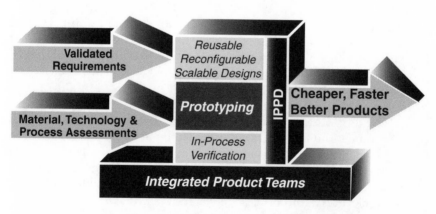

Figure 8.3 Key Elements of IPPD

➤ An underpinning of integrated teams that include all the relevant stakeholders, not limited to product and process development engineers, but including, possibly, customers, operations personnel, and financial stakeholders.

➤ Exploring and Validating Market Requirements

The first step in delivering a profitable product is to understand the customers' requirements sufficiently that you can build a product and give the customers enough value to justify their paying you your cost plus a good profit margin.

Understanding requirements is easier when they are for improvements in established products for which there is an observable market. Customers, development engineers, and manufacturing engineers all have ideas on how to improve the product—the issue is one of costing and prioritization of improvements. Companies have structured the requirements definition process in many ways. The scale of the product, the size of the development investment, and the target market may dictate different tools for requirements gathering. Software packages are now available to perform much of this work. Many companies use market surveys and focus groups to obtain preliminary data. Automobile companies can use that kind of data, which can be refined as customers are exposed to exterior style alternatives, to computer displays of possible interiors, perhaps even to virtual reality presentations in which they can experience the ride and handling of a proposed vehicle.

It is not as easy to understand requirements for new innovative products entering the market. These are instances when entrepreneurs have to predict the success of products even before the reasons were fully articulated for which customers would buy them.

In the 1940s, Tom Watson predicted there might be a market for a small number—less than 10—of the earliest large electronic computers, and IBM took the plunge anyway. Less than two decades later, Tom Watson, Jr., "bet the company" that customers would buy general-purpose computers with a standard architecture and operating system. In the next decade, Digital bet that there was a market for smaller computers with real-time operating systems. The following decade PC pioneers bet that there was a consumer market for desktop machines more powerful that Watson's behemoths. And the next decade brought the World Wide Web, the Web Browser, and a continuing stream of new products that could not have been imagined 50 years ago. Who besides the entrepreneurs operating with gut-level faith, at the start of each of those ventures, would have predicted the transforming success of information technology?

The signs pointing to success were there, however. Large companies needed to keep up with accounting data; the large data processing machine was an obvious answer. Companies trying to control complicated processes needed a way to coordinate the results from hardwired controllers. While no one could imagine the ubiquitous spread of PCs, their utility could be seen. The World Wide Web and the Mosaic browser filled a niche need—a way to improve collaboration among scientific researchers, especially computational scientists. This net turned out to be a great way for grandmothers to communicate with grandchildren a thousand miles away, or for Gen-Xers to order books, too.

The Japanese have developed a process that uses the open market and efficient small-lot manufacturing. Sony and other consumer electronics manufacturers test the market for a new product by putting small batches on the market and collecting customer responses. If the response is favorable, the product enters a series of successive improvements and enhancements. If the response is unfavorable, the companies probe deeper to understand why, and then either redesign the concept and product or abandon it altogether.

Usually the customer wants many things, things that may be difficult to satisfy simultaneously. I want a laptop that includes a high speed processor, lots of RAM, a big hard disk, a bright, high-contrast, high resolution display, a DVD drive, and a DSL modem, that will operate on a battery for a trans-Pacific flight, doesn't weigh much and doesn't cost much. But I can't have the fastest, biggest, newest, lightest, if I'm willing to pay only $1000. What are my priorities? How fast is fast enough? Can I live with 600×800 pixels? Can I live with a 3 Gigabyte hard disk? What's the best compromise so that my needs are met, affordably, so that I walk away with a product that delivers value for me? The next person will probably have a different set of priorities. Understanding the customers' individual priorities is key to your success.

Dialog with the Customer

Innovative, never-been-seen-before products, or products derived in never imagined ways from other product streams, are increasingly important. Never-the-less, any good requirements definition process starts with the customer.

The best way to find out what the customer wants is to ask. The days of "we know what the customer wants—and he'll jolly well buy it from us!" are long gone.

Now companies look to their customers to tell them, explicitly or implicitly, what they want. They understand that the customer is the arbiter of a product's acceptability—that the ultimate measure of quality is how the customer values the product. The goal is for customers to tell you what is important to them, and for you to tell them what you can deliver to them—and still make a profit.

Everyone in a company who encounters customers can be part of the requirements process, just by observing the customers' use—or misuse—of the product. You can see when customers grow frustrated by product deficiencies; you can listen to the emotion in their "wish" lists. An alert service organization can provide lots of insight into customer needs or the ways customers abuse the product. Some companies go further, assigning product developers to talk with product users, even to the point of working within the customer's operations.

Surveys by mail or phone can provide a great deal of raw data. Increasingly, computerized databases provide even more. Microsoft

CHRYSLER USES EMOTIONAL RESPONSES TO DESIGN THE PT PROWLER

Chrysler used a hybrid process to help nail down the functional and styling requirements for the PT Prowler, a product that doesn't fit an established market segment. With retro styling reminiscent of the 1940s "woodie" station wagons, it isn't quite a minivan, not quite a compact sedan, not quite a light SUV. Since its market niche didn't exist, Chrysler couldn't start with the successful designs and ask potential customers in focus groups how they would like it improved. Instead, Chrysler convened focus groups to evoke emotions and feelings in response to the PT Prowler's early designs. The focus groups didn't sit around a table discussing product features. Instead, members of the focus groups lounged on comfortable couches with their eyes closed, listening to the PT Prowler concept. They pictured their emotional responses, sometimes in words, sometimes in drawings. Psychologists helped guide the translation of these responses into recommendations for changes in the product concept and then into suggestions for changes in the design. Chrysler was immensely successful in pioneering a market segment with its minivans—it remains to be seen if the PT Prowler will open another segment for them.

gains data on me when I register a new purchase to obtain its warranty. It gathers more data when I let Microsoft inventory all the applications software on my machine. Microsoft can use data mining technology to identify gaps in my inventory. It can even predict the products I and others like me will need next. Microsoft continues the dialog when it releases Beta versions of its products. Customer critiques lead to changes in the final product that make it more congruent with customer wants.

The first of the QFD matrices can be used to structure the dialog with customers if the customers are involved. Shapiro describes the use of Quality Function Deployment (QFD) and Customer-Oriented Product Concepting (COPC) as ways to translate customers' qualitative "wants" into measurable product attributes and manufacturing processes. If your customers are involved actively in the translation of their wishes into technical specifications, there are fewer opportunities for your product development team's natural biases to creep into the product design.

Boeing went further in the design of the 777 by including experienced airlines flight and ground operations personnel on the design teams. Boeing's customers were there as the early design decisions were being made. They were able to say, "yes, that looks good, but what we really meant here was . . . " And Boeing was able to say, "you want this, but that's going to cost a bunch. What if we did . . . " So in the end there was less need for costly redesign as the plane neared production.

MIT's Dorothy Leonard calls the endpoint of this dialog with the customer *empathetic design.*[4] Empathetic design is a team sport—a design effort in which the designer learns enough about the way the customer perceives his or her needs that the designer begins to be able to "feel" what's good—or what's bad—about a product concept. At the same time, the designer brings the art of the possible—the ways a wide range of materials, parts, and processes might be combined into a responsive product—and elicits the customer's feelings about the design alternatives.

Requirements Definitions

The customer wants value—they are giving you a scarce resource, their wealth, in return for something that will help them do what they want to do. Value is based on the product's function, its quality, and its timing (see Figure 8.4).

What is the *value* of the function to the customer? How much will the customer pay to acquire the product? to use it? In an era of

---

WHAT NEXT? THE QUANDARY OF SUCCESS

Our friend, a senior development manager for a Silicon Valley success story—0 to multibillions in 10 years—was talking about his latest task force assignment: find out what the customers want!

His company started in the proverbial garage. A bunch of techies and Stanford graduate students who saw a real need if the Internet was ever going to be a commercial success. They found the venture capital, then survived the months of 20-hour days needed to get their first product to the market—and the market thought it was great. They were there first and they cornered the emerging market. They knew how to improve their product, and they did—staying ahead of competitors who entered the market later. But now they have, by Internet standards, a mature product line and their competitors have closed the gaps in product functionality and quality. Worse yet, the competition is biting into their profit margins.

What to do? How can the company sustain its high profit margins and ever-increasing revenue growth? It may be years before the first set of products plays out, but what then? That's when the company decided it needed to learn from its customers!

---

environmental constraints, how much is the customer willing to pay for disposal of the product when it no longer has value? Is the customer more concerned about the acquisition cost or the operations cost? Is the customer open to alternatives in the distribution of cost over the product lifecycle?

What does the customer want to do with the product—that's the product's *functionality*. That's a different question from the equally

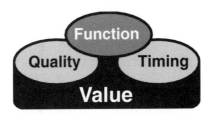

Figure 8.4 The Customer Wants *Value*

important one of what does the customer wants the product to do? Ultimately it's the functional specification—what an architect would term the *architectural program*—that embodies the value of the product to the user.

So it works. Is it hard for the customer to use? What are the human factors, the ergonomics that must be considered? Is the customer willing to pay the cost in time and thought to learn how to use the product? Will the customer be irritated or satisfied by the placement and visibility of gauges and controls?

What about design? Is it stylish? Did the dramatic styling of the Ford Taurus of the late 1990s cost it market share, or did it attract buyers who otherwise would have bought Chevys? How much design innovation is too much innovation? how little is too little?

Can the product fit within the customer's systems? Has the customer developed a way of using other products that predisposes him or her to a specific style of operation? Will your product have to work with other products the customer already has? Does he live in a Windows98™ or a Macintosh™ world? Think of the single mom who has just been promoted to a job with customer contact, realizes she needs to augment her wardrobe, and wears a size 6 blouse and a size 10 skirt—the classic requirements for "plug-and-play," "mix-and-match." She's likely to prefer a line of clothes with size and color flexibility that fits with her prior purchases.

When does the customer want to gain value from the product? That's *timing*. Value is a temporal thing—it doesn't last any longer than the customer's perception of value. You may have a lot of money tied up in a product in inventory, but it doesn't have any value unless the customer thinks so. And value is a *now* thing. If it's September, the customer who wants a lightweight backpacking tent for hiking the Muir Trail next summer may be willing to wait for several months for your new design—but if it's early June, forget it.

Part of the customer's assignment of value is how confident the customer can be that the product's value will be available whenever and for as long as the customer wants it. That's *quality* for the customer. You may think of quality as the number of defect-free toasters you make, but the customer judges quality by the toaster's ability to take the wear and tear of years of normal use—maybe even abnormal use—and still make presentable toast when the customer's mother-in-law comes to visit. If that toaster provided good toast longer than expected, when the customer finally decides to replace it, she'll buy your newest model, at the same time telling her friends how faithful the old one was.

Tracking Requirements

Requirements are in the present—when the customer contracts to buy the product. Whatever the customer said in the past, the requirements that count are the ones that surface as the desire is established and the commitment is made. A year ago, you told yourself and others—maybe even automobile manufacturers—that you wanted a beautiful new sport sedan. You could describe it in detail. But as the time came to buy, you realized that attractive as that sport sedan was, a four-wheel-drive sport utility vehicle fit your needs better. The requirements that count are the ones you have when you sign the check or the contract.

Complacency. Companies suffer from assumptions that customers don't change. "We went out and talked with our customers. Now we know their needs. We'll go back to the development lab and have just what they want on the market 18 months from now." Right, except in 18 months consumer fadism will dictate that instead of green widgets with hard edges, they really want blue widgets with rounded shapes. If you stay open to customer requirements, if you continually revalidate the requirements, you can know 9 months from now, before your tooling and dye operations are fixed, that the widget fashion trend is to soft blue shapes. You can make middevelopment changes instead of having an idle production facility or a pile of unsold green things.

➤ Material, Technology, and Process Assessments

There was a time when products were not so technology-rich. A hundred years ago, a garage mechanic had command of most of the technology needed to build an automobile, or even an airplane. The repertoire of materials was equally limited. There was a time when a new technology or a new material crept slowly into products and processes. No more. The waves of change in technology and materials can sweep products onto—or off—the market in weeks.

An important input to IPPD is an early and accurate assessment of the technologies that can best contribute to a successful product or process. In Chapters 13 to 15, we will consider Knowledge Processes more generally. Technology and Materials Assessments are a specific outcome of the Knowledge Supply process, intended to provide usable knowledge as it is needed.

There are two kinds of assessments. First, there are assessments of the technologies, materials, and processes that the company uses now or can predict will become important. These might be thought of as being part of the company's *portfolio,* and should be the subject of on-going assessment within a tracking function in the company's research and development organization.

These on-going assessments involve maintaining awareness of the related R&D literature, having access to academic and industrial R&D labs, considering the improvements and alternatives offered by vendors, and developing a repository of best practices from competing companies and related industries. For example, a company that makes body panels for automobiles would want to maintain on-going assessments of steels, aluminums, and even composites. They would want to understand the latest quality measuring technologies, employing those that promise the most economical maintenance of product quality. They also would want to track the latest stamping and molding processes.

The results of adopting new materials and technologies as they become practical can be dramatic. IBM recently adopted a new process using copper instead of aluminum for the connectors within integrated circuits. It's a subtle, but important, change that enabled IBM to gain a 20 percent or more performance advantage in the dog-eat-dog competition for high-end mainframes.

The second kind of assessments are the *ad hoc* ones needed when in the course of product or process development, other technologies or materials may emerge unexpectedly as candidates for inclusion. These must be subjected to ad hoc assessments. At these times, immediate access to expert knowledge sources becomes important. On-line access to public data bases, to university research, to reports of pre-competitive R&D consortia, and to other knowledge resources can accelerate the assessment.

The assessment of a technology or material should include:

➤ *Functionality*—what are its basic parameters? How can it be used?

➤ *Coverage*—what is its range of application, relative to the foreseeable uses a company might have? The more the coverage the better the return on an investment in it.

➤ *Quality*—what are its inherent quality characteristics?

➤ *Degree of readiness*—is this a technology or material that is just emerging from a research lab and whose adoption carries high risk, or is it proven and low-risk? Do handbook descriptions of its applications exist, or will the company be "writing the book" if it uses it?

➤ *Costs*—what are the capital costs of introducing it? the training costs of learning how to use it? the operational costs? the costs of integrating the technology or material into existing processes or with processes that will remain unchanged?

➤ *Availability*—how plentiful is it? or can it be created on demand? Could availability become a factor in meeting the market demands?

➤ *Alternatives*—with what alternatives should the technology or material be compared? Are any of the alternatives considered "best practice"?

➤ Design Economics and Design Repositories

In the early days of computers, every new model computer meant an entirely new design. Each design was costly. Costs came down as companies standardized computer architectures and application program interfaces (APIs). Proven circuit designs were used in many different models, as were proven modules of the operating system. The emphasis shifted from the re-invention of basic pieces of the design to the innovation required to make the designs more reliable, more flexible, and less expensive.

Today, innovation is at a premium, but not for its own sake. Innovation is important to differentiate products, for new products, for less costly processes. But if a part, embodying a function that is found in most of your company's products, is redesigned for each product variation, then it is wasteful of your time and your creative talent. Redesign should accommodate as many of the old applications as possible. Better to use the designer's time and creativity on the parts that will be unique, or that will have special wear, or which otherwise give an important, differentiating value for the customer.

The economics of design dictate the use of designs that are:

➤ Reusable in many product or process applications.

➤ Parameterized and scalable so that their technical attributes can be sized appropriately to the need.

➤ Adaptable to differing materials and technologies so that the designs do not inhibit use of less expensive or better processes.

➤ Modular and reconfigurable, with defined interfaces, to provide flexibility in production and encourage interchangeability.

Early on, Toyota and Honda showed the value of designing a common *platform* that can support a host of product variations. Chrysler's venerable "K Car" platform, used for compact-class sedans, sports sedans, convertibles, the first of the modern minivans, and stretched for quasi-luxury sedans, saved Chrysler from extinction because the platform was so versatile.

It is simply not a good business practice to redesign all the parts of a transaxle for every model General Motors car. It makes more sense to have a few basic transaxle designs, especially if experience has proven them to be reliable, and to augment those designs with vehicle-specific, or engine-train-specific, modifications. Then the cost of one major design effort can be spread across many different car models.

Even if each product must be a custom product, the design need not be a custom design. In the early 1990s, a mid-sized manufacturer of industrial pumps designed a new pump for each order it received. As a well-respected vendor, the manufacturer enjoyed a good reputation. But its unit costs were high and competitors could offer good value for less. Better to do business by standardizing on a family of platform designs and using creativity to ensure that the design sold to a customer was the one that best fit the customer's need.

To be competitive, the Next Generation Manufacturing enterprise will use an electronic backbone for communication of product and process designs, formulae, and performance characteristics. The information will be stored as digital models. As we will discuss next, each data element in the design must carry an unambiguous definition, and the interfaces with other components must be specified precisely, so that there is no confusion when a design done in Toronto is used in Colombo or Capetown.

➤ Prototyping

Integrated Product and Process Development places a strong reliance on prototyping; that is, on models and simulations. The modeled and simulated prototypes are not just of products and their functionality, but of the processes by which the product will be manufactured and serviced. Over time, NGM companies will build *virtual factories*. The myriad of design decisions will be made, integrated together, and shown to work before any physical process is put in place, even before a factory is built.

Much of IPPD is already automated. Modeling and simulation will become the primary tools for decision making throughout the enterprise. They will be used for product models and simulations, for simulations of manufacturing processes including inspection and testing, simulation for product support, and increasingly for models and simulations of the extended enterprise. Simulations will provide essential information for the choice of alternatives. As models and simulations become more realistic, and as the cost of computing decreases, IPPD will increasingly become a process of multiobjective optimization.

Virtual Prototypes

Virtual prototypes are complete descriptions of a whole product, of an entire process, or if the product and process development is truly integrated, of the transformation from feedstock to finished product.

Virtual Product Prototypes

The virtual product prototypes are product models that have been integrated from models of component subsystems and parts. The component models should be parameterized and have well-specified interfaces. They should be cataloged and easily accessible for reuse from a design repository.

Virtual Process Prototypes

Similarly, virtual process prototypes are integrated from models of unit processes. These, too, should be based on process models retained in the design depository, again with standardized interfaces. Process modeling is a less developed discipline than product modeling, but many companies and vendors are developing reusable models of equipment and some standard equipment applications. As these models grow in applicability and span a larger scope of application, they may provide a basis for standards and libraries.

Computer-aided production engineering (CAPE) tools are used for the planning, simulation, and optimization of production lines. They can be used to simulate operations, subject to physical, time, and cost constraints, including graphical or virtual reality representations so that engineers and operators can "see" the benefits and limitations of alternative layouts and processes. For example, engineers can see the effects of a surge in workload or of unexpected maintenance actions or of delays in parts supplies.

Above all, simulation and modeling become the tools of choice for identifying and defining interfaces in product and process. Without clear definitions of interfaces, interchangeability and transparency become hollow words.

Ultimately, the virtual factory consists of a detailed simulation in space and time of all of the process operations—on and above the floor—that result in the finished product.

PRODUCT PROTOTYPING AT JOHNSON CONTROLS

Johnson Controls is using a powerful, integrated suite of 3-D CAD tools.[5] They are part of a process that introduces analysis early in the development process, leverages standard parts and proven design, and captures product data to be used in process development and for supplier specifications and contracts. The suite includes modules for:

➤ 3-D modeling of subsystems and components.

➤ 3-D visualization.

➤ Finite element analysis.

➤ Product and process data models.

➤ A repository of geometries of standard parts.

➤ A facility to capture the geometries of custom parts.

The suite also has access controls to facilitate disciplined communication among design team members and version control that maintains the integrity of the current version. The updating and version control permit others to recreate the step-by-step design process.

The 3D models and finite element analysis enabled design-intent analyses and helped in the development of assembly procedures. The design-for-assembly features forced designers to consider how the parts they were working on would fit together with the rest of the parts in the assembly. These features led to a substantial reduction—as much as 40 percent—in time and development cost.

The suite is Internet-capable, so that members of the design team need not be physically co-located.

The Virtual Factory

The models and simulations for IPPD will be aggregated into a *virtual factory* (see Figure 8.5). Because manufacturing will be geographically dispersed, the virtual factory will have to include many extended enterprise relationships.

The virtual factory is a digital representation of real products and real processes. The value of the virtual factory depends critically on the accuracy of the models and simulations being commensurate

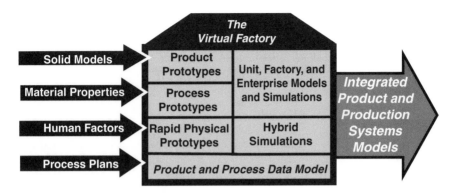

Figure 8.5 Modeling and Simulation: Basis for the Virtual Factory

with the detail needed to respond to the questions being asked. For example, if the need is to estimate the number of parts of a given specification that can be shipped from a factory, then an event-driven simulator incorporating estimated times to complete unit operations may be a sufficient guide for scheduling deliveries. But if the need is to optimize the design of a racing yacht to be used in the America's Cup competition off the coast of New Zealand, the requirement is for a very detailed model that describes the dynamics of the hull and sails under variable wind and sea conditions.

Simulation Assessment Validation Environment. The Simulation Assessment Validation Environment (SAVE) is an integrated set of simulation and process-development tools that is a prototype virtual factory.[6] SAVE is being developed by Lockheed Martin Aeronautical Systems and nine other companies, with support from the U.S. Air Force's Materials and Manufacturing Technology Directorate, to help development of the Joint Strike Fighter (JSF). The JSF will be produced with four major variants for the U.S. Air Force, U.S. Marines, U.S. Navy, and the U.K. Royal Navy. The four variants will have more than 90 percent commonality and are to be manufactured on a single production line.

SAVE is an environment for quickly assessing and validating part and process decisions. These design goals for SAVE were a system that could:

➤ Assess the effectiveness of the design process, reduce design changes, and eliminate undesirable changes.

➤ Evaluate the capability of designs to meet functional and cost objectives.

➤ Reduce the need for design changes after production begins.

➤ Reduce product variation, fabrication and assembly inspection, and scrap and rework.

➤ Evaluate corrective actions.

The net effect is to reduce cycle time and eliminate nonvalue-added activities.

Key components of SAVE, shown in Figure 8.6, are:

➤ The common desktop for the user interface.

➤ The workflow manager and the electronic collaboration design notebook.

➤ A common data model and system of translators. The common desktop provides access to the system and all the requisite data that is stored in multiple databases including a repository containing the SAVE database of design/product data, models, libraries, and documentation.

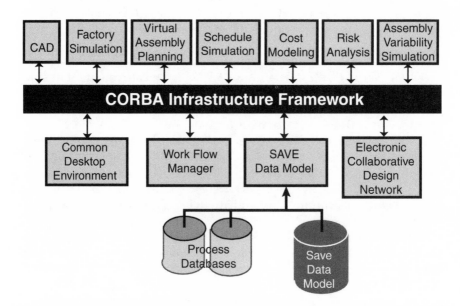

Figure 8.6 The Simulation Assessment Validation Environment

➤ A communications infrastructure that uses the Common Object Request Broker Architecture (CORBA—see Chapter 17).

To demonstrate SAVE, the project team integrated a number of commercial packages: Dassault's CATIA™ CAD system, Deneb's IGRIP™, Ergo™ and Quest™ software, Pritsker's FACTOR/AIM™ system, Cognition's Cost Advantage™, SAIC's ASURE™, IBM/Technomatix's VSA, and Decision Dynamics Design/Production Model using CORBA as the glue. The intent is to enable any applications to be used in the environment so long as they have a CORBA interface and use consistent semantics. This will allow the users to apply collaborative virtual manufacturing concepts to reduce the life cycle costs, schedule requirements, and risks associated with product development.

In its first phase, SAVE was tested and validated on the F-16 fighter's horizontal stabilizer. In the second phase, SAVE is being used with specific subsystems of the F-22 fighter. Based on a 1998 demonstration of the use of SAVE for the redesign of an F-22 gun port assembly, use of SAVE for the Joint Strike Fighter is projected to save more than $1 million in unit cost and 2 percent to 3 percent in lifecycle costs, or a savings of more than $2 billion over the lifetime of the JSF program.

Rapid Physical and Hybrid Prototypes

It is unlikely that all pre-production issues can be resolved with virtual prototyping, at least until companies gain more experience and confidence with such techniques. Companies will use physical prototypes for validation studies: validation of the virtual prototypes, of integrated processes, of new materials used in the processes, of new processes, and of overall performance.

For example, the introduction of a process change into a model run, say of an automobile, has been so difficult that companies generally wait until there's a model changeover or plant shutdown to make the change. A company can use virtual and hybrid simulation to model the changed process and simulate its operation. The simulation first can be done virtually, assuming ideal process measurements and controls. Then a hybrid simulation can use the real measurements and control signals from the processes that will remain unchanged with the digital simulation of the changes. This hybrid simulation provides an evaluation of the adequacy of the fit of the change into the existing production line, while preparing operators for the changes.

Where physical prototypes must be used, IPPD will take advantage of emerging rapid prototyping technologies and of hybrid simulation. Several rapid prototyping technologies will be considered in Chapter 10. Some are suited primarily for design prototypes, able to demonstrate spatial relationships and stylistic features, but not so robust that they could be used functionally. Others are robust enough that they can be used functionally and can lead to programmable, lot sizes of one, production.

Hybrid simulations, blending models of proposed innovations with the actual operations of physical processes will be used to validate designs and to prepare production workers. IPPD will increasingly become a real-time activity, as machines and processes become more flexible, even programmable. Together, IPPD and more agile processes and equipment will enable greater and more timely product customization.

ON-LINE IPPD FOR HIP REPLACEMENTS

Cornell University engineers and doctors have a powerful demonstration of a virtual factory that results in the rapid production of one-of-a-kind hip replacements. Typical hip replacements are made by matching one from a standard assortment of steel hip replacements and then shaping the residual bone to fit. Over time, the mismatch in shapes leads to wear on the site of the replacement, sometimes to the point of incapacitating the recipient or necessitating a second replacement.

The Cornell research includes computer tomography (CT) scans of the hip to be replaced at Cornell Medical Center in New York City, use of the Cornell Theory Center's supercomputer to translate the scans into a solid model that represents the site of the replacement, to match the properties of the hip replacement to the specifics of the recipient's body, and to develop a solid model of the appropriate hip replacement. The solid model of the hip replacement is then translated to a numerical control order stream for the machine shop at the Cornell Medical Center. The customized hip replacement, shaped specifically for the recipient, is then implanted.

In principle, a customized hip replacement can be fabricated in a matter of hours from the time the replacement is determined to be necessary.

➤ **In-Process Verification**

Rapid Product and Process Realization (RPPR) demands first-time quality, so no time is wasted between production and delivery and so no rework costs are incurred. Much of quality can be designed in, but tools wear, materials have flaws, and data gets corrupted. There are many ways in which even the best designed processes can fail.

Instrumentation will be designed into next generation manufacturing processes, perhaps into products, so that the quality of the critical processes can be measured and adjusted in real-time. Instrumentation, such as built-in sensors, plays many roles. First, in the virtual factory, it can serve as the basis for simulated control actions that can validate, or invalidate, the utility of a proposed process when integrated with others. Second, it can provide realistic inputs for operator training simulators. Third, in the process itself it can provide signals to the controller that can lead to a diagnosis of problems and to corrective control actions, including, if necessary, shutting down a malfunctioning machine before it does significant damage.

Another aspect of in-process verification is in-use verification. Smart products that diagnose themselves are becoming common. For many years, railroads have monitored bearings on rail cars and over-the-road transport companies have monitored the on-road performance of their tractors. General Motors is advertising its OnStar product in which the car notifies a GM help center if it has suffered a catastrophic event.

The consequence of this phenomenon is that all product and process producers, from simple components and materials to factory tooling and test equipment, are expected to have an understanding of instrumentation, problem analysis, and control.

➤ **Integrated Product Teams (IPTs)**

Underlying IPPDs are integrated product teams (IPTs). As we have noted earlier, the need is to bring all the knowledge to bear on the product that can maximize its chances for success. The idea is that at any point in the in the Product Realization process the right knowledge and skills are available and used.

The QFD model provides a guide to the composition of the IPTs. Who are the right people to contribute to the solutions of the issues posed in any given matrix? Unless the company is a small one, the chances are that different people should participate in each exercise. The project manager, the chief product designer, the chief process

THE WOLFPACK AT MILICRON

Milicron, Inc., has made the transformation from a company, then called Cincinnati Milicron, with a core competency in machine tools to one whose core competency is in plastics. A major element of the transformation, which started in the late 1980s, was the *Wolfpack,* a team formed with people from design, engineering, production, finance, manufacturing, and logistics.[7] The team designed a new injection molding machine, the Vista, taking the design from concept to prototype in nine months. The machine cost 40 percent less than its predecessor, performed with significantly higher quality, and was faster to assemble since it had fewer parts. The Vista grabbed market share and gave Milicron a platform for continual innovation.

designer, the production manager, the chief tool designer, the quality manager, and the individual responsible for customer support may be the only people to participate in all the QFD-mediated discussions, with experts brought in when the discussions require their particular expertise.

There is an important exception. QFD discussions provide an excellent way to broaden the experts' perceptions and may challenge them to be more creative within their own area of expertise.

Especially on matters dealing with the functionality trade-offs, ergonomics, and the economics of acquisition and use, it is important to hear the voice of the customer. As Boeing found, when they included customers on the design teams for the 777, they saved rework time, effort, and expenses.

It is just as important to hear the voice of other "customers" for the production processes—namely, the tool designers, the operators and assemblers and others who will make the processes work. It makes no sense to design a spiffy new product if the processes are so clumsy that workers cannot produce them efficiently, reliably, and with high quality.

Finally, it is important to hear the voice of the financial stakeholders. An essential aspect of the modern manufacturing company's success is the confidence that the financial stakeholders have in the company's products and processes. Major financial trade-offs are especially significant for the development of products that represent a major departure from the existing product lines or the introduction of "you-bet-your-company" processes. When trade-offs must be made, the financial community can provide guidance to minimize financial risks and convey confidence to the investors.

The Enterprisewide Computing Environment to Support IPTs

The IPT's will need an integrated, enterprisewide computer environment that is robust enough to support all the subprocesses of IPPD and to make the decisions made by each IPT or function immediately available to all the other IPTs and functions. An enterprisewide computing environment consists of:

➤ Workstations that can support functional activities, such as product or process design, logistics and supply chain management, business operations, and so forth, all linked with facile communications and shared knowledge.

➤ Comprehensive data bases that provide a consistent representation of all of RPPR.

➤ Transparent networks linking customers and suppliers.

➤ Total configuration management and control.

➤ Real time access.

➤ Protection of intellectual property and business information.

We will consider the enterprisewide computing environment in detail in Chapter 17.

■ BETTER, FASTER, CHEAPER

There are now countless examples where Integrated Product and Process Development has led to products that provide better value to the customer. The ultimate arbiters of quality are better satisfied when product design incorporates an understanding of their needs. The customers are better satisfied when the best combination of materials, technologies, and processes, are combined with proven platform designs that have been customized with them in mind. They are better satisfied when the value they want is there when they need it, and when the product is right the first time, and all the time. IPPD is the way NGM companies will ensure that their products are indeed *better, faster, cheaper.*

■ EXERCISE

With a group of colleagues, choose a new product your company is considering or one you would like the company to develop. Alternatively, by default consider this product: a space-saving combination washer/dryer that can replace today's conventional clothes washers and dryers, at a cost of 75 percent of that of the typical pair of appliances.

Select roles—as customer, marketer, product designer, process designer, operations worker, customer support representative, distributor, first tier supplier, investor—to form an integrated product team. Use QFD matrices to:

1. Identify the most significant product technical requirements from the marketing requirements. Where does the team have to be sure to "get it right" in order to have a successful product?

2. What are the alternative component or subsystem designs? Which will best meet the product technical requirements?

3. Considering the possible processes for the components and subsystems, which will best realize the chosen designs?

4. How can the processes you have chosen best be organized for production?

Given the results of Step 4, iterate back to Step 1. Do the decisions your team made still look good, or did you find that modifications were needed as you worked through the results of your early design decisions? Be sure to keep an audit trail on why your team made the decisions it did.

■ NOTES

1. M. Larry Shapiro, *Advanced QFD: Linking Technology to Market and Company Needs* (New York: John Wiley & Sons, Inc., 1994).
2. J.R. Hauser and D. Clausing, "The House of Quality," *Harvard Business Review* (May/June 1988) pp. 43–63.
3. Tim Stevens, "Method to the Madness: Structure Breeds Success as Companies Reap the Benefits of Specific Design Methodologies When Creating New Products and Processes," *Industry Week*, vol. 245, no. 4 (November 18, 1996) p. 34.
4. Dorothy Leonard-Barton, *Wellsprings of Knowledge: Building and Sustaining the Sources of Innovation* (Boston: Harvard Business School Press, 1998).

5. James F. Manji, "CAE Tools Slashes Time and Cost for Automotive Supplier," *Managing Automation* (January 1999) 60D.
6. Ray Chalmers, "SAVE Saves Millions for Fighter Program," *Manufacturing Engineering* (May 1999). Also see the SAVE Project's Web pages. Available at: skipper.mar.external.lmco.com/save/
7. "Milicron's Secret Weapon," *Manufacturing Engineering* (July 1999) p. 18.

Chapter *9*

Modeling and Simulation

TUESDAY, 1:30 PM: SEEING THE FUTURE

There was a break in the task force presentation as you had a short telephone conversation updating you on the delicate negotiations for a ten-aircraft order in Hungary. Your people had made sure Egret could fill their needs, although as usual there were some special design modifications. There was always that lingering doubt—could the modifications be made safely? Would they add a lot of cost? Would they really work?

You wished life were as easy for BAI as for a company like CapitalOne. They could create 30,000 product ideas each year, try them out in simulation, discard most of the ideas, but still come out with over a thousand profitable products. Of course, creating different credit card products is a very different business from creating large manufactured systems. They have a huge database that gives them intensive knowledge about narrow market segments—they really understand their customers' preferences and behaviors in a deep way. Their simulations are very accurate, so that when they offer a product, it has been thoroughly tested.

On your way back to the presentation, you thought about the Virtual Factory—the closest thing you could have to CapitalOne's simulation capability. It could be the way to make sure you could build the modified Egrets for the Hungarian customer. Of course, the Virtual Factory depended on having models and simulations you could trust.

116

■ INTRODUCING MODELING AND SIMULATION

In the NGM Enterprise, modeling and simulation (M&S) will reflect a new way of doing business rather than a supporting technology. It will make virtual production a reality. All production decisions will be made based on modeling and simulation methods, rather than on build-and-test methods. M&S tools will move from being the domain of the technologist, to being a tool for all involved in the product realization, production and business processes.

M&S will eliminate the need for developing hardware prototypes and allow for lot sizes of one. This will dramatically decrease time-to-market for new products and services. It will provide products and services optimized for the customer and other stakeholders. It will require significantly fewer resources in the development process than build-and-test methods.[1]

Modeling and simulation (M&S) is the use of computer tools for the design, analysis, performance testing, and implementation of products, manufacturing processes, business processes, and enterprise processes. In the past, these tools have been used by specialists to evaluate specific aspects of a product or a process and to support specific decisions. The use of M&S has been limited by the burden of data model creation and updating, and by the lack of interconnectivity between different modeling methods and simulation tools.

This is changing. In the NGM company, M&S will provide the integrated tools for the design and operation of the virtual factory. But M&S will reach beyond product design and manufacturing process simulation to guide decisions on the formation, operation, and dissolution of the extended manufacturing enterprise, and of the enterprise's logistics and business processes and operations.

No Surprises

Recently a Boeing executive talked about the assembly of the fuselage of a lot-size-of-one prototype of the proposed Joint Strike Fighter (JSF).[2] The assembly occurred without difficulty and ahead of schedule. "Our assembly simulations modeled the joining of the forebody and the mid-fuselage a year and a half ago—just as it happened here," Frank Statkus, Boeing vice president and JSF general manager is quoted as saying. "There were no surprises."

No surprises: The reason to build models and do simulations is to find a "right-the-first-time" solution and avoid the waste of rework and the quality risks of "bumping and fitting." Every function in the enterprise has to make timely, accurate decisions. Today, some functions use models routinely. Others use models and simulations as an advisory adjunct in the decision-making process. Examples of the use of M&S today include:

1. *Product design.* Drawings, which are two-dimensional models, and three-dimensional solid models are the norm for discrete part design. The most elaborate models are those that describe complete designs, such as the models of the Boeing 777 and the Dodge Intrepid introduced in 1998. In these cases, the models were not just static representations of the dimensional properties of the product. The models were dynamical and described various performance factors. In these cases, the models were so complete that production processes could be designed without reference to a physical prototype.

   Logic and physical simulators are routinely used to validate models of very complicated integrated circuits (ICs)—for example, microprocessors containing millions of individual circuits. The IC models are themselves a compilation of models of individual circuits guided by functional requirements.

2. *Manufacturing process design and control.* Factory, cell, or line layouts are simple models that describe spatial relationships in processes. More elaborate event simulations describe the flow of parts through a process, the movement of parts through the spatial elements.

   Equipment controllers embody at least rudimentary models of the processes accomplished by the equipment. The intelligent closed loop process controllers discussed in Chapter 10 incorporate more elaborate descriptions of processes.

   Some companies like General Motors are now doing detailed process modeling, modeling of physical properties at a level of detail that permits the dynamic simulation of operational manufacturing processes.

3. *Financial analysis.* At the very least, companies routinely use spreadsheets to model their financial operations with an ability to parameterize inputs so that the effects of change can be predicted.

   Often the financial models roll up operating unit models and model the effects of alternative investment decisions.

4. *Business process design and operations.* Much of business process re-engineering is based on the use of simple models or simulations that describe the required process. The description of the required process is compared to the processes in place and appropriate adjustments are made. The re-engineered model of the process can identify unnecessary work and eliminate bottlenecks.

Operational models for specific functions include models for Equipment Maintenance, Staffing, Training Requirements, Support Service, and Lifecycle Ownership and Operating Cost Model.

5. *Enterprise design and operations.* Modeling techniques are used in some companies to describe the relationships among functional units and to guide organizational design.

The Simulation Assessment Validation Environment (SAVE) introduced in Chapter 8 provides for the integrated simulation of the product as it undergoes manufacturing processes. Further extensions of SAVE will lead to the capability for *virtual product development,* a process that includes not only traditional product and manufacturing process design, but also the business and enterprise processes, and spanning the extended enterprise.

Most of the models and simulations that companies use are still tied to isolated functions. In the NGM company, they will have to fit together. M&S will assume a central role in decision making when models using standardized semantics become more available and better integrated with the company's design and operational databases. The models may not be fully integrated in the sense of all models having access to the data from all other models, but they will have to be consistent, so that the enterprise can be assured that they will work together on the same set of enterprise goals.

Verified models will become accessible through the company's own efforts, vendor offerings, industry consortia, and industry/government cooperation.

As the e-commerce technologies evolve, the Internet and internal Intranets will be essential distribution mechanisms. The capabilities of commercial software tools will be extended to include tools for embedding customer requirements and market analysis, planning and execution aids, and process optimization in IPPD. Integration frameworks (see Chapter 17) will help users to fluidly couple discrete software packages and data for the construction of models, the simulation of systems, and the multimedia presentation of results.

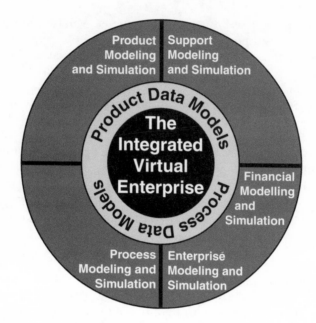

Figure 9.1 Modeling and Simulation for the Virtual Enterprise

If the goal for M&S in IPPD is to build the virtual factory, then the goal for M&S in RPPR is to create the virtual enterprise (see Figure 9.1). This integrated set of models and simulations will allow decision makers in every part of the enterprise to try out ideas that will affect all parts of the company and its suppliers.

■ THE EVOLVING STATE OF THE ART OF MODELING AND SIMULATION

We want to use a virtual enterprise so that every aspect of the product, the manufacturing processes, and the business processes is on time and right the first time. We can't build general purpose virtual enterprises or factories today, but the state of the art of M&S is evolving, in two important ways, to meet the goal (see Table 9.1). First, the applications are moving into the mainstream of development and operations. To date, models have been used to help solve narrowly defined issues. Financial models have been used to evaluate business plan alternatives. Solid models are the norm for product development.

Table 9.1   The Evolution of Modeling and Simulation

M&S Technology		M&S Applications	
From	To	From	To
"Point" solutions	Integrated package solutions	Hardware prototypes	Virtual (software) prototypes
Costly, idiosyncratic models	Libraries of easily accessible models	Planning	Shop-floor operations
Proprietary M&S tools	Interoperable, networked M&S tools	Hard tooling	Model-based programmable tooling
Event-based simulations	M&S incorporating time, dimensional variation, and physical properties explicitly	Fixed capacity	Managed variable capacity
		"On-the-Job" Training	Education and training using simulators
		Finished product quality control	In-process verification
		M&S assists in a support role	M&S imbedded in all decision-making

Dynamical models are used to validate specific product attributes, such as the flex of a wing in turbulence or the trajectory of a read head flying over the surface of a hard disk.

The merger of the worlds of mathematical modeling and programmable processes, tooling, and equipment makes it possible for your company to prototype not just product features or even entire products, but also to prototype the manufacturing of the products. More data is available because more of your operations depend on automated systems. As the programmable operations become better defined digitally, you can program controllers for a wide range of process applications. It is becoming possible to automate tooling operations and in some cases to modify the tooling itself under program control. This means that more and more operations can be modeled, at increasing levels of detail. The scale of the models can be greater, more inclusive of complete operations, even at the enterprise level.

The lines between modeling and simulation of processes and process control are getting blurred. The models can be used within real processes, notably as comparison standards for data acquired during process operations. Such data can be used for verifying the process quality, driving controller actions, and for adjusting plans for downstream processes. And the data from real operations can feed simulations to validate the "fit" or simulated modifications of the real processes.

A second major thrust of M&S is the development of more standardized tools and models. These will make it possible to build up libraries of models that are less idiosyncratic; that is, limited to a single function, to a narrow range of products, or even to a single product, and to a narrowly defined application procedure. The trend is toward representations of functional modules intended to be integrated in plug-and-play fashion into dynamically variable cross-functional models.

The technologies—especially visual, object-oriented programming and graphical user interfaces—used for modeling and simulation promote flexibility and ease-of-use. As models and simulations become easier to assemble and use, they will be used:

➤ Both as planning tools and as operational tools, to prototype products, processes, quality assurance plans, and entire factories before any physical effort is made.

➤ To validate interfaces between subsystems.

➤ To optimize the human-machine interface (HMI), especially for complex human-machine systems.

➤ For risk, safety, and reliability analyses and then systems validation and assurance testing.

➤ As vehicles for education and training.

In the long run, the distinction between model, simulation, controller, process, and equipment will fade. Prototypes may at one time take a completely digital form, at another a full physical realization, and at another a hybrid form in which, for example, data from real cell operations is used as input to a simulated process modification.

Models and simulations require two things: algorithms and data. Increasingly, they will require something else: representations of human behavior.

Algorithms

In the enthusiasm for modeling as an important tool for operational decisions, the quality of the underlying *algorithms* is as important as the quality of any of the physical processes.

All models and simulations start with a set of assumptions about the way the world works. They include, implicitly, a set of value judgments. Usually the assumptions and value judgments correspond to good practice. Your starting point as a user is to be sure that your assumptions and those embodied in the software are similar. You encode your assumptions in algorithms that are only as good as your assumptions.

Models and simulations aren't reality. They are representations of reality. To be useful, those representations need to be so close to reality that, for the purposes of design or control decisions, there is no difference in the results. How close is "close enough"? The differences start with the precision with which physical quantities are measured and with which numerical quantities are represented. These inherent differences, compounded perhaps by small calibration errors, propagate through a model or simulation. A good algorithm is one in which the user can have confidence that the result of the model is within some tolerable, rigorously determined, error band. The user should be able to assess quickly the possible range of errors and to ensure that it is much less than the variations in the design or control parameters.

Many operational simulations incorporate heuristic models because the processes being controlled have not been modeled accurately from physical principles. Often process controllers operate around a *set point* and the process model is a linear one—the controllers apply corrective action proportional to the deviation from the set point. Higher order models fit curves to experimental data on the effects of corrective actions. Even more sophisticated heuristic models incorporate rule based or other knowledge-based technologies. The limitations of such models should be well understood before they are used in operations, especially when they influence the inputs to other control functions.

Many algorithms are iterative. You start with a trial solution, see whether it fits the inputs as they are constrained by the boundary conditions. If the trial solution doesn't fit the inputs, as it likely won't, the algorithm modifies the trial solution and tries the fit again. The process is repeated and eventually converges to the point where there is little variation in the fit from successive trials. The questions then are whether the fit is "good enough" and whether the convergence is to the best solution or just to a mathematical artifact, a question which the algorithm should answer unambiguously. Numerical analysis has matured since the advent of the computer. Many older M&S systems used numerical methods that are suspect, but for which more rigorous algorithms can be substituted.

Models of complicated physical processes, especially dynamical processes subjected to stochastic inputs (e.g., an aerodynamic surface subjected to turbulence, or even the trajectories of several robot arms subjected to loosely coupled autonomous controllers) may not be provably correct. That is, although the results of the models appear to mimic physical reality most of the time, one cannot say with mathematical assurance that the models will always mimic reality. Such models may prove very useful in all realistic situations, but nevertheless should be used with caution when inputs change greatly.

Not only should models be provably correct, they should be computationally efficient. The way a model is mapped into the computer's memory and the ways the algorithms' instructions are represented will determine to a great degree if a given simulation is practical to perform. Carefully matching computer representation to the problem being solved can impact execution time by 3, 4, or more orders of magnitude—or a 1000-fold, 10,000-fold, or greater decrease in computer time. The company with the efficient models may have a commanding competitive advantage.

The Semantics of Data

The second requirement for useful models and simulation is *data* that has precise meaning. Virtual prototypes will depend on accurate models where the meaning (semantics) of the variables (data objects) is precisely and universally defined in standard ways.

Over the years, many applications have grown up around specific operations or a vendor's algorithms. One result is that when one tries to use these models in an integrated way, as is needed for a virtual factory, there are slight mismatches in the semantics. As we will see repeatedly, the problems posed by semantic mismatch are the biggest and most costly inhibitors to integration.

What does General Motors mean when it specifies the horsepower or torque of car? What does your local gas station mean by octane? What does Koret mean by Size 10; does Koret have the same definition as Liz Claiborne's? Is the 3-D solid modeling program's understanding of tolerance the same as the equipment controller's? Is the process planner's definition of final exit consistent with that of the enterprise resource planner? Is the process planner's definition of just-in-time the same as that of the supply chain manager? Are there any conversions required (of measurement units, for example)?

RPPR demands that all members of the extended enterprise operate with the same definitions and data model. Horror stories abound of suppliers who have had to make large, redundant investments in CAD software in order to accept the solid models provided by different prime contractors. In the next generation of manufacturing, it will be the rule that companies will participate in several extended enterprises simultaneously. Specialized vendors outside of the extended enterprise may be also be used to supply models that incorporate their core competency, but in any event *the semantics of their models must be the same as those used in the rest of the enterprise.*

Semantic data models on which there is widespread agreement do not yet exist. The establishment of standards such as ISO 10303, the Standards for Exchange of Product model data (the STEP standards) together with application dependent auxiliary standards, are a move in the right direction. Standardization of process data definitions will be more difficult because of the wide variation in processes. However, efforts to develop these standards will accelerate the vision of "plug-and-play" modules for virtual factories.

Representations of Human Behavior

We can characterize machines and processes precisely—or at least precisely within well-understood statistical bounds. But manufacturing systems also include people, and if we want to model such a system, we have to have some sort of representation of the ways in which people interact with systems.

Ergonomic models are useful when dealing with usability issues—what are the difficulties that short or tall, thin or heavy, weak or strong, or even disabled people will have when using a product or operating a process?

Cognitive models are useful in understanding how people will make decisions and take actions given the communications they can expect to receive from the system—will the information flow in the system be insufficient for crisp decision making? Or will there be so much information that people can suffer cognitive overload? Will operators recognize the patterns that forewarn of equipment failures?

Ultimately, a lot of what goes on in a manufacturing system is people interacting, directly or through machines, with other people. Simple transactional models can adequately represent some of those interactions. Situation theory is a mathematical way to represent the subtleties of human interaction, but there are no fully satisfactory models.

■ MODELING AND SIMULATION IN THE MANUFACTURING ENTERPRISE

The history of modeling and simulation in manufacturing has at least three important sources. Product modeling started with computer-aided drafting. Manufacturing process modeling started with simple algorithms for linear control around set points and with event simulators. Logistics process modeling started with bill of materials processing. The three sources have provided a basis for evolutionary development over 40 years. The development was usually contained within organizational silos and therefore usually incompatible. Only recently have people begun to see the power that comes through an integrated understanding of how the effects of a product innovation will propagate throughout the enterprise.

Over the past 40 years, sophisticated CAD programs, incorporating accurate three-dimensional solid modeling tools, have proliferated. As the cost of computing has come down, CAD has become the predominant medium for design. CAD is used together with visualization and virtual reality for presentation of digital product models for human review.

Process modeling is more of an art than product modeling, but there are modeling tools resulting in accurate, dynamical models of some physical processes. Companies are building up libraries of unit process models that can be used as building blocks for larger process models. There are now many tools for modeling and simulating business processes in support of business process re-engineering.

Logistics programs have also become much more inclusive and sophisticated. Material Requirements Planning (MRP) provided inventory control for materials, parts, and finished products. Manufacturing Resource Planning (MRP II) extended MRP by integrating product scheduling and related applications, including decision support, material requirements planning, accounting, and distribution. MRP II systems proved inadequate for the integrated resource management needs of large manufacturing companies. Because MRP II systems do span inventory, production, job costing, scheduling, materials ordering, all tied into a general ledger and accounts payable/receivable system, they can still be useful in smaller companies.

In the early 1990s, it was recognized that there needed to be, at least, Product Data Management (PDM) to provide consistent digital product representations to all the applications that dealt with the product. PDM has evolved further into Product Development Management or PDM II. Vendors call the integration of three-dimensional solid modeling with Bills of Material and the product structure as the basis for virtual product development management (VPDM). PDM II combines product data management (PDM) with VPDM. VPDM makes possible the creation, release and communication of multi-CAD assembly models across the enterprise's development and delivery chains. VPDM provides the tools to help define, configure, and optimize products and manufacturing processes, while PDM has the tools to manage product data and documents. Together they represent the state-of-the-art of commercial products for the virtual factory.

PDM II vendors assert that by combining the virtual product development management function with product data management, a PDM II implementation can provide an integration platform for the design, manufacturing, and maintenance functions, each having a different view of the shared data set. The result should enable the design, development and manufacturing disciplines to access data sooner, collaborate better, and reduce costs. Commercial PDM II offerings are discussed further in Chapter 12.

A parallel step in the evolution of logistics programs was to the modern Enterprise Resources Planning (ERP) system. (See Chapter 12.) ERP integrates manufacturing including suppliers, financial, human resources, sales force automation, data warehousing, document management and postsales service and support. ERP systems have had the reputation of being large, expensive, and difficult to implement. They are being re-architected for use of Internet technologies by extended enterprises, resulting in more open, modular designs and implementations. These are more accessible to and affordable by smaller companies, and more adaptive to change in larger organizations.

The trend now is to integrate models and simulations so that a change in one, say a shift in materials from a plastic to a composite, can be evaluated for its effects on product maintenance, or on logistics and supply chain requirements, or on profit margins. Rather than build very large integrated models, the trend is also to "plug-and-play" modules that can run on workstations and be integrated using electronic networks. The long-term key to M&S success is that models, simulations, and supporting infrastructure be flexible and scalable, growing or shrinking as needed for the specific needs of a given extended enterprise.

➤ M&S for Product Development

The ultimate goal of virtual prototyping is to eliminate the need for hardware prototypes in the development process. There are only a few examples of large-scale models or simulations that integrate all the functions of a product, a manufacturing process, or an enterprise. We think immediately of the Boeing 777 or Chrysler's 1998 LH replacement products, but these represent exceptions where the value clearly was worth very substantial investment. The Boeing 777 development, avoiding the need for physical prototypes, cut a year from the product realization cycle and started the revenue stream a year earlier; the Chrysler effort cut nine months out of the cycle.

The current generation of virtual prototyping technology makes possible the three-dimensional visualization of complete products, not just single parts. Using high-speed visualization techniques or animation, your engineers can "fly" through the product design using advanced "fly-through" technologies.

Just as important, your engineers can work simultaneously to develop the product, with each knowing the changes the others make—that is, they can work in a collaborative environment that keeps them all focused on the latest design. Virtual prototyping can be shaped to provide a disciplined and natural way for concurrent engineering teams to define products. It provides a natural design methodology and is the focal point for storage of specifications, engineering rules, operational parameters, and simulation results. Disciplines working in concert with the design engineers—manufacturing and maintenance engineers, and technical publishing specialists for example—can also use the digital mock-up as the appropriate place to store their own data.

We're undergoing a transition from traditional, file-based, digital mock-ups that are constrained to just the part being designed. We are moving to digital representations that access all the information relationships which define a product—its mechanical contacts, the dependencies between the geometry and related NC programs, electrical connections, links between geometry and knowledge stored in documents, and other attributes. Virtual Product Development Management (VPDM) systems are intended to provide the infrastructure that allows engineers to develop shared models which capture both product geometry and product behavior.

A typical VPDM system is a suite of offerings that enable the enterprise to:

➤ Optimize the end-to-end development of competitive and innovative products.

➤ Manage detailed product information such as features and relationships generated by assembly and configuration modeler tools.

➤ Optimize existing products and processes; realize a high degree of collaboration; simultaneously define, configure and optimize designs, processes and operations.

➤ Explore the impact of changes and new ideas on the complete product, alert the integrated product team as the changes are adopted, and propagate changes consistently throughout the enterprise.

➤ Establish and access a broad range of knowledge during the product development process.

Hybrid Prototyping

Virtual prototyping requires that all aspects of the behavior of the components and the system are well understood and can be modeled. This is a demanding goal that may not be achieved in the near term in many applications. Hybrid prototyping is a step toward the goal.

Hybrid prototyping involves coupling digital models with physical devices to simulate the complete behavior of the system. When no suitable models exist, the hardware components are integrated into the simulation. The total system can then be modeled and analyzed. Hybrid prototyping also provides for systematic integration of software and hardware, where components can be added in stages, with modeling and analyzing performance at each stage. It also enables training concurrently with system implementation. For example, a trainee can use the actual controls of a machine, but the performance of the machine will be simulated. Hybrid prototyping also provides another tool to enable model validation and verification.

Commercial software is currently available to support hybrid prototyping although in general these tools are used for systems integration rather than product development.

➤ M&S of Manufacturing Processes and Equipment

The product guys have this crazy idea that we can sell a bunch of actuators for high temp applications if we change the dimensions from 6″ × 4″ to 4.5″ × 2.75″, use a ceramic base instead of plastic, and change the pressure pads to a ¼″ diameter composite from a ½″ diameter stainless steel—no change in unit price, of course. We claim to be the industry's "can-do" people. Can we really make these suckers and still make a profit? Can we do it using the cells we use for our regular product lines? Could we even mix production—sometimes the regular products, sometimes the high temp actuators?

Those are the questions a process engineer brought back from an early meeting of an integrated product team beginning new product development for market expansion. The engineer has some choices on how to answer the questions:

Make educated guesses based on experience and on what worked the last time.

Take a leap of faith and adopt a new process documented in a handbook or a repository of best practices.

Go to a model shop and have them build prototype parts—then take a cell out of production to prototype several alternative processes.

Digitally model the existing and new processes—then use the models in simulated operations.

There are significant advantages in using computer modeling that renders hardware, facilities, or processes into computer-based images, data, and simulations. For example:

➤ Savings in the time and cost of product development.

➤ Detailed understanding of a process or an event.

➤ Assessments of design or process alternatives, including resource requirements.

➤ Early optimization and validation of designs for cost targets, manufacturability, and resource utilization.

➤ Virtual prototyping to eliminate the need for costly hardware prototypes.

➤ Elimination or significant reduction of product testing.

You can get your designs and processes right because you can see them working. You'll know their real-world results before you invest in building them. Your company will use M&S capabilities in the product-realization cycle to design for manufacturability, cost, and continuous product or process improvement. You will use M&S to test responses to changing customer requirements. You will apply M&S to manufacturing issues ranging from the dynamic loads resulting from machine-tool chatter to the flow of material through a complex production line, and from preparation of a CAD file for part fabrication to a full-scale virtual manufacturing simulation. You will use M&S to optimize your resources, including human resources.

At least this time the process engineer was involved from the start—maybe this Integrated Product and Process Development stuff was going to work. Last time this happened she received the product design after it had been "finalized"—well, finalized until she pointed out the features that were impossible to make—and she cobbled together a set of processes that were like ones that had worked in the past—of course, not exactly in the same application, not exactly in the same configuration. She had used M&S only after problems had developed and everyone realized they didn't understand why the process worked the way it did. By that point, the company had spent a lot of time and resources and all it had to show was a product realization deadlock. She had found a solution, one that she realized she probably would have found if she had done the simulations earlier in the cycle. Then she read the NGM Report encouraging the NGM Company to insert M&S of products and processes at an earlier stage in IPPD.

Your company will find the benefits of M&S compelling. You will apply M&S to your processes routinely. You'll do this to realize time and cost savings, to gain a better understanding of your products and processes, and to communicate your competencies to your partners and your capabilities to your customers. Your company's culture will evolve to encourage more and more applications, whether you manage the evolution formally with explicit R&D funding or less formally as individual managers use workstation-based M&S to better their functional activities.

The application of M&S to advanced manufacturing processes and equipment has advanced significantly. It will become even more important and widespread as computational power increases and software capabilities improve—and as users gain confidence in the results of M&S. The use of parallel processing, distributed computing, or other emerging high-performance computing methods is enabling larger, complex three-dimensional simulation problems to be accomplished routinely. Technologies to ensure synchronized multi-platform computing will assure rapid turn-around of large problems. The dream of optimizing the design of a complete product and all the processes to make it will soon be within reach computationally, even if the models themselves are not yet complete enough.

Simulation used to be event simulation—certainly good for eliminating the buildup of work in progress (WIP) or for scheduling just in time (JIT) parts delivery. Simulation now includes the use of animation, a powerful tool for helping the user to "see" how a process will work—to watch it as it unfolds in time, to see where the bottlenecks can occur. Animation and visualization make simulation results accessible to and believable by relatively unsophisticated users.

CHARACTERIZING PROCESSES USING M&S

Two generic examples show how M&S methods that are broadly applied have transformed the way basic processes are understood. These two examples were the result of joint government/ industry efforts in which government funding was used to perfect the performance of software for simulating metalworking processes and industry developed the required databases and provided validation studies.

In the first of these examples, most major forging companies have adopted linear and nonlinear finite-element methods for the simulation of metalworking operations to aid in the design and validation of forging die designs. A forging geometry, designed by applying long-established rules, is simulated to test forge-ability performance. The die designer can iterate the evolving geometry to minimize input of raw material, to achieve a specific microstructure, or to arrive at some other target. The verification of the forging process can be discussed with the part designer during IPPD, assuring cost and producibility goals are met before the part design is complete. In most cases, the forging dies are machined and the first forging is acceptable for production.

In the second example, the casting industry is acquiring a similar capability with FASTCAST, an investment casting software system that includes prediction of material flow through molds (process modeling), optimum placement of gates and risers (equipment design), and prediction of cooling schedules to minimize residual stresses during solidification (process modeling).

More efforts of this sort will build up the library of basic process models, reducing the burden on individual companies to do the R&D to characterize the processes and then to build the models.

Even though current M&S capabilities are impressive, they still tend to be point solutions for specific process modeling or equipment design objectives—and are often electronically disconnected from the rest of the product realization software. M&S capabilities should be integrated into the product realization process so that manual or software "translators" between applications—and the mismatches in semantics that are endemic in their use—are unnecessary. Integration software (see Chapter 17) will be developed that is compatible with iterative process design or process feedback for manufacturability assessment or optimization. This software will be suitable for use by non-modeling specialists, highly modular for custom application, fully coupled across discipline boundaries when needed (i.e., electro-thermomechanical couplings), and sufficiently general to address the complexities of three-dimensional and nonlinear behavior.

The projected inclusion of process analysis and simulation into an optimization environment for design and manufacturing analyses will accelerate the RPPR process. You will be able to demonstrate cost, schedule, resource, and capability trade-offs, to support rules-based design capabilities, and to greatly shrink the time needed for product design. Simulation methods that are compatible with system-level optimization will enhance the product design environment. Achievement of this high-level integration and application flexibility will bring the technical community closer to true virtual manufacturing, where the engineer can perform desired product development assessments quickly, inexpensively, and with complete confidence.

The accelerating use of modeling and simulation by next generation companies will force equipment vendors to make available geometric (CAD) and behavioral models of their equipment, models that can be integrated by the user into larger process models. The equipment models will be derived from product models the vendors create during the development of the equipment. These models should be responsive to a variety of product characteristics and specifications (e.g., tolerances, materials, environment).

Some of the M&S techniques NGM companies can expect to use a decade from now are:

➤ Computationally-driven materials development where existing materials development practices are radically changed by the ability to model and simulate vast combinations of elemental and process variables to discover engineered material systems tailored for specific applications.

➤ Process mapping of phenomena to reveal both optimum processing parameter regimes and regimes that satisfy failure criteria will allow simulation to verify stable process conditions that ensure robustness.

➤ Model-based process control, in which the knowledge of localized conditions within a part being processed (defined from simulation) is used adaptively by an intelligent control device to vary process parameters in order to maximize quality and minimize time.

➤ Enterprise M&S that includes the interacting functional entities that comprise the total enterprise. Managers make strategic decisions using product flow, resource availability, business drivers, and product insertion opportunities.

M&S for Petrochemical Manufacturing Processes

There is a long, parallel history of product and process modeling in the petrochemical industry. Product modeling, especially of pharmaceuticals, has become common as computers have become powerful enough for the modeling, from quantum mechanical first principles, of very large organic molecules and their reactions. While not yet completely reliable as a predictor of effectiveness in any given application, these models permit the investigation of many, many alternatives before companies start incurring the costs of physical experimentation with selected candidate products.

Process modeling has moved from university- and industry-based R&D consortia efforts to commercial availability. For example, MIT's ASPEN effort has evolved into commercially available simulation software. The petrochemical industry is notoriously capital-intensive. Companies use models and simulations to predict how changes in materials or production processes will affect end results from new or existing plants. In addition, the models can guide improvements in process control, the troubleshooting of plant operations, and the evaluation of alternative operational strategies.

The process model serves both for off-line process design and evaluation and for on-line process optimization and control. Using the same model in both applications improves the rigor of the overall design and saves the time of entire engineering teams that would otherwise duplicate each other's work. As market requirements demand smaller batch sizes, the models can be used to automate and control the transition between batches. A plant switching between batches or products will often produce off-spec product for hours before the plant has fully transitioned to producing the desired product and grade. Entirely automating this transition is the best way to minimize the amount of product that must be sold at a reduced price, reprocessed, or discarded.

Simultaneously with the development of advanced simulators, there has been a development of integrated tools for developing the manufacturing plan, executing the plan, and using real-time information to evaluate how well the plan performed and then to make improvements for the next cycle. These tools help companies anticipate demand, manage inventory, schedule manufacturing activities, and allocate production across plants. The tools are based on models that reflect economic, chemical and physical constraints, provide a common decision support system from the plant floor to the supply chain, and allow the system to adapt to real-time changes in supply and demand.

Unified batch modeling and management capabilities allow plant engineers to feed real-time plant data into the off-line modeling system, where it can be analyzed to determine the best processing sequence. Integrating modeling, scheduling, and data acquisition capabilities enables engineers to make better production-execution decisions and shortens cycle times.

Combined steady-state simulation and process information management capacity allows engineers to feed operating data into the simulator to examine specific cases or hypothetical scenarios. Engineers can then make decisions about changes in production in minutes rather than days or weeks.

➤ Modeling and Simulation of Business and Enterprise Processes

NGM companies will use a continually improving suite of M&S tools to enable more accurate and sophisticated analysis of enterprises, business practices, plants, equipment, operations, products, processes, and product support. At the enterprise level, these tools will be used for strategic planning, gaming the enterprise's alternative business models. Given a strategy, M&S will be used for tactical planning. These tools will contain more accurate mathematical representations of physical reality; better cost analysis methods that span the product life-cycle; more robust manufacturing process models; high-level product models; and advanced, interactive, user-friendly interfaces.

Organizational Modeling

The modern manufacturing enterprise is a complex system whose organizational structure will greatly influence its performance. Just as products need to be designed for function, quality, cost, assembly, maintenance, and any number of additional attributes, organizations need to be designed to give the best results. Understanding the impact of a change in the organization (due to customer specifications, new market needs, and so forth) is a major design challenge. The dynamics of the workforce—multifunctional teaming, shifting personnel—compound the challenge. This challenge will become even more significant as your company moves toward distributed, multiorganizational projects and virtual enterprises that operate with many geographically dispersed partners. You'll need to keep track of the ways one team is dependent on another and provide active channels for coordination services. Some of the most promising design documentation systems focus on facilities for dependency maintenance and for producing sharable, self-explaining design models and process simulations.

In the future, the entire NGM enterprise, spanning not just your company but the multiple organizations in an extended enterprise, will be modeled and simulated before production. The tools will be especially important for the formation of extended enterprises where they will guide important decisions on partner selection and risk/reward structures. Trade-offs will be made at all levels to optimize the product design, the plant, the equipment, and the production processes. It will take time to develop robust M&S concepts and methodologies as well as software engineering methodologies for developing complex simulation environments to support the rapid development of new simulations that are also needed. These tools must be available and affordable for small as well as large manufacturers.

Business Process M&S

The best business process engineering is done using M&S tools that give assurance that the benefits of changing to the new process design will outweigh the inevitable costs of change. Effective modeling tools will be flexible and will enable your company to develop enterprise-wide business processes that are optimized for their specific needs. In some cases, you will use modeling tools linked to software development tools that can generate the software to support the process. Workflow models serve as the starting point for outlining how users want their processes to proceed.

Traditional enterprise management systems offer application templates for engineered business processes. In some cases, these are restrictive, constraining the processes to the vendors' preconceptions. However, they can integrate process components, operating policies, system and ISO/QS quality certification procedures, and standard practices to provide a complete description of the re-engineered process. They can go further and include evaluation of a process for its operational and financial effects.

IDEF

IDEF is a suite of methods for modeling the information flows in enterprises. IDEF was first developed by the U.S. Air Force's Integrated Computer Aided Manufacturing (ICAM) program and is widely used in the federal government. A first step in modeling information flows is modeling the processes at work in an enterprise. IDEF has also been adopted in tools for business process re-engineering. IDEF1X97, or IDEF Object, is an emerging standard (IEEE 1320.2) for object-oriented function modeling. The standard describes two styles of modeling:

1. The key-style is used to produce information models that represent the structure and semantics of data within an enterprise and is backward-compatible with the earlier IDEF1X93 function modeling method, which was not object-oriented.

2. The identity-style is consistent with the key style, but includes techniques that provide a robust set of modeling capabilities for all of the static and many of the dynamic aspects of the object-oriented approach to modeling. The standard also includes a rich approach for defining business rules. With suitable automation support, identity-style modeling can be used to develop an executable prototype of a target object-oriented system. The identity-style can be used with object-behavior modeling techniques, as found, for example, in the Object Management Group's (OMG) Unified Modeling Language (UML), to produce complete object-oriented models.

IDEF Modeling tools typically support both styles of modeling, integration with UML behavior modeling, and automation support to generate executable prototypes in software languages such as JAVA, C++, and in Object Management Group (OMG)-compliant distributed business object frameworks.

■ SUMMARY

Data, models, and applications must be integrated before M&S can demonstrate its full impact on the Rapid Product and Process Realization process. The infrastructure required to support virtual production is similar (if not identical) to the infrastructure that supports actual production. The integration technologies discussed in Chapter 17 are needed to provide seamless input to M&S applications, to visualize the output of these analyses, and to enable cross-functional tradeoffs. Because M&S ultimately will span the distributed operations of the extended enterprise, the supporting information systems must be integrated across disciplines, vendors, supplies, customers, and so forth, probably using Internet-based information technology.

■ EXERCISE

Consider the last important decision you made in your company. Construct a model of the decision process and consider the information flows into and out of it.

➤ Sketch the steps in your decision-making progress.

➤ How did you evaluate alternatives?

➤ What information did you need for your decision? Where did it come from?

➤ In what sequence did you use the information?

➤ What information came out of your decision-making progress?

■ NOTES

1. NGM Project, *Next Generation Manufacturing: Framework for Action* (Bethlehem, PA: Agility Forum, 1997).
2. Press Release, "Final Assembly Begins Ahead of Schedule for Boeing Joint Strike Fighter Demonstrator" (Seattle: The Boeing Company, April 8, 1999).
3. Ray Chalmers, "SAVE Saves Millions for Fighter Program," *Manufacturing Engineering* (May 1999). Also see the SAVE Project's web pages. Available: skipper.mar.external.lmco.com/save/
4. The process simulation software is available from AspenTech, Inc., Cambridge, MA. AspenTech's Plantelligence™ system is an example of a commercially available system for model-based plant operations.

Chapter

Next Generation
Processes and Equipment

MONDAY, 2:30 PM: TURNING TO PHYSICAL REALITY

Later, you asked a set of questions intended to fix clearly where BAI stood in the race to use modeling and simulation as a tool for decision making at all levels of the business. The picture was spotty; good in some areas, less good in others, certainly not yet up to the "pervasive" standard set by the NGM Report, and not "integrated" yet.

Now it was time to turn to the hardware. All manufacturing gets down to physical things: machines and processes working on raw materials and parts. NGM has something to say about these things, too.

■ CONNECTED FACTORY SYSTEMS

Crucial to RPPR is the availability of the equipment and processes that the enterprise can use to translate designs quickly into reality. Your company will have to anticipate customer requirements and be prepared, with knowledge if not with physical equipment and processes, for market demands.

The processes and equipment that next generation manufacturing companies will use will be reconfigurable, scaleable, and cost-effective manufacturing processes, equipment, and plants implemented using the best knowledge of the science of manufacturing. These processes and equipment will be interconnected into factory systems and will enable a company to adapt rapidly to specific production needs.

Figure 10.1 shows the concept of a company that is electronically connected to its partners in an extended enterprise. In Chapter 17, we will consider the information systems technologies that the company will use for the connected factory system. Within the conceptual company of Figure 10.1:

➤ Design efforts are conducted on high-performance product design workstations, perhaps linked to specialized computational servers, that model many product features and optional product configurations, including manufacturing, environmental, and disposal/reuse issues.

➤ Standardization of product and process data files that makes it possible to search their own and their partners' archival files to locate historical process plans of similar components, and thereby avoiding needlessly repeating work.

➤ Complex processing steps requiring many unit processes may be performed on modular processing equipment that would be assembled from standardized components owned by the company, by others in the extended enterprise, or rented from equipment vendors.

➤ Existing and new machine tools or specialized processing equipment can be configured for the duration of a production

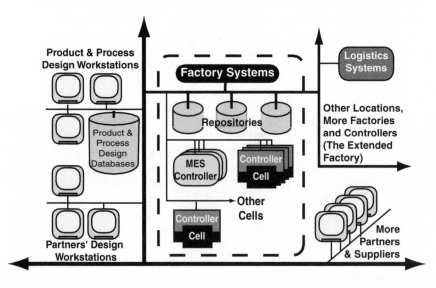

Figure 10.1 The Connected Factory System

run and then disassembled, with its component parts to be used for future production activities.

➤ Standardized and fully characterized processing components will allow near-autonomous process planning to be conducted and would assure with high confidence that the assembled processing equipment will perform as expected when making the first component.

➤ Quality standards can be defined by modeling and effectively controlled through process monitoring and real-time process adjustments.

➤ Inexpensive computer modeling of manufacturing processes will become routine and will allow small-lot-size production runs (even lot sizes of 1 item) with high confidence of success.

In this conceptual company, the design repositories and process prototyping capabilities of IPPD will drive the semi-automated construction of detailed process plans, using software that captures the specialized knowledge of skilled craftsmen, engineers, supervisors, maintenance personnel, and process planners. Virtual prototyping capabilities will allow many alternative manufacturing processes and equipment configurations to be simulated and evaluated before work is released to the floor.

The company's equipment and processes will match the agility of virtual prototyping. Equipment, machine tools, and controls that are modular will allow rapid configuration and reconfiguration of factories. Modular processing equipment will allow complex processing machinery to be assembled from smaller, well-characterized subcomponents. Open-architecture controllers will be automatically programmed and configured to operate for any lot size based on information contained in detailed process plans. When a production run is completed, the processing equipment will be reconfigured or disassembled and stored for reuse in similar or new configurations— depending on the requirements of the next production run.

Of particular importance are three categories of NGM processes and equipment that companies should track now for early inclusion in their repertoire:

➤ Flexible, modular and in-line processes and equipment. The cost of flexible manufacturing is still relatively high, but ROI should be viewed not in absolute terms but as modified by the advantages created by flexibility, namely improved response time to market.

➤ High-speed machining processes that can save time and space.

➤ Rapid prototyping technologies that can greatly accelerate product realization.

A fourth category of technologies that appears very promising, although further in the future, are the micro- and nanotechnologies considered in Chapter 20.

■ SENSORS AND ACTUATORS

The mechanisms by which factory systems interact with equipment are sensors, which obtain data from the equipment, and actuators, which transmit physical commands to the equipment. Sensors are devices that can detect the change in the state of a process or product. This change in state can be reported as a measurable signal that can be transmitted to a controller. After analysis, the controller can transmit a signal to an actuator that causes a change in the operation of the process.

➤ Sensors

A sensor can provide the input to a control device the output of which can report either a failure, a potential failure, or a command to make an adjustment in the manufacturing process. In the past, the main function of sensors was to report a failure, that is, to ring an alarm and cause the operator to stop the process. The shutdown would then allow the operator to locate the source of failure, effect the appropriate repairs, and restart the process.

With the advances of microelectronic technology, more intelligence is integrated into sensors and much more detailed data is being returned to the control systems. "Smart" sensors include network capabilities. With the expanded use of sensors, it is becoming commonplace to see cell- or floor-level distributed measurements and control systems, integrated into factory or manufacturing execution systems (MES).

In recent years, sensor technology in conjunction with modern control theory has provided much greater opportunities to reduce manufacturing costs by providing new tools for quality management. We can now use sensors not simply for alarms, but to effect continuous control of a process (i.e., "make a part right the first time" or control a process within the predetermined limits of quality standards).

An entire gamut of devices can be used for sensing. One of the determinants for selecting a particular sensing device is the state of the process material, whether it is as solid, liquid, or gaseous, or whether its state is changing as it is going through the manufacturing process. Another important factor is the method selected for sensing. Required sensitivity—how fine a control is needed—is another factor. Is the sensing to be an observation as with an optical device or is the sensor embedded in the final product? An example of the latter is a sensor embedded in a casting or molding to monitor and control temperature or the flow of material during the casting or molding process.

The availability of sensors for achieving closed-loop control has provided the means for improving yield enormously. The concept is applicable both to continuous process control and to discrete parts manufacture. Examples of continuous process control can be found in the pharmaceutical, the petrochemical, and the food processing industries in particular. One important application of sensors is in monitoring the condition of effluents to detect the presence of contaminants. Discrete process control can be found in stamping operations where, for example, audio sensing is used to determine die wear.

Process control sensors provide the data for performing predictive maintenance and thus provide a tool for reliability modeling. Reliability modeling depends on the use of historic equipment performance data and real-time input from sensors placed at various critical locations on the equipment to continually update failure probability predictions. Recent advances in sensor technology, information utilization and exchange, system integration, and reliability modeling can be used to develop optimized maintenance practices.

Sensors are also used extensively in the inspection of partially completed parts and finished products. It was not uncommon to subject finished products to 100 percent inspection; sample inspection is still very much part of the manufacturing process to confirm compliance with prescribed quality standards. Where in the past measurements were performed manually by the inspector and in selected cases recorded, today the measurements are performed automatically and recorded continuously in a data base for diagnostic analysis and product liability protection.

Sensors can be inductive, ultrasonic and photoelectric proximity devices, galvanically isolated barriers, position recognition and level measurement devices. Output data from sensors are fed into controllers to perform diagnostics, compare the input signals to preprogrammed standards, determine the need for corrective action and send corrective signals to actuators which then effect the corrections in the manufacturing process.

APPLICATIONS OF SENSORS

In Boeing's Seattle engineering laboratories, a sheet of networked sensors covering a wing provides a profile of stress patterns as the structural integrity of the wing is tested. In Austin, a developer downloads a new Java applet that provides a fuzzy logic control algorithm for an actuator plant in Beijing. In Holland, a warning system blinks on the dashboard of a tractor-trailer as temperature and pressure sensors in the tire system transmit information about a problem with the trailer axle. These are examples of smart sensing and control technologies that are actually being deployed.[1]

The sensors and controls usually are connected by wires. Often the costs of the wires and conduit are higher than those of the sensors. Once in place, the wires are a constraint on cell and plant layout that reduces the factory's agility. There is a trend toward wireless communication using transmitters incorporated into sensors.

Microelectronic devices, a class of mechanical sensors, which are microscopic in scale and are typically fabricated by the techniques used in the manufacture of integrated circuits, are rapidly finding more applications. They are an outgrowth of an area of technology referred to as Micro-electromechanical Systems or MEMS.

➤ Actuators

Actuators are devices that translate a command received from the controller into a rectilinear or rotary motion. Actuators can be mechanical, hydraulic, or pneumatically operated depending on the function they are to perform and the power they need. They can be microscopic in size such as a MEMS device needed to bring about microscopic displacements.

Actuators, especially when used on machine tools, are positioning devices for the work piece and therefore have to be capable of performing this task with a high degree of precision and repeatability. The increasing requirement in modern manufacturing for greater accuracy and consistency in performance requires that actuators be equipped with feed-back loops (i.e., sensors feeding the position of the work piece back to the controller). This information serves the dual purposes of validating the static position of the work piece at any given time and providing information on the conformance of resultant shape to the specified dimension, within the specified tolerance, as material is removed.

As with any precision devices, sensors and actuators require periodic calibration to ensure that their results are reproducible and that no defects in them affect the processes or products.

■ QUALITY, MAINTENANCE, AND SAFETY

Connected factory systems will provide unprecedented knowledge for quality, maintenance, and safety. The controller will provide the factory systems with real-time data the systems can use to determine the state of the equipment and process.

➤ Quality

Quality is a pervasive requirement for manufacturing. You won't stay in business unless you meet or exceed your customers' quality expectations. The customer is interested in durability, utility, and reliability of performance. Performance translates into availability. You want your car to start-up whenever you get into it, to go to work, go to the store, pick up the kids from school, or go on a vacation. And whenever you use the car you want to know that it will get you there and back. When you use a product in your business you are not only concerned about acquisition and operation costs, but also your maintenance costs and the possible cost of time lost due to equipment breakdown. You are concerned about lifecycle cost, and that translates into a definition of quality that stretches across the entire useful life of the product.

Is there a cost of quality? Certainly there is. Most companies have learned that the costs of ensuring that they deliver high-quality products far outweigh the longer term costs of customers who are dissatisfied because of poor quality. The traditional way to ensure quality has been to inspect the product before it is shipped. Although you may deliver a quality product, you can incur large, unrecoverable costs by spending too much time on rework and on scrapping bad parts. Mercedes-Benz in the late 1980s had the reputation of delivering very high quality automobiles, but a significant portion of their cost lay in inspection and rework.[2] Quality doesn't cost as much if you've designed a process that yields quality products the first time, all the time. You will increase your profitability substantially if you can make first-time quality products during the time that you normally spend on reworking parts that require repair, or spending time in making parts that have to be scrapped. That kind of quality cost savings goes straight to the profit line!

The Big Three automotive companies lost market share in the 1970s in part because competitively priced cars from Japan and Europe had higher quality. Even as the quality of U.S. built cars has improved to the point where there is little difference with that of cars built elsewhere, it has taken the Big Three years to overcome the residual reputation for poor quality.

In many companies, continuous improvement is synonymous with improving quality. Continuous improvement programs make it easier for the workforce to internalize the quest for quality. So do programs that institutionalize total quality management (TQM), or use the Six-Sigma approach—an especially useful approach when quantitatively significant measures can be used. Also useful are programs of self-assessment, such as those based on the Baldrige Award[3] criteria. The Baldrige Award criteria are for the enterprisewide quality processes that provide companies with a comprehensive checklist. The international ISO 9000 standard imposes quality criteria on business and manufacturing processes. Meeting the ISO 9000 standard combines self-assessment with external certification, and is required in some countries and by some customers.

Quality programs carry inherent risks, of course. The biggest risk is a lack of commitment based on poor communication of the need for the program and of its practical benefits. It's hard to take quality programs seriously if the company's leaders don't set the example and if the followers don't understand the need and the benefit.

➤ Image Processing and Quality

Image processing technologies provide tools for measuring spatial relationships. The most common image processing systems are vision systems, whose cost has been reduced dramatically as an extension of the PC cost structure. For example, vision systems can use the increased speed and capabilities for signal and graphics processing of microprocessors like Intel's Pentium III processors with a specialized instruction set for multimedia signal processing.[4] The vision capability can be used to monitor alignment, even surface quality, matching what the system sees to an ideal numerical model and identifying unacceptable deviations. Applications[5] of vision systems include:

➤ *Robot guidance*—Identifying part locations as inputs to the robot controller.

➤ *Dimensional gauging*—Measuring the dimensions of part features.

➤ *Flaw detection*—Identification of defects such as chips or scratches.

➤ *Print verification*—Matching labeling to ensure print quality.

➤ *Code reading*—Tracking parts using OCR or bar code identifiers.

➤ *Assembly verification*—Verifying that all parts are present and assembled correctly.

➤ *Sorting*—Identifying parts as input to sorters.

➤ *Parts alignment*—Orientation of parts in preparation for next operation.

The image processing algorithms of vision systems can be used with other spatial sensors that can "see" inside parts: x-rays, ultrasound, magnetic resonance, or tomographic imagery using various forms of radiation.

➤ Predictive Maintenance

Predictive maintenance is maintenance based on the prediction of failures using real-time data. It is preferable to preventive maintenance—and both are preferable to emergency maintenance. The idea is to use real-time data to develop an estimate of the probability of an equipment failure during some future time interval. If a failure is predicted within the time interval, then maintenance can be scheduled when it is least disruptive to production and performed before the failure occurs. Enabling selective downtime and avoiding overly conservative preventive maintenance schedules optimizes the throughput of the fabrication equipment. Predictive maintenance can significantly improve equipment reliability and availability. It assures the readiness of equipment to meet changing customer demands. Expanded predictive capabilities also can be used to drive the continuous improvement process by identifying sources of the most frequent failures, improving the source, and thus increasing the meantime-between failures.

Maintenance of accurate logs that operators keep on the performance of each piece of manufacturing equipment is a simple but highly useful tool for anticipating common, recurring problems. The operators' familiarity with normal equipment operation, equipment idiosyncrasies, and output quality can serve as a qualitative source of early warnings of impending problems. If you couple this practice with regularly scheduled machine inspection and preventive maintenance, you can substantially reduce the risk of catastrophic failure.

The approach depends on problem repeatability and on the operators' knowledge, attention, and sensitivity to equipment. It can be both unreliable and costly because of its subjective, sometimes conservative, and intermittent nature, and because it cannot anticipate new problems.

Sensors that detect anomalous parameters associated with machine operation provide the basis for better approaches. The simplest is to sound an alarm when the parameters exceed acceptable limits. This approach is an improvement over databased or reactive methods, but still depends on the operators' observation, problem analysis, and intervention.

An emerging extension to predictive maintenance is parallel to in-process quality verification. The signals from sensors on the equipment provide measurements on the quality of the process. Some of these same signals can provide continuous feedback to the tool-positioning mechanisms and thus maintain tolerances with the originally established band. The performance of the equipment can be inferred if the product, process, and equipment are modeled in adequate detail.

Future extensions of this technology include the application of predictive maintenance and system reliability modeling to the complete equipment inventory of an NGM Company. Real-time output from the reliability modeling will be integrated into an analytical server in a factory-level system to recommend alternative equipment and material routing through the factory in anticipation of scheduling particular production machines for maintenance or repair. In principle, the server could provide information regarding reconfiguration scheduling and costs, production rate impact, operator requirements, and other metrics that demonstrate the functional and fiscal benefits of implementing the reconfiguration.

> **Safety**

Your company must view safety as having intrinsic value—certainly, the safety of the customer and of the workforce is valuable. Safety is an essential part of your company's business systems.

A safe product is one that meets the customers' explicit and implicit expectations on usability without doing them harm. The customer may have radically different expectations for product use than you do, so you must be alert for both expected and unexpected safety hazards. The public standards for product safety have increased to the point where you cannot afford to trade off safety for incremental cost—as seen in the recent multibillion dollar award against General Motors and others.

Safety is also a major factor on the factory floor and in processes. Workforce safety is a mandatory requirement when you are laying out your facilities and designing your processes. No company can afford the disruption caused by a series of safety incidents. No company can afford the immediate impact on the workforce, the long-term burdens of workers' compensation, the potential for even greater liability, or the delays as processes are redesigned for improved safety standards.

■ DEVELOPMENT OF PROCESSES AND EQUIPMENT

Mass production started in the nineteenth century. Many of the common unit processes of discrete manufacturing, such as cutting, drilling, welding, and forging, existed before the industrial revolution, but they underwent standardization and integration as mass production took hold. Two concepts form the foundation of mass production: the interchangeability of parts and sequential construction and assembly. The unit processes themselves were refined using time-and-motion studies and improving quality standards.

The knowledge of manufacturing processes was held first by tradesmen and guilds. Even when the early power-driven tools augmented hand tools with a level of automation, the worker's skill and experience still determined the quality of the final product. The human served as the controller, taking corrective actions when indicators—some explicit measurements, others more based on experienced observation of machine behavior—showed a variance from the accepted quality standards.

Computer-controlled equipment expanded the capability of machining operations—equipment became more complex—and allowed some of the "manufacturing skill" requirements to be hard-wired or programmed into manufacturing equipment. Operators replaced skilled craftsmen in automated manufacturing facilities—but that led to the need for numerical control (NC) programmers who could prepare the programs for the machinery. In general, NC machining provided a means for improving repeatability of dimensions and thereby improving interchangeability. The first programmable equipment, machine tools with numerical control, were demonstrated four decades ago. Machine tool users could coordinate the movement of multiple axes and produce high-quality workpiece contours. NC machine tools were constructed with two, three, four, and even five axes of motion (i.e., five degrees of freedom). They were quickly put to use in making jigs, fixtures, and tools and in the machining of complex components such as aircraft wings and turbine blades.

The usefulness of these machines was expanded with the advent of computer numerical control (CNC) and direct numerical control (DNC). During the 1980s and early 1990s, NC machine tools were equipped with complex push-button consoles with proprietary operator interfaces. The tool path was computed off-line and downloaded to the machine tool. These efforts demonstrated that programmable, advanced closed-loop control strategies were required for special-purpose machinery and robotic equipment used under realistic conditions—not easy with the current generation of propriety controllers. Enhanced process control techniques, additional process sensors, and advanced control algorithms are needed to achieve higher product quality and more robust and agile operations—and that requires controllers with a more open architecture.

There has been a parallel development in automated process planning and in using machine intelligence to control processes. Gradually, process engineers learned more of the science of a process and worked as a communications bridge between the product designer and the NC programmer. The manufacturing process for a new part was usually tested off-line before being introduced into an existing process line. The off-line work generally involved the construction of several prototype parts or assemblies to determine both part-to-part dimensional consistency and assembly incompatibilities. This trial-and-error approach to process development required substantial investments of time and money.

Modern machine controllers can be reconfigured easily and rapidly to accommodate changes in geometric design. These devices can control processes in which features are added or deleted to meet customer requirements. Sensor signals can now be inputted to perform unique on-machine process changes and to perform self-diagnostics to verify operational performance and make necessary adjustments.

Open architecture controllers (OACs) incorporate the user interface technologies of personal computers. The operator will be able to reconfigure tomorrow's manufacturing equipment to perform unique tasks for each part type processed. When used with accurate process models, reconfigurable equipment will allow operation in a near-optimal configuration even when only a single part of a given configuration is required (lot size of one).

Programmable equipment coupled with high-speed communications makes it possible for factories to become distributed and transitory. The specific processes required to assemble a given small-lot-size job may be distributed physically but can be operated with instructions from a computer anywhere in the extended enterprise. The NGM Report predicts that *remotely operated* or *remotely initiated* processing will "mark a transition in manufacturing as profound as numerical control when it was first demonstrated. It will also allow true manufacturing agility and the ability to fabricate parts in a lot size of one as easily and efficiently as a lot size of 1000 or more."

■ UNDERSTANDING MANUFACTURING PROCESSES

Your company needs to get everything you can out of your equipment and processes. That means you need a deeper understanding of the manufacturing processes, the required machine tools, and the computing equipment controlling the machines that represent your core manufacturing competencies. You need the skills to identify the additional competencies you need from other companies to produce a given product. You have to understand how your processes and those of your partners can affect the quality, producibility, reusability, and disposability of products.

If a company understands the variables and their relationships in a process that determine quality, cost, and performance, then it can enhance its competitive position by improving predictability of the quality of the product. The characterization of a process includes:

➤ An accurate assessment of the output from the unit manufacturing operations.

➤ The identification, measurement and control of critical process parameters.

➤ The development, or acquisition, and use of a model that reliably defines the process-quality inter-relationships.

➤ The description of any special instructions or training required by the workforce.

➤ Costing of the process.

You need to have a standard way to describe processes so that you can characterize alternative processes at comparable levels of detail. Then the company can make better trade-off decisions on the suitability of equipment or process development options for current and potential future needs, the appropriateness of process, equipment, and capital investments, and the impact of processes on a factory floor's flexibility and agility.

Companies that do not have well-understood and characterized processes frequently suffer when markets demand more sophisticated, higher quality products. Often the problem does not lie with people or equipment, but with a lack of understanding of how best to use the company's equipment and processes. If your people do not understand the processes and the equipment you now have, you may be wasting your money by buying new equipment.

EXAMPLES OF PROCESS CHARACTERIZATION*

A manufacturer of turned components with hemispherical profiles wanted to improve the accuracy of the workpiece contours. The existing part contour accuracy was approximately 0.002 inches. One proposed solution was to purchase new machine tools. Before doing so, the company characterized the capabilities of the existing machines. It discovered that the machines had a tool-path accuracy of approximately 0.0002 inches under ideal conditions. The challenge then was to find the reason why the actual machining performance didn't match the inherent capability of the machine. Further testing identified cutting-tool wear as the major source of process error. In this situation, acquiring a machine tool capable of producing a perfect tool path would not have made a significant improvement in contour quality. Instead, the company developed a system that characterized the cutting tool form after each machining pass and automatically compensated for any wear errors.

A large manufacturer of off-road equipment had an ongoing 2 percent camshaft scrap problem. This was a topic of concern for more than 5 years before the cause was understood. The manufacturer used a process plan that allowed the operator to increase the feed rate on the first pass in each batch until it caused grinder burn. At this point, the operator reduced the feed to a safe level to run the rest of the batch. Thus, one part per batch of 50 parts became a reject, creating a scrap rate of 2 percent.

In another case, a component supplier to a large locomotive manufacturer had problems producing consistent properties in heat-treated products. The company traced the difficulty to variability in the sand quench process that followed the heat-treating operation. They improved product quality by enhancing the uniformity of the sand covering.

*Source: NGM Report's Imperative on NGM Processes and Equipment.

The NGM Report gives examples (see box) of the power of process characterization. In each of these cases, the solutions were not difficult—once the process was understood. The challenge came in understanding the process in sufficient detail. Traditional methods for understanding manufacturing processes and equipment have been focused largely on statistical process control (SPC) techniques, such as control charts. These are powerful techniques, but they are intended to characterize production lot characteristics, after the process has run to completion. They are techniques inherently suited for mass production since statistical sampling and analysis makes the best sense when it applied across large numbers of pieces. The trend toward mass customization and small lot sizes makes the interpretation of SPC results less reliable or even impossible. In the cases described in the box, equipment operators and process planners teamed to understand what was happening to the individual workpieces, and then took appropriate corrective action to resolve the problems.

The NGM Report cites another example of machine characterization. The examples show that many manufacturing operations can easily be characterized when applying analytical methods. The best way to characterize a manufacturing process is to build a model at a sufficient level of detail that the output of the model is an accurate representation of the output of the real process. The NGM company will decide on manufacturing processes using reliable models that accurately predict the consequences of process designs and modifications. The company will monitor the quality of manufacturing operations in near-real time using process sensors and models. Sensor data and specific application models may be used for other operations, providing information such as the exact positional relationship between a workpiece and the tip of the cutting tool, the temperature of a

---

UNDERSTANDING THERMAL EFFECTS

The accuracies required today often mean that machining operations must be done in temperature-controlled environments. One company characterized the performance of a machining center in a non-uniform thermal environment. They traced unwanted geometric deviations to specific, temperature-sensitive, machine components. The company modified the machining center to minimize the machine geometry errors associated with variations in temperature. The results were affordable enhancements to the accuracy of existing machines.

specific location in a high-temperature furnace, or the shape of a rapidly moving part.

➤ **Benchmarking of Manufacturing Processes on a Global Scale**

There you are in your factory in Trenton. You've figured out the bottleneck in your manufacturing process. You have been soldering part A to part B and the solder joints are failing. You haven't been able to see the failures, but because a side effect of the failure of the joint is an intermittent electrical fault, you've known there was a problem somewhere in your process. So you studiously characterized your unit processes and now you have a plan for improving the quality of the solder joint. It's going to cost you $50,000 in new equipment and another $25,000 in engineering, but you'll stay even with unit costs and cut warranty costs by $10,000 per month. Good ROI. Never mind that your competitor in Barcelona has just licensed a process that eliminates the need for the solder joint. They will be able to cut their unit cost by 10 percent and have quality just as good as yours.

In the past, companies have operated on the premise that they have the required knowledge within the corporation. Today, it's not enough to know your own manufacturing processes well enough that you can predict their behavior and control them. In the globally competitive world of advanced manufacturing, you also need to know that your processes are as good or better than the next guy's. And when you find out you aren't better, you need to consider whether it is time to invest in a change. If you want to be world class or compete with the companies that are recognized to be world class, you need to compare your processes with those of the world's best, through individual and cooperative benchmarking. Internal information is not sufficient for setting the targets for process improvement.

Your company should know "how high the bar is set" in every area of strategic importance. Then you can prioritize your investments of scarce resources to enhance your processes. You should benchmark individual processes and equipment, process design, process and equipment modeling and simulation methodologies and tools, and process optimization strategies.

You should use benchmarking to bring knowledge to the manufacturing engineer, the process planner, and even the operator. Benchmarking should stimulate the continuous improvement process. In this usage, benchmarking is not part of an audit or management control process, but rather it is part of the knowledge supply process we will discuss in Chapter 15. Your manufacturing engineer may want to adopt the benchmarked process. More likely, he or she will use the knowledge to help question your company's existing repertoire of processes, picking up ideas for improvement through the benchmarked process.

A cautionary note: What works well for your competitor, or even in your company's plant on the other coast, may not be right in your plant. A best practice in Chrysler's Sterling Heights Assembly Plant might not work in Mercedes-Benz' Sindelfingen plant. The blind use of best practices without thinking it through can lead to problems. What are the underlying assumptions of the documented best practices? does your plant fit those assumptions? What was the culture in which the best practices were employed? is their culture a match with yours? Rather than adopt a best practice "out-of-the-box," what modifications should you make to adopt it to your operation to ensure success? Your understanding of best practices should be deep enough to stimulate your innovative juices, so that your process becomes the new best practice.[6]

➤ Equipment Standards

Machines are the building blocks of manufacturing processes. An *equipment standard* is a machine tool industry design standard that gives assurance that the equipment can fit into processes. There are equipment standards for commonly used machine bases, power units, tooling, material conveyors, and fixturing. Using common footprint dimensions, mounting hole patterns, standardized fasteners, interchangeable tooling, compatible controls hook-ups, and standardized power transmission devices has several benefits. It reduces:

➤ The cost of obtaining and servicing production equipment.

➤ Lead-time requirements for fixturing and tooling changeover.

➤ New equipment installation lead-time.

Equipment standards create opportunities to reduce service and spare part costs, encourage competitive pricing, facilitate rapid tooling changeover, and lead to greater equipment residual value. They make "plug-and-play" workstations feasible.

There is a continuing need for the refinement of specifications and standards. For example, the DMIS standard for dimensional measurement provides a sound basis for determining the instrumentation required for in-process verification of part dimensions. The European DIN standard has been employed in the design of fixture and pallet base footprints for some time by machining system designers and

RESOURCES FOR BENCHMARKING

One electronics manufacturing center uses benchmarks of best industry practices as the basis for its continuous improvement effort. The center used the traditional benchmarking technique after visiting more than 40 other sites to establish a pilot benchmarking database. In its initial efforts, the manufacturing center found redundant and unfocused reports. The center then developed a disciplined process to conduct and evaluate benchmarks. A Benchmarking Coordination Team was established. The team found that the center needed a dedicated focal point for benchmarking, that the database had to be easy to use and maintain. The team trained the groups doing benchmarks, coordinated and focused multiple efforts, publicized the database, trained database users, and served as the champion as benchmarking was adopted within the business units.

Many industry associations and R&D consortia, such as the Consortium for Advanced Manufacturing—International (CAM-I) and the National Center for the Manufacturing Sciences (NCMS), conduct cooperative benchmarking efforts. The results are shared among members of the association or consortium and reduce the cost of benchmarking for the member companies in the consortium.

The Best Manufacturing Practices Center of Excellence (BMPCOE)* is a U.S. Navy sponsored center that identifies, researches, and promotes exceptional manufacturing practices, methods, and procedures in design, test, production, facilities, logistics, and management.

For smaller companies in the United States, the NIST-supported Manufacturing Extension Partnership has established a nationwide network of technology transfer centers that can provide best practices information in their areas of expertise. Similar centers exist in most developed countries.

---

*Internet access to the BMPCOE available: www.bmpcoe.org

builders. The HKS-63 tooling specification has been adopted as a standard for high-speed spindle applications.

Some companies have made a corporate commitment to standardize a variety of automation devices that have wide application, especially for equipment used in a number of discrete manufacturing processes such as the use of pick-and-place and indexing units.

For example, if a slide is going to be used at several sites worldwide and used in a number of diverse applications, a significant benefit can be achieved in designing one single slide or a family of slides with well-defined variants.

Another example is Honda's use of the same indexing unit to drive a chain conveyor in the heat treating operation and an automatic handling device in subassembly. The obvious advantages to Honda are that maintenance people need training to service a single indexing device, and that the spare parts inventory is minimized. Unit costs drop because new engineering is necessary only for the unique fixturing or tooling of components required for a specific application.

■ CONTROLLERS

At the heart of a manufacturing process is the controller (see Figure 10.2). Manufacturing process control systems have four major functional components: process sensors, process actuators, process controllers, and the human operator. The sensors provide the data for monitoring product and process variables. The actuators provide the means for interacting with the manufacturing process to control specified product and process parameters. The process controller accepts sensor signals, uses process models, together with control

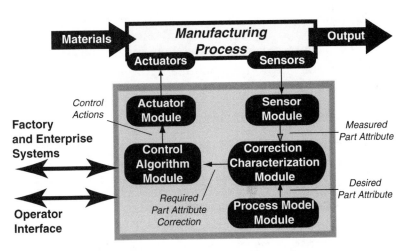

Figure 10.2 Intelligent Closed-Loop Processing (ICLP) Model

strategies and algorithms, to actuate control actions. The sensor signals may come from simple counters, other tactile measurement tools, and from non-invasive tools—interferometers, vision systems,[7] and so forth. The process controller also provides an interface to the human operator's knowledge base and communicates product and process information to factory and enterprise systems. The human operator provides supervisory control.

Traditionally, controllers have been designed to work with a particular piece of equipment in one or a few fixed ways. The controllers have had a mass production culture wired into them. They were intended to control specific pieces of equipment that would be used in set ways to perform the same task over and over.

Next generation manufacturing companies will not have the luxury of operating processes with long-term stability. The next generation of manufacturing processes will have to adapt quickly, easily, and affordably to current and future production needs. The world of mass production had a seductive simplicity about it—but the simplicity of hard wiring has given way to the complexity and the need to accommodate rapid changes in the use of equipment. In a world of programmable controllers, simplicity takes on a different set of attributes:[8]

➤ Lower system costs—your company will ask how the controller can help lower total system costs.

➤ Improved systems reliability—the controller should not be the weak point in the system but should aid in identifying problems in machines.

➤ Reusable logic and applications that enable a shorter order lifecycle—you will need programmable controllers with proven libraries of control algorithms that adhere to accepted standards.

➤ Agility and flexibility—but the agility of your controllers should not make them more difficult to use.

➤ Motion control that is seamlessly integrated with machine logic.

➤ Human-machine interfaces (HMI) that are integrated with application logic.

➤ Open Architecture Controllers

Intelligent closed-loop processing (ICLP) (see Figure 10.2) is an important way to achieve process agility and affordability by enabling advanced, flexible, nontraditional controls. ICLP controls the process with real-time accuracy using adaptive control algorithms and detailed product and process models, updated with real-time sensor data.

You have a problem when the process controller has static models and algorithms, either hardwired or protected by impenetrable software interfaces. Those controllers can't respond well to new conditions, new needs. One solution is to borrow from the "open" concepts of information technology and implement controllers that can accept, in plug-and-play fashion, nontraditional models and algorithms. Open-architecture controllers (OACs) are an important enabling technology for flexible and responsive ICLP. The most common implementations of OACs are on personal computers running a Microsoft Windows™ operating system and communicating via open standards based protocols like TCP/IP and Ethernet.

Early adopters of ICLP haven't waited for commercially available OACs, nor are they depending on the characterizations of their equipment provided by the manufacturer. They are doing experiments that allow them to determine the "footprint" or "signature" of the specific pieces of equipment. Having such a detailed characterization of the equipment permits the development of more finely tuned models that can be incorporated in control algorithms.

The Open Modular Architecture Controller (OMAC) User Group,[9] which includes end-user companies, technology suppliers and integrators, and OEMs, is one organization working to ensure that OACs evolve as agile and flexible, while becoming robust and reliable in the industrial setting. Ideally, OACs should have a plug-and-play capability for both hardware and software modules. For example, if you have a better signal processing algorithm for conditioning sensor data, you should be able to unplug the algorithms that came with the controller and plug in your new ones—without making any other changes. While plug-and-play introduces agility and flexibility, it also introduces a dependence on industry-wide standards. It introduces a need to ensure the integrity and correctness of interchangeable modules. Each module must meet well-defined interface specifications and provide complete, rigorously defined functions.

Although the concept of an OAC is accepted in advanced manufacturing, there is still a need for formal or de facto standards. Several organizations in the United States, Europe, and Japan are working to define application programming interfaces (APIs) for open architecture controllers. An interim API standard, suitable for initial hardware and software development, was made available in 1998 and third-party software modules initially were written using the interim standard.

SAVING TIME AND MONEY THROUGH MACHINE CHARACTERIZATION

A heavy equipment manufacturer had a process requiring very accurate operations on a very large vertical mill. They only had one vertical mill—about 50 years old—large enough for the job; but the built-in controller, up-dated in the 1980s, could not control the mill well enough to achieve the required accuracy. The choice was a multimillion dollar investment in an entirely new mill or augmenting the controller with additional sensor inputs to an industrialized personal computer running an advanced ICLP algorithm at a tenth the cost. Because the mill was inherently capable of delivering the required accuracy, the company saved millions by moving to ICLP. Since one of the important measures investors use to evaluate the company is Return on Assets (ROA), the action was reflected in the investment community's generally favorable view of the company.

The NGM Report provides two examples of the use of ICLP controllers.

General Motors' Powertrain has adopted a conservative implementation plan for introducing OACs—often module-by-module in new manufacturing programs requiring upgrading of existing machines or purchase of new machines.

The combination of sensors, controllers, and actuators together with the software to operate the closed-loop system are an invaluable tool to significantly improve yield and consequently reduce manufacturing costs. Experience shows, however, that for ICLP to be optimally cost effective it must be designed from the top down, starting with a definition of the expected end results. In most instances, the intended system will have several sensors. The concept should then be modeled to define the characteristics of each of the sensors, the controller, and the actuators, based on the particular application.

■ ADVANCED PROCESSES AND EQUIPMENT

As you design processes, you select materials, equipment, and treatment processes. Many of these have worked satisfactorily for decades—and if the result meets your customers' current and projected value needs, you should not rush into newer processes. But often changing

USE OF ICLP CONTROLLERS

A company makes turbines. It must inspect turbine rotor shroud gaps since overall wear is sensitive to the total gap. The smaller the gap, the less the wear. These gaps, therefore, are closely controlled by dimensional limits. The company measured the gap manually using feeler gauges. The method was slow and extremely sensitive to the individual skills of the inspector; it produced reading variations. To accelerate this process and provide a more reliable inspection method, the company worked with an outside vendor with laser application and gauge design experience to help build a laser inspection gauge. An instrument was developed to inspect shroud gaps accurately and repeatably to within 0.0005 inches. The new instrument has provided accurate and consistent measurements and a significant cost saving. Inspection time has been reduced from 30 minutes to 3 minutes per wheel.

An aerospace company has a well-established distributed numerical control (DNC) system to which they upload machine tool data. A machine-monitoring unit also uploads analog and digital data from 15 to 20 sensors placed on each machine tool. These sensors provide readouts of vital signs such as coolant level, hydraulic pressure, and spindle temperatures. The data can be used to provide notice of conditions that warrant action, from routine maintenance to an immediate shutdown.

requirements will lead you to consider advanced processes and equipment. Note, however, that a cautious approach is often the right approach. General Motors made a massive commitment to robotics in the mid-1980s. Chrysler picked its investments in robots very carefully, investing only when convinced there was no cheaper way to get the job done. Yet Chrysler can build a new car with fewer labor hours than Buick can.

Often we equate advanced, or at least re-engineered, processes as being *lean*. In the narrow sense, lean manufacturing means using processes in which every activity adds value, and furthermore where the result is achieved with the lowest cost activities consistent with the required product quality. These ideas have been taken well beyond the factory floor, but they are best exemplified by the Toyota Production System. Lean processes sometimes suffer from a lack of agility—once tuned for volume production, they can be difficult to change.

➤ Flexible, Modular, and In-line Cellular Processes and Equipment

The key word of next generation manufacturing is *responsiveness*. If you use flexible and modular equipment, you will be able to change a specific manufacturing process to accommodate a large family of different products and a variety of production volume rates. If you can do this rapidly, you will increase your company's ability to anticipate and meet changing needs and customer requirements. Flexible and modular equipment may employ open-architecture controls and industry standard mechanical designs.

Flexible manufacturing equipment and processes are characterized by the speed with which they can be reconfigured and their ability to handle a variety of manufacturing processes. They have their roots in the need to improve capital utilization rates and to support just-in-time (JIT) inventory objectives by reducing changeover time and expense.

The product lifecycle and projected volume rates will determine your strategy for flexibility. If you really are going to turn out a million identical flanges each year for the next five years, dedicated production equipment probably will be more cost-effective. The trend to shorter product lifecycles, reduced inventory levels, reuse of equipment, and higher equipment utilization rates, however, increasingly points to flexible, cellular lines or stand-alone flexible machining centers.

In-line manufacturing is a straight-line transfer of in-process material through sequential and automated production operations, resulting in a continuous flow of product. Examples include both dedicated and flexible transfer lines that feature multiple individual workstations, mounted on modular bases that employ either central or distributed process control systems. The benefits of in-line/cellular manufacturing are improved quality control, reduced floor-space requirements, reduced work-in-progress inventory, and perhaps simplified material handling.

One common measure of leanness is flow efficiency (FE), (see Figure 10.3). Flow efficiency is the ratio of the time a part is actually undergoing a manufacturing process to the elapsed time from its arrival at the process station to its arrival at the subsequent process station. If the ratio is low, the part is either wasting time on a machine while waiting for something to happen, or it is sitting in a work-in-progress area. Either way, there is an associated cost. The MIT Lean Aircraft Initiative surveyed seventeen aerospace companies to compare flow efficiency in three different sectors: airframes, electronics,

FLEXIBLE MANUFACTURING

One automobile company has developed a flexible transfer line to produce engine blocks. The line can produce any mix of the three cast-iron blocks. Each machine can process one type of block and then adjust automatically to accommodate different block heights, with no downtime for tool-changing or fixturing reconfiguration. The controller adjusts fixturing and tool depth automatically to accommodate different block heights.

Another company developed a machining system with a two-spindle tool changer design. The design allows the tool on one spindle to be changed while the other is cutting metal. On completion of an operation, the working spindle is exchanged with the second spindle, now gripping the tool for the next operation. Chip-to-chip time in this design was under 3 seconds. Combined with quick-change fixturing, this design allowed the customer to process a family of different small engine blocks in relatively small lot sizes.

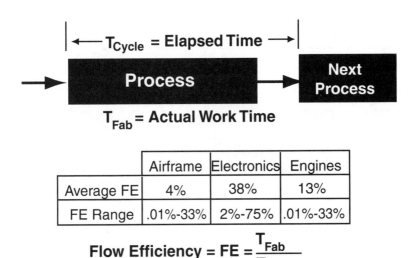

	Airframe	Electronics	Engines
Average FE	4%	38%	13%
FE Range	.01%-33%	2%-75%	.01%-33%

$$\text{Flow Efficiency} = FE = \frac{T_{Fab}}{T_{Cycle}}$$

Figure 10.3 Flow Efficiency Is a Measure of "Leanness"

and engines.[10] The results are summarized in Figure 10.3. The MIT study found that the flow efficiency in job shops averaged less than one-tenth of one percent, whereas the flow efficiency in shops with in-line processing averaged nearly 20 percent.

The cost of flexible equipment is still high, relative to fixed machinery, so a trade-off analysis needs to be done before one is chosen over the other. Much work remains to be done in developing industry design standards that reduce new design costs, and servicing costs that allow for greater interchangeability of flexible modular units. Standards are needed for base dimensions, mounting-hole patterns/locations, fasteners, fixturing, tooling, and control hardware/software.

The vision of a truly agile machine stretches current manufacturing technologies in a number of respects. The ability to "plug-and-play" intelligent work cells rapidly into an in-line configuration will require standardization of cell footprints, quick disconnects for integrated utilities and controls, materials-handling automation, seamless software interfaces, and environmental control equipment.

➤ High-Velocity Machining

High-velocity machining combines much higher spindle speeds, feed rates, and traverse rates, with faster acceleration and deceleration. High-velocity machining allows an NGM Company to increase manufacturing throughput, increase equipment utilization, and maintain higher machining tolerances (see Table 10.1).

Table 10.1 Thresholds for High Velocity Machining*		
Attribute	Today's Typical Machining	High Velocity Machining
Spindle speed	<6000 RPM	10,000 to 50,000 RPM
Feed rates	2–5 m/minute	10–30 m/minute
Traverse rates	10 m/minute	Up to 60 m/minute
Acceleration/deceleration	2–3 m/sec^2	10 m/sec^2
Accuracy		Measured to bi-directional VDI standard
Reliability		>6000 hours/year

*Data from Carl Barthelson, "High Velocity Comes to Die Machining," *Manufacturing Engineering* (July 1998) and Jean V. Owen, "Transfer Lines Get Flexible," *Manufacturing Engineering* (January 1999).

New technologies such as spindles incorporating integral motors, linear motors, integral positioning scales, composite machine bases, ceramic spindle bearings, hydraulically-balanced spindle bearings, and advanced controls systems can be combined with higher spindle speeds to achieve enhanced productivity. Greater volumetric removal rates are achievable with a single high-speed machining center and provide a shorter return on capital investment and reduced floor space requirements.

The benefits for die and mold makers, can be dramatic. When coupled with interchangeable spindle units, high velocity centers require fewer tools, sustain less wear and tear, and yield longer tool life. The time to complete finished dies can be reduced by 30 percent or more.

Many argue that the combination of linear motors and high-speed spindles, used in conjunction with near-net-shaped components and advanced control/feedback systems, will become the standard machining system for the early twenty-first century.

More field testing of new high-speed machine tools in actual production settings is essential to evaluate fully the long-term durability of linear motors and the ability to hold their original accuracy. Because of the high feed/speed rates of these machines, chip removal is a constant challenge. Spindle speeds of 40,000 to 50,000 rpm can cause problems such as whipping with long tools. Preventing the tool from flying out of the tool holder is both a performance and safety concern. Finally, the ability of high-speed machines to process ferrous-based

EXAMPLES OF HIGH-SPEED MACHINING

A machine tool company has recently developed a machining product with up to 60 percent improvement in cycle time over conventional machines. An industry-standard HSK-63 spindle taper and a 36-position tool changer supports the tooling. The machine also incorporates linear motor technology because conventional servo-driven ball screws cannot feed the ultra-high-speed spindles fast enough. Another machine tool company also has developed a system that uses linear motors to drive axis motions. Using a hollow-shank, short-taper tool holder, they claim improved axial repeatability by a factor of three over conventional tool holders, 0.01 mm under ideal conditions. Run-out is a third of high-accuracy steep-taper shanks (0.003 mm). And the system demonstrates improved dynamic stiffness with simultaneous face and taper contact between the tool adapter and the spindle.

materials needs to be explored and developed further, because to date most high-speed applications have been with aluminum and nonferrous alloy parts.

➤ Flexible Transfer Lines

The traditional transfer line has been built for mass production. Since the expectation was on long, high-volume, production runs, investing in fixed, dedicated equipment made sense. But manufacturers now can't count on long production runs and they can't afford to invest in dedicated equipment that isn't being used. They need modular and flexible transfer lines that permit manufacturers to mix and match high-speed machining (HSM) equipment as modules. The machines themselves may often have multiple spindles, and are designed for fast retooling and reprogramming.

For example, Renault is using such centers in its Spanish four-cylinder engine plant with the objective of changeover of less than 15 minutes to produce a different engine variant. BMW Munich has found that replacing its 1980s machines with HSM machines can cut cycle times by as much as 80 percent.[11]

➤ Near Net-Shape Processes and Rapid Prototyping

Near net-shaped processes are processes by which parts are formed to dimensions that require few or no finishing operations. The goal is to use programmable tooling to convert a three-dimensional solid model into a finished part. One effect of near net-shape manufacturing is to reduce or eliminate the waste of time, materials, and energy of finish operations.

One set of programmable technologies for near net-shape manufacturing is often termed *rapid prototyping* (RP). These are processes in which material is incrementally or continuously and selectively added, one layer at a time, to a preliminary foundation. Parts are generated directly from software that reads and interprets CAD solid models to form three-dimensional solids requiring minimal clean up and generally no secondary fabrication processes.

More than 25 different RP processes are in use or are in development. These include:

> ➤ Stereolithography, in which a laser beam is scanned across successive layers of a pool of a photo-sensitive polymer liquid to "grow" parts.

➤ Laminated object modeling, in which successive layers of a laminate are cut by a laser and fused to form the part.

➤ Selective laser sintering, in which a laser melts and fuses particles of plastic, wax, or metals.

➤ Three-dimensional printing, which sprays a binder directly onto ceramic powder.

Commercial RP equipment can be interfaced electronically with CAD design software to provide a prototyping service, with remote access handled similarly to the way desktop-publishing files can be submitted to an electronic print server.

The uses of parts produced by RP processes are usually non-structural since most are made from materials that have very limited load-carrying capability. As the rapid prototyping name implies, however, these parts can help significantly in the early stages of product development, product conceptualization and visualization, manufacturability assessment, and part assembly fit check.

RP parts are also useful for functional models, displays, scale-model testing, mold or casting patterns, and even for non-structural functional parts. The NGM Company should assess continuously the value of implementing and integrating RP processes into their product

---

CUTTING THE DEVELOPMENT CYCLE IN HALF*

HPM, an Australian company that is one of the world's largest producers of extension cords and other electrical outlets found itself under significant pressure from its competitors to manufacture low-cost extension cords suitable for personal computer users. HPM had had an 18-month development cycle, from the time it laid out the functional specification until it gained certification for the product from the Australian government laboratory charged with product safety assurance.

HPM used CAD tools and stereolithography to produce early prototypes of their new product. The prototypes guided the development of production dies that were right the first time. They also were used to accelerate the testing cycle in the product safety lab. HPM cut nine months out of the development cycle, met the window of opportunity, and survived a major competitive challenge.

---

*Presentation by Stuart Romm, CEO of HPM, IMS Australia Symposium (March 30, 1996).

realization cycle, particularly when there is a need for physical prototypes and customer interaction. Prototypes generated from modern RP processes can significantly shorten the early stages of product development and greatly enhance product visualization for effective customer interaction, thereby reducing costs and strengthening customer relations.

Additional challenges for continuous improvement of these processes include increasing production speed while maintaining or further improving part quality, increasing part size, integrating new materials, and automating or minimizing postfabrication clean-up.

The RP process is currently being extended into direct fabrication (DF), the construction of metallic, structural hardware that can be used in delivered products. Several private-sector companies and federal laboratories are developing direct-to-functional-part manufacturing processes. They involve the use of metal powders that are fused through laser sintering, thermal spray processes, or thermal metal jetting. These processes can produce full-density parts ranging in size from tenths of millimeters to meters. Metals ranging from solder alloys to aerospace superalloys have been used successfully to fabricate both perimeter and solid objects.

The RP technologies that produce functionally usable products may prove over time to be the economically most viable way to do small-lot production. They can also provide for parts and assemblies that meet immediate availability requirements—say you need a replacement part for your 20-year-old tractor. There may be a time when instead of scrounging in junkyards, your neighborhood machine shop will search a national database of CAD data and then produce the part using an RP process. Or it will use a vision system to reverse engineer the defective part—and then use the RP process to duplicate it. RP processes, since they usually are processes which build up structures from a continuous flow of raw materials, involve less waste than do processes where a block of material is cut to shape. There is an expectation that RP processes will demonstrate significant economic and environmental impact advantages.

■ EXERCISE

Think about the last time your company starting making a new product or underwent a major model changeover.

> ➤ Could you use existing equipment? Did you have to modify it?
> ➤ How long did it take to recover the costs of new equipment or of the modifications?

➤ How much down time was there as you installed the new equipment or made the modifications?

➤ Did you build parallel facilities so you could keep production going on the old model as you prepared for the new? How much space did that cost?

➤ What about tooling? Were you able to reuse existing tooling? Could you modify any of the existing tooling for the new use?

➤ How about your processes? Did you have to design all new processes?

■ NOTES

1. "Smart Sensor Networks of the Future," *Sensors Magazine* (March 1997).
2. James P. Womack, Daniel T. Jones, and Daniel Roos, *The Machine that Changed the World* (New York: Rawson Associates, 1990).
3. The criteria and other information on the Baldrige Award are available at the NIST web site, www.quality.nist.gov
4. Sharon Hogarth, "Machines with Vision," *Manufacturing Engineering* (April 1999) p. 100.
5. John Teresko, "New Eyes in Manufacturing," *Industry Week* (April 19, 1999) p. 47.
6. Michael Schrage, "When Best Practices Meet the Intranet, Innovation Takes a Holiday," *Fortune* (March 29, 1999).
7. Sharon Hogarth, "Machines with Vision," *Manufacturing Engineering* (April 1999) p. 100.
8. Bryan A. Graham, "PC Controls: An Unfulfilled Promise," *Managing Automation* (July 1998).
9. Jerry Yen, "GM and OMAC in Partnership," *Manufacturing Engineering* (July 1998).
10. J.T. Shields, *Factory Flow Benchmarking Time* (Cambridge: MIT Lean Aerospace Initiative, 1996). Available: lean.mit.edu/public/index.html
11. Jean V. Owen, "Transfer Lines Get Flexible," *Manufacturing Engineering* (January 1999).

Chapter 11

Extended Enterprise Collaboration

MONDAY, 3:15 PM: $2^2 = 9$

Wow! There was a lot of meat in the "how to" part of the Product Realization Task Force's presentation—the part that dealt with the design, engineering, and production processes.

But then in the last part of the presentation, the Task Force turned to the "who does it" question. You realized that they had subtly expanded your job description. Turns out that you are more than the CEO of a manufacturing company. You are the leader within multiple extended enterprises (see Figure 11.1), each created when BAI started working with a new customer, or started working on a new product, or even when you took on jobs to convert used aircraft for different uses. RPPR isn't something contained within BAI. It is spread over many companies over which you don't the have direct control that you have over BAI. The result is that in addition to the more or less hierarchical management relationships you have at BAI, you are engaged daily in collaborative management, where your negotiation and influence skills come to play. That has been the part of your job that always gives you the feeling of "herding cats," although of course BAI has lots of procedures, contracts, and other infrastructure scaffolding in place which diffused the feelings.

If only reality were as simple as the diagrams on the charts!

Jason Biggs, the Special Projects guy from Operations, spoke about characteristics of extended enterprises—the things that

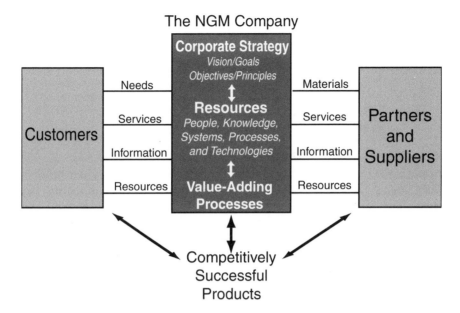

Figure 11.1 A Next Generation Manufacturing Extended Enterprise

made working in an extended enterprise different from simply working in a large, geographically distributed, but vertically integrated company.

Jason summarized the changes that BAI was undergoing as a result of its participation in extended enterprises. There is the emphasis on so-called core competencies—the make-or-break things at which BAI just had to be the best. There is the divestiture of groups whose competencies were not essential for BAI, but could be better managed by others. There are the still-confused legal and financial ground rules for extended enterprises. Finally, there is the need for business and manufacturing systems that could treat other companies' work as if it were being done by a BAI unit.

Finally, Jason talked about trust and ethics as the essential ingredients in holding extended enterprises together and making them work, relating trust to ethical behavior. Pretty deep stuff, but you felt it was good to think about it since the rules for building and operating extended enterprises weren't as clear cut as the rules for, say, old-style contracts with suppliers. Maybe you should use that tonight with the Supplier Council—especially the scary stuff like sharing intellectual property and shared risks and rewards.

■ PRODUCT REALIZATION IN EXTENDED ENTERPRISES

The NGM project states:

> An Extended Enterprise *is the seamless integration of a group of companies and suppliers (industrial, educational, investment, and governmental) that collaborates to create and support a timely and cost-effective service or product, that responds to the customers' needs.*[1]

In many cases, your company will want to respond to a market opportunity, building on an existing relationship with a customer, or building on a successful product line, or building on improved processes. But then the company will realize it doesn't have all the knowledge it needs to produce the product. Maybe it can commission its R&D function to learn what is needed, but how long will that take? Or the company will realize it does not have all the physical capabilities needed to produce the product. Again, the company can build new facilities, but how long will it be before they are put into production? Sometimes there just isn't enough time. Or maybe there isn't enough money to invest in the R&D or the new facilities.

So does your company give up? Or does it decide that splitting the profit with someone else is better than no profit at all? In these cases, your company will have to collaborate with others to complement its knowledge and capabilities. Your company must organize itself so that it can make important decisions quickly. It must find and include the companies that together have the knowledge and capabilities needed to make the product in time to meet the customers' needs. That is, your company needs to know how to create and collaborate in an *extended enterprise*.

Figure 11.2 shows some of the important enablers for extended enterprise collaboration. The centerpiece is *trust*—each member of

Figure 11.2 Enablers of Extended Enterprises

The VP-Marketing and the VP-Development of a specialty integrated circuit vendor were leaving the office together. The VP-Marketing said: "Just got off the phone with the CEO of Really Good Customer (RGC), Inc., who say they can sell a bunch of miniaturized remote-controlled vehicles if we can add an RF transmitter to the chip we make for them—the one with the control circuitry. They think they will have a competitive lead if they can get the first copies on the market in four months—after that it may be too late for them. Can we do it?"

The VP-Development said one of the following:

➤ "Sorry, we can't do the job in four months. We don't have the RF expertise or the capacity. We'll have to pass on this one."

➤ "Stall them. We don't have any RF expertise. It will take us about four months for our R&D people to spec up on RF circuits and another two months to prototype a circuit. We'll have to build up some more capacity, too. So tell them we'll deliver in nine months."

➤ "Gee, we don't have any RF expertise. Maybe we can hire someone to do the design. 'Course, then we'll have to build up capacity. Four months would be pretty dicey, but tell them we'll do our best."

➤ "Hmm. RF/IC, Inc., is really good with RF transmitter design. If we can get them to do the design in, say, a month, then maybe the university's research institute can build a prototype the following month. In fact, if we don't have enough capacity, maybe the institute can even do early production runs. Let me make some calls in the morning and see if we can put a team together. Then let's talk with RGC to coordinate our schedules with theirs."

Which answer is most likely to get the VP-Development a year-end bonus?

the collaboration will have to rely on the integrity, strengths, and abilities of the others. It will have to do so even if there are significant differences in corporate or national cultures. They will need to develop standards of behavior and performance, perhaps certifiable, that will facilitate the rapid establishment of trust relationships.

■ THE EVOLUTION TO NETWORKED EXTENDED ENTERPRISES

The next generation company will view its relationships differently than in the past (see Figure 11.3).

Yesterday's companies often took the macho attitude that they could do it all. Ford's River Rouge plant was the extreme example of vertical integration, where raw materials, often brought in using Ford-owned ore carriers and rail cars, were transformed into finished automobiles ready for the customer to drive away. More typically, companies supplemented their vertically integrated structures with a pool of suppliers. IBM found it needed to supplement its vertically integrated capabilities with vendors who could provide second sources for components, as insurance against catastrophic failure of an internal plant or to meet peak demand. With these traditional supply chains, the companies typically did all the design work, even specified manufacturing processes, and put the finished specification up for bid. They encouraged fierce price competition among suppliers to achieve the lowest unit prices. The company often isolated itself

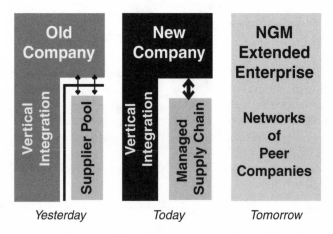

Figure 11.3 The Changing Structures of Manufacturing Enterprises

from its suppliers with self-contained business processes. They relied on static contractual agreements with rigid terms and conditions to govern what often became adversarial relationships.

As companies have moved from high volume mass production toward lower volume responsiveness, the time and cost overheads of vertical integration ate into their competitiveness. Companies began to see suppliers as allies able to reduce inventory and other costs, improve overall product quality, and reduce time-to-market.

➤ Managed Supply Chains

Companies replaced the grab bag of supplier pool relationships with a managed process, supply chain management. The supply chain is managed in that suppliers are selected according to formal criteria, such as:

➤ Suppliers should be proven providers of high-quality components.

➤ Suppliers should meet their delivery commitments, often commitments for just-in-time (JIT) delivery.

➤ Suppliers should have competitive prices.

➤ Suppliers should have a history of continuously improving products.

One result of longer term, less adversarial relationships is that suppliers contribute more of the intellectual contents of products, participating in the design and engineering of products and processes. They develop specialize competencies related to the particular components they provide. Contemporary thinking about strategically managed supply chains has evolved into a set of axioms to tap this potential:[2]

1. There is a shared specific focus on satisfying the common end-consumer.

2. There is an alignment of vision.

3. There is a fundamental level of cooperation and performance to commitment (trust).

4. There are open and effective communications.

5. Decisions are made by maximizing the use of the competencies and knowledge within the supply chain.

6. All stakeholders are committed to generate long-term mutual benefits.

7. There is a common view of how success is measured.

8. All members are committed to continuous improvement and breakthrough advancements.

9. Whatever competitive pressures exist in the environment are allowed to exist within the Extended Enterprise.

First-tier suppliers now are likely to take broad responsibility for the design, engineering, and production of entire subsystems. The functional requirements and the interfaces with other subsystems may be the result of shared decision making, but the detailed knowledge needed for the subsystem lies with the supplier, not the company. Increasingly, these first-tier suppliers are behaving as peer members of the company's integrated product realization process. The result is that manufacturing is evolving toward *networked extended enterprises,* with a hybrid organization. In addition to traditional supplier relations with suppliers of commodity goods, the organization may include more peer-to-peer relationships, especially among the companies whose contribution is a high-value, intellectual one. In this new world, the company's strategic goals will be realized by partnering into successful and competitive extended enterprises.

Like Boeing's commercial aircraft business, the enterprise of the future will collaborate with the customer as an active participant, not just the writer of a purchase order. Companies in the enterprise will pool their knowledge with others to optimize the resulting product. These relationships often cannot be defined in traditional contracts. Risks and rewards are shared in nontraditional ways. The intellectual assets relating to the product and customer are co-mingled. That's a scary notion that raises significant issues relating to the protection of the company's knowledge base, loosely defined as its explicit and tacit intellectual property.

➤ Japanese *Keiretsu*

For many years, we viewed the massive Japanese *keiretsu* as the most effective examples of extended enterprises.[3] There are really two ways to think about *keiretsu*—one is of the six horizontal families of large companies, spanning most of the major industrial and financial sectors, that have equity positions in one another and interlocking directorates. The horizontal *keiretsu* oversaw and dominated the growth of the Japanese economy for decades.

The second view is of the vertical *keiretsu*, consisting of a major manufacturing company together with its supply chain. It is this

Chrysler has transformed its traditional supply chain, filled with animosity, into an extended enterprise in which there is much greater trust and a commitment to work for the good of the entire enterprise. There have been two important aspects of the transformation. First, Chrysler had to transform itself, breaking the old organizational model of functional silos that worked sequentially. Chrysler created cross-functional platform teams— including design, engineering, manufacturing, procurement, marketing, and finance—that worked concurrently. Second, Chrysler invited and motivated its suppliers to join the platform teams.

Dyer describes the essential aspects of Chrysler's new approach as:

➤ Reliance on cross-functional platform teams—leading to more stable relationships, improved continuity, better coordination, and trust within Chrysler and between Chrysler and its suppliers. Use of the teams has trimmed years out of Chrysler's development cycle.

➤ Use of presourcing and target costing—with first-tier suppliers selected early in the development of a new vehicle and given a target cost of a component for whose design, fabrication, and quality the supplier would be responsible. Assuming the target cost is met, or a negotiated alternative agreed on, Chrysler and the supplier enter into an agreement that can extend through—even beyond—the model run.

➤ Focus on total value chain improvement—Chrysler's Supplier Cost Reduction Effort (SCORE) program helps to reduce total vehicle costs without damaging suppliers' profit margins. At first voluntary, Chrysler now expects all its suppliers to participate. The SCORE program invites suggestions from suppliers—they can make them online—and evaluates them. If the suggestions are accepted, Chrysler shares the benefits with the suppliers, either by giving them up to 50 percent of the savings or by increasing their supplier rating for additional opportunities. In its first six years, SCORE saved Chrysler $1.7 billion.

---

*Jeffrey H. Dyer, "How Chrysler Created an American Keiretsu," *Harvard Business Review* (July 1, 1996) p. 42.

> ## CHRYSLER'S EXTENDED ENTERPRISE (CONTINUED)

> ➤ Enhanced communication and coordination—bringing the suppliers' engineers into Chrysler's facilities early in the development cycle and developing an intranet that spans the supplier base. Chrysler's longer term commitments have encouraged suppliers to make investments in information technology and in plants sited close to Chrysler's facilities, also improving coordination.

> ➤ Make long-term commitments that extend for the duration of the model run, perhaps beyond. The assumption is that the supplier will have the business as long as cost, delivery, and quality targets are met, encouraging them to make investments and take risks on behalf of Chrysler.

> The results are dramatic, making Chrysler prior to its merger with Daimler-Benz, into a far more successful company. In less than 10 years, Chrysler cut vehicle development time by 40 percent, reduced overall costs for new vehicle development and production, reduced procurement costs, and significantly improved the bottom line—with increased market share and profitability.

second view that is often taken as a model for a managed supply chain and leads, for example, to think of Chrysler and its supply chain as a U.S. analog of the *keiretsu* (see box). The two views are often intertwined and in recent years the difficulties of the horizontal *keiretsu* have had significant impact on the workings of the vertical *keiretsu*.

The great strengths of the both forms of *keiretsu* were the relationships among its members, often extending back to Japan's post-World War II reconstruction. The trust levels were so strong that every member of a *keiretsu* could expect the others to help if he got in trouble, just as he expected to help the others succeed when they faltered. In the horizontal *keiretsu*, the companies pooled their assets to shore up weaknesses and to provide the resources for expansion. The manufacturing companies adopted strategies focused on gaining market share, in part because the banking and finance companies could be depended upon to provide the needed investment capital.

The vertical *keiretsu* have been held together by an even more complicated blend of people, financial resources, information, components and products, and technology. They, too, have been characterized by strong loyalty and mutual support for one another, even when the major company holds a negligible equity interest in a supplier. With loyalty and mutual support came the expectation of extraordinary efforts to contribute to the success of the *keiretsu*.

The vertical *keiretsu* provided an ideal setting for the introduction and refinement of the lean paradigm for mass production. The stability of the *keiretsu*, to which each member had a long-term commitment, encouraged continuous improvement and cooperative optimization of production processes (for example, through just-in-time parts supply). At times, the *keiretsu* were also agile—because of the high trust levels, problems, especially production problems involving many suppliers could be solved quickly with little regard for corporate boundaries or strict accounting.

The *keiretsu* member's mutual commitment was reflected in the mutual commitments the companies had with their workforces—in return for the company's long-term commitment of employment, workers gave their loyalty to the companies and often worked extraordinarily hard. Even when there was little work to be done, the mutual commitment was honored.

In the 1990s, the horizontal *keiretsu* ran into trouble. The financial assets—real estate and shares in the various member companies—that held the *keiretsu* together lost value. Major investments, such as Mitsubishi Electric's nearly $3.5 billion investment in production of 64 megabit memory chips, led to overcapacity that now is draining profitability. The Japanese began to talk of the bubble economy, the bubble being real estate and share values that, in retrospect, had risen to unsupportable levels. When the bubble burst, the *keiretsu* members no longer had the financial resources to support one another through rough times.

One effect has been for the major manufacturing companies to shift their strategic goals away from long-term growth and market share and more toward shorter term profitability. As this has happened, some smaller companies in the supply chains have suffered greatly, laying off employees, even declaring bankruptcy. Even in the horizontal *keiretsu*, cracks have emerged. Increasingly, members act autonomously as they look outside the *keiretsu* for alliances, often with non-Japanese companies, that will improve their competitiveness. The lifetime employment model has eroded in some large Japanese companies, with some outright layoffs and forced retirements, and with younger Japanese workers less accepting of the work ethic engendered by strong company loyalty.

Some would argue that the Japanese *keiretsu* will survive, that the next economic upturn will see them regain strength. That may be true, but it is more likely that the new *keiretsu* will be more dynamic, more fluid, more like international models.[4] Partnerships will still be based on trust relationships. However, the partners will have more autonomy and a greater propensity to modify their participation in the *keiretsu* as conditions change.

➤ Networked Extended Enterprises

Every participant in a networked extended enterprise is a *stakeholder.* They all contribute something to the product. They all make commitments and assume some risks. They all expect benefits and rewards. These stakeholders (Figure 11.4) include customers, equity holders, employees, and collaborative partners. Each will need the ability to create, sustain, and amicably dissolve relationships with partners possessing diverse business practices and cultures. They must also be willing to accept more shared risks, with commensurate potential rewards, to optimize the return to all the stakeholders.

Most NGM companies will build and sustain multiple simultaneous cooperative relationships, some of which will compete with each other. Some participating companies may compete directly with one another on other products even during the lifetime of the extended enterprise.

The extended enterprise will change as soon as the customers' need is met, perhaps even before. By comparison with today's strategic

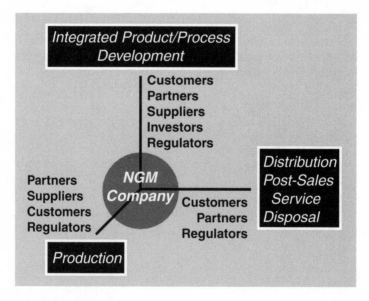

Figure 11.4 Members of the Next Generation Extended Enterprise

alliances, the dissolution or reconfiguration of the next generation extended enterprise will be preplanned to occur after the specific needs of a customer have been satisfied. Many of the decisions on when and how to change the extended enterprise will be triggered by prearranged criteria, reducing the need for time-consuming negotiations. (See the discussion in the section, *Lifecycle of a Networked Extended Enterprise,* that follows.) Processes are being developed to make the end of the life of the extended enterprise a graceful one. The goal is for the member companies to quickly focus on new market opportunities, working either as a reconstituted enterprise or along separate paths.

Your company's management has a crucial role in establishing the vision for your company and for the roles your company will play in extended enterprises. The CEO and management team, through the metrics and reward systems they institute at the strategic, operational, and process levels, continuously reinforce the vision. Part of the vision will be providing a learning environment that is open to change, with active support for risk taking and commensurate rewards.

The NGM networked extended enterprise will:

➤ *Be capable of globally integrating the processes of manufacturing.* These include all processes from gathering marketing requirements through product recycling.

➤ *Easily and dynamically change to accommodate changing environmental factors.* Drivers for change might include new materials, socio-economic upheaval, ecological or "green" issues, niche opportunities, and so forth.

➤ *Have collaborative leadership methods.* These will allow matching products and/or services to customer desires while maximizing long-term benefits to all the stakeholders.

➤ *Have the vision and commitment to think and act globally while adding value locally.* This will permit serving markets anywhere they exist.

➤ *Have the skills of competitive anticipation to envision and create new markets.* They will use the marketing expertise of all members to provide necessary information.

➤ *Be comprised of suppliers and customers in a variety of teaming relationships and commitments.* These will be easily reconfigured and will provide benefits to all stakeholders.

➤ *Effectively manage cultural differences.* They will seek to understand and honor cultural differences, even borrowing those practices that can help build the company.

Agile Virtual Enterprises

For many companies, the networked extended enterprises in which they participate will be transitory and dynamic—so called agile virtual enterprises (AVEs). An AVE has been defined as an opportunistic aggregation of entities working toward a common goal. The entities could be individual corporations, separate divisions in a corporation, or even consumer groups or labor unions. Goranson[5] has identified several different types of aggregation:

1. An aggregation formed in response to an opportunity. In its pure form, one entity identifies an opportunity which takes advantage of a core competency. Then an entity—usually the one which found the opportunity—acts as an organizer to identify and integrate partners having the required core competencies.

2. A relatively permanent aggregation of core competencies that largely pre-exists, and which seeks opportunities. Often new members are added to round out the competencies needed to address the opportunity.

3. A supplier chain which, while using relatively conventional business relationships, exhibits agility in responding to market needs.

4. A bidding consortium. Such a group relies on relatively conventional business relationships in its interactions, but employs agile practices in response to market needs. It acts as an extended enterprise in presenting its collective capabilities to a customer.

Each of the four types could result in extended enterprises that are useful and profitable but not agile. An Agile Virtual Enterprise (AVE) is one that responds well (quickly and with low costs) to unexpected change. Roughly speaking, an AVE is formed to meet a market opportunity and then dissolve or quickly and cheaply reconfigure in direct response to a change in the opportunity.

■ COLLABORATION AND CORE COMPETENCIES

As the business environment moves through the discontinuous changes from mass production to mass customization, from regional to global competition, from traditional to innovative markets, technologies, and business practices, your company will need strategies to cope with the resulting disruption and unpredictability. In this environment, the speed of response—the clock time it takes to field a solution—is the problem. Rapid innovations and quick changes are the answers.

➤ Collaboration

Most companies are choosing to concentrate resources on a reduced number of functions and processes, but being good at an activity usually is not "good enough" to prevent a superior competitor from usurping the market. In the next generation, that competitor will probably be an extended enterprise. Companies will link to create and support a service or product for its service life including final disposal. Integration is required so that people and processes of the collaborative partners can combine their competencies to provide *solutions* to meet their customers' needs.

Few companies will have the resources to provide complete solutions of uniformly high quality, as perceived by the customer. The cost of maintaining a complete set of vertically integrated competencies that can compete with the best competencies in the world is prohibitive for most industries, making partnering mandatory. Technology is changing so fast that most companies that continue to integrate vertically will soon reach resource limitations. Extended enterprise collaboration is a way for individual companies, in association with other

---

WHAT ARE SOLUTIONS?

More than a decade ago, the word *solution* entered the business buzzword lexicon. Some even use *solution* as a verb! But the word denotes a very serious shift in thinking about the nature of business. It placed the focus of business on the goals of the potential customers—on what the customers wanted to accomplish. If a company could figure that out, it could offer not just a product, but a solution that would give, or help give, the customers what they wanted directly. Thinking about solutions stimulated companies to think about the uses customers made of their products and to provide services that would help customers use the products in ways more attuned to their goals. Many companies have found that offering solutions, tailored packages of products and services, is lucrative because they allow customers to more quickly satisfy their goals.

companies, academia, and government, to improve the odds. The forces acting on companies will require most to collaborate actively.

Globalization is also accelerating the trend to collaboration. Global markets demand local presence in multiple markets. The local presence may be a marketing, distribution, and service presence tuned to local language and culture. Or the local presence may be dictated by governmental policies. Many of the less developed countries with limited foreign exchange resources require companies to make long-term investments in the countries' economies, through joint ventures, before they can market their products.

Increasingly, no country's manufacturers will have all the knowledge and all of the capabilities required to meet their customers' needs. Better technology, unique facilities and processes, more cost-effective production, co-production requirements and a closer understanding of country- or region-specific customer requirements will accelerate the trend toward trans-national extended enterprises. Thus the RPPR process will be globally distributed.

Collaborative relationships are the dynamic linkages that enable NGM companies to work together in extended enterprises. The collaborative relationships will be formalized in any of several forms: value networks, webs, or chains in which the partners may be sharing and exchanging other resources in addition to value-added material.

The keyword is *collaborate*—to work together with others. Collaboration is required so that people and processes are dynamically connected and combined effectively and efficiently among the extended enterprise's partners. Collaboration maximizes the combined competencies of the partners to achieve each partner's strategic goals and to provide solutions to meet customers and stakeholder needs.

➤ The Complexity of Collaboration

Life used to be so simple. When we didn't know what was going on in India, and they didn't know what U.S. industry was doing, a machine tool company in, say, Endicott could establish a set of routine practices and processes that, once learned, stood it in good stead for years. It could operate much of the time on autopilot. Now that company may partner with a company in Madras that does control software, or with a partner in Bangalore in a joint offering to the Indian market.

There is a significant increase in operational complexity for companies that participate in extended enterprises. The extended enterprise must manage a host of issues in addition to the usual coordination issues experienced within a company. Hierarchical command-and-control practices may not work when there may be vast cultural differences and when there are business systems and accounting practices that are incompatible. Different organizations may have different approaches, even different definitions and meaning, for common business concepts, such as *overhead*. They may have different approaches to managing production and to sharing and protecting intangible resources such as reputation and intellectual capital.

Education, training, and automated support can help reduce the negative effects of these and other complex issues. Employees will need skills for maintaining collaborative relations, such as:

➤ Understanding the need for extended enterprises and the principles for ethical partnering.

➤ Assessing potential partners' commitment to extended enterprise principles.

➤ Building trust rapidly.

➤ Maintaining trust efficiently.

➤ Facilitating mutually beneficial teaming relationships within the company and across the extended enterprise.

➤ Developing longer-term collaborative relationships.

➤ Making decisions within the bounds of clearly defined responsibilities.

➤ Communicating intent, decisions, and results clearly.

This is a challenge that will require continuing attention and investment by society as well as industry, especially in small and medium-sized companies. Among the critical needs is the capability to simulate future results through a network of dynamically connected processes spread across a series of collaborative partners. The simulation should establish the ways processes and companies need to interface with each other to accomplish both the enterprise's and the companies' goals.

➤ The Sourcing Dilemma

When to collaborate? When to go it alone? You have to protect your intellectual property and your core competencies. You need to collaborate to get the product out the door. Many companies have aggressively adopted outsourcing strategies. IBM adopted an outsourcing strategy for most of the components of its Personal Computer, notably including the operating system. Over time, the decision to outsource the hardware components has proven an excellent model for the industry. But the decision to outsource the operating system without controlling it was questionable. In retrospect, building operating systems and their extensions proved more lucrative for Microsoft and its founders than building PCs did for IBM.

➤ Tools for Collaboration

The extended enterprise may be widely dispersed geographically. It will require standards for communicating about its business and processes and methods for sharing its common intellectual property. Adaptable standards that apply throughout the system will significantly ease the implementation of innovations and will minimize the unnecessary disruption they can cause. The extended enterprise requires effective data, information, and knowledge-sharing technology that protects each partner's proprietary intellectual property and provides secure access to the shared intellectual property of the extended enterprise.

The more open, accessible, and affordable the information infrastructure is, the greater the likelihood that individuals within the extended enterprise will share information and learn from each other. Groupware and other methods of communication that support long-distance group learning and decision making will increase the rate of mutual learning and adoption of new ideas and augment face-to-face learning.

This subject is more fully addressed in Chapters 17 and 19.

➤ Core Competency

The concept on which extended enterprises are built and operated is that of *core competencies*—the capabilities that provide the greatest value to the company. In the PC example cited earlier, Microsoft's core competency lay in understanding and meeting customer needs for PC operating systems; IBM's core competency lay in the design, assembly, and marketing of the PC. Core competencies tend to gather around skills, talents, or resources that are rare, valuable, and usually incorporate cross-functionality. They are difficult to emulate but usually have a significant influence on the capability of the entire company.

One company may have perfected the techniques for designing and building top quality microprocessors. If they have extra R&D dollars they use them to design faster, more reliable circuits, or to improve the quality of the lithography, or to increase the yield. They do this because although they are better than their three or four other serious competitors, they know they have to stay a step ahead. Other companies recognize their competence because of their products' leading edge quality and competitive prices.

Another company specializes in computer memory—building the best high-volume memory chips in the world is its core competence. Someone else's core competency is integrating microprocessors and memory. Another company provides the best operating system implementation, and another the best CAD software. The resultant design workstations may be sold to customers by an organization whose core competence is as a distribution channel. These companies have combined their core competencies, via various kinds of collaborative relationships, in an extended enterprise.

Many companies consider core competencies as the building blocks of their corporate strategies. The strategies include not only products or markets, but also certain technical or business process competencies. Competitive success, in turn, depends on transforming these core competencies into strategic capabilities that provide superior value to a customer. An NGM company's core competencies are its entry into collaboration. Participation in collaborative extended enterprises will enable the NGM company to maximize the value of its competencies as well as those of its partners.

The first thing a company needs to do is understand what it is good at. Even if the best of what the company does is not world-class, its list of core competencies provides a basis for improvement—both in the quality of the competency and in its scope of application. *The second thing a company needs is an understanding of the core competencies it must have to achieve its vision and strategic goals.* Then the company must create a plan to build on existing core competencies and to acquire the additional ones it needs.

Management by core competency permits the company to focus on the crucial elements that will maximize its potential value for collaboration. Note, however, that a list of core competencies is no substitute for a strategic vision—the core competencies are only means for reaching the goals. A company may find itself, as Westinghouse did, with world-class manufacturing competencies that could not help it achieve its goal of becoming a world-class broadcasting company. Westinghouse divested itself of its manufacturing competencies and even changed its name to CBS. Other companies thought Westinghouse's manufacturing competencies were the stuff that could make their strategic visions real and bought them. Other management rubrics for core competencies are:

➤ Maintain a consistent strategic view of core competencies so that management uses them as the basis for linkages within extended enterprises.

➤ Form a capability to anticipate changing core competence requirements.

➤ Establish a repository of benchmarks that can be used to demonstrate the qualifications of the company's core competencies.

➤ Articulate credible standards for identification, evaluation, and normalization of the core competencies of potential partners.

➤ Develop processes to identify how and when to use the core competencies of partners in the extended enterprise.

The identification and management of core competence has received much attention in the efforts to "rightsize" organizations by focusing on the processes, activities, and resources that add the most value to the company. Management has the responsibility to implement a strategic architecture (such as that described in Chapter 3) that guides the development and acquisition of competencies. Historically this process has been used to reposition companies, or the processes and product lines within a company. This process begins with a strategy—the combined ability of a group to see where it wants to go, assess where it is, and identify what must be done to close the gap—that must be consistent with and supportive of the company's long-term business objectives. This is a dynamic, on-going process.

As you go about the business of re-engineering, business process simplification, and resultant downsizing, you must create a balance. You have to sustain and grow your core competencies. But you also have to have the resources to support the work of the core competencies. We often call those resources *infrastructure*. Sometimes we overlook investment in infrastructure in favor of those activities that are demonstrably part of our core competencies. Many companies have learned—sometimes the hard way—that the building blocks of corporate strategies are not just products and markets, not just core technologies and unit processes, but also include integrated business processes. Companies need to build the supporting infrastructure and functions that will enable it to gain maximum benefit from its core competencies.

■ LEGAL AND FINANCIAL FACILITATORS

Collaborative extended enterprises will bring together complementary sets of competencies to address a market opportunity. Companies will require new skills and new business processes and practices if they are going to successfully participate in collaborative extended enterprises. They will need to posses the ability to create, sustain, and amicably dissolve relationships with partners having diverse business practices and cultures. They will need to have willingness to accept increased risk in order to optimize the potential returns to all the stakeholders of the extended enterprise.

➤ Legal Relationship Facilitators

Contractual and other legal practices can promote—or impede—dynamic collaboration and the formation and operation of extended enterprises. More than one company has found itself watching a market opportunity disappear because it could not complete the negotiations with its prospective partners. That's unacceptable today. Streamlined company-to-company negotiation practices are a prerequisite for success.

Many writers view the historical financial and legal systems and practices along with the related laws and regulations as the most serious inhibitors to successful transformation to the NGM extended enterprise scenario. In fact, however, companies have found successful paths through the plethora of legalisms. Both the legal and financial professions are trained to operate from precedent and often act as if they were creating business systems for the last decade, not the next. In the past decade, however, pioneering precedents have provided a basis for extended enterprises. This basis will be simplified and improved, but it is sturdy enough to support practical enterprises.

Extended enterprise collaboration, particularly in peer-coupled web or matrix configurations, requires a different view of the legal frameworks for customer-supplier relationships. The current legal system allows for dynamic partnering, but large customers, especially customers used to dictating their vendors business models, may have to change acquisition procedures to take advantage of them. The U.S. Department of Defense (DoD) is one such customer that is undergoing the painful evaluation and reform of its procurement practices to bring them into better conformance with the practical realities of next generation manufacturing.

There may also be new kinds of legal underpinnings—for example, reinterpretation of antitrust law—that encourage rather than inhibit teaming, that encourage rather than inhibit innovation, and that permit more collaborative sharing of risks and rewards. As NGM companies gain experience with dynamic partnering, they will develop commonly accepted contractual templates for the rapid creation, change in composition, and dissolution of the extended enterprise. These will include consideration of creating a legal entity to have fiduciary responsibility and resolve the joint and separate liability responsibility.

Standard, accepted, forms for agreements will consider sharing of revenue based upon value contributed, data rights, compensation for excess capacity maintained for the good of the extended enterprise, and many aspects that have not been common in customer-supplier agreements. Ways to constructively and expeditiously resolve controversy and avoid litigation—both among partners in an extended enterprise and with third parties—need to be in place so that partners can act in good faith and remain whole during and after participation in an extended enterprise.

Intellectual property, as we shall see in Chapters 13 to 15, will be the defining and most valuable assets of most next generation manufacturing companies. Companies will require strong protections for their intellectual property, protections backed by the force of international law as well as by trust in the ethical behavior of the company's partners.

➤ Financial Relationship Facilitators

Historical financial systems and accounting practices were based upon the assumptions that products had high physical labor content, that capital utilization was roughly the same for each product unit, and that capital investments had an extended value (i.e., machines whose useful life was measured in decades). Those assumptions were valid in the era of mass production. They don't accurately reflect the reality of most next generation manufacturing companies. What is needed are:

➤ Management policies and business practices that support shared risk/reward and teaming, both within the company and in extended enterprises.

➤ Accounting methods for valuing intellectual assets.

➤ Flexible business agreements for the extended enterprise.

➤ Financial incentives that facilitate mutually beneficial teaming relationships, at all levels and in all relevant processes.

➤ Structures and methods which allow the extended enterprise composition to be dynamic without undue penalty to past, current, or future partners.

To maximize return or profit, systems and practices are needed which can support decisions such as:

➤ Determining the value to the company of time savings.

➤ Determining the net return to the business of one percentage point of market share.

➤ Providing a financial value for intangible but real assets such as knowledge and organization strength.

NGM companies and extended enterprises will turn to techniques such as activity-based costing, target costing, and time-based costing. Time-based costing may hold the greatest promise to facilitate extended enterprises, but will not become the generally accepted practice without further trials. All the partners in an extended enterprise will need to use not only the same general accounting method but will also need to use common assumptions so that their cost and price structures are consistent, so that they accurately reflect the method of operation of the NGM company, and so that equitable profit distributions can be made among the partners.

Methods to value human talent and other intangible assets remain a mystery—but a mystery that the stock market is attempting to solve. In start-ups, knowledge is usually all that a company brings to potential investors. As companies mature, accounting practices focus on tangible things—machines, buildings, land, inventory—and lose sight of the intellectual asset base. Yet when those companies are merged into another company, there is invariably an attempt to retain the people whose knowledge and skill constitute the company's true asset base. In many companies, the real assets prove to be the knowledge base and the people capable of exploiting it.

Traditional metrics have made it difficult to link short-term goals with long-term strategy. Manufacturing technology investments have been usually justified financially to meet tactical goals without considering long-term flexibility and reusability. Standard measures of performance are being augmented to bring a broader perspective to investment decisions, reflect true environmental costs, show other hidden costs, and include the benefits of time reductions. Focus on total time, on nonproductive activities, and on dynamic response of the system will sharpen with the use of these new tools. Use of a balanced scorecard (see Chapter 18) will introduce new management processes that contribute to linking long-term strategic objectives with short-term actions.

■ ETHICS AND TRUST

You live with a set of ethics that guide your behavior. And your company has a set of ethics, which may be expressed, implicit, or both. Your company uses its ethics to guide its behavior. Your company's ethics guide your relationships with others in the company. They are part of a shared corporate culture and you depend on the others in your company to behave in ways that are consistent with them. Your personal ethics may not be the same as your company's, even if you are comfortable with them. And your company's ethics likely are not be the same, in detail, as those of the company down the street. The behavior of your company, derived from its ethics, almost surely will differ from what its European, or its Asian, or its African partners regard as ethical behaviors.

➤ Ethics

To the extent that ethics are shared, they provide an axiomatic basis for trust.

The world's dominant ethical systems have a minimal set of common rules that are applicable in business:

1. Avoid doing things that are harmful to others. Like Asimov's robots, neither people nor corporate "persons" ethically may damage other people or companies.

2. Each individual, and by extension each company, is to be accorded the respect due an autonomous peer. In the great religions, this is phrased in terms of the Golden Rule: "Treat others as you would want them to treat you." It is not ethical to usurp another's autonomy. If a company cannot act with autonomy, it cannot enter into a morally binding contract.

3. If an autonomous person freely enters into an agreement, the person is ethically bound to honor it. We extend that to corporate bodies: if an autonomous company freely enters into an agreement, the company is ethically bound to honor it.

4. Lying is unacceptable and no person or company is ethically permitted to lie. Note that this is not quite the same as being ethically committed to tell "the whole truth."

These principles are viewed as a minimum set to govern the ethical behavior of companies that are operating within so-called free markets.[6] Some people and some companies, add two *welfarist* ethical principles:

1. It is the ethical duty of an individual or of a company to promote the well-being of others.

2. It is an ethical duty of individuals and companies to treat others fairly and equitably.

While the minimal ethical set is generally accepted globally, the ways in which it is interpreted and applied differ from culture to culture and company to company. There is evidence that different cultures use different reasoning patterns and emphasize different cultural values as they interpret the minimal set.[7] Husted et al., examined moral reasoning in the United States, Mexico, and Spain, and came to two conclusions: The attitudes toward ethically acceptable behavior are quite similar, but the reasoning by which the attitudes are formed is strongly influenced by culture. They consider the following scenario:

> *Suppose that U.S., Mexican, and Spanish executives sign a contract with the notion that it is unethical for either party to break any of the agreements contained in the document. For the U.S. businessperson, a deal is a deal and an agreement is an agreement (especially one reduced to writing). To the Mexican, on the other hand, the relationship with the other person is the most important aspect of the business deal, certainly more than the contract, but the contract is signed as a "formality" (or as one Latin business person was heard to say, "Now we can throw this away and get down to working together"). Some time passes with no problems and suddenly something happens that has a direct and negative impact on the Mexican executive, his or her organization, group, or even friend. So, a part of the contract is "broken" in order to deal with this new development and surely the other person will understand, because understanding is a central part of a good business relationship. After all, it is only a deviation from one part of a contract that has many parts! However, the U.S. executive does not see it this way, charges the other with being unethical and the conflict is off to a running start. It is even likely to spiral out of control once the countercharges of a lack of flexibility and understanding are made.*

Here the U.S. executive is giving precedence to Rule 3, the keeping of agreements, while the Mexican executive is giving precedence to Rule 1, not harming others, or Rule 5, promoting the well-being of others. Both are shaped by the culture in which they are doing their reasoning. If they focus, as Husted et al. assume they will, on their differences, the agreement and the collaboration are likely to fall apart. If instead they focus on the minimalist set of ethics and on the reasoning processes they have used, it is possible that they can find mutually acceptable ways to complete the collaboration.

In collaborative cross-cultural relationships, Donaldson suggests companies need to maintain fidelity to the minimal set of ethical principles, but that in their application they should adhere to three principles:[8]

1. Respect for core human values, which determine an absolute moral threshold for all business activities.
2. Respect for local traditions.
3. The belief that context matters when deciding what is right and what is wrong.

That is, there is a set of immutable axioms for business ethics, but there are also many shades of variation in the ways businesses reason from and apply those axioms. Hence it is wrong to accept "anything goes" in cross-cultural collaborations, but it is equally wrong to assume that there is only one way to apply business ethics. Just as in making ethical end-of-life medical care decisions, a whole panoply of considerations is required before making decisions that involve ethical conflict. For example, what is ethical behavior relating to child labor for a company operating in Indonesia? what is ethical behavior relating to the employment of women in Saudi Arabia?

Cultures are not contained within national borders. Suppose a manufacturer whose roots are in Cincinnati's German-American community collaborates with a Mexican-American manufacturer in Los Angeles. How do the ways the two apply business ethics align? For that matter, do the "good ol' boy" cultures of the southern United States apply business ethics the way orthodox Jewish manufacturers in Brooklyn or Mormon manufacturers in Salt Lake City apply them? The issues may exist within national borders.

➤ Trust

Your company needs the abilities to establish trust quickly, to create a vision for your roles in a collaborative extended enterprise, and to agree with your partners on a common set of goals, metrics of success, and a shared risk/reward agreement if you are going to address market opportunities in a timely manner.

Ideally, when you give a partner in an extended enterprise your trust, you do so because your partner adheres to a set of ethical business practices, preferably held in common with the other partners.

Such a set of practices, even if arrived at by different culturally affected reasoning mechanisms, can define an ethic for the extended enterprise's corporate culture. When differing societal cultures prevent the development of a common ethic, each of the partners' sets of ethics need to be articulated so all know what they can expect from the others.

An understood set of ethics is just a starting point for trust. Trust is iterative. You build on it through experience. Trust in one's partners can be reinforced by performance across seven dimensions:[9]

1. *Accountability.* Each partner has a specific role in the extended enterprise, a role that is well defined, understandable, and measurable for all to see.

2. *Currency.* Each partner makes the current state of its activities relative to the extended enterprise available to the other partners, has the current state of the extended enterprise available to it, and bases its commitments and efforts on a truthful rendering of the current state.

3. *Accessibility.* Each partner is accessible quickly, at the convenience of the other partners.

4. *Accuracy.* Each partner's data, information, and knowledge are factually correct.

5. *Completeness.* Each partner's input to the extended enterprise includes all of the necessary information, including context, assumptions, and qualifiers to allow the other partners to understand the input in the context of their own activities.

6. *Integrity.* Each partner's input is uncorrupted with irrelevant matter or by information motivated by hidden purposes.

7. *Security.* Each partner respects the property and interests of the other partners.

If, as measured by these dimensions of trust, a company meets its commitments fully and reliably, then others will consider it to be trustworthy.

There is a less demanding view of trust. If you are confident that a partner will give consistent and predictable results using understandable and workable business processes, you can trust them to always produce results of the same character and quality. This begs the question of whether the character and quality match the properties you need. Some folks mess up so much that you can be confident that they will mess up any job you give them. But if you find that the work of a company, while not trustworthy according to the seven dimensions given above, is good enough for the extended enterprise's purposes, you may want to include the company in an appropriately fenced relationship.

The extended enterprise may not have the luxury of relationships only with those who have proven themselves in long-term relationships. Competitive pressures may require a greatly reduced "time to trust"—maybe reduced by orders of magnitude. Companies are turning to prequalification, benchmarking, and trusted agents or brokers as ways to accelerate the trust process.

■ A PROCESS MODEL FOR NETWORKED EXTENDED ENTERPRISES

The networked extended enterprise of the near future will be a dynamic entity.[10] Time will be an explicit variable. The enterprise will be designed for change and for going out of business once a customer need is met. The Agile Virtual Enterprise (AVE) Reference Base[11] provides a process model describing the lifecycle of such an extended enterprise, its formation, operation, and change or dissolution. The basic processes of an Extended Enterprise, put together to meet a particular customer need, are shown in Figure 11.5.

The initiation activities involve processes that are often developed through trial and error. They mirror the processes companies use

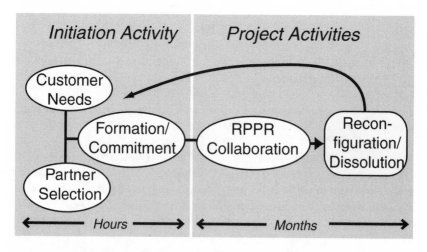

Figure 11.5 A Process Model for Extended Enterprises

when they enter into strategic alliances or other partnering arrangements. However, competitive time pressures mean these processes must be executable in hours or days instead of months or years. During the major part of its lifecycle, the extended enterprise will execute RPPR, engaging in product realization processes that are spread across the member companies of the enterprise. Networked Extended Enterprises will grow increasingly dependent on enterprise modeling and simulation to game business models, including partner selection and risk/reward structures.

If change is the hallmark of the competitive environment, then the extended enterprise should be designed with change in mind. As partners complete their tasks in the enterprise, they may leave it, and be replaced by partners whose core competencies now are needed. At some point, the customer need for which the enterprise was formed will be satisfied. The process model recognizes this by explicitly including the processes for reconfiguration and dissolution. The dynamic nature of extended enterprises is illustrated by the inclusion of a feedback loop from the reconfiguration/ dissolution processes to the initiation activities.

The five major processes, subdivided in the AVE Reference Base into 26 subprocesses, don't operate in a vacuum. The processes are supported by the social and cultural, legal, physical, and knowledge infrastructures we discuss in other sections and chapters.

➤ Opportunity Identification and Partner Selection

The Opportunity Identification and Partner Selection Processes are concurrent and interactive processes meant to define what the product offering will be and what companies or groups will produce it. The resultant "package" is formalized in the Formation/Commitment Process.

Opportunity Identification

In Chapter 6, we discussed the start of Integrated Product and Process Development (IPPD) as listening to the *voice of the customer*. The Opportunity Identification Process assumes that either a potential leader for the extended enterprise or some designated agent is listening and identifies, refines, and characterizes the opportunity. The most prevalent way this happens today is for a company that has an essential relevant core competency to identify and refine an opportunity. Then that company uses its understanding of the characteristics of the opportunity to define the requirements of the extended enterprise which must be formed in response. There are four sub-processes: Opportunity Strategy, Target Marketing, Search, and Exposure. These are interrelated processes with Opportunity Strategy as "first among equals."

Opportunity Strategy

The initiating company's strategy for identifying opportunities should be explicit and well reasoned, because its results will be examined by potential partners in the extended enterprise. Since each partner will be deciding whether to commit to the enterprise, there should be no question of the assumptions behind the company's analysis. The strategy should be based on a consistent method for defining and determining core competencies and there should be a simple relationship between characteristics of the opportunity and the core competencies of the partners.

Targeted Marketing

Would that customers knew what they wanted! Often, however, an initiating company may sense a market opportunity that is just beyond the horizon for new applications perceived by the customer. The initiating company may need to incubate the opportunity by integrating the customer into the extended enterprise at an early stage to facilitate product understanding and acceptance. This is more than just opening a communication channel, since many customers may not know what could be possible, or may not have recognized the opportunity afforded by the new product.

Search

Sometimes the opportunity is not apparent. Each company should be constantly searching for new opportunities, new ways to leverage its competencies. A company should always be investigating many possibilities, including very unfamiliar ones. Christensen[12] has described many instances where innovators have moved across traditional product boundaries with great competitive success. Therefore, there should be a set of processes that looks for new, perhaps unconventional, markets made possible by new partnerships.

Exposure to the Market

Unless the opportunity has first been identified by potential customers, the initiating company needs a mechanism to inform the customer set that the company plans to pursue the opportunity. Ideally, the customers would be active stakeholders in the extended enterprise.

Partner Selection

In some cases, the partners in an extended enterprise will be fixed by long-term relationships or by an agreement among companies to seek opportunities that use their combined competencies, and this process can be omitted. Often, however, the initiating company will first identify, in a preliminary way, a market opportunity, and then seek to put together a partnership team. There are four subprocesses (Figure 11.6).

Sometimes, your company will take the lead in seeking partners. At other times, others will seek out your company. Your company will need strategies for searching out potential partners, and also for making itself easy to find and evaluate. You will find it advantageous to have multiple methods for searching—relying on traditional networking is not likely to be adequate in an era of rapid change.

Partner Qualification

The company needs a standard method for defining its core competencies and the core competencies it is seeking in the proposed extended enterprise. Over time, the standard method needs to be shared with other companies so that there evolve standard ways for objectively describing, with a high level of confidence, a candidate partner's core competencies (what gives them value as a partner) and associated quality, technical, capacity, and financial indicators. The compatibility of management styles may also be a criterion.

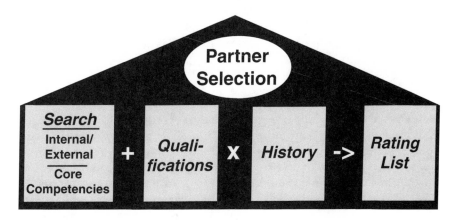

Figure 11.6 The Partner Selection Process

Partner Performance History

An essential factor in forming extended enterprises is *trust*. (See the previous section on trust.) The Partner Selection Processes are essentially decisions on whom to trust. A potential partner's history of proven quality, delivery, and other criteria can provide assurances of trustworthiness. Given the time-driven nature of competition, the partner's history of response to change may also be a significant determinant.

This subcategory differs from Partner Qualification by focusing on specific performance data from the past. Special analytical tools may be required to map past situations to the current ones since today's may differ widely.

Ordering

The Partner Selection Process should yield a prioritized candidate list of partners for each of the required competencies, based on the formula shown in Figure 11.6. Reality is that the top-rated candidate for any given competence may not be able to participate in your extended enterprise, so there is a need for alternatives.

➤ Formation and Commitment

Having identified the opportunity and partners, the extended enterprise must detail the business case and establish the required commitments. It is at this point that major resources are committed. The responsiveness of the Formation/Commitment Process will depend on the enterprises' ability to reuse prior templates and established infrastructure components; to scale the needed core competencies to the size of the opportunity; and to self-organize with limited direction, with minimal negotiation, and with loose coupling among partners so no dependencies are built up except in pursuit of the specific market opportunity.

Vision/Strategy Development

An explicit vision and purpose provide the rationale for building an extended enterprise. Your company should not participate unless the stated purpose aligns with its overall strategic plan. The vision and operational strategy of an extended enterprise is likely to be mission-based and differ from the company's vision and strategy for itself. The vision for the enterprise should incorporate a sense of its life span, of how it is going to change in response to expected conditions, and of how it is going to respond to unanticipated change. There should be strategies for continually assessing the competition, existing and potential customer needs, and related technology development. Finally, there should be a common set of ethical standards that can facilitate an environment of trust and cooperation.

Partner Commitment

This is the actual selection of and commitment to partners. This process establishes the go/no go decisions of the potential partners and may require catch-up processes of filling in the gaps and clarifying all the roles.

Enterprise Metrics

The enterprise needs a balanced set of metrics. These may be based on traditional financial and operational metrics but also should be capable of identifying not only whether goals are being met, but also predicting problems or the need for change.

Resource Commitment

This process deals with the detailed determination of who commits what capital (and other assets) and with the commitment of those assets. New financial/legal infrastructure may be needed before there can be rapid, smoothly functioning, implementations of the process. The partners will need to agree upon a method for valuing intellectual property or other dynamic assets as the enterprise is operated and the values change.

Product Liabilities

Who is liable, and for what? All anticipated product liabilities, including those which are improbable, need to be assigned. Note that there is a separate class of liabilities, addressed below, associated with the production processes (lawsuits concerning ecological or social impacts, for example) which are not bound to the product.

Risk/Reward Strategies

When the enterprise makes a profit or otherwise is successful, who is rewarded? Presumably, risks and rewards will be co-defined, with reward based on risk. Risk should be included as part of the Enterprise Metrics. Those metrics should be capable of identifying failure modes as a way of assessing negative reward. The process should accommodate risk contributions that may not be naturally expressed by a dollar amount; name, image, goodwill, and market intelligence. The resultant risk/reward structure should be capable of responding to change in an orderly and inexpensive way.

Operating Structure

The extended enterprise will require a shared operational infrastructure, created to support the relationships which partners have with one another. Reporting and supervisory relationships need to be established. The hierarchy of partners needs to be explicit. The procedure for filling leadership positions needs to be set out. The structure may require a mechanism for dispute resolution. There may be need for a scorekeeper/adjudicator, a role which may be supplemented by processes which anticipate and neutralize conflict.

Dissolution Plan

At the outset, each enterprise should plan for its dissolution. One necessary component of the plan is the set of threshold conditions, presumably tied to Enterprise Metrics, which would trigger dissolution.

➤ RPPR in the Extended Enterprise

Once the extended enterprise is formed, it must execute the rapid product and process realization (RPPR) process. It should look like a single organization from the outside. The operation should have an external view that looks like a conventional organization. The way RPPR is done should be similar or identical to the operation in a large, decentralized manufacturing operation.

Performance Measures

This collection of processes will be the basis for the metrics which measure individual components at the micro level, but these should combine at macro levels, rolling up to Enterprise Metrics. The metrics should support the predetermined risk/reward structure. Since the metrics are applied to processes that may span more than one company, they may expose activities normally contained within a single company to the entire enterprise.

Customer Relations

The extended enterprise must appear as a unified organization to the customer and its processes must support this transparency. Presumably, some of the risk/reward structure will be based on customer satisfaction. This necessitates a metric that measures satisfaction, traceable to specific components and processes. Processes also have to recognize and measure intangibles such as goodwill, including those giving back to the community, society, and environment.

Operating Practice

Once the extended enterprise is operating, it will need a set of practices and processes that make it possible to function without regard to company boundaries.

➤ Reconfiguration and Dissolution

The time will come when the market opportunity has been fully satisfied or changes qualitatively. That is the time to dissolve or radically reconfigure the Extended Enterprise. Ideally, the time will be apparent to all the partners because of the triggers preplanned during the Formation/Commitment Process. If the extended enterprise is to be reconfigured, the lifecycle will iterate back to the Initiation activities.

Identification of Need

If the earlier processes were done right, the extended enterprise will have predefined sunset conditions. A process is needed for monitoring those sunset conditions to identify when the formation of the extended enterprise should be reviewed. This process will trigger (and provide information for) fundamental change of both the nature and the structure of the extended enterprise.

Residual Liabilities

Whether the extended enterprise is dissolved or reconstituted, there should to be a set of processes to identify and assign responsibility for residual liabilities. Examples would include warranties, environmental concerns, employee benefits, and product liabilities. Note that even normal operations or changes in the extended enterprise may require liability reassignments. It is possible that the assignee might not have been an original partner in the extended enterprise, is a partner acting in a new role, or is a successor extended enterprise.

Asset/Equity Dispersal

A series of processes are required to distribute assets and equities. These processes are likely to be more metrics- and cost-based. However, assets could also include intangibles such as intellectual property and goodwill. This subcategory does not include profits dispersal, since that should have been handled in normal operation. Moreover, the assets may form the basis for reconfiguring or otherwise reconstituting the extended enterprise.

➤ Supporting Infrastructure

The processes of the extended enterprise don't exist disembodied in the abstract. They live within a set of infrastructures provided by the partnering companies and by society. They include codes of ethics, psychological behaviors, social mores, community cultures, and business cultures. They include the legal and regulatory framework. They include accepted standards and tools for business plans and workflow management. They include the knowledge infrastructure we shall discuss in Chapters 13 to 15. They include the logistical and transport infrastructure. Because these infrastructures extend beyond the boundaries of any potential partner in the extended enterprise, they are a community or societal concern—critical to the economic survival of the community as well as the company.

MONDAY, 5:00 PM: TO THE SUPPLIER COUNCIL DINNER

The Task Force finished up; you had a half-hour with Jose, Diane, and Adolfo on incorporating the Task Force recommendations into the discussion at the Executive Leadership Team meetings on Thursday and Friday. You left the ELT Conference Room, dealt with the accumulation of "must call, must sign, must decide" things that couldn't wait, and turned your attention to the Supplier Council. Your consciousness had certainly been raised as you thought about your suppliers.

For several years, BAI had hosted a conference for its suppliers. It was an opportunity to make sure everyone understood the standards expected of them, to give the suppliers some tools for meeting the standards, and to show how they fit in the big picture—and it was also an opportunity to reward the best of the suppliers. There had been a curious evolution in the meetings. At the start, BAI people would make the presentations—mostly on what the suppliers had to do to continue getting business from BAI. The only supplier voices heard from were those who had a spectacular "best practice" BAI wanted all the others to adopt.

Somewhere along the line, some joint presentations showed up on the agenda. Working together, BAI and a supplier showed such-and-such a practice. The real change came when the Supplier Council—senior executives representative of BAI's first-, second-, and third-tier suppliers—was formed. One of their duties was to orchestrate the agenda for the Supplier Conference. Now the conferences included what the suppliers thought they needed to know and BAI's candid discussions of not-yet-solved problems.

In parallel, the notion of supply chain management had gained credence. The Task Force presentation pushed you further in your thinking. In managed supply chains, your suppliers had in limited ways become your partners. You didn't tell them everything and expect them blindly to do whatever you said. You expected them to add value through their own process innovations, maybe even through participation in the design process. But now you, and they, were going to have to behave more as peers, sharing knowledge, sharing risk, and sharing rewards.

As you drove to the Plaza del Sol for the meeting, you knew two things—you were going to have a good dinner, but it was going to be interrupted time and again by candid discussions. Your leadership—and followership—skills were going to be tested.

■ EXERCISE

Is your company ready to collaborate in extended enterprises? You can assess the readiness of your company with these metrics:

1. What is the percentage of the people in your company who have training in the skills needed to participate in multicultural extended enterprises?

   —Teaming skills

   —Communications skills

   —Skills for multicompany decision making

2. What is the percentage of your company's competencies that have been designated as "core"? Are they documented and validated at a level such as to be useful in a national or international registry?

3. How long would it take to identify the competencies needed for your next product? How long would it take to identify sources of the needed competencies inside and outside your company?

4. How long would it take you to establish an extended enterprise to produce the next product your company wants to put on the market?

5. How many of your company's attempts to form extended enterprises, of any mix of customers, partners, and suppliers, have been successful? List the five most important reasons for the failures.

■ NOTES

1. NGM Project, *Next Generation Manufacturing: Framework for Action* (Bethlehem, PA: Agility Forum, 1997).
2. The "Axioms of the Optimized Supply Chain" were developed within the CAM-I Strategic Supply-Chain Management (SSCM) Program and the DARPA Qualification Criteria for Agile Enterprises (QCAE) Project. © Doyle, Parker, Zampino, & Boykin, 1996.
3. Hiroyuki Tezuka, "Success as the Source of Failure? Competition and Cooperation in the Japanese Economy," *Sloan Management Review* (January 1, 1997) p. 83.
4. Peter Drucker in "Management's New Paradigms," *Forbes Magazine* (October 5, 1998) p. 152, traces the origins of keiretsu back to Will Durant's assembly of General Motors, to Sears Roebuck, and to Great Britain's Marks and Spencer.
5. H.T. Goranson, *The Agile Virtual Enterprise: Cases, Metrics, Tools* (Westport, CT: Quorum Books, 1999).
6. See, for example, Dennis P. Quinn and Thomas M. Jones, "An Agent Morality View of Business Policy," *Academy of Management Review,* vol. 20 (January 1995) p. 22.
7. Bryan W. Husted, Janelle Brinker Dozier, J. Timothy McMahon, and Michael W. Kattan, "The Impact of Cross-National Carriers of Business Ethics on Attitudes about Questionable Practices and Form of Moral Reasoning, *Journal of International Business Studies,* vol. 27, no. 21 (June 1996) p. 391.
8. Thomas Donaldson, "Values in Tension: Ethics Away from Home," *Harvard Business Review* (September 1996) p. 48.
9. Taken from the NGM Report.
10. This section borrows heavily from the work of the Agile Virtual Enterprise Executive Develop Group, organized and supported by the Agility Forum in 1994–97, especially an unpublished 1997 report presented at the 1997 Agility Conference. This work used materials and ideas gener-

ated in the course of a Defense Advanced Research Projects Agency (DARPA)-funded project with Sirius-Beta on *Metrics for Agile Virtual Enterprise,* a project that focused on understanding and measuring agility and which is discussed in Reference 6.

11. The AVE Reference Base is described by H.T. Goranson (Bethlehem, PA: Proceedings of the Fourth Annual Agility Conference, Agility Forum, 1995).

12. Clayton M. Christensen, *The Innovator's Dilemma: When New Technologies Cause Great Firms to Fail* (Boston: Harvard Business School Press, 1997).

Systems Support for Extended RPPR

Rapid Product and Process Realization (RPPR) is conducted across the extended enterprise. Today, companies are using a number of commercially available systems to support Integrated Product and Process Development (IPPD) and other business processes. These will evolve to support RPPR. If they were seamlessly integrated, they would provide a basis for the virtual factory and virtual prototyping within the next generation manufacturing extended enterprise, as well as the tools for enterprise resource planning and management. These systems (see Figure 12.1) include:

➤ Computer-Aided Design (CAD) and Computer-Aided Engineering (CAE) systems that support Integrated Product and Process Development (IPPD).

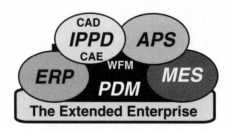

Figure 12.1   The Overlapping Systems That Support RPPR

➤ Advanced Planning and Scheduling (APS) systems that opti-mize both local factory operations and enterprisewide supply chains.

➤ Manufacturing Execution Systems (MES) that monitor and control operations at the factory level.

➤ Enterprise Resource Planning (ERP) systems that monitor and control operations across the enterprise.

In turn, these systems are supported by Product Development Management (PDM) repositories and tools for managing product and process data. Often, PDM includes Work Flow Management (WFM), which usually involves document flow and processing.

Each of these systems has evolved from a different starting point. As point solutions to specific functional needs, they stood alone. As companies expressed the need for greater integration, vendors grew these systems each in functionality to the point where now there is significant overlap. If properly implemented any one of them could be the backbone for the complete integrated support systems com-panies need. Now, however, integration is usually a clumsy exercise, requiring a significant amount of custom systems integration effort.

Many vendors provide proprietary interface tools that facilitate interoperability among systems. As has been typical in computing, interoperability may come at the cost of significant customization. Standard interfaces do not yet exist for much of the functionality in-corporated in these systems.

■ PRODUCT DATA

The focus of many commercial product data management (PDM) systems is on the text-based data required for engineering release. They incorporate functions for:

➤ *Documentation management.* The best PDM systems provide a product data model that has a single image for all the users. The product data model is a virtually centralized, but physically dis-tributed, facility for collecting, controlling, storing, and deliver-ing design and development data. The PDM systems should also interface with the document preparation and display tools that are used in the enterprise.

➤ *Product management.* Product management includes change management and configuration management. Change management manages the design and release process within an enterprise, providing automated processes for communication and approval of engineering change requests. Configuration management focuses on defining and maintaining the product definition data, product structure, features, and variants, and their overall configuration management across the design, the customer order, the manufacturing plan, the manufacturing operations, and the delivery processes. If linked to maintenance, this function can include field modifications and upgrades.

► *Data support.* PDM systems should support the enterprise's major CAD, CAM, and CIM systems with database distribution, replication, and linking capabilities so that all the systems used for integrated product and process development (IPPD) use the same data.

While PDM started as a way to manage the data for engineering release, its real power is as a repository for the representations of the product that everyone needs—not just the people who approve engineering releases.[1] For example, Enterprise Resource Planning (ERP) is the principal application used today to manage logistical flows for manufacturing, including the supply chains. If the cycle time for product realization is to be reduced, suppliers need the knowledge contained in product designs and PDM needs to be integrated with ERP. In some PDM systems, there are links to the enterprise's manufacturing execution systems (MES) and ERP systems. One advanced feature is proactive updating in which the PDM system notifies the other systems whenever there is a change in product data that will affect the functions of those systems.

Today, integration is possible, but it is inhibited by the proprietary interfaces between proprietary PDM systems and proprietary ERP systems. NGM enterprises may find insufficient flexibility in proprietary systems with "hard-wired" interfaces. The answer lies in more modularized systems that can be used, plug-and-play style, on the Internet.

■ PRODUCT DEVELOPMENT

Product data modeling and management systems are evolving into Product Development Management,[2] which has been given the somewhat confusing acronym PDM II (see Figure 12.2). The goal of PDM II is to accelerate product realization by managing all the data generated throughout the development process. The expectation is that the

IBM developed its own ProductManager™ PDM system, which has been commercialized by the ENOVIA Corporation as EN-OVIApm.* During IBM's initial implementation at seven locations, approximately 100 million design records were loaded into the database, for use by 3,300 users. "ENOVIApm is a strategic application within IBM's Integrated Product Development process re-engineering project. Design, manufacturing, commodity and cost engineers, product planners, procurement and others are integrated into the release process electronically," Johnny Barnes, director of hardware common tools for IBM, is quoted as saying. "ENOVIApm is playing a significant role in helping us reduce the normal 40 to 60 steps needed to release a product to 15 steps or less. We expect to cut the time we are spending in recreating and interpreting engineering data by 50 percent or more." Barnes adds: "We are already seeing benefits that amount to millions of dollars a year in increased productivity and reductions in I/T, scrap and rework costs. We are also recognizing much more value from accurate engineering information being leveraged downstream in manufacturing."

When Hughes Electronics, a commercial unit of General Motors, started the transition from defense contractor to commercial products, it restructured into a flatter, decentralized company focused on specific markets with an objective of dramatically cutting operating costs. As part of this initiative, Hughes moved to a client/server computing environment that enables cross-functional integrated product teams to access relevant information from manufacturing, engineering or finance systems. One of the first applications to leverage this client/server system was an ambitious PDM system, which fosters collaboration among business units. The $70 million initiative uses a commercial PDM system from Inso Corporation to put engineering documents and drawings, parts lists and bills of material online. The system consolidates a variety of incompatible PDM systems that were running on mainframes

---

*Enovia Corporation is a subsidiary of Dassault Systemes. Enovia's products were partially developed for internal use by IBM and are now marketed and sold by IBM Corporation. Dassault Systemes is the developer of CATIA-CADAM product design tools.

(continued)

EXAMPLES OF PDM (CONTINUED)

within the old Hughes operating groups and incorporates previously paper-based data. With this system, Hughes has seen an increase in productivity because engineers no longer have to spend time tracking down or redrawing part graphics. In addition, the system's security options let Hughes connect to its suppliers and customers, enabling each group to track the progress of each order. With this feature, Hughes has cut communication times, especially when dealing with offshore suppliers.

Datel manufactures power supplies and data equipment that had used a manual engineering change order (ECO) process. By the mid-1990s, the process had become a bottleneck with an increasing number of in process ECOs, but with no similar increase in the number completed. Datel automated the ECO using the ConsenSys Rapid PDM software serving the design services, quality assurance, prototyping, manufacturing, and planning departments. Everyone can see the status of designs simultaneously and work together to better forecast work, resolve problems, and create plans.

Product Definition Management
Product Creation and Design
Reuse of Part Designs
Bills of Materials
Functional View Management
Variant Management
BOM Editing, Export and Import

Manufacturing Process Management
Process Plan Representation
Mapping of Components
to Processes
Support for Distributed Factories
Management/delivery of Process
Plans and Instructions

Change Management
Change Control
Change Requirements
Change Item Creation
Change Impact Analysis
Change Process Flow
Change Notification
Online View and Markup

Visualization Management
Product Design
Process Design
Cell and Floor Layout
Collaborative, Interactive 3D
and Graphical Visualizations

Documentation Management
Support for Distributed IPPD
Configuration Management
Organization
Search and Access Control
Publication

Figure 12.2 Product Development Management (PDM II)

data may be generated by integrated, but perhaps physically disbursed, product teams. The teams define every attribute of a product in an all-digital format. As the product design matures, the Product Data Manager, incorporated as a part of PDM II, ensures that the correct data is received by all the groups in the extended enterprise who share in the responsibility for transforming the design into a finished product.

The objective of PDM II is to enable enterprises to define, configure, manage, and optimize:

➤ Product development, starting with the "voice-of-the-customer" and market requirements definition, through concept design and detailed engineering design, including product-manufacturing and maintenance process design and execution.

➤ Manufacturing and human resources definition and tracking.

➤ Plant definition, which includes plant designs, plant manufacturing and maintenance processes, and all associated plant information.

PDM II systems should provide access for anyone in the extended enterprise needing product information, whether to control the product over its lifecycle, to work on the virtual product model, or simply to visualize product data.

PDM II is still evolving. There is general agreement that PDM II includes the applications and application library services shown in Figure 12.2, but the competing offerings do not include a uniform set of functions. Furthermore, the interfaces among functions are not well enough defined to support mix-and-match interoperability among the offerings. Since NGM companies will work in collaborative teams, the PDM II systems will have to provide, or be built within, interactive, collaborative, work environments.

■ ADVANCED PLANNING AND SCHEDULING

Advanced Planning and Scheduling (APS) systems will be a critical part of Rapid Product and Process Realization (RPPR). APS systems give companies the scheduling flexibility they need to be customer-responsive.[3] They support the NGM paradigm in which customer orders drive plant scheduling, not long-term forecasts or production plans.[4] APS also lie at the heart of managed supply chains.

Trek Bicycle Corporation is a rapidly growing company—with annual sales of more than $400 million—that designs and assembles several lines of bicycles—mountain bikes, road racing bikes, and urban recreational bikes, using components from suppliers all over the world. The key for Trek is to assemble the best available components into products that meet the changing needs of bicycle riders. The business is both technology driven with new materials, new designs, and suppliers competing to improve component technologies, and market driven with increased market segmentation. It is a dynamic market for which the specifications of the "best" bicycle change all the time.

Using a PDM II system from Matrix One, Trek's 50 engineers have doubled their productivity. The greatest time savings came from automating the specification change request (SCR) process—the time for SCR approval was reduced by 30 percent and for SCR tracking by 50 percent. The more disciplined communication of designs and specifications with suppliers has reduced errors that at one time led to costly rework, even to the procurement of components made obsolete in later designs. Overall, Trek's design cycle has been reduced by four months.

Calor is a mid-sized European company with annual sales of about $200 million that makes small appliances. Windows of opportunity open as customers develop new interest in novel functionality and new convenience or style features—and then the windows close just as quickly. New models are not that much different from the old ones—many are just variants. There's added complexity because Calor builds country-specific variants, which must meet country-specific regulations, for the European, North American, South American, and Middle Eastern markets.

Also using Matrix One's PDM II system, Calor reduced the time to define product specifications, create detailed designs, developing customized country-specific variants, and producing manufacturing documentation from four months to one month. Part of the time savings came from the increased reuse of older designs that had previously been hard to access. Engineers now focus on designing truly new components and on performing cost and quality analyses of new product designs.

In the 1990s, vendors have developed APS systems that use heuristic search techniques from artificial intelligence and efficient, global optimization techniques from management science. These systems build on the Theory of Constraints[5] to guide the search for schedules that best meet the constraints imposed by limited resources. The Theory of Constraints helps reduce the optimization calculation by focusing on the most important potential bottlenecks, such as equipment shutdowns, labor shortages, parts shortages, and the lack of availability of tools and materials.

The algorithms in APS systems also run in near real time. A company can optimize its next day's—maybe even its next hour's—schedules based on today's reality, not on what it thought a month ago, what that reality was going to be. Companies can also reprioritize work—say, an emergency order comes in from your best customer—and almost immediately develop a schedule to get the emergency work, and the rest of the work too, done.

Typical APS systems for the shop floor include features that permit:[6]

➤ User definition of machine, cell, or plant-specific scheduling rules.

➤ Optimization of machine utilization by combining multiple orders to reduce set-up times or splitting orders into smaller lots that will permit use of small intervals of time on machines, time that might otherwise be idle time.

➤ Splitting of complicated operations into segments where each segment is defined with its own resource requirements, its own lags, and its own time requirements.

➤ Balancing of production lines by splitting operations to run on multiple machines simultaneously.

➤ Generation of machine loading queues optimized on user defined order characteristics (e.g., priority), and optimization of schedules based on order attributes.

➤ Balancing of the workload on flexible machining centers by scheduling different orders on each station in a multistation center.

➤ Definition of order- or operation-specific start dates and of the resource requirements of support functions.

➤ Dynamic adjustment of the time required to complete a job when that time is dependent on the specific assigned resources and dynamic assignment of intraoperation delays, for example to

---

HERMAN MILLER GETS PRODUCTION RIGHT

Office furniture manufacturer Herman Miller Inc., reports that with the use of i2 Technologies' Rhythm scheduler, it has improved on-time delivery from 65 percent to greater than 98 percent, reducing late orders from $10–$12 million in 1993 to $300,000 in 1996. The scheduling spans all of the company's plants. One result of the APS is that Herman Miller's plants focus less on meeting weekly production schedules and more on fulfilling the needs of customers. Another result is the coordinated shipment of orders directly from the plants to the customer, rather than incurring the time delays and extra overhead of consolidating shipments at a distribution center. And still another result is a nearly 80 percent increase in inventory turns.

---

ensure that an operation starts on a specific day or specific time of the day.

➤ Minimization of make time by running operations simultaneously and of changeover time by defining part families with common operations, such as set-up.

➤ Automatic selection of the resources that would result in the earliest completion of an operation.

➤ Scheduling orders for ASAP completion or for completion at a specific time.

➤ Constraining part combinations so that parts of different configurations are not scheduled in the same work center at the same time.

Schedulers for supply chain management have similar flexibility in developing optimized schedules for the entire extended enterprise.

■ MANUFACTURING EXECUTION SYSTEMS (MES)

In the semiconductor industry, individual equipment controllers are often networked into manufacturing execution systems (MES) to provide a plantwide view of critical production process and product data for operations, management, and other functions in the enterprise.[7] MESA International, a trade association of MES vendors, has identified the principal functions of MES:

Dispatching production units	Operations and detailed scheduling	Resource allocation and status
Document control	Work in process (WIP) tracking and history	Performance analysis
Human resource allocation and tracking	Maintenance management	Process management
Quality management	Floor-wide data acquisition	

The essential element of MES is the control and coordination of cell and equipment controllers to optimize overall plant efficiency. Where MES have been implemented, plant floor control systems serve as the core production systems and provide near real-time data to:

➤ Enterprise Resource Planning (ERP) systems that require production performance data for evaluation of the current plan and guidance on future planning.

➤ Supply chain management to adapt the supply pipeline to meet actual needs.

➤ Sales and service management needing timely order status data for distribution and delivery planning.

➤ Product and process engineering with data for evaluation of product quality and process efficiency.

MES or their equivalents—for example, refinery control systems in the petroleum industry—are most highly integrated in continuous and quasi-continuous process plants, such as semiconductor fab lines. In many plants, some functions listed above are done manually and others are automated in individual software packages. Still other functions are not done at all, either because they are unnecessary or because the need for them hasn't surfaced.

A survey of companies, coming from seven industry segments weighted toward discrete manufacturing, that have implemented MES[8] identified the eight kinds of benefits as:

Benefit	Quantification
Reduction in manufacturing cycle time	Average: 35%. Range: 10–80%
Reduction of data entry time	Average: 36%. Range: 0–90%
Reduction of work in process (WIP)	Average: 32%. Range: 0–100%
Reduction of paperwork between shifts	Average: 67%. Range: 0–200%
Reduction of lead time	Average: 22%. Range: 0–80%
Reduction of defects	Average: 22%. Range: 0–65%
Reduction of lost paperwork and drawings	Average: 55%. Range: 0–100%
Empowers plant operations personnel	Anecdotal evidence that personnel make more and more timely local decisions

The significance of MES is that they promote a systems understanding of the plant. In the NGM company, as intelligent closed loop control becomes the norm, MES will become more sophisticated, incorporating models of the entire plant at a sufficient level of detail that most routine operations can be conducted quickly and effectively. The difficulty of MES, one that has inhibited widespread implementation, is the great variation in the functions needed from plant to plant and manufacturer to manufacturer. The need is for MES to be better chunked into plug-and-play modules with standard interfaces.[9]

■ ENTERPRISE RESOURCE PLANNING (ERP)

Enterprise Resource Planning (ERP) systems, ideally, automate and integrate the company's major, enterprisewide, business functions—generally the finance, inventory, logistics, and human resource functions. Companies have turned to ERP when they have found it too difficult and too expensive to maintain systems that are specific to a few business processes, especially when those processes need to share time-dependent data and to exchange results with other processes.

Implementation of ERP has helped many companies, not just by integrating information flows, but often by forcing business process rationalization and re-engineering. Companies that have successfully implemented ERP report reduced inventories, improved workforce utilization, enhanced productivity, better order management and reduced order-to-payment cycle times, reduced information technology costs, reduced procurement costs, and better cash management.

Not all implementations have been successful. For many companies, early ERP packages were analogous to computer mainframes—large, expensive, rigid, and difficult. They often incorporated, implicitly, a fixed business model—fine if it was like your company's, not so good if yours didn't line up with the one in the ERP package. They were effective for large companies that could afford the time and financial investment, but not so good for smaller companies, especially if there were time pressures.

In the world of organizational change, mergers, and divestitures, it has become common for what had been two autonomous companies to have to integrate their ERP systems.[10] This has been a challenge since the proprietary ERP packages were not developed with interoperability in mind.

Next generation manufacturing needs the functions of an ERP system, but it also needs the ability to change its processes quickly. Next generation manufacturing also needs systems that can support the RPPR processes spanning dynamic extended enterprises. These needs are driving ERP more toward a distributed computing model with modularized functions that can be implemented in peer-coupled client-server networks, where functions can be implemented on a module-by-module basis.

ERP systems span most of a company's business processes, but not all. As companies see the power of integration, and as they automate more of the knowledge-based processes, they are finding need for additional functions—functions that sometimes are added to vendor packages and sometimes found in other offerings that are "bolted" onto ERP. Some of these are described next.

➤ Customer Relationship Management (CRM)

The company's interface to the customer is its Customer Relationship Management (CRM) system. Companies—Dell is a premier example—are using the World Wide Web as their interface to their customers. The Web-based CRM system provides a portal through which customers can explore the company's products, configure the product that best meets their needs, order it, track its progress in the factory, arrange for its delivery, provide payment, and obtain service.

Much of the data the customer sees, of course, should come out of the ERP system and the Product Data Model.

The Web will not be the only interface to customers—some may prefer other channels to communicate with your company. So your CRM system will have to accept go-betweens—account representatives, customer service centers that answer phones and even letters, distributors and services retailers—and still reach into the rest of the company's automated systems.

➤ e-Commerce[11]

Great savings can be obtained for both the manufacturer and the customer by conducting business transactions electronically—if the electronic links between them extend back into the manufacturers business systems and forward into the customer's asset management systems. CRM systems provide one approach for business-to-consumer and business-to-business e-commerce. In the business-to-business arena, automated procurement packages are more specialized, but are evolving toward being procurement *portals,* entry points accessible on the World Wide Web where everything a contracting vendor needs to know is made available. A thesis of this book is that next generation manufacturing will employ e-commerce for its primary business systems and that today's pioneering commercial packages will be overtaken by systems with enterprisewide functionality.

➤ On-Line Analytic Processes (OLAP)

On-Line Analytic Processes (OLAP) are processes intended to support decision making for complicated decisions. OLAP applications allow business users to access critical information, to model sophisticated business problems, to predict the outcome of decisions, and to implement the decisions.

Integrated Decision Processing (IDP)[TM12] is one approach to combining flexible data access, powerful business modeling, and multivariable "what-if" analyses with process automation to produce an end-to-end decision processing system. OLAP applications can support IDP for such complex processes as brand management, portfolio management, enterprise risk management, and customer relationship management. In the past, these areas have required a great deal of human intervention and hands-on analysis. The resulting gaps in the decision process led to delayed decisions, which were often based on inadequate data, faulty analysis, and inconsistent business measures.

➤ **Enterprise Application Integration (EAI)**[13,14]

Companies have legacy systems that were developed in the "islands of automation" days. These systems are frequently so big and so costly to rewrite that they must be used until they can no longer be forced to match the company's changing business processes. Until those systems are rewritten as modular, flexible, open systems, with standard design and process semantics, as we will describe in Chapter 17, companies will struggle with integrating the legacy systems with their ERP and PDM systems. Enterprise Application Integration (EAI) is a term used to describe *middleware,* software packages that provide pragmatic solutions to today's problems—interfaces and conversion tools for integrating legacy systems with modern ERP, APS, and PDM systems. This is tough work—the heavy lifting of practical enterprise integration—because the variability of semantic meaning from system to system introduces immense levels of complexity. Nevertheless, using EAI packages can reduce the cost of integration as much as 50 percent.

■ SUMMARY

Existing commercial packages generally have pre-NGM and pre-World Wide Web origins. They represent the vendors' understanding of their sphere of application with little thought given to interoperability. But interoperability of functional modules from competing packages continues to increase in importance. We can expect to see the evolution of these large packages into the lean, agile, reconfigurable modules that will track the NGM paradigm.

■ NOTES

1. Jeffrey Zygmont, "PDM Expands Its Role by Linking to ERP," *Managing Automation,* (August 1998).
2. George Shultz, "PDM Sees More Integration, New Adherents," *Managing Automation,* (August 1997).
3. Doug Bartholomew, "MRP Upstaged: New Planning and Scheduling Systems are Threatening the Very Existence of Manufacturing Resource Planning Systems," *Industry Week,* (February 3, 1997) p. 39.
4. George Schultz, "Rapid Response Is a Strategy, Not an Application," *Managing Automation,* (April, 1997).
5. William H. Dettmer, *Goldratt's Theory of Constraints* (Milwaukee, WI: ASQC Quality Press, 1990). See also, Eliyahu M. Goldratt, *The Goal* (Great Barrington, MA: North River Press, 1992).

6. Adapted from the marketing literature of TigrAPS.
7. "New Views of MES," *Managing Automation*, (1999).
8. *The Benefits of MES: A Report from the Field* (Pittsburgh, PA: MESA International, 1997).
9. Erin Calloway, "A Second Chance for MES," *Managing Automation*, (December 1998).
10. Suzanne Hildreth, "ERP Woes," *S/W Expert*, (June 1999) p. 59.
11. Emily Kay, "Electronic Commerce," *Managing Automation*, (June 1999) p. 46.
12. Trademark of WhiteLight, Inc., Palo Alto, CA.
13. Ira Breskin, "Middleware," *Managing Automation*, (June, 1999) p. 42. Note that the term, middleware, has many meanings in information systems and the reader should always understand the context to know which meaning is in use.
14. Eric Keller, "How to Cut through the Hype of EAI," *Managing Automation*, (June 1999) p. 72.

Chapter 13

The Innovative NGM Company

TUESDAY, 9:00 AM: FACING THE NEW WORLD

Back to the ELT conference room. Yesterday you focused on the tangibles—on developing winning products and getting them out the door. Today, the focus will be on the intangibles: knowledge and the ways people get it and use it.

One of the two-pagers on Next Generation Manufacturing (NGM) that Angela gave you this morning had the quote:

> A fundamental thesis of NGM is that the only competition that counts will be knowledge-based. In a worldwide free market for ideas and products, the company that uses knowledge to build a product better and more profitably will be the one that succeeds.

The introductory chart (Figure 13.1) of the morning's presentation was already on display. BAI needed to do everything it could to gain competitive advantage.

It is people who get the job done, who get the product into the market. They use what they know, pouring that knowledge into the product. New ideas come from people. Some of the best ideas you've had, the ones that made a real difference to BAI, came when you took pieces of knowledge—from a technical journal, from an internal BAI report, from a chance remark by a customer or colleague—and on a hunch you wove them together. You had been lucky. Your bosses gave

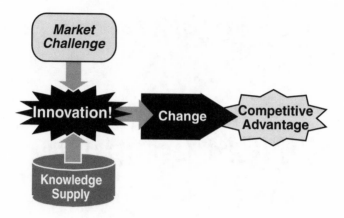

Figure 13.1   Knowledge Leads to Competitive Advantage

you the freedom to test your ideas—and you hadn't had many failures, so they seemed to put up with the ideas that went down in flames (as long as it was ideas, not aircraft or sustained profits, that crashed).

The experience with the EagleII's weight had taught you how much knowledge you had to tap to be competitive. Four years ago, early in the development of the EagleII, Gigantus Leasing wanted a plane it could lease to tour operators, for whom the key issue would be operating costs, especially the fuel/seat mile. All things being equal, that would be the biggest factor in Gigantus' decision. Getting Gigantus' order was important, maybe crucial, for the profitability of EagleII. Gigantus was a leader. If Gigantus ordered, others would follow.

You were the COO at the time and your folks were discouraged. If they used the design and manufacturing processes they had used for the original Eagle, EagleII was going to eat too much fuel, more than your competition would. BAI needed to take weight out of the plane. You formed the "EagleLite Tigers," an ad hoc team of design and process engineers, and told them what Gigantus wanted. You told them to wrack their brains and "steal" good ideas from anywhere they could be found. You even set aside some lab resources so they could try out their ideas.

Turns out there weren't any big ideas that made the difference for EagleII's success—but many little ones. One engineer was thumbing through a journal and realized that there was a stronger alloy that would allow BAI to cut 1,000 pounds out of the EagleII's structural members. A designer and a process engineer realized that if they tweaked the design and manufacturing process for an interior cabin mount they could save 200 pounds/plane. One engineer who had been on a benchmarking trip had seen a better way to design the landing gear—and cut 300 pounds/plane. An aerodynamicist suggested a change in the wing design—turned out to be too costly a change from the existing design, but the engineer filed it away and was using it now on the preliminary work on the SuperEagle. By the time the EagleLite Tigers finished their work, BAI had learned a lot and you had a plane, packed with knowledge, that Gigantus could buy.

There had been some blood on the floor, though. It was fascinating how people held on to the older ways. "We've always done it this way!" "Our people can't make *that* change!" "Those people don't know as much as we do!" You had had to use a combination of persuasion and coercion to get people to do what was needed. In time most of your people had accepted the new ideas, but at least one very experienced veteran, whom you could use now, had taken early retirement and left grumbling about how BAI was going to the dogs.

The EagleLite Tigers were a success. They had responded well to Gigantus' challenge. Of course, there is a similar challenge waiting in every conversation with every customer—the implicit, "Unless you can give me thus-and-so, I'll do business with the guy down the street (or half a world away)."

You wished everything BAI did had as much innovation in it as EagleII had. That was why you had asked for this morning's presentations: What can BAI do to maintain a steady flow of the kinds of ideas that will keep BAI ahead of the competitors? You figured it had to do with bringing the things you'd done with the EagleLite Tigers into BAI's corporate culture, with systematizing the processes you had used to guide the changes, working through the cultural issues so that folks wouldn't quit in a huff.

■ INNOVATION

Innovation can mean two things:

1. Innovation is the process of creating something new. But it is more than that. It is the process of creating something new and then of using the new to achieve a useful result. The process, innovation, combines invention and implementation.

2. An innovation is a result. In practical terms, an innovation is something new to the company, not necessarily new to the world—something the company hasn't seen or done before.

We'll use the word both ways.

The techies will tell you, often at length, about technical innovations—a better material, a new process, novel product features. The R&D folks talk about the process of innovation and describe the progression from basic research in the physical sciences, to applied research in academic engineering, to industrial development in their companies' labs.

Technical innovation can be very important, of course, but it is just one type of innovation. An innovation can just as well be a new business practice, or a new way to deliver products, or a different way of organizing work.

Where does innovation come from? It comes from the human mind. It is an exercise in problem solving at a deep, creative level. Each person has a unique understanding of his or her domain within the enterprise, and so each has unique insights into solutions to its problems and ways for coping with changing conditions. Your company will need all the brainpower it can garner if it aspires to thrive, so it should demand innovative contributions from all its employees.

The research and development (R&D) function used to be the place to find people who are paid to be innovative, but the traditional R&D silos are undergoing major changes. A wide separation between many companies' R&D functions and their operations grew up in the post-World War II era until R&D seemed irrelevant to profitability. In reaction, companies have forced R&D to be tightly aligned with operational needs and even distributed the R&D resources throughout line operations.

While established R&D labs will continue as a significant source of innovation, NGM companies expect good ideas and practical solutions to come from anyone. You may not be a technical specialist, but you probably know more about some aspect of your work than anyone else in your company does. So you are in the best position to know the weaknesses of that aspect of the business—and once you've identified the weaknesses, you probably have good ideas on how to eliminate them.

There is no magic to innovation. Very few ideas are truly new. It is almost true that "there's nothing new under the sun." Drucker[1] tells us that we often overlook the homely questions we should ask to stimulate innovation—questions that arise out of our daily activities but that we often overlook in our quest for the "home run" that will transform us into instant leadership:

➤ Some of our ideas work better than we expect. Can we apply them elsewhere? Can we sell them?

➤ Some ideas don't work the way we expect. What can we learn from the incongruity? How can we apply what we learn?

➤ We take many processes for granted—we've always used them. Do we know their weaknesses? Do we need different, better processes?

➤ What is happening in the rest of the industry and in the structure of markets that is likely to affect us? What do others do better than we do? Are we ready for the future markets?

➤ How can we best respond to demographic trends that affect our markets, our partners and suppliers, even our own workforce?

➤ We know the economy has its ups and downs that affect the mood and fashion trends in the market. How well prepared are we for these cycles?

➤ What new knowledge is going to prove important in our industry? How can we use it?

The new process you need to improve your fabrication may be a best practice at the shop down the street. The new product feature you think will differentiate your product may be a feature on a complementary product offered by your Polish competitor. The agreements for strategic alliances that will build a new relationship with your first tier suppliers may be similar to the joint venture arrangements an Argentinean company and your key competitor's suppliers are using to enter your market.

Christensen[2] teaches us that there are two fundamental classes of innovation (see Figure 13.2):

➤ *Sustaining innovations*—innovations that help us serve our target customers better by enhancing our existing products, processes, and business models.

➤ *Disruptive innovations*—innovations that force paradigm shifts, that enable new products, processes and business models to serve customers in different ways, with radically different value equations.

Christensen writes of *value networks,* complexes of customers, companies, and suppliers who aggregate around an innovation. In the 1960s and 1970s the banks, insurance companies, and the other customers for mainframe computers, together with the major manufacturers, their suppliers, and software companies, made up one such value network. The customers for minicomputers, the minicomputer

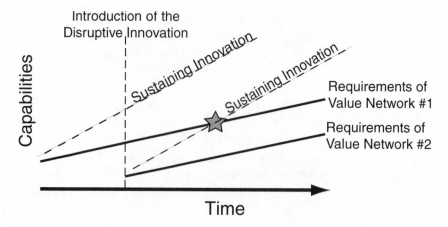

Figure 13.2 Why Innovations Can Be Disruptive

manufacturers, their suppliers, and associated software companies formed another value network around the cheaper, lower margin, minicomputer. At first the two value networks didn't overlap, but as the minicomputer underwent a series of sustaining innovations, it grew in capability to the point where it could meet a significant portion of the first value network's needs. The minicomputer value network operated around a lower price point. Result: disruption!

The two classes of innovation both will be important for the NGM company, in spite of the tension that results. To stay ahead of its competitors in its existing markets, the company will need a continuous stream of sustaining innovations. To stay ahead of paradigm shifts in the global business environment, the company will have to identify, create, track, and adopt destructive innovations. This can be a major challenge for the leaders of an NGM company. They cannot let a focus on continuous improvements (which are just incremental sustaining innovations) blind them to an understanding of the threats and opportunities afforded by disruptive innovations.

If your company is going to be competitive in the next generation manufacturing environment, the entire workforce must participate in modern innovation strategies and practices. Innovation is a very human process. You can teach and you can learn corporate, team, and individual innovative behavior. Motivated people, set in a culture that encourages innovation, see a need, a problem, a challenge—pick your euphemism—and use their explicit and tacit knowledge to forge a response. Your company must create an organizational structure, culture, and measurement and reward systems that encourage innovation. This includes placing value on risk-taking and learning from failure in the creative process of innovation. It also includes balancing investment in sustaining innovations and in disruptive ones.

■ BUILDING AN INNOVATION CULTURE

➤ Choosing a Strategy

Every organization—not just businesses—needs one core competence: innovation. *And every organization needs a way to record and appraise its innovative performance.—Peter Drucker*[3]

You can assume that innovation will just happen when you need it—or you can set a strategy (see Figure 13.3) and then plan and manage a culture and a discipline for the innovation you need. NGM's thesis is that companies that foster an innovation-driven culture, apply a systematic approach to innovation, and rapidly make use of emerging technologies, processes, and business practices will dominate their markets.

NGM companies need to develop and maintain an environment that promotes, fosters, and rewards creativity and innovation. But no company can do it all. No company can be on the forefront of materials science for all materials, on the forefront of computational science for all modeling and simulation, on the forefront of manufacturing science for all processes, and on the forefront of market development for all markets. Companies have to pick and choose, to guide innovation in the ways that best fit the company's strategic goals.

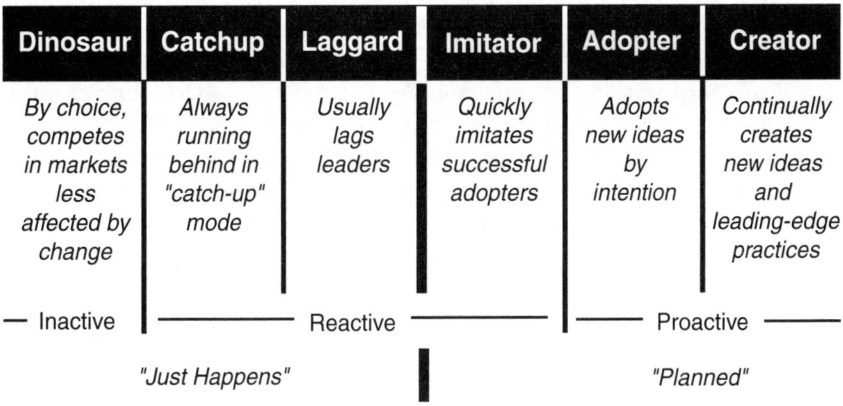

Dinosaur	Catchup	Laggard	Imitator	Adopter	Creator
By choice, competes in markets less affected by change	Always running behind in "catch-up" mode	Usually lags leaders	Quickly imitates successful adopters	Adopts new ideas by intention	Continually creates new ideas and leading-edge practices

— Inactive ——————— Reactive ——————— Proactive ——————

"Just Happens" ▮ "Planned"

Figure 13.3 A Continuum of Enterprise Strategies for Change and Innovation

The NGM Project developed a continuum for innovation strategies (Figure 13.3). Companies must make strategic decisions as to where to place themselves on the Continuum. The strategies should be aligned with corporate goals and the understanding the company has of its core competencies.

The Dinosaur, by choice or by instinct, chooses to graze off the *status quo,* willing to risk extinction usually because it feels little threat. The Dinosaur doesn't know if there is a train leaving the station. The Catch-up is the little kid who has always just realized the train is leaving the station, and has to run like the dickens to stay with the market. The Laggard dawdles along, usually getting on board before the market disappears into the distance. The Imitator keeps its eyes open, assesses the optimum time to jump on board with the least risk and the biggest benefits. The Adopter is the company that makes sure it has a seat in the front car of the train, leaving the old early, getting to the new early. The Creator is the company that makes the train go.

This train analogy is outdated. Maybe we should use the airplane analogy. That adds to the sense of urgency. It's hard to walk in the tracks of an airplane to the next station and the Pilot/Creator has a lot of freedom to take the plane anywhere. But even that analogy is wrong. Today it's a question of whose electrons are ahead.

The double line in Figure 13.3 between "Laggard" and "Imitator" indicates a critical point in the ability to get on the electronic train. A company with a core competency should always have a strategic position for that competency to the right of the double line so that it will be less surprised by a competitive threat. In a global and dynamic environment, companies that lag or do worse will be overwhelmed by those that quickly imitate or do better. While it is possible to allow processes that aren't part of the corporate core to drift to the left, the company system should continually review and decide whether even those processes need innovation.

Time compression means that the lines between Creator, Adopter, and Imitator have gotten fuzzy. Imitators used to have the luxury of waiting for months, maybe years, to decide to adopt a new idea. Today the window of opportunity—say in the PC business—may be so short that early adopters will have to act in a matter of hours and imitators in a matter of days.

Your company needs a holistic, enterprise systems-level innovation strategy, with conscious decisions made based on core competencies, technology advances, and market developments. You must manage your innovation portfolio to achieve the best sustained return on investment. You do this in a context of playing off technology innovations against business innovations. You will have to put more effort into integrating the economic, behavioral, and technological factors. You'll find natural resonances for innovation as you simultaneously build stronger customer involvement in rapid product and process realization (RPPR) and better harness your company's intellectual capabilities.

The NGM Report outlines what your company needs to do to make innovation management a core competency:

➤ Make innovation management an explicit priority in all strategic planning.

➤ Clearly articulate the concepts of innovation and link them to the business success of the company.

➤ Manage change so that the workforce is motivated to enhance innovation.

➤ Demand innovation in every aspect of the business, not just in product development and manufacturing processes.

➤ Develop and implement metrics and performance measures that encourage innovative team work.

➤ Avoid punishing failures when an attempted constructive innovation falls short.

➤ Use innovation when designing, implementing, and operating extended enterprise relationships.

VALEO'S COMMITMENT TO INNOVATION[*]

Valeo SA is a profitable $7 Billion French multinational automotive parts supplier that has adopted a vision for operational strategies called the 5 Axes: involvement of employees, supplier integration, constant innovation, total quality, and a lean production system. The 5 Axes means that Valeo is on a never-ending quest for continual improvement.

The quest for constant innovation is backed up with metrics and measurements. There is a goal of soliciting an average of 15 suggestions each year from each of the company's 50,000 employees. And the suggestions don't sit on the shelf. The target is that each will be evaluated within five days of submittal. Valeo doesn't accept all the suggestions, of course, but it accepts enough that its major customers, like General Motors, credit Valeo with many improvements that they, in turn, can use to improve the cars their customers buy.

[*] Andrea Knox, "From an Also-Ran to Front-Runner," *Industry Week,* (April 19, 1999) p. 18.

■ THE LANGUAGE OF INNOVATION

The language of innovation is dynamic. Companies have defined invention and innovation in many ways. We adopt the notion that invention is just the first stage of the total process of innovation, that an innovation hasn't happened unless it has been implemented in routine operations.

> *A scientific invention may be viewed as a new idea or concept generated by R&D, but this invention only becomes an innovation when it is transformed into a socially usable product. Lay persons, probably because of the mystique which surrounds science, generally view invention as a relatively rare event, and assume that once it has occurred, the process of innovation can be completed in a straightforward manner. In actuality, the converse situation occurs.*[4]

➤ Invention

Invention is the creation of something new. Classically, an invention is an idea that is well enough described that, from the Patent Office's point of view it has been "reduced to practice." But as any frustrated inventor knows, it is a long way from reduction to practice to royalties. The purpose for an invention may not yet be defined, except in some fuzzy way by the inventor. Some invention is done out of necessity, some out of chance.

There are two ways to perceive invention:

1. The first view is from the perspective of patents, prototypes, and discrete deliverables.
2. The second view is broader and includes the notion of idea creation and new insights, which may lead to new or improved products, processes, practices, and services.

Because there is as much creativity in market development and company operations as there is in product or unit process development, we adopt the broader view.

➤ Innovation

There is much confusion in the literature of innovation. Some writers focus on the big innovations that change the industrial, even the social, paradigm—things like mass produced automobiles, the jet airplane, and electronic file transfer. Others focus on the little innovations of, for example, the continuous improvement programs adopted by many companies. Others, as we have noted, focus on innovation as a process rather than a result. Again, some focus on innovation as the restless search for the next paradigm, others on the continual refinement of today's paradigm.

Systemic Innovation

> Innovation is a process, not a product. For example, the innovation of xerography was more than Chester Carlson tinkering for a decade in his basement. Success took design refinement, capital, distribution, service, and charging by the copy rather than selling machines. . . . A monumental innovation such as the automobile is a social movement as much as a machine.[5]

This is an example of a *systemic innovation*—one that required many inventions woven into a production, marketing, educational, and business system before it became viable.

Incremental Innovations

Some systemic innovations give your company a giant leap ahead of the competitors in your value network or let you establish an entirely new value network. But many innovations are incremental—they move a little bit at a time. Over time, these *incremental innovations* add up.

Sustaining Innovations

Christensen has clarified the distinctions among innovations.[6] A *sustaining innovation* is one that gives greater value to an existing value network of customers and applications, suppliers, and partners. The innovations often are incremental advances, like the ever-smaller linewidths of conductors in integrated circuits, which are predictable from trend curves.

The innovations of continuous improvement programs are sustaining, incremental innovations, each intended to make a small contribution toward bettering the competitive position of the extended enterprises within the established value network.

Christensen reports that the market leaders within established value networks are the companies with the strongest record of sustaining innovation. If you started in the business by piloting the plane, you are likely to be the company that makes the midcourse corrections. And if you were a laggard who barely caught the train as you left the station, it is unlikely you will ever get to the front of the pack.

Disruptive Innovations

Christensen also describes the *disruptive innovations* that are big enough to move markets and ruin what would otherwise be judged as good business plans. Often these innovations come from unexpected sources and nontraditional competitors.

Examples of innovations that changed the world by stimulating entirely new value networks fill the history of innovation. The value network for minicomputers was different from that for mainframes—different customers, different applications, different technologies, different price points, and margins. Similarly, the value network for PCs was different from that for minicomputers. So these disruptive innovations were established and proven as economically viable—and then they underwent "mission creep." Sustaining innovations refined the disruptive one—to the point where it made sense for medium-sized businesses to replace mainframes with minicomputers, and now with networks of PCs—even to the point where supercomputers are built with PC technologies.

Christensen describes the effects of disruptive technology innovations on the leading companies in established value networks. Few survived unscathed. IBM, for example, had to reinvent itself—with much pain—when the cheaper CMOS technology, which had been refined with sustaining innovation overtook the exquisitely refined, but much more expensive, bipolar technology of mainframe processors and knocked the established value network on its ear. Companies without the mass and will of an IBM would not have survived.

The Xerox machine is another example of a disruptive innovation that, although initially more expensive, replaced many alternative copying technologies: carbon paper, mimeographs, even small printing shops. It led to a value network centered on copier technology, including maintenance technicians, suppliers of print cartridges and paper, even facilities for storage of copies files. Part of the disruption came from the relative ease of making copies and distributing information, often involving many people in the information distribution process who really did not have the need to know!

➤ Technology

Technology is a specialized body of knowledge that can be applied to achieve a mission or purpose. The knowledge can be in the form of methods, processes, techniques, tools, machines, materials, or procedures. Technology can therefore be defined as the means by which knowledge is applied to produce goods and services.[7]

> *The technology of a society represents the composite usable knowledge that the society applies and directs toward the attainment of cultural and economic objectives. In essence, technology is how things are accomplished. Different societies will use different methods, varying in degree of methodological sophistication to reach goals . . . Technology is a product of invention and innovation.*[8]

By this definition, technology is not just a means for transforming tangible materials, through some production processes, into products. Instead, technology includes learning, knowledge application, management systems, and the increasing role of services in the process. Technology exists in the mind as well as the physical world because of its ability to build on itself and perpetually produce new things.

➤ Types of Innovation

Dell chose an innovative way to sell computers—no patentable invention there. Johnson Controls chose to organize its workforce into teams—challenging and new to the company but, again, not patentable. There is a lot of new that enters into a company. The principles and processes of innovation are generic, equally applicable to transforming all types of invention into competitive results.

Innovation is a factor for the company's vision and strategic goals. It is essential for all four of the NGM operational strategies. There are many types of innovation, including:

1. *Strategic and management innovation*—to improve or create a better organizational environment for achieving strategic goals. This may include introducing new concepts into the corporate strategies as well as into corporate policies, practices, organization, and resource allocations.

2. *Product innovation*—to improve or create an actual item and its components or a supporting service provided to the customer.

3. *Human resource innovation*—to better leverage the capabilities of the workforce. This may include teaming structures, human resources practices and policies, even what we term new social contracts in Chapter 16.

4. *Knowledge process innovation*—to better acquire, distribute, manage, and use knowledge.

5. *Manufacturing process and equipment innovation*—to improve or create specific manufacturing processes within an

organization. This includes the creation of new and improved equipment, material, and processes to deliver specific products and services.

6. *Business process innovation*—to improve or create specific business processes within an organization. This may include radical business process re-engineering efforts that lead to re-invention of the processes required to meet corporate goals. An important subset of this is *marketing innovation* intended to improve or create the means by which the organization and customer communicate and exchange goods. The wants and needs of its customers will shape the NGM company and marketing innovation is likely to play an increasing role as the company responds.

Systemic innovations may span several of the types of innovation, but it is convenient to use the types to drive home two key points:

1. Much of the stuff of innovation has nothing to do with new hardware or software.

2. Everyone, in every function, in a company can contribute to innovation. In fact, in the NGM company, everyone will be expected to contribute.

■ MANAGING FOR INNOVATION

Companies can manage for innovation. They can't guarantee success for every attempt. They still may have to make difficult choices, choosing to cut off funding for a promising innovation when other corporate needs loom more significant. But they can build cultures and systems designed to capitalize on the insight and imagination of every employee in the company—indeed, of every member of the extended enterprise.

To be successful, your company will depend on the motivation of the workforce and the synergy of their interactions. Given the natural tendency of people to take comfort in the status quo, you must keep the need for innovation in front of the employees—to make it the new status quo. Companies may need to "shake things up" strategically and constructively to stimulate the innovation they need to achieve their goals. Seemingly radical changes can be controlled through good management of the workforce, the technology, and the extended enterprise.

DELL—A MASTER OF INNOVATION

Dell Computer has gained competitive success through innovation. Dell has pioneered disruptive innovation while maintaining a flow of sustaining innovation.

Dell's direct-to-the-customer business model, facilitated by the Internet, is a disruptive innovation that has established a new way to do business. The model has cut Dell's costs and those of its customers (Ford is said to have saved $2 million by moving its Dell business on-line) in its order-entry process. The business model left Dell's competitors struggling.

But Dell's innovation culture didn't stop with the new business model. In the factory, Dell has used incremental, sustaining, innovations to reduce cost and complexity and to speed up production. As a result, the number of times a worker has to touch a computer as it is being assembled has been cut in half, assembly processes have been redesigned to reduce the number of operations (one screw to attach the motherboard to the chassis instead of six), and automated transport has replaced manual efforts.

Innovations, particularly those in business practices, have many different applications. They come from many places and many people. What works for Amazon.com may also work for Caterpillar. Practices relating to integrating avionics into aircraft that work for Boeing may also work for Ford as integrating "auto-onics" into cars becomes more important. Innovation, whether sustaining or disruptive, increasingly means companies must look "outside the box," paying attention to other industries and cultural developments.

➤ Leadership for Innovation

Successful innovation demands management leadership and support. It starts at the top. The board of directors must not accept business as usual, but should expect the company's leadership team to be innovative themselves and to encourage innovation throughout the company. In turn, the leadership team should understand how to leverage the creative juices of all employees at all levels of the company.

You can find innovation leaders in all the company's functions, from finance through services. Each profession is wrestling with the same challenge—how best to integrate the economic, behavioral, and technological factors of the company so that it can compete and succeed. Innovation will be the result of a network of activity. One person's or function's solutions will both draw from and influence the solutions from other functions. The function that implements a new collaborative design process requiring the features of Version 3.0 of a groupware program may impact the other functions who are happily using Version 2.0. So, the leadership should be collaborative and involve the diverse competencies of functions throughout the company.

Management's view of risk-taking is crucial to the innovation process. Management needs to take the fear out of presenting unconventional ideas. Innovation depends on the nature of creativity, experimentation, and discovery—it is the exploration of the unknown. And if you explore the unknown, you take a risk, a risk of wasting your time, a risk of wasting company resources, a risk of failure. Your company shouldn't inhibit innovation with policies and procedures that punish out-of-the-box thinking. Unsuccessful risk-taking should be treated as an investment, a learning of what doesn't work. Responsible risk-taking should be encouraged and continually reaffirmed.

■ ENABLING INNOVATION

Creativity and innovation rely on people who have the freedom to think of and express new ideas. They rely on people who have enough of a grasp of the entire system, from creation through commercialization, to articulate the value of the innovation to the enterprise. Companies can improve the chances of those people making successful contributions by adopting an innovation process that provides the mental "space" for new ideas and which openly shares the knowledge resources of the whole enterprise. This comes when the innovation process is an explicit part of the corporate culture and is defined as a corporate value.

A few companies have broken the structural barriers to communication and knowledge in an attempt to build an innovation culture. Most find structure is required, certainly as they grow beyond the size of an "everybody knows everybody else" team. In any event, the corporate structure should facilitate, not inhibit, communication, knowledge sharing, and formal and informal cross-functional problem solving. The company should be flexible enough that it does not hold onto existing structures when innovations dictate a need for change.

The willingness to restructure in response to better ways to achieve corporate goals is a symbol of an innovation-friendly company.

Internal and external teaming can facilitate innovation. The corporate culture should encourage bringing together individuals and resources into teams that include all the disciplines, all the competencies, required to exploit the innovation.

➤ Organizational Culture and Structure

The old-style hierarchical company often discouraged innovation. Or if it did encourage it, innovation was management's prerogative— managers or their designated experts did the new stuff. Or, in R&D-oriented companies, hardware and software technology innovation was done in a separate, designated, organization. In these organizations, the coupling between technology innovation and business process innovation was often overlooked.

Innovation depends critically on people. People are creative and innovative when they are expected to be innovative, when they are given the resources to be innovative, and when they are rewarded for their innovations. Many company cultures have a negative impact on innovation. A rigid organization that puts too much emphasis on "the way things are done here" inhibits employees' attempts to try new ways.

A more insidious inhibition on innovation is the company's view of its human resources. Does your company view its employees as physical components in a production system—cogs in the machine, automatons on the assembly line, liabilities on the corporate balance sheet? These employees may meet your company's expectations: They do their jobs as they are told to do them, they fit into the system, quietly—maybe even comfortably—accepting the wisdom of the hierarchy without question, and they certainly don't rock the boat by offering ideas that might have risks or costs.

Although command-and-control systems of hierarchically organized companies foster a sense of accountability and logic to the decision-making process, they will be too rigid for NGM the company. In today's work environment, they encourage employees to "do things the right way" rather than "do the right things."

The emphasis on re-engineering and restructuring on the model of lean manufacturing has had mixed results for innovation. The emphasis on total quality management (TQM) and continuous improvement has often stimulated a stream of incremental sustaining innovation. But it has also led to less time and resources being devoted to discretionary innovation efforts. In some cases, re-engineering has led to a loss of knowledge that is discovered only after the fact to be part of the company's core competency. The results may be a "corporate anorexia" leaving companies too lean to innovate.

Re-engineering efforts that focus on rigid implementation of today's best practices can impose new structural barriers to innovation. Here the innovation of re-engineering, often imposed on people rather than sourced from the people themselves, seems to preclude further innovation. Even if organized well, innovation requires a sense of freedom from rigid self- or management-imposed structures. As re-engineering is done, it should take into account and attempt to quantify soft-side innovation enablers such as behavior, workplace environment, and creative idea generation.

The old attitudes live on even as more companies attempt to flatten the hierarchy. Many employees continue to live by the old paradigm. Empowerment for innovation can create a sense of confusion or loss in some employees. This problem is magnified in larger companies where even improved structures do not keep employees from feeling lost in the system. Ultimately this can result in fragmentation and competition for internal resources rather than strategies for a collective vision and common goals.

➤ Overcoming Resistance to Change

Innovation is *proactive change*. How do you react to change? Almost all humans, be they executives, middle managers, or line employees, react negatively to changes for which they are unprepared. The activities in most companies mature to the point where employees think they are working in a stable environment. The more comfortable they become with their work, the more unwilling they are to accept change. Choosing to innovate means "rocking the boat."

Resistance to change is natural for most people. Your company must have sustained management reinforcement of the need for continuous innovation to overcome this natural *status quo* mentality. Most often, this resistance is pervasive at the operational and process levels and therefore is a companywide cultural issue.

There may be a direct correlation between the lack of access to new resources and the inability to be open to new ideas. Those who are not able to follow through with ideas—or who have lost faith that their ideas will be implemented—are unlikely to generate or share new ideas.

A company with an innovation culture is one whose workforce is comfortable with change—hopefully comfortable enough to welcome it. Overcoming the resistance to change will be so important in NGM companies that we devote an entire chapter, Chapter 14, *Managing and Measuring Change*, to it.

NIH—Not Invented Here

People struggling to do a job well learn what works for them. They adopt practices, refine them, gain confidence in them, and make them their own. Then somebody comes along with an innovation, a suggestion for change. The NIH—*not invented here*—barrier goes up, almost instinctively. "I know this process better than anyone. Stay away! Don't interfere with me as I apply my knowledge to making it better." The NIH problem is tough enough that unless they are trained to look for solutions outside themselves, people use all their capacities on building their own solutions.

Overcoming NIH is a challenge not to be taken lightly. The solution is to promote a culture in which taking innovations from any source is made part of the company's problem-solving discipline. The aim should be for people to "own" the ideas even if they were first generated by outside sources.

➤ Skunk Works—Protecting Innovation

Companies traditionally set up special teams for very important projects that require significant new ideas, new technologies, and new processes. These teams are often successful because common corporate barriers have been specifically lifted to facilitate a quick and effective result. The prototypical example is the Lockheed Martin Corporation's Skunk Works facility which produced classified military systems such as the P-80, Air Force's first production jet fighter, the U-2 and SR-71 reconnaissance aircraft, and more recently the F-117 Stealth fighter—all outside the visible Lockheed bureaucracy.

Historically, the Skunk Works concept was applied to the underground activities of those projects not yet legitimized in the corporate business plan. The idea crept into more general practice, leading to various forms of independent business units not subjected to all the bureaucratic oversight of core operations. Examples include IBM's personal computer organization of the early 1980s and Chrysler's platform teams of the early 1990s—both located away from the corporate development site.

Skunk Works have many characteristics that are *must haves* of NGM companies—they are lean, agile, and filled with cross-functional knowledge. The implementation of Skunk Works can provide models for entire companies. In the early-1990s, Ford designed a Skunk Works with the following characteristics:[9]

> ➤ The cross-functional team was comprised of seven engineers of proven competence, with management experience, selected from the operating divisions and on extended loan from them.

➤ The Skunk Works was located in rented quarters, physically separate from other parts of the company, but within easy driving distance from company resources.

➤ The facilities were designed and laid out to promote creativity and facilitate product exhibition.

➤ There was absolutely *no* bureaucratic red tape! Paperwork was minimal; time use was therefore very efficient.

➤ "Reverse-engineered" hardware was the primary deliverable.

➤ Sufficient funding was provided from the start. It was not necessary to spend time hunting for money.

➤ There was strong support from the group executive and the general managers of the operating divisions.

➤ Management chains were very short.

➤ Performance Metrics

People respond to the metrics by which they are measured. For metrics to serve the intended purpose, they must be easily understandable, clearly defined to the people to whom they apply, understood by them and accepted as appropriate means to measure a given function. If a marketing rep has a quota of 500 PCs/month, the rep will find a way to sell them. If a production manager has a target of 27 hydraulic pumps a day, that's where his or her energies are focused. If the board has told the CEO to cut headcount by 25 percent, that's what will happen, even if some core competency has to go. If a company has an implicit "no failures" policy, people won't fail, but they won't take risks either.

Start-up companies typically reward innovation—by giving their employees a share of the rewards of their creative work—through mechanisms like stock options based on the employees' and the company's performance. Start-ups are small enough that management has first-hand knowledge of employee contributions. Larger companies give bonuses, awards, or, having seen the successes of the start-ups, stock options for successful innovations—especially patents or specific product developments—that are traceable to specific people. Only a few large companies, like Microsoft, have built cultures that not only encourage but demand innovative contributions from all their employees, and find ways to reward them.

There are fewer metrics that can catch the incremental innovations. The problem is that few companies have formalized the audit trails linking new ideas with profits. At the heart of the issue is how the company accounts for its knowledge assets. Companies tend to use traditional accounting metrics, but they may be the wrong indicators of success. In many companies, especially high-tech manufacturing companies, there is a significant difference between book value and market value. Leading economists think that the difference is mostly due to the company's intangible assets, what we call knowledge assets. These assets are not easily quantifiable in financial terms and not reported on the balance sheet. The practice of accounting for knowledge assets is in its infancy and will take years to mature.

We will discuss metrics for innovation again in Chapter 18.

➤ Knowledge, Knowledge-Sharing, and Information Technology

The raw material of innovation is knowledge. Innovation comes when the mind makes connections among the pieces of knowledge it needs to have the "ah ha!" of a new idea. The more complete the assembly of knowledge, the more likely the "ah ha!" will lead to a successful implementation.

Your company needs a knowledge infrastructure to support innovation. Some of the factors in creating a knowledge infrastructure are knowledge leadership, defined roles, and a culture of creativity, learning, and dialogue. Some companies have formalized the central role of knowledge by naming a "Chief Knowledge Officer" to shepherd knowledge as a precious corporate asset. Successful knowledge and innovation leaders need good conceptual capabilities, an ability to see connections among a myriad of factors, and skills in communication with an extensive network.

The world is so complex that although all employees should have a general idea of how their company functions—and thus how a new idea might fit—the devil is in more details than a single mind can comprehend. And the knowledge we need for today's "ah ha!" is not likely to be all the knowledge we need for tomorrow's. We need help to make our idea work. We need knowledge that others have, and they need our knowledge as they solve their problems. We all need an easy way to share knowledge.

An essential tenet for innovation will be "the right knowledge, at the right place, at the right time, and in a useful format." Information technology (IT) is an important enabler of the innovation process. It is the fast way to share knowledge over distance. In this view, IT is an essential part of the supporting infrastructure, a knowledge superhighway for the flow of ideas and rapid learning, not just an information superhighway. The role of the innovation enabler places requirements for flexibility, transparency, reconfigurability, and reusability on your company's information systems.

In 1991, Gillette's now retired CEO, Alfred Zeien committed Gillette to be a world leader, or have a committed plan to become one, in all of its core businesses.* The commitment is symbolized by Gillette's investment of 2.2 percent of its sales revenues in research and development. By 1998, Gillette had had consistent revenue growth and had become a world leader in 13 product categories that account for 80 percent of its revenue. One technique used by Gillette has been to set up competing development teams, choosing to use the best results from all the teams in the final product design. Complementing the focus on technological innovation in product design, Gillette has focused on meeting annual cost reduction targets using innovative process design. One result is that, through incremental improvements, Gillette cut the manufacturing cost of its flagship Sensor™ razor blades by 30 percent between 1993 and 1997. More recently, Gillette has developed a manufacturing system for cartridges for its new Mach3™ razor product. The system will produce cartridges at twice the rate as the one for Sensor cartridges, but at lower costs.

3M is a well-established company that has long been respected for its continuous stream of innovative products. It is one of only a few companies that have had a stated and working procedure for innovation. This critical difference has a strong impact on the culture and resulting effectiveness of employees.

At Electronic Data Systems (EDS), customer relationships are defined to fit into one of five levels. At the first level, interaction between the two companies is minimal and based on an agreed service and fee. The levels progress with increasing amounts of interaction. Ideally, the relationship will progress to level 5, where there are specific near term goals but in which the companies work together in a partnership of innovation for the longer term. The companies invest today in a relationship that will reap unspecified gains in the future.

---

*"Gillette's Edge," *Business Week,* (January 19, 1998) pp. 70–77. Also, see Gillette's web site.

■ INNOVATION INVESTMENT STRATEGIES

The funds allocated to research and development (R&D) are a good indicator of a company's commitment to innovation. Companies that cut their R&D budgets are often perceived as being unsupportive of innovation. R&D funding in the United States since the 1960s has exhibited an S-shaped curve, with rapid increases in the 1970s and 1980s followed by a leveling off of funding in the 1990s. There is an indication that at the turn of the century, R&D investment is rising again.

In the past decade, many companies have reduced, even eliminated, the formal research functions. The basic research activities of AT&T's Bell Laboratories, before the spin-off of Lucent Technologies, and of IBM's Research Division have been cut back. Lester Thurow, the MIT economist, has flatly stated that there will be no more Nobel prizes won for work done in industrial labs.[10] This is a daunting statement in light of the Nobel Prizes won for the transistor that created the microelectronics industry and, more recently, for the tunneling electron microscopy that is pointing the way to nanofabrication (see Chapter 20). In the industrial labs, applied research also has been targeted to nearer-to-market product development from high-risk, medium-term applications. Exploratory product or process development activities were focused on core competencies.

It is easy to bemoan the loss of R&D investment as a symbol of shortsighted rejection of innovation. The question remains, however, whether the traditional R&D investments were managed well. At their peak, the research output from Bell Labs and IBM's T.J. Watson Research Center was among the very best in the world—witness the Nobel Prizes. Much of that research did find its way into the parent companies' product lines. But much of it was irrelevant to AT&T's and IBM's businesses, a sunk cost that was more appropriate to commercially neutral research facilities in universities or publicly funded laboratories.

The funding tied up in irrelevant R&D can have a greater impact on the company's vitality if it is used to support less formalized innovation conducted throughout the company. But cutting the investment in formal R&D should be done judiciously. Questions should be asked: Is what the R&D functions are doing truly irrelevant to tomorrow's core competencies? Will the investment in innovation be diverted to better achieve corporate goals or will it simply be cut as "fat" in a rush to corporate leanness? What is the message the stakeholders will perceive about the company's commitment to innovation if there are dramatic cuts in formal R&D budgets?

IBM has struggled through this process, toying at one time with distributing all of the resources devoted to its Research Division to the line organizations.[11] Instead, IBM radically refocused the Division on customer needs and on what IBM required for its future success. The result is a more vital R&D operation that is making leadership contributions to IBM's bottom line—but which is making fewer contributions to the public store of scientific discovery.

For U.S. industry, there is a shadow player in innovation investment: the federal government. Although there are protests that the federal government should not have a technology policy, in fact it does have an implicit policy. The policy is manifested through the choices made by the Congress in the budgets for the Departments of Defense, Energy, and Commerce and for independent agencies like the National Science Foundation, the National Institute of Health, and the Environmental Protection Agency. In the mid-1990s, arguments about the government's role in technology development were perceived to have dampened the national interest in innovation.

> ➤ **Choosing Targets for Investment**

As early as 1969, IBM had a choice—to invest in improvements in the mainframe product line or to invest in an innovative personal computer. Christensen calls this the choice between investing in sustaining innovation and investing in disruptive innovation. IBM made the formal investment in the stream of sustaining innovation, while killing the nascent PC with the kindness of "well, that's interesting, okay if your manager wants to divert his discretionary funds (there were discretionary funds in those days), but that's not where we're competing hard and making our bucks." Lucky for IBM, the PC ideas kept floating around and allowed IBM's PC independent business unit to be an aggressive imitator in the early 1980s.

Investments in sustaining innovation are clearly important when a company is competing head-to-head for a lucrative market that is the centerpiece of a value network. Yet once a disruptive innovation, with its value network, has begun to intrude on the established market, companies need to carefully assess whether continuing investment in sustaining innovation will indeed extend the life of a cash cow or whether the investment will be lost in the rush to the disruptive technology.

The decisions aren't easy. At the end of 1999, Compaq had not yet been able to find the right investment strategy in the face of Dell's innovative PC marketing and distribution system. The stream of innovations in silicon-based semiconductors and in magnetic data storage media have sustained the viability of those technologies in the face of potentially disruptive gallium arsenate and solid state memories.

■ INNOVATION IN AN EXTENDED ENTERPRISE

Whether the extended enterprise is operating in joint venture, partnership, or ordinary customer-supplier relationships, its companies should encourage cross-enterprise innovation. Each partner offers a set of competencies for which it is the enterprise's expert. Each partner is valued for its knowledge base and its ability to use it. Innovation will be stimulated when all these competencies are brought together in new or unusual combinations. The flow of ideas and knowledge can be as important—or more important—than the flow of finances or materials. The recognition of the creative value in extended enterprises has led to the view of the enterprise as a value network or "system" rather than a value chain.

The extended enterprise includes customers as sources of knowledge—not just as purchasers of products and services whose only contribution to the enterprise is payment. The resulting balance of technology-push and market-pull means the enterprise focuses on doing the things that enable the customer's success, for example, in serving their customers, and their well-being within the enterprise. This refocus on the customer has been particularly important for companies in the business of providing technology solutions.

The challenge for the extended enterprises is to recognize that different company practices, and thus organizational cultures, have to be integrated in ways that protect proprietary rights while optimizing the performance of the enterprise. Cross-boundary thinking has promoted many process innovations, some because of quality and re-engineering priorities. It has been driven or influenced by simultaneous supply-chain processes, collaborative marketing agreements with distributors, new forms of alliances and joint ventures with partners, and innovative approaches to customer interaction. There are numerous examples of companies expanding their perspective on what constitutes the enterprise that foster new forms of stakeholder innovation.

■ TOOLS FOR INNOVATION

Two important classes of tools can help channel innovation and creativity toward the enterprise's needs and instill an innovation culture: disciplines for group innovation and information technology (IT).

➤ Disciplines for Group Innovation

We can let innovation happen spontaneously. After all, there are people who always seem to have new ideas. They walk through a factory and suggestions drip from them. All we have to do is follow them around, select their best ideas, and then run with them. Well, maybe . . . Maybe the ideas are okay as far as they go, but they don't provide a complete solution. Or maybe they lose something in translation from the casual idea-generator's sketch to the serious problem-solver's specification. Or maybe they could create other, worse, problems. Or maybe they are ideal technical solutions, except they would cost too much. Or maybe they just are not relevant.

Better to use a disciplined technique, a technique that brings all the important skills to bear on the innovation process. There are several processes described in the literature. Some, like "Breakthrough Thinking,"[12] provide a design for innovation. Breakthrough Thinking describes seven principles for innovative problem solving:

1. Treat each problem as if it is unique. What worked on the last problem you solved may not work on this one, even if the problems seem similar. Start with a clean sheet and work the problem-solving process.

2. Grasp the big picture. Understand the purpose of the function that is presenting the problem before trying to solve the specific problem. Understand what you are trying to achieve from the customers' point of view and then work on the processes to meet the customers' needs. It may be that you shouldn't solve the problem, that there is a better way to meet the function's purpose.

3. Build a vision of the ideal way to meet the purpose. Use that as a guidepost for problem solving. Each incremental innovation should take you toward the ideal.

4. Think about the problem as part of a system, and think of the effects of your solution on the rest of the system. Any sustaining innovation that works is one that fits with the rest of the value network.

5. Use the knowledge that is readily available—what you know and what can be delivered to you in a usable form. Don't waste time in overanalysis or waiting for the "perfect" answer. Do the "nickel experiment" to try out a solution, a rapid prototype, and refine it if it proves successful.

6. Look at the problem from many points of view—that's a value of teams. The knowledge base for problem solving is broader if there are more inputs for innovation.

7. Even if you implement intermediate solutions, don't stop upgrading the solution until you achieve the ideal—and then ask whether the ideal needs to be revised.

➤ Software

We have already talked about IT as making knowledge available, ideally whenever and wherever it is needed, more ideally making it available in a form that the user can use naturally. There is a spectrum of tools available, starting with simple database query languages that allow users to formulate structured queries. Repositories of best practices provide resources: "Hmmm, they solved their problem that way . . . not the same problem I have, but close enough . . . bet that if I tweaked their solution, I could solve my problem."

Data mining techniques expand the kinds of queries and analyses available to an end-user, often ferreting out unexpected correlations and insights. Data mining software can sometimes identify important patterns in acquired data, patterns that can lead to insights on product utilization and wear, process effectiveness, and areas for improvement.

Innovative ways to display multidimensional data patterns, such as those based on parallel coordinates, can augment the insights gained by these techniques.[13] They do so by presenting the patterns in the data visually. The power of parallel coordinates is that patterns of data with many dimensions can be represented in two, so that needles can be found in multidimensional haystacks. These techniques have been used to guide analyses of statistical process control (SPC) data[14] to find sources of error in manufacturing processes. Combined with rule finding algorithms, the parallel coordinate methodology can be used for computationally efficient pattern classifiers.[15] These classifiers can pick the characteristics of processes out of masses of data.

Corporate "portals," analogous to the portals—like AOL, Yahoo!, or Excite—in which casual World Wide Web users find all manner of useful knowledge, are becoming the entry points to the rich sources of corporate knowledge that are being made accessible via intranets. Consulting companies use portals, knowledge repositories, centers of expertise, and groupware to enable a consultant anywhere in the world to access all the expertise in his company.

Expert systems can provide expert knowledge in response to general queries, although usually in narrow domains. Case base systems can provide expert knowledge reasoning from a repository of similar cases and best practices. In each case, the hope is to use the IT tools to broaden and deepen the knowledge base an innovator has available.

Some software is designed specifically to support a discipline for innovation. For example, one tool is based on the Theory of Inventive Problem Solving, or TRIZ (its Russian acronym), created by G.S. Altshuller. Altshuller believed that in most cases problem-solving engineers looked for answers in only their narrow domains of specialty when better solutions often could be answered by casting a wider net over the knowledge base.

> [M]ore than 90 percent of the problems faced by engineers have, in some analogous form, been previously solved at sometime, somewhere. Sometimes the solution has been developed in a different department of the same company; sometimes in an entirely different and unrelated industry.[16]

Altshuller studied thousands of patents and found patterns in the problems the patents were intended to solve. By having engineers recast their problem in one of the generic patterns, the TRIZ method guides them to a wider "space" of solutions, making it easier to recognize that, for example, a problem in a flow manufacturing process in an aerospace factory might have a solution sourced from the petrochemical industry. Modern computer technology has been used to automate the TRIZ methodology, helping companies to stimulate higher quality innovation.

■ SUMMARY

Innovation doesn't happen by accident. It may be the result of a serendipitous "ah ha!" a creative thought of a single individual. But it takes a nurturing environment to transform that creative thought into a bottom-line contribution. Your company must have a combination of leadership, discipline, resource commitment, and freedom to nurture and shape productive innovation.

■ EXERCISE

Suppose your company announces that it wants to ready itself for a substantial expansion that will include competing globally. Your

Steelcase used a cross-functional design research team—working in close collaboration with customers to apply progressive notions of real-time learning to the work environment. This resulted in the implementation of the knowledge channel, an entire new line of products and services, and a new marketing campaign positioning the company as facilitating smarter places to work. In the process, Steelcase transformed itself and created a stronger image for the value added by properly designed workspaces.

If there is no explicit innovation function, it is up to the CEO to manage the process. Buckman Laboratories, a provider of extensive technical service and advanced chemical treatment technologies, helps solve complex industrial problems. The CEO sets the direction, communicates the benefits, and leads by example. The company's advanced communications enhance the innovation process by delivering the company's global expertise to the customer interface. Buckman's intranet contains knowledge bases in the form of information libraries, bulletin boards, discussion forums, and virtual conference rooms. A Buckman associate working with a customer can tap the reservoir of knowledge and access colleagues wherever they might be.

In the early 1990s, Dow was awarded over 1,200 patents a year at an annual cost of $30 million. After systematically reviewing its portfolio, Dow saved over $1 million in 18 months by licensing patents that it holds but does not use. It has developed a six-phase intellectual asset model that links intellectual assets to the business needs: (1) contribution to business strategy, (2) competitor assessment, (3) asset clarification, (4) valuation of intellectual assets, (5) investment strategies to enhance value, and (6) intellectual portfolio management. Using this framework, Dow's target is to have innovation show a profit, with annual licensing revenue targeted at more than $100 million by the year 2000.

Analog Devices has taken the position that the rate of learning is the only sustainable competitive advantage. It has grown from a focus on quality to a process for innovation using orga-

(continued)

PRACTICAL INNOVATION STRATEGIES (CONTINUED)

nizational learning theory. As Analog Devices pursued its quality objectives, it developed a common language for strategy formulation. All Analog's chief executives participated in week-long training during which they explored strategies for incremental and breakthrough improvements. They benchmarked and developed predictive metrics to improve the performance of the financial and accounting services. Management cut time-to-market by promoting a collaborative community of inquirers—learning from one another—supported by groupware tools worldwide. After implementing these strategies, Analog's net income and profits increased by 60 percent and 53 percent, respectively.

management says innovation will play an essential role. Now suppose you've been named to a task force to recommend initiatives the company should undertake to make itself more competitive. In preparation for your assignment, answer the following:

1. What have the explicit and implicit company policies been regarding doing innovative things?

2. What changes would you recommend to the existing policies?

3. In what three areas in your company is the introduction of innovation needed the most?

4. What are the key bullets you would propose for a plan for the introduction of innovative ideas and concepts?

5. What would you do to maximize acceptance of the innovation process among the company employees?

6. How would you measure the effectiveness of the innovation process?

7. Where would you look for innovative ideas potentially suitable for use by your company?

8. Would you deem it necessary to involve your suppliers ? Why?

9. How would entering a global market influence your thinking in developing a plan for innovation?

■ NOTES

1. Peter F. Drucker, *Innovation and Entrepreneurship* (New York: Harper-Business, 1985).
2. Clayton M. Christensen, *The Innovator's Dilemma: When New Technologies Cause Great Firms to Fail* (Boston: Harvard Business School Press, 1997).
3. Peter F. Drucker, "The Information Executives Truly Need," *Harvard Business Review,* (January/February) 1995.
4. Michael J.C. Martin, *Managing Innovation and Entrepreneurship in Technology-Based Firms* (New York: John Wiley, 1994) p. 4.
5. Robert Hall, *The Soul of the Enterprise: Creating a Dynamic Vision for American Manufacturing* (New York: HarperCollins, 1993) p. 172.
6. See Note 2.
7. Johnson A. Edosomwan, *Integrating Innovation and Technology Management* (New York: John Wiley, 1989) p. 10.
8. Daniel D. Roman and Joseph F. Puett, Jr., *International Business and Technological Innovation* (New York: Elsevier Science Publishing, 1983) pp. 3–4.
9. Arthur W. Single and William M. Spurgeon, "Creating and Commercializing Innovation Inside a Skunk Works," *Research-Technology Management,* (January/February 1996) pp. 38–39.
10. Lester C. Thurow, *Building Wealth: The New Rules for Individuals, Companies, and Nations in a Knowledge-Based Economy* (New York: HarperCollins, 1999).
11. Robert Buderi, "Into the Big Blue Yonder," *Technology Review,* (July/August 1999).
12. Gerald Nadler & Shozo Hibino, *Breakthrough Thinking, (2nd ed.)* (Rocklin, CA: Prima Publishing, 1994).
13. Alfred Inselberg, "Don't Panic . . . Do It in Parallel!" *Computational Statistics,* vol. 14, (1999) p. 53.
14. Tova Avidan and Shlomo Avidan, "ParallAX—A Data Mining Tool Based on Parallel Coordinates," *Computational Statistics,* vol. 14, (1999) p. 78.
15. E.W. Bassett, "IBM's IBM Fix," *Journal of Industrial Computing,* (1995).
16. G.S. Altshuller, *Creativity as an Exact Science: The Theory of the Solution of Inventive Problems* (translated by Anthony Williams) (New York: Gordon and Breach, 1984).

Chapter 14

Managing and Measuring Change

Chapter 13 was all about innovation. As Figure 14.1 shows, *change* is often the result of an innovation. When the innovation is an informed and knowledgeable response to changing market conditions, to the changing global environment, or to the introduction of new technology, we can structure change as an orderly process. The innovation culture is by its very nature going to generate the need for change. If your company successfully masters the process of innovation, it will also need to master the process of change.

But change often happens in another, less orderly, way. When things are going badly—say product designs do not meet functional

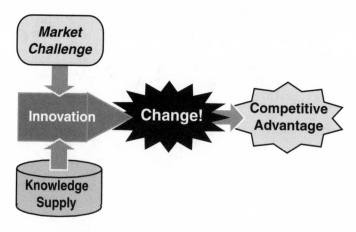

Figure 14.1   Innovation Leads to Change

254

requirements, or there are customers unhappy with product quality, or costs are unexpectedly high, we say, "Something's got to change!" Often we fix on something—the most obvious something—and change it. Maybe we fire our product designer and hire another. Maybe we institute a crash quality program. Maybe we order an across the board 10 percent reduction in expenditures. We act. We make a change.

However it happens, a barrage of changes is going to beat on your company. Change will happen to a company's strategic direction, to the processes by which work is done, to the content of the work, to the company's culture, and to the behaviors of the individuals in the company. Some changes will be big, systemic, changes—such as IBM ending its "full employment" policy. Other changes will be incremental—say a new way to order cable harnesses electronically.

The way companies cope with change, the way they manage the change process will be a defining discriminator for the company's sustained success. The ability to change effectively is going to be like quality—a *given* if you want to survive. Just as the company needs an "innovation culture," it needs a "change culture" into which is embedded a systematic methodology to accept change into the organization. The companies that can manage change and embrace innovation, proactively, while minimizing negative effects on existing operations, will gain competitive advantage.

Change will happen. Your managers can stand back and hope the process reaches a successful end—less and less likely in an age of growing complexity. Or your managers can accept change as something to understand, shape, and manage intentionally. Shaping change means prioritizing the changes the company will accept—with a focus on meeting the company's strategic vision and goals. It means coordinating the changes so that the interaction of one with another is constructive and does not lead to destructive side effects. Change will happen all the time and so will change management. One change will hardly be implemented when the next comes. The rate of change is accelerating. To respond effectively, the NGM company must have a robust change process that yields quick results. The mechanisms for change management are incorporated in emerging process models which:

➤ Recognize the need to change.

➤ Define and articulate a desired future state.

➤ Develop a clear and detailed assessment of the current state.

➤ Design an integrated plan for the transition period.

➤ Focus and sustain commitment of the organization to change in the direction of the vision.

➤ Continuously reassess the need for change, whether or not the vision is being achieved, and adjust the process accordingly.

Changes outside the company can have an enormous impact. The collapse of a market in Thailand may threaten the financial health of your supplier in Brazil, and you face difficult decisions: do you bail out your supplier or do you seek a replacement? If so, what will happen to your market in Brazil? The European Union told you to conform to ISO 9000—now they say you must conform to ISO 14000. You are going to be hit by changes at what will feel like an exponentially growing rate. The NGM Project has defined the "proficiency to capitalize on the inevitable continuous change" to be essential for the successful NGM enterprise.

We can't say for sure what changes will happen in the competitive environment in the next decade. They will come to us quickly—information technology will see to that. Since we can't predict what the world will look like in 10 years, the company must have a change process that can continuously re-tune business processes to support the corporate vision. The vision must be articulated by the corporate leadership team and communicated to all the stakeholders—employees, partners, customers, equity holders, and so on. They need to see the vision as a constant even though the company is in a continuous state of change.

■ CREATING THE ENVIRONMENT FOR CHANGE

Your company's management must lead the company's transformation. Change requires that many people, in many separate actions each day in their work, perform in a manner different from what they have come to believe is "normal." These actions are rarely defined in specific detail in procedures or manuals. The guiding force for these people is their understanding of the company's goals and objectives and the picture of the future that they carry in their mind. If they do not have a consistent, clear picture of the future state toward which the company is driving, their daily decisions will not help move toward the vision.

➤ Vision and Leadership

It's the executive leadership's job to project a clear vision if they expect the workforce to respond in the robust, continuous change processes required for transformation. John Kotter, in *Leading Change,* tells us that complacency, weak guidance, under-communicating the vision, allowing obstacles, and not anchoring the changes in company culture are the principal modes of failure to achieve and sustain change successfully.[1] The company's leaders must help the stakeholders in the extended enterprise understand that although the change process for a specific task will have a point of completion, with metrics defining success, there is no end to the total business change process.

➤ Recognition of the Need to Continuously Change

Your company needs to build mechanisms to anticipate, or at least detect quickly, the need to make changes in its business. You shouldn't ignore this, even if your company is enjoying success—Christiansen teaches us that these are the very times when you are the most vulnerable to disruptive innovation.[2] This is a good time to adopt the paranoid attitudes of Intel's now retired CEO, Andrew Grove.[3] You must understand that today's methods of success may be obsolete tonight—and certainly will be obsolete before you retire. Your company must identify the disruptive innovations coming from technology or new competitors from areas outside their immediate market segment. A company's way of viewing its world creates a framework for determining what types of information are considered important. Information outside this framework is generally considered of small importance or is ignored completely. The company needs a wide scope in its observational framework.

➤ Change Champions

The NGM company needs senior leaders who are champions of change. Few systemic changes happen unless they are championed by senior leaders who are willing to articulate the vision and take the risks needed to achieve it. The champion leads the change process and fights the battles encountered in implementing the desired action. In general, the higher the champion is in the organizational hierarchy, the greater the chances of success in fully deploying the change. One function of a company's board of directors is to encourage senior executives to lead change processes. The board can provide an environment for supporting change in addition to the new ideas for change they bring to the company. Change championship is a skill to be taken seriously. The role should not be given to a "wannabe" unless the change is discretionary and its failure would not affect the achievement of the corporate goals.

➤ Change-Comfortable Culture

The greatest hurdle to change is embedded in the corporate culture. It's not *change* that's so difficult and painful for us—it's *changing*. A change-comfortable culture is one that:

➤ *Minimizes inertia*. Particularly in older, established companies, inertia on the part of managers unaware of the need for change and on the part of employees resistant to change can strongly inhibit change processes. Your company's leaders must listen to customers, operations personnel, and first-line management to identify the most urgent changes that are needed—and then they need to act with confidence and alacrity. Employees need to know that their success flows not from the particular tasks they have been doing but to their contributions to the success of the company as their tasks change.

➤ *Has trust and is trusted,* so that each individual is able to enter into risk with a sense that all in the enterprise will work to transform that risk into a positive result.

➤ *Has change competencies*. A workforce that has no exposure to world-class business models and change methods can hardly be expected to break out of a "comfortable" structure. The entire workforce needs to understand the change model that the organization is going to use. Knowing the origin and the destination is not enough. Everyone needs to know the route, so they can all pull together in the right direction.

➤ *Builds decision-making skills,* placing decision making where it can be most effective. The decision support structure must permit long-term strategic decisions to be made at a corporate level, tactical decisions to be made at the point of engagement, and operational decisions to be made on the "factory floor."

➤ Resources Commitment

Change won't happen without a commitment of time and resources. Employees and leaders must have time to develop or learn the new methods, tools, and skills required. They need time to recognize the impacts of the change and to plan and develop mitigating efforts for the most disruptive impacts. This creates a time offset between the implementation of the changes and realization of the benefits. Companies need to be prepared for the time lag between costs and savings. Companies that do not address this issue effectively often do not provide sufficient commitment to the change efforts. This lack of commitment may show up as a shortage of funding, a shortage of time to plan and implement the change efforts, or as an unwillingness to invest sufficient resources (people, tools, equipment, systems, funding) to implement the change successfully.

■ THE UPS AND DOWNS OF A CHANGE

Most companies aren't so "on track" that they will meet their strategic goals just by doing what they have always done. Most need to make strategic changes. But strategic change doesn't come just with the wave of a hand or the pronouncement of a strategic vision—it is the cumulative result of many, many tactical changes. The tactical changes should be planned, step by step, to achieve the strategic change. Or the tactical changes may be made by people autonomously responding to the strategic vision.

Either way, the tactical changes should be undertaken deliberately, with an understanding of how the change will support strategic goals. Where possible, there should be an audit trail that leads from the benefits resulting from the tactical change to the company's strategic goals. This may be especially important for investments in corporate infrastructure.

Consider the lifecycle of a change (see Figure 14.2). The company perceives an opportunity, or a challenge, or a threat, or a problem.

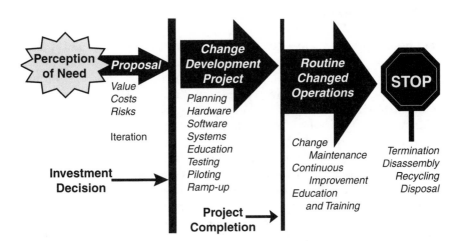

Figure 14.2 Lifecycle of a Change

Someone comes up with a good idea: "If we change such-and-such, we'll profit from the opportunity, or meet the challenge, or blunt the threat, or solve the problem. We'll win." People focus on the positives. There's a burst of enthusiasm as people begin to form expectations about the outcome of the change.

The creative burst of energy should lead to a proposal, one that presents the expected value of the change, but that also considers its costs and risks. The proposal should be thorough enough to evoke a commitment to invest in the change process.

Modern U.S. culture is prone to hype and fadism. Often what starts as a realistic set of expectations is blown way out of proportion. Sometimes the group with the idea claims more for it than is warranted. That's a natural response—you are so focused on the problem at hand that you don't realize it is just one of complexities that lie between a company and its goals. Sometimes uncritical adherents grab hold of the idea and trumpet it. The rush to hard automation in the 1970s, to artificial intelligence solutions for knowledge delivery in the 1980s, to robotics in the early 1990s, even today's rush to e-commerce set expectations very high. When the expectations aren't met, the crowd turns ugly.

Even when change leaders manage expectations realistically, as the change is developed and implemented, people will start pointing out the negatives, not only the flaws in the change vision itself, but also the possible negative side effects. Attitudes toward the change will become more pessimistic. A good change leader will listen and evaluate the validity of the negative concerns—but move ahead with courage.

The development and implementation of change is a human endeavor, so it will be flawed. Technologies won't work quite the way the book—or the salesman—says. The work will probably take longer than hoped for. Fine tuning will be necessary in the implementation. Just as we tend to be overly optimistic when we plunge into a change, we can be overly pessimistic when we run into problems. Strong and consistent leadership may be necessary to keep the change team focused—this is a time for the leadership team to be confidently visible.

Finally the change is implemented. You haven't fully implemented the change until your company has gone through the learning curve and the pain of doing things differently has faded into comfort with the now routine new mode of operations. It is well worth the effort then to look back and celebrate the achievement, the successful results. And it is worth reminding all in the enterprise that they will be called on repeatedly to accomplish change successfully.

There will come a time, inevitably, when the change becomes irrelevant to the newest realities of the business. That's the time to let go of that creative idea and move on to the next change.

■ THE CHARACTERISTICS OF CHANGE

➤ Many People Dislike Change

Change is a very common, very human phenomenon—and most humans don't like it. Children may approach change with a spirit of playful delight and a sense of adventure, but most adults have scar tissue from uninvited changes for which they were unprepared. There are some who embrace change because they choose it—they have a sense of ownership, even control. But most of us view change—especially if it is imposed on us—as something to be avoided. It is a disruption. It causes extra work. People usually see it as unsettling, risky, and unrewarding.

People need to get comfortable with change—both with the specifics of a particular change and with the notion that they live in a world that is constantly changing. That is a process of education. The more people know, the more comfortable they can become—unless they feel threatened by the change and are unable to find a way to cope with it. Continuous education is a powerful way to reinforce the understanding of change as continuous, inevitable, and perhaps even, as our children know, fun. There is a practical need for employees to expand their personal knowledge of new technology and business processes. The more employees know, the better able they will be to maintain and grow their long-term employability.

Your change management process should focus on the problem to be solved, on the need for creativity and collaboration to find the best solution, and on the personal rewards and opportunities that can come from the change. Most employees do want to contribute to their company's success and will participate pro-actively in the change process when they understand it to be in the company's, and their own, best interests.

➤ Change Is a Process, Not an Event or a Product

Change is a process that requires planning, preparation, development, training implementation, and evaluation. Since change is a process, each change should be accompanied by a process plan that is crafted to ensure that the change achieves its goal with minimum organizational disruption and costs, and maximum effectiveness.

➤ Change Takes Time

Change always takes time. In the NGM world, time is likely to be more valuable than money. One of the major risks in today's fast-moving, competitive environment is that a change will not be in place in time to be effective. A timely change may provide strong competitive advantage; a delayed change may result in a window of opportunity being lost forever.

Often change takes more time than first estimated. There are many reasons for this. Any change is a move into the unknown, maybe just a small step, but often a leap. Sometimes the development of the components of change and their integration into a system takes additional time. Often we underestimate the psychological impact and the time it takes the company's employees to internalize the change.

➤ Change Has Financial Costs

Any change, large or small, has costs. At the end of the day, the decision to make a change should be based on achieving reasonable and foreseeable benefits that exceed the costs. The costs may include:

➤ Scrapping work in progress.

➤ Write-off of undepreciated assets made obsolete by the change.

➤ Releasing employees made redundant by the change.

➤ New assets required by the change.

➤ Recruiting and orienting new employees required by the change.

➤ Education, training, and retraining of employees to accommodate the change.

➤ Education and training of suppliers and others in the extended enterprise.

➤ Education and training of customers.

➤ Psychological costs of change.

➤ Not All Change Is Good

Those people resisting change may be right! There is always some risk that the change will prove ineffective, or worse. It is important to identify failure as quickly as possible in the change process and adjust to it. It makes no sense to make further investments of time and resources in a change that cannot succeed. The implementation of an unproductive change may result in disastrous effects on the organization—no matter how much ego we have invested in the change.

A newsworthy example of this was a change in flight and crew scheduling that Federal Express tried to implement. Like all airlines, FedEx has a challenge in maximizing utilization of its aircraft. FedEx tried to use an optimization program that had been used successfully by other airlines, although those airlines used a different set of constraints in their input to the program. FedEx implemented the change without understanding the very significant impact it had on its flight crews. Rather than test the result in a controlled way, FedEx implemented the optimized scheduling across its whole system. While the program did an excellent job of scheduling aircraft, it resulted in very demanding crew schedules. The resultant effects on the crews are cited as one reason FedEx pilots voted to authorize a strike. FedEx abandoned use of the scheduling program until more reasonable—from the point of view of the crews—constraints were imposed.

➤ **Change Should Be Chunked**

Most changes that companies undertake are complicated enough that they involve many steps. The design of a change should be similar to a good product design, modular with well-specified interfaces between modules. The change project should be viewed as one more project to be managed, with timelines and milestones, resource allocation and tracking, and periodic reviews.

Where possible, the change project should be designed to generate early intermediate results. There are three reasons for this:

1. Early positive results will demonstrate that the project is on schedule and delivering results to the company as promised. This leads to confidence on the part of the change project team, the organization, and its executive leadership that the change is on track.

2. Early results can illuminate the need for additional refinement, either in the completed module or in the work yet to be completed.

3. In rare cases, the early results from a completed chunk may demonstrate that the change was a bad idea. The change that seemed so promising may prove to be the wrong solution. Killing the effort early on saves the company money and the people a demoralizing sense of failure.

➤ Chunks Should Be Measured

Each chunk should include measurements. Think of the analogy with unit testing for subsystems that will ultimately be integrated into a system. The project plan for the change should include checkpoints at significant points in the development or implementation of each chunk. When there should be intermediate results of a change—for example, when the implementation of a chunk leads to a different way employees work—the effects should be measured and evaluated. Even when intermediate results are not desired, there should be measurements to permit in-process verification against the change plan.

➤ Change Has Side Effects

Even when the change mimics the best practices of other companies, a change made in any given company is likely to have idiosyncratic results. Some unpredicted effects may prove beneficial; others less so.

For example, in the 1970s IBM developed VNET, its internal network analogous in many respects to the Internet, so that product developers could share design data. The capabilities of the network, however, led to profound changes in business processes and systems that have provided IBM with unpredicted competitive advantages. The FedEx ample cited earlier provides an example of negative side effects.

■ CHANGE CONSIDERATIONS

There are many kinds of change and many ways to make change happen. In their book, *Managing Organizational Change* Connor and Lake describe a framework—a way of thinking about change processes—by considering the three dimensions: the objects of change, the methods of change, and strategies for change[4] (see Figure 14.3).

➤ What Is Being Changed: The Objects of Change

In old-style manufacturing companies, changes in *individual task behavior* focused on simplifying jobs, reducing them to simple repetitive tasks. Now the emphasis has shifted to helping employees cope with processes that are inherently complicated, master multidimensional tasks, make knowledge-based decisions, and take knowledge-based actions. The characteristics of tasks that are of the greatest interest are skill variety, task identity, task significance, autonomy, feedback, and opportunities for interaction.

DaimlerChrysler faces the daunting task of integrating two large companies with proud histories of accomplishment, both in its own way extraordinarily successful. This is the ultimate change challenge—combining two large organizations, each with its own cultures, into a single $40 billion company. DaimlerChrysler has a set of principles to guide change that include:

1. *Maintain the base.* During the change process, make sure the customers are served.

2. *Focus on "value-drivers."* Prioritize activities so that the things that are done first are the ones that will create the greatest near-term customer value.

3. *Maintain and build on the strengths of both companies.* The integrated result will be greater than the sum of its parts if everyone draws on the entire enterprise's knowledge base.

4. *Decide and act fast.* Time really is money, and indecision has overhead costs to morale and productivity, so crisp decisions should be followed by equally crisp implementation.

5. *Affected parties are participating parties.* That is, if a group is going to be affected by a decision, it should participate in the planning process so that it "owns" the consequences.

6. *Pragmatism comes before perfectionism.* Perfection takes infinite effort so the goal is to maximize the results of finite effort.

7. *Post-merger integration is transient.* The effort and urgency of this change doesn't mean that as soon as it's finished there won't be another change challenge in front of DaimlerChrysler. There will be.

---

*"Automotive Megamergers Auger Changing Roles for Suppliers," *Manufacturing Engineering,* (March 1999).

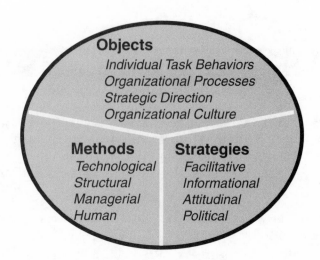

Figure 14.3 A Framework for Describing Change Processes

Frequently, basic *organizational processes*—such as control, reward, appraisal, and decision processes—*are* targets of change. Control processes can be preemptive, attempting to influence the company's environment and to shape its direction, or reactive, focusing on the company's operations performance and its deviation from standards. Reward processes—who is rewarded, for what behavior, and how—are crucial to all members of an extended enterprise. The models for decision making have changed greatly from the days of centralized hierarchies. Employees now are expected to participate as members of a network of decision makers. This leads to the question of responsibility and authority—to who contributes how much, and in what way, to what decisions.

A change in *strategic direction* entails a change in the corporate vision and goals. Your company expresses its vision and goals in the claims it makes for itself. These are made real through the company's offerings of products and services and through its positioning within the marketplace. A change in strategic direction often means changing the firm's structure, its management, or even its collective identity.

Culture is the pattern of beliefs and expectations that are shared across the enterprise and that shape the behavior of individuals and groups in the organization. Culture comprises the company's behavioral patterns, concepts, values, ceremonies, and rituals. Cultural values provide employees with a sense of what they ought to be doing and how they should behave—the emotional, intangible part of the company.

➤ How Change Happens Tactically: The Methods of Change

Change is usually multidimensional, a combination of four distinct change methods:

1. *Technological change* is changing the technologies used in producing the company's output. Examples may be specific to a unit process, say substitution of rapid prototyping for model building, or enterprisewide, such as the introduction of an enterprise resource planning system.

2. *Structural change* involves altering the various organizational bounds within the company. Structural change can occur along any of the following dimensions: complexity and simplification, formal procedures and autonomous actions, centralization and decentralization, and direction and coordination.

3. The two most commonly used *managerial change* methods are reward systems and labor/management cooperation. Reward systems can give a clear indication of the company's commitment to change. Beginning with something near and dear to the heart can focus energies on making changes stick. Revising or overhauling a reward system lays helpful groundwork for change. Labor/management cooperation—concerned with improving employee morale, solving production and work or technology problems, developing training programs, and the like—can facilitate positive and constructive change that meets both corporate and labor goals.

4. *Human change* methods effect change through people by education and training and through organizational development. Education and training upgrades people's knowledge, skills, attitudes, and even beliefs. In addition to specific task-related skills, these programs cover everything from managing stress to improving communication skills. Organizational development involves intervening in individual, group, and systemwide processes and practices, with the goal of improving organizational and employee climate, values, health, functioning, and well-being.

➤ Change Strategies

Connor and Lake say there are four types of strategies to effect change: Facilitative, Informational, Attitudinal, and Political. Your selection of a change strategy will depend on the time available for the change, the extent of the change (the number of people and groups affected, the number of behaviors to be changed, and the emotional impact of the change), the characteristics of the change target, and the resources available to implement the change.

Facilitative strategies help the group that is the target for change use of its own abilities or resources in making the change. These strategies work best when the group has a good sense of what it wants to do, but lacks the specific skills needed to get to where they already know they need to be.

Informational strategies assume that if you give the target groups adequate factual information they will recognize the problem and develop a mutually agreeable solution. These strategies can work when you can accurately assume that the group lacks the information they need, or possesses information that is incorrect or misleading, and that they will know what to do when they do have correct information.

Attitudinal strategies presume that people will change their behavior if they change their attitudes. These strategies depend on the change champion to articulate persuasive messages in many different ways and to use other attitude-changing techniques. These strategies can be useful when there is no requirement for speed, the planned change is extensive, the target group is suspicious of the change, and when the change champion has persuasive, attitude-changing skills.

Political strategies depend on giving, withholding, competing, or bargaining for resources. They can be coercive: "Do it or else." Or they can be subtle: "You scratch my back, I'll scratch yours." The resources may be budget, personnel, knowledge, new equipment, even opportunities for promotion. Coercive strategies fit when the proposed change is needed "now!" when the change is not extensive, and when the target group is resistant. More subtle and complex political strategies fit when speed is not necessary and when the change is more extensive. In either case, the change agent must control the "carrot," the necessary and valued resources.

■ THE STEPS OF CHANGE

Change starts when there is a perception of need. The need may come crashing in as an immediate competitive threat, or it may come as a sense that there must be a better way to achieve corporate goals. You must think through the proposed response, perhaps using the change considerations of the previous section as a checklist.

Then the benefits, costs, and risks must be evaluated, usually in an iterative process. Once the investment decision is made, you can manage the change effort as a development project. At some point, the change will be accepted as part of the way your company operates routinely. Even then, the change will live on, through continuous improvement and maintenance efforts. Finally, the change will have lived out its usefulness—all that will be left will be the effort to tie up loose ends, to dispose of equipment and intellectual baggage that is no longer needed.

Change is a process to be accomplished deliberately. Table 14.1 outlines a process for managing change. Since companies need to know whether a change accomplished its goals—and furthered the company's corporate goals, we emphasize the metrics and measurements by which a company can evaluate the success of a change initiative.

➤ The Planning Phase

Align Change Goals

The first step in a change process is to recognize the need for change and to choose from the alternative ways the need can be met. One way to do that is to recall the company's strategic goals described in Chapter 3, a balanced set of goals relating to the financial, customer,

Table 14.1	A Discipline for Change and Change Measurement	
Phase	**Step**	**Metrics and Measurements**
Planning	1. Align change goals with strategic goals.	Change metrics and targets
	2. Develop project plan.	Progress metrics
Execution	3. Develop change components and system.	Progress measurements
	4. Implement change components and system.	Progress measurements Interim change measurements
Assessment	5. Analyze results.	Change measurements
	6. Evaluate strategic effects.	Corporate strategic measurements
Completion	7. Integrate into continuous improvement process.	Change metrics

internal operations, globalization, innovation, and learning perspectives. There is a need for change when there is a misalignment between the company's operations and the results the company needs to achieve to realize its corporate strategic goals. Our feelings that a change is needed are symptomatic. We may have an intuitive grasp of the change that is needed. Intuition based on experience may be a good guide, but it does not in itself provide the justification for a change. Our instincts should be confirmed by relating the goals of a change to the company's strategic goals.

For example, suppose the XYZ Company, getting on the e-commerce bandwagon, proposes to develop an on-line direct retailing distribution channel for its consumer electronics product line. If this proposed change in the way factory operations are linked to customer wants does not increase financial measures, or improve customer satisfaction, or reduce internal operations complexity, or open the XYZ Company for a more global reach, or develop bottom line results from new ideas, or provide a platform for the company's growth, then it is surely questionable. In its analysis of the change initiative, XYZ Company should align the change goals with its corporate goals, as shown in Table 14.2.

Note that the matrix for this example has entries for all six perspectives. Many valid change projects will address fewer perspectives.

Set Metrics and Targets

Once the change goals have been articulated, appropriate metrics must be defined. How will we know the change has been effective?

Table 14.2   The Change Goal Matrix for the XYZ Corporation

Strategic Perspective	Balanced Strategic Goals	Change Goals
Financial	Improve profit margins.	Reduce the cost of sales.
Customer	Improve customer retention.	Reduce time for delivery.
Internal operations	Reduce inventory costs.	Tailor production to real-time demand.
Globalization	Increase offshore revenues.	Test global markets.
Innovation	Grow revenues with innovative value-adds.	Provide new delivery mechanism.
Learning and growth	Increase number of distribution options.	Train a cadre of experts in online operations.

The metrics may be obvious or subtle, but should be linked to the change goals. The definitions of the metrics must be unambiguous. In some cases, of course, the definitions will be governed by standards. For example, many financial metrics are governed by accounting standards. While the significance of any given metric may be a matter of debate, the definition of the metric itself should be clear enough that there is no debate over what is being measured.

How do you know you have made a meaningful change? You cannot see the difference a change has made unless you know where you started. Baseline measurements determined before you start the change project will allow you to confirm the benefits (or determine the losses) of a change.

The measurements may be common ones that already exist explicitly in historical records. In other cases, it may be possible to derive the measurements from historical records. Because a change may introduce a new variable into the company's operations, it may be that data does not exist from which one can derive measurements. There may be time while the change is being developed and before it is made operational to make specific baseline measurements.

How much of a change is enough? Or too much? The benefits of change must outweigh the organization's costs—its use of time and other resources. Preliminary targets for change should be large enough to justify the change effort. On the other hand, targets should be realistic.

The key to understanding the effects of change is consistency. The change metrics should reflect the change goals and be aligned with the corporate strategic goals and metrics. All measurements—whether baseline measurements taken before the change project, intermediate measurements taken while the change project is being executed, or operational measurements taken after the project is completed—should obey the same definition of metrics. One should make sure that one compares apples to apples and not apples to oranges.

Develop the Project Plan

There is no substitute for good project management based on the use of appropriate project management tools. The typical project plan will cover the development and implementation of the change, including not just the mechanics of changing equipment or procedures, but also the education, training, and learning required before the change is internalized in the company's operations. Included in the project plan should be:

➤ *Change project overview.* The overview should provide a synopsis of the change project. The overview should describe the chief goals, targets, and benefits. It should sketch costs, project timing, and resource requirements. It should also outline the major risk factors. It should define the roles of all the players in the change—the executives and other change leaders, the change team, the employees who will have to accommodate to the change, and where appropriate, the customers, suppliers, or others affected by the change.

If the change is a major organizational one, the plan should describe the vision of the changed company. It should specify the organizational structure, reward system, personnel policies, authority and task-responsibility distributions, managerial values and practices, performance-review systems, relationships with external groups, and expected performance outcomes. A test of this future state is that it can be supported by a credible schedule and activity plan.

➤ *Readiness, goals, targets, risks, and benefits.* The activity plan will build on the company's present situation and systems. It is important to set priorities for change, identify relevant subsystems, and assess their readiness and capability for the contemplated change. The activity plan will incorporate this scenario of the transition to the changed state.

This section should include the analysis of change goals as developed in Step 1, a statement of the targets defined in Step 2, and a presentation of the benefits to the company of achieving the targets in Step 3. The discussion of benefits should consider time. If the change is being made to meet a window of opportunity, then it is especially important to assess the value of an early completion of the change, or the cost of a delayed completion.

Since change involves moving into the unknown, any change carries risks. The project may be too challenging technically for the organization. People may not be able to accommodate to the change. There may be side effects; the change may have negative impact on other of the company's operations. Not making the change carries risks, too, so the risk analysis should include that alternative look into the unknown.

➤ *Work breakdown plan.* The activity plan will specify the critical activities and events of the transition period—what must be developed in preparation for the change, how it will be developed, what has to happen as the change is implemented, and what resources are required. The plan should include contingency planning if, for example, resources do not prove to be available, and actions to mitigate risk. The plan should have a logical sequence of events designed to achieve the change within the window of opportunity. Assuming that the change has been broken into "chunks," each should be described separately, with the their sub-plans rolled up into the project plan. As mentioned earlier, the interfaces of the "chunks" must fit as the pieces in a picture puzzle.

➤ *Schedule.* The schedule should show the logical sequence of activities and events and include important milestones. It should identify critical precedence and other constraints. Each chunk of the change should be described by its own subschedule. PERT scheduling and Critical Path Analysis are invaluable tools for creating a practical and effective scheduling system.

➤ *The communications plan.* The project plan should include a communications plan. Change can affect many people in a company, often in ways that are unpredictable. The acceptance of a change (or lack thereof) can be the critical factor in the success of a change project. Communications are required to condition the organization for change, to reduce the uncertainty employees have about change and replace them with reasonable expectations, and then as part of the education, training, and learning curve. The plan must cover internal and external communications to achieve an optimum system. A suggested outline for a communications plan follows:

A. Sectors and Goals
   1. Company Personnel
      a. Executives and Managers
      b. Change Project Team
      c. Affected Employees
      d. Everyone Else
   2. Customers
   3. Distribution Channels
   4. Suppliers

B. Communications Scenario (by Sector)

C. Communications Events
   1. Crosscutting Events
   2. Events by Sector
   3. Schedule and Milestones

D. Roles and Responsibilities

E. Communications Measurements

Communications, starting with communications from the executive management, will lubricate the process and help ensure success. Depending on the magnitude of the change, the sectors of the enterprise targeted for communications can be extensive. The communications should be designed to get enough understandable knowledge to each sector so that it can play its role in ensuring the enterprise's success as it undergoes its change.

➤ Execution Phase

Once the commitment has been made to a change project, the Execution Phase begins. There are two principal parts of the Execution Phase: the development of the hardware, software, and systems needed to support the change, and then the implementation of the change itself.

Leadership is essential during the execution phase. This is the time when the company will be most doubtful about the change, the time when investments are being made but before results are seen. Leadership, coupled with a continuous assessment of the change process to ensure that it is on track toward the overall vision, and if it is not, to determine what corrections are required to stay on course.

Progress against the Project Plan

Measurement is important during a change project to ensure that it doesn't go off track. There are two aspects of measuring the progress of a change process: the measurement of the change process itself and the measurement of any planned intermediate results.

Progress on the Work Breakdown

A change project is like any other project and all the familiar tools of project management should be employed to keep the project on target. The project plan for any but the simplest changes should include milestones, definable results mapped against time and cost. The simplest measures then are binary: did the project reach the milestone on time and under budget? There are often other measures contained within the project plan, for example, percentage of resources consumed, availability of resources for completion, and so forth. Critical Path Analysis will be most helpful in measuring progress.

The measurement of progress against the plan can lead to confidence that the project will in fact be completed as planned or may indicate problems that must be addressed. Is the change more difficult to achieve than thought? Will the change be completed in time to make a difference? What changes should be made to aid in the success of the change?

Achievement of Intermediate Results

For many change projects, the implementation of a "chunk" means that some new function is operationalized. A part of the change has been made and we can begin to measure the effectiveness of the change. These intermediate results provide early validation of the change or indications of problems with the change. They can also be used to demonstrate to the enterprise that the change is beginning to yield the promised results.

You should be cautious about intermediate results achieved before the change is fully operationalized. They can be indicators of eventual results, but should not be taken out of context. For most changes, the last chunk is implemented and results flow from the whole change effort. Measurements made during this time should be considered intermediate results until the company has internalized the changes.

When Is a Change Project Finished?

When do we "declare victory" and say that a change project is complete? Is it when we have switched from the old way to the new way? Is it when we no longer carry a budget item for the change; that is, when we've completed our investment in the change? Since the results of the change should be improved upon through the company's continuous improvement efforts, do we say that the change is never complete?

We arbitrarily define completion as that time when the change is accepted as part of the company's routine operations and is subject now to the continuous improvement efforts. That is, completion is after all the development of new processes, systems, and procedures is complete. It is after all that is new is implemented. It is after cutover. It is also after the learning curve is asymptotically complete. Only at this time will we know whether the change has been effective—only then will the measurements provide us with the quantitative indicators of success (or failure).

➤ Assessment Phase

The temptation, especially in small companies, is to make a change, see that it seems to be working, and go on to the next most pressing problem (and there always is a next most pressing problem). However, the results should be analyzed and evaluated to:

➤ Learn what is good about the change.

➤ Learn what is bad.

➤ Package the lessons for application elsewhere in the company or for use in other change projects.

➤ Understand the unpredicted consequences of change.

Comparison of Actual Results with Targets and Baseline Measurements

The comparison of actual results with targets and baseline measurements should be straightforward. If the actual results come close to meeting our targets, everyone can go away feeling good. But usually results are mixed: some targets are met, we fall short on others, and occasionally we over-achieve. The comparisons flag important questions:

➤ When we haven't met our targets is it because we were naïve? was there a failure in the project planning or execution? or were we late into the window of opportunity? or was there an unexpected change in the external environment that blind-sided us?

➤ When we exceed our targets, the questions are usually more subtle: Were we just lucky? What new opportunities does over-achievement make available to us? What lessons can we apply to our other change efforts?

Unexpected Results and Side Effects

One of the old saws of change management is that the solution of one problem inevitably introduces new problems. Some cynics claim the growth in new problems is exponential. While careful change selection and change project management can minimize new or unexpected problems, the analysis of a completed change should identify new problems and side effects.

Effects on Strategic Goals

Finally, although the effects may be indirect, was alignment with strategic goals achieved? A significant change effort should at least show up as a blip in the measurements of the corporate metrics.

➤ **The Completion Phase**

Completion of a change project—when the change is accepted as part of the company's routine operations—does not mean that the change is "cast in concrete." It means that the change has become part of the company's routine operations. NGM companies will have some sort of continuous improvement program as part of their quality effort. The change is truly operationalized when it is just one more target for continuous improvement, either to reduce costs or to enhance function.

The completion phase is, of course, also a starting point for the next change effort. While a company should celebrate a successful change, it should maintain vigilance, looking for changing conditions that will render the new, recently implemented, situation out-moded.

■ EXERCISE

Change leaders must "think systems" as a prerequisite for managing change. The list that follows shows seven aspects of the company that can be affected by change. Use the list to rate your company (on a scale of 1 to 5–5 being most proficient) on the aspects:

1. Changes *in the environment:*
   - Physical workplace structure
   - Organizational adaptability
   - Change in technology and its impact on the workplace
   - Change in technology and its impact on the marketplace
   - Increased requirements for employee safety
2. Changes *in organizational priorities:*
   - Market- versus technology-driven
   - Quality versus price priority
   - Continuous education and training for all employees
3. Changes *in structures:*
   - From functional to brand, business, or matrix structure
   - Parallel structures and temporary systems
4. Changes *in the ways work is done:*
   - People managing their own work
   - Inspection closer to work

5. Changes *in personnel policies:*
   —Rewarding innovation and creativity
   —Rewarding productivity and quality
   —Diversity issues and management
   —Credible employability vs. guaranteed employment
6. Changes *in roles:*
   —Entrepreneurship within the company
   —Decentralized tactical decisions
7. Changes *in culture:*
   —Elimination of traditions
   —Reexamining current beliefs, assumptions, norms and customs
   —Recognizing and adapting to social changes
   —Recognizing and adapting to legal changes
   —Explicitly espousing core values
   —Valuing intangible assets (people, information, knowledge)
   —Supporting individual and agile leadership.

■ NOTES

1. John P. Kotter, *Leading Change* (Boston: Harvard Business School Press, September 1996).
2. Clayton M. Christensen, *The Innovator's Dilemma: When New Technologies Cause Great Firms to Fail* (Boston: Harvard Business School Press, 1997).
3. Andrew S. Grove, *Only the Paranoid Survive: How to Exploit the Crisis Points That Challenge Every Company* (New York: Bantam Books, 1999).
4. Patrick E. Connor and Linda K. Lake, *Managing Organizational Change* (Westport, CT: Praeger Publishing, 1994).

Chapter 15

The Knowledge Enterprise

The theme of the presentations on innovation and knowledge was *knowledge in action.* People take knowledge and use it. They get results with it. Yet they have trouble understanding what it is. It's easy to understand physical assets—equipment and the physical processes associated with Rapid Product and Process Realization (RPPR) are tangible. They may not be easy to manage, but you can, in principle, see them, feel them, and understand them with all your senses. People are tangible, too—very complicated and a continuing challenge to your leadership skills, but you can go eyeball to eyeball with someone and really get a good understanding of them.

But knowledge is something else—it's intangible. Knowledge reminds you of the mythic understandings of life. Knowledge is like a flux, a lifeforce that energizes the company as it flows through the company's processes. On that philosophical note, you turned your attention back to what your people called "the Knowledge Enterprise."

■ THE KNOWLEDGE ENTERPRISE

Today, the only remaining sustainable source of competitive advantage is implementation of new knowledge.—Lester Thurow[1]

The productivity of knowledge is increasingly going to be the determining factor in the competitive position of a country, an industry, a company . . . The only thing that increasingly will matter in national as well as international economics is management's performance in making knowledge productive.—Peter Drucker[2]

279

Two of America's leading thinkers are telling us that intellectual content—knowledge—is now the competitive discriminator among products. All other things being equal, we are most likely to buy the "smartest" product, the one that knows our needs well enough to anticipate them. All other things being equal, we are most likely to buy the product that was produced by the most efficient and timely processes— the "smartest" ones. Knowledge is the essential enabler of innovation, of productivity, and of the ability to meet the customer's needs.

Knowledge is an asset. It takes a whole enterprise—different from the extended enterprise that conducts the RPPR processes—to create and distribute knowledge assets. We call that enterprise the *knowledge enterprise* (see Figure 15.1).

The knowledge enterprise consists of:

➤ *Knowledge sources*—the labs and vendors who develop and package knowledge, and the on-the-job experiences that provide knowledge of lasting value.

➤ *Knowledge supply chain*—the mechanisms by which knowledge gets from its source to the company's knowledge repository or directly into the heads of the knowledge users.

➤ *Knowledge repository*—the company's store of ready knowledge.

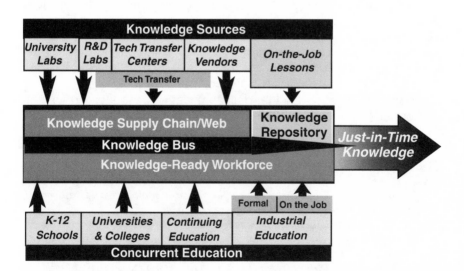

Figure 15.1 The Knowledge Enterprise

➤ *Concurrent education*—the educational entities—K–12 schools, community colleges, colleges, and universities, continuing education, and formal and on-the-job industrial education—that provide education about newly developed knowledge and its uses as quickly as possible at whatever level is appropriate for the user.

➤ *Knowledge-ready workforce*—the people who need the knowledge cannot be expected to use knowledge, no matter how well packaged, unless they are prepared.

➤ *Knowledge delivery technology*—the infrastructure that communicates knowledge throughout the enterprise, especially to the person using it.

The processes of knowledge creation, distribution, and utilization require investment by all the individuals, companies, and institutions in the knowledge enterprise. Recognizing those investments and measuring the returns is good management, even though we do not yet have well-established yardsticks to do this.

➤ Knowledge

There are many types and sources of knowledge—formal and informal, explicit and tacit, commercial, cooperative, and academic. When you think of your company as part of a knowledge enterprise, you will seek the best sources for the particular kind of knowledge you need.

Formal and Informal Knowledge Sources

Formal knowledge is generally explicit, discussed first in scholarly papers from academia, government labs, or industrial labs. This is refined into documented, even codified, knowledge presented in textbooks, reports, tutorials, and procedure manuals, using a number of types of media: books, journals, audio- and video-tapes, etc. It is the stuff of fact-based education and training programs.

Informal knowledge is more experiential. It is gained as a by-product of the problem solving all companies have to do in response to change and to operational challenges. Over time, this knowledge, which often is unexpressed and retained in employees' brains, becomes part of the company's tacit knowledge base. It is transferred primarily by observation, exposure to examples, and on-the-job training. Many companies fail to convert these knowledge assets to explicit knowledge.

Explicit and Tacit Knowledge

As noted, some knowledge is described explicitly. In addition to the formal results of scholarship, sources of explicit knowledge may include a company's corporate databases. This explicit knowledge is delivered as the company's vision and mission statements, strategic and operating plans, internal operating reports, and measurements taken from the many perspectives of the business.

Other knowledge is tacit. Often the knowledge that defines a company's culture is tacit, never really written down, but encoded in the core of knowledge that the company's employees share. Much of the informal intellectual content of the work employees do is not fully "worked out," but done uncritically, almost subconsciously, because "it worked this way the last time," "it feels right," "everyone knows this is the best way."

One way to acquire valuable tacit knowledge is to hire new employees. We are moving toward a model for employing talented employees in the high-tech industries similar to the free agency of star athletes.

➤ Knowledge Assets

It is hard to think about knowledge as an asset. It seems so ephemeral, so difficult to measure. But we are beginning to understand that knowledge, by analogy to more tangible assets, is a transferable commodity. The more we explore this idea, the more we understand that the concept applies to both *explicit knowledge*—books, defined procedures and processes, codified information—and the *tacit knowledge* embodied in the experience and learning of people.

One of the truly inventive aspects of the NGM Project was the realization that a company could use supply chain management principles to improve its knowledge acquisition process. Knowledge is something that can be "sourced," thought of as a transferable commodity, specified and acquired. Your company can source knowledge in response to a specific "pull," where your needs provide the impetus and motivation for knowledge delivery.

If knowledge is your company's lifeblood, you will need to ensure a healthy knowledge supply. While there are many eternal truths, the knowledge that provides competitive advantage is new knowledge or old knowledge that is used in new ways. Your company cannot afford to acquire and stockpile knowledge. It is too costly to acquire all the knowledge that the company might need or want to use in the future—and often the knowledge you acquire is obsolete before it can be used. This is especially true if the knowledge does not contribute directly to the company's core competencies.

Your company needs to develop "pull" processes that:

➤ Identify the need for new knowledge. "New" is used here broadly to mean knowledge that is not readily available to the user in his or her knowledge base. It may sit in some data repository in the company, in a coworker's brain, or in some source outside the company, or it may be truly new, derived from a recent discovery or invention.

➤ Contain a chain of knowledge suppliers reaching back to research universities and laboratories and including public sector institutions (such as the National Institute of Standards and Technology) and specialized knowledge vendors.

➤ Include delivery mechanisms that will transport the required knowledge quickly and in a usable form to the user.

Your company will miss opportunities if it copes with its needs by grabbing at knowledge that is indiscriminately "pushed" by knowledge sources. When industry acquires a physical commodity it drives, or "pulls" the system by establishing a demand, defining clear specifications, fixing processes and responsibilities, and measuring results. When industry acquires knowledge, however, it is often less demanding. Industry's knowledge demand signals are less clear, its specifications are often abstract, and its expectations for the deliverable are not so high—for example, the knowledge processes are not often subjected to a Six-Sigma quality requirements.

Thinking of knowledge as the object of a pull system, instead of as something being pumped out of the knowledge sources onto a mass of indifferent users, has the potential to:

➤ Reduce knowledge "shortages" by using supply chain management principles to help ensure continuous availability of the knowledge essential to enterprise operations.

➤ Improve the productivity of the knowledge acquisition process if the 20 percent cost reduction and 50 percent cycle time reduction achieved by material supply chain concepts can be duplicated by knowledge supply chain practices.

Outside-the-box thinking is encouraged when the company considers knowledge acquisition and delivery as enterprisewide processes that are managed with a set of principles, such as those suggested below for knowledge supply chains. A user's need for knowledge then becomes a challenge to the entire knowledge enterprise, not to any single entity. Meeting the need becomes a collective goal and the entities involved are more motivated to adjust their roles in achieving it.

Thinking about knowledge as the output of a knowledge enterprise organized and managed as we would an extended enterprise means that we can employ many of our well-understood management tools. Quality initiatives such as Total Quality Management (TQM) can be used to refine the knowledge processes. TQM and similar ideas are slowly being assimilated into academia's operations, making the inclusion of academic institutions within quality-driven knowledge enterprises feasible.

A high-quality focus implies, though, that the user has a good understanding of what knowledge is needed. To get a high quality response, the user has to ask a high-quality question—that is the user has to be smart about what he or she asks for.

➤ Knowledge as a Valuable Commodity

Knowledge is what you need to know to get the job done right, on time, under budget, so that the customer is well satisfied. The cost of inadequate knowledge is prohibitive. The company with inadequate knowledge will not be able to compete with the knowledge-rich company. In material terms, inadequate knowledge is an unacceptable shortage. The first responsibility of the company's knowledge enterprise is to eliminate shortages by ensuring the on-time delivery of its specified "commodity."

Although valuing knowledge seems a formidable task, a starting point for a company is to identify and quantify its annual investments in activities that support the knowledge processes. The cumulative investments for knowledge processes are huge—$1 trillion or more in the United States for research and development (knowledge creation) and for education and training (knowledge transfer). The NGM Report asserts that the typical Fortune 500 company spends over 10 percent of its annual revenue on officially accounted for knowledge processes. The actual cost could be far higher if all of the nonqualified or misallocated costs were properly considered.

Given the chaotic way knowledge is managed in many companies, it is reasonable that a more orderly way to manage the knowledge enterprise could yield a higher return on the knowledge investment. For example, if your company does spend 10 percent of its revenues on knowledge processes and if it could achieve the 20 percent cost savings seen in managed materials supply chains, it could increase its margins by 2 percent.

In many cases, your company can point to discrete pieces of knowledge and can assign costs to their production and use. You can also point to revenues or cost-savings that result from their use. This is knowledge that clearly can be considered as a commodity. Other knowledge seems too nebulous to be thought of as a commodity— there is so much tacit knowledge that enters the equation. But as your company grows accustomed to thinking of knowledge in measurable terms, as you think of the value of people in terms of the value of their individual knowledge contributions, your company may be able to include more and more categories of knowledge in the measured knowledge base.

➤ **The Knowledge Cycle**

Knowledge is the output of a cycle that involves generation, development, transfer, and application (see Figure 15.2). Since the value of knowledge lies in its application in a specific, often dynamic, situation,

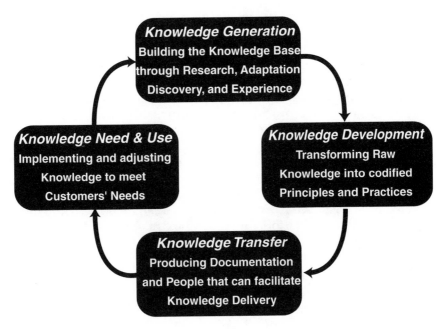

Figure 15.2 The Knowledge Cycle

it can not be separated clearly from the creator, the teacher, the learner, or the doer. The elements of the knowledge cycle include:

➤ *Knowledge generation*—the process that creates or discovers new knowledge. Formal research is an example of a knowledge-generating process. The process of sharing and adapting best practices is another effective way to generate new knowledge.

➤ *Knowledge development*—the process of making new knowledge transferable by developing and documenting it in explicit or codified terms that can be understood by others.

➤ *Knowledge transfer*—the process that distributes the knowledge in a variety of knowledge forms so that users can efficiently apply it. These forms can include documented knowledge available through printed or electronic media; education and training activities; and the embedded knowledge acquired with an individual.

➤ *Knowledge need and use*—the process that makes knowledge actionable as it is applied to meet a need. Sometimes the explicit knowledge itself is the product, but more often the new knowledge must be combined with other knowledge and transformed into a product or service. The knowledge process loop is closed when the product of that knowledge satisfies the ultimate customer's needs. When the needs are not met, or new needs are identified, the process starts again.

Knowledge is created when something new is implemented, usually to meet a specific need. New knowledge is combined with existing knowledge to create a new solution. Innovation depends on a knowledge-generation process that discovers, creates, and transforms new ideas and concepts into explicit knowledge that can be transferred to a wide body of knowledge users.

A company may use knowledge, either as codified knowledge or as knowledge embedded in technologies, in management practices, or in people in an innovative product or by producing an existing product or service faster, cheaper, and more reliably. The company's ability to use knowledge for competitiveness depends on how quickly the knowledge can be employed.

The efficacy of the knowledge cycle depends on the knowledge supplier understanding the real needs of the knowledge user. This usually is accomplished best as a collaborative process that integrates the customer's tacit and explicit knowledge of their needs with the tacit and explicit knowledge of how the products and services of the supplier can be adapted to meet those needs—the knowledge analog of the *empathetic design* process we discussed in Chapter 8.

The efficiency of the process is a function of how well each step is integrated with the others. When the process involves only an individual or a team integrated by a common need, the boundaries between these steps blur, and the knowledge flow appears efficient and seamless. However, given the diversity and quantity of potential knowledge uses and users, most systems lack integration, and the process takes the characteristics of a "push" system with each step focusing on its individual task as the end product. Unfortunately, this pattern of "functional silos" has become so well entrenched that it limits the participants' ability to recognize and capitalize on their interdependencies, even when the "pull" of a larger unifying purpose exists.

■ KNOWLEDGE SOURCES

The first sources of knowledge to which your company should look are its own knowledge bases of explicit and tacit knowledge—since you've already made that investment, use it! But the internal knowledge bases won't provide all the knowledge you need, so you must look outside for new knowledge, for updates to the knowledge already in your knowledge bases, and especially for the knowledge you need to fuel innovation.

➤ Commercial Sources

Consulting firms constitute an important source of new knowledge. Large firms provide core competence with major initiatives, such as the design and implementation of an enterprise resource planning (ERP) system. Small firms provide knowledge on specific topics. The motivation and culture in these companies is likely to fit into the notion of a knowledge supply chain with well-developed specifications and deliverables, and measures of success related to the success of the ultimate customer.

A second group of commercial companies provides instruction and training, usually focused on narrowly defined, often highly technical, topics. The courses they offer may provide the quick injection of knowledge needed, for example, to implement a Windows NT network or to deal with import regulations for your products in the European Union.

Your company can be a significant knowledge source within your supply chain or web. Your engineering and manufacturing organizations may have knowledge far beyond that existing among your smaller suppliers. When they encounter a technical problem, they often simply do not have the knowledge that is needed to solve their immediate problem. You can package your knowledge, leveraging it within the supply chain, or even packaging it to generate revenues. Similarly, you may look to your customers to provide you with specialized knowledge you need to fulfil their requirements.

➤ Cooperative Sources

Most industries have cooperative trade associations and many have R&D consortia. Many of these associations provide repositories of best practices, ripe for translation to meet your company's specific needs. The R&D consortia do research on the generic needs of their industries—often these studies lead to prototypical architectures for a company's major systems, such as shop floor systems, information systems, human resources systems, even cost accounting systems.

In addition, there are international, national, and regional consortia (see box for examples) in which companies cooperate, usually on so-called pre-competitive or generic knowledge—the sort of knowledge that will keep the company up on the competitive forefront if at the appropriate time it is brought in-house for the company's proprietary applications.

Cooperative consortia are sometimes formed around the activities of government laboratories—the labs benefit by learning how companies will use what they develop, while the companies benefit from the government's high priority applied research projects. Formal cooperative agreements provide for the transfer of new knowledge to companies willing to invest in its commercialization.

Cooperative consortia are also often formed around specific academic programs and research centers. MIT's Leaders for Manufacturing (LFM) program, for example, brings about 15 major manufacturers together with academics interested in the leadership needs of manufacturing enterprises. LFM is a part of each of those companies' knowledge enterprises in two ways: by providing talented management candidates and by conducting research on jointly defined problems. The Agile Manufacturing Research Institutes at Rensselaer Polytechnic Institute, University of Illinois at Urbana–Champaign, and University of Texas–Arlington are the nuclei for consortia centered on electronics packaging, machine tools, and the aerospace industry, respectively.

➤ Noncommercial Sources

Academic R&D provides the most important source of new knowledge. Many companies search out the academic centers of excellence

Consortium for Advanced Manufacturing—International (CAM-I)

CAM-I was the first cooperative R&D consortium formed in 1972 after the relaxation of anti-trust law permitted industry to join in precompetitive R&D. With an international membership, CAM-I fostered the development of standards for numerical control, created the original algorithms used in machining contoured, sculptured surfaces, the solid modeling extension of IGES, the Application Interface Standard for numerical controls, and pioneered feature-based modeling. CAM-I's technical programs continue this tradition, balancing R&D of production processes with standards development. CAM-I's management programs have pioneered the application of activity-based costing and target costing.

National Center for Manufacturing Science (NCMS)

Formed in the mid-1980s, NCMS has managed a large portfolio of nearly $500 million worth of industry- and federally-funded collaborative R&D projects. The projects have covered a wide range of industrial needs. The current emphasis is on advanced electronics technology, environmentally conscious manufacturing, enterprise integration and management, manufacturing processes and materials, and production equipment and systems. NCMS has a special focus on the automotive industry and defense manufacturing.

The International Intelligent Manufacturing Systems (IMS) Program

Active since the early 1990s, the IMS Program is an umbrella organization for nearly two dozen collaborative R&D projects involving companies from Australia, Canada, the European Union, Japan, South Korea, Switzerland, and the United States. These projects range from large enterprise integration projects, to projects with a more limited focus, such as wood manufacturing processes and adaptive, flexible materials handling systems. The projects are overseen by an international committee that includes industry and government representatives and that provides help in establishing collaborations under intellectual property agreements that have governmental sanction.

in their specific areas of need. Others often work in close cooperation with a local university as a primary provider of new knowledge.
From the point of view of the company, the best of these arrangements are those in which the university exhibits flexibility in building competencies in areas of importance to the company. Regionally
established knowledge centers attract knowledge seekers—industrial
enterprises—and thus create new job opportunities. Some noncom-
mercial institutes affiliated with universities serve broad sectors of
industry. The Software Engineering Institute at Carnegie Mellon University is a federally-funded institute that serves the industrial community by establishing disciplined management and technical
practices for software engineering.

Smaller companies often find great value in knowledge transferred by technology transfer groups, such as the NIST-supported
Manufacturing Extension Program, the Consortium of Federal Laboratories, and the Manufacturing Technology Information Assessment
Center (MTIAC). These groups, which are often associated with a community college or university, are found in every state in the United
States with analogs in most countries. They work to translate the new
knowledge that is driving competitive manufacturing in large companies into the chunks that can be used by small- and medium-sized
enterprises.

➤ Communities of Knowledge

Some communities accidentally or intentionally have been engineered to be *communities of knowledge*. The knowledge enterprise has
nearly been institutionalized. These regional communities are typi-
fied by the university-related industrial spawning grounds, such as
Silicon Valley, North Carolina's Research Triangle, Boston's Route
128, and Virginia's Fairfax County and by the strong linkages that the
leaders of state-supported research universities are forging with industry. The need is for even stronger partnerships with knowledge
creation as an interdependent, albeit segmented, process spanning
the integrated knowledge enterprise.

A good starting point is to recognize the existence of the larger
common or unifying purpose. The economic development of the
community depends on the systems it puts in place to maximize the
resources it has for invention and implementation. Industry's
problem-oriented research depends on the fundamental knowledge
that comes from basic university research. In return, it is often the
"pull" of problem-oriented research that stimulates the need for new
areas of basic research.

In this scheme of things, it is the needs of the economic end-user—not the needs of government—that drive and fund university research. While economic development often provides a common focus today, a real and committed partnership within a knowledge enterprise won't happen unless it provides tangible benefits for all participants. The value of viewing R&D in the context of the innovation process is that it facilitates collaboration between the knowledge sources and the knowledge users. Adopting this view:

1. Gives industry better access to generic knowledge that could have a major impact on product and process development.
2. Accelerates the transfer of basic research into products and services.
3. Accelerates the acceptance and value of basic research by:
   —Ensuring a closer coupling of the relevance of that research to ultimate customer needs.
   —Improving the speed and quality of knowledge requirements from the users back to the academic researchers.
   —Improving academia's access to practical information about an industry's commercial applications.
   —Helping academia keep abreast of leading-edge industrial practices.
4. Reduces the costs of the R&D process through the more efficient use of core competencies, of people, and capital assets.

■ KNOWLEDGE SUPPLY CHAINS

The NGM Report asserts that knowledge is a transferable commodity, like an engine block or a silicon wafer, whose value is realized when it satisfies a practical need in a timely, cost-efficient manner. Companies can manage their knowledge assets by applying the same principles of supply chain management that manufacturers have applied to material acquisition over the last decade.

➤ The Structure of Knowledge Supply Chains

A *knowledge supply chain* is an integrated process that uses the core competencies of industry and academia to provide an enterprise with the information and wisdom it needs to run its business profitably, and to educate and train its workforce. A competitive NGM enterprise will depend on continuous access and efficient distribution of knowledge. Its knowledge supply chain will include industrial, academic, and governmental knowledge-generation systems in addition to its own internal systems and processes. Figure 15.3 compares the steps in the material supply chain with those of the knowledge supply chain.

Both chains require the steps of creation or generation, development, needs identification, transfer, and use. Both chains move from a concept to a final utility by adding value to the unit as it moves through the process. Both chains employ a transformation that converts the concept into a state that can be used by the end consumer. Both chains depend on a rich, efficient, continuous flow of information and knowledge across all the steps of the chain. Finally, both chains typically extend beyond any one group or institution.

A well-managed supply chain is one managed by the principles shown in Table 15.1, which compares them with a set of principles adapted for a knowledge supply chain.

These principles apply whatever the form of knowledge. It can be knowledge from an established knowledge base such as a library, web

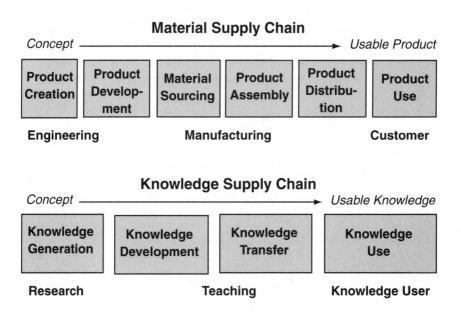

Figure 15.3 Comparing the Material Supply Chain with the Knowledge Supply Chain

Table 15.1 Management Principles for Material and Knowledge Supply Chains

Material Supply Chain	Knowledge Supply Chain
Treat the system as a continuous, integrated process.	The knowledge process is managed as an integrated system, with all links of the process actively involved.
Operate with a purpose focused on the ultimate customer.	The partners are focused on delivering the knowledge the ultimate user needs.
Provide benefits for all supply chain partners.	Each partner benefits from its participation, with rewards consistent with the partner's values and reward structure.
Ensure a free flow of information and knowledge across the entire supply chain.	Each partner has all the information and requirements specifications it needs to maximize the value of its contribution.
Optimize the total process by integrating and using the core competencies of each partner.	Each partner's core competencies are recognized and utilized for the best mutual benefit of the enterprise and the partner.
Measure results against clearly defined needs.	There is quick feedback from the user to each knowledge provider on the efficiency and effectiveness of the knowledge exchange.

site, or company database. It can be new skills and learning acquired through formal education and training. It can be knowledge or skills "embedded" in newly hired people. It can be new knowledge derived from the sharing of best practices or consulting with relevant experts. Or it can be new knowledge generated by formal R&D processes.

The knowledge supply chain focuses on managing the interdependent steps and partners that provide knowledge on demand, not on the knowledge content. The knowledge supply chain disciplines knowledge acquisition and use so that the company invests in knowledge intentionally, with a well-defined use in mind, instead of making broad investments in a grab-bag of knowledge.

Benefits of the Knowledge Supply Chain Approach

Well-managed knowledge supply chains can provide more effective and efficient access to knowledge, reduced technology development and deployment cycles, improved ROI on enterprise's knowledge investment, reduced waste in knowledge-acquisition process, and increased workforce and workplace functionality.

The actual benefits depend on the enterprise's ability to work with its appropriate knowledge supply chain partners to develop the appropriate cost, time, quality, and functionality goals. A knowledge supply chain, like a material supply chain, should provide reductions in costs and delivery times, as well as increased functionality and higher quality. These benefits can only come when the knowledge user sets high expectations, then pulls on the system to deliver the results that meet those expectations.

The benefits that apply to the larger, national system are harder to quantify, because they are a function of the aggregate set of knowledge supply chain actions taken by individuals, enterprises, academia, and communities. It is important to recognize these systemic benefits, however, to demonstrate that benefits from knowledge supply chains apply to more than just the enterprises that use them. The American Society for Training and Development (ASTD) estimates that $25 billion of the $150 billion spent by industry on training in 1991was spent on remedial training, training that had to be done before the employees could accept and use new knowledge. Even the nation's best research universities make significant investments in remedial education. In terms familiar to a material supply chain, that's a lot of *rework*.

The underlying need is to manage the knowledge enterprise better so that rework is minimized. A lot of remedial work is engendered by the lack of educational standards and the lack of uniformity when standards exist. Some academic institutions, even public K–12 schools, are adopting Total Quality Management (TQM) or other quality initiatives similar to those exhibited in well-managed material supply chains.

➤ Implementing Knowledge Supply Chains

Knowledge supply chains are tools to integrate the knowledge enterprise better. Knowledge supply chains, like product supply chains, do not have to be built from the ground up. Most entities already exist, although they are often isolated. The value of knowledge supply chains, like physical supply chains, is their focus on the specific need and on those partners who can contribute to meeting it. Focused knowledge supply chains require only the agreement and participation of those contributing to the specific area of knowledge.

1. *Specify the type of knowledge required to meet a defined need.*
   The better the need is defined, the better the expectation that a knowledge supplier can meet the need efficiently. "We need

to understand Enterprise Resource Planning" is likely to evoke broad and vague responses. "How can we integrate the factory systems we use in Sao Paulo, Nogales, and Riga with the corporate system in El Paso to accurately reflect a project's engineering costs?" will narrow the knowledge search.

2. *Build a linkage between knowledge supplier and user that is well defined.* Having defined a specific need, your company needs to find a primary information supplier expert in the type of knowledge specified. This may be a technology transfer institute, a consultant, a university's engineering or business school—or maybe another company. Early on, you will want to qualify knowledge suppliers as you would material suppliers, evaluating them on their expertise, reliability, and integrity. An important caveat in building a knowledge supply chain is that alternative knowledge sources often contribute from more points of view than any single source can.

3. *Compensate for the inhibitors that impact a knowledge supply chain.* Since the concept of knowledge as a commodity that can be subjected to a supply chain discipline is not a familiar one, the partners in the supply chain will need to overcome:

   —The natural human reluctance to think that the acquisition and delivery of useful knowledge can be managed and the lack of first-hand experience in the knowledge sector with the supply chain concept.

   —Our collective inexperience in specifying, quantifying, valuing, and protecting knowledge, and our limited abilities to measure the flow of knowledge or to know when the knowledge transfer is complete.

   —The difficulties in characterizing transition points from one link in the supply chain to the next.

   —The investment of time required to develop the new processes and measurements implicit in the knowledge supply chain concept.

   —The difficulties in balancing open sharing of knowledge with proprietary rights and values.

4. *Apply supply chain principles.*

   —Integrate process with purpose. The knowledge supply chain must have a clear, shared, vision or objective that provides a common purpose for all of the supply chain partners. It must have an equally clear understanding of the roles of the partners.

—Focus on the ultimate customer. The ultimate customer is that customer who provides the pull and purpose that unifies the process, establishes standards, and measures results. Focus on the ultimate customer forces the system to operate to meet a common and measurable objective.

—Develop processes that bring benefits to each partner. A successful and sustainable knowledge supply chain is one that yields benefits for all the participants. This can be a complicated challenge because of the mix of motivations among the people, the companies, and the not-for-profit entities in the knowledge enterprise.

—Ensure a free flow of information and knowledge. The partners in the knowledge enterprise must operate with mutual understanding, respect, and trust. The knowledge users and suppliers must engage in a dialog through which the suppliers will gain an understanding of the user's needs and of the context for those needs. *There must be a balance between the needs of the company to protect its intellectual property rights for competitive advantage and the demands of academic freedom and academia's public role in doing basic research.* The potential conflicts of interest as knowledge makes the transition from pre-competitive to competitive applications also must be managed.

—Measure results. The knowledge enterprise must have metrics for the knowledge processes, balancing objectives for the cost, time, quality, and functionality of the knowledge it delivers (see Figure 15.4). Table 15.2 provides representative

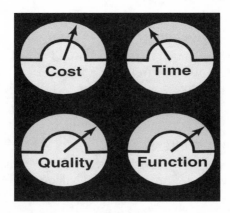

Figure 15.4 Balanced Metrics for the Knowledge Enterprise

Table 15.2   Representative Knowledge Supply Metrics

Perspective	People-Embedded Knowledge	Explicit Knowledge
Cost	Training cost/hire	R&D ROI
	Skill content/job level	Education and training ROI
	Restructuring/reorganization costs	Cost/unit of education
		ROI of company-funded academic R&D
Time	Hiring cycle time	Knowledge acquisition cycle time —> "just-in-time knowledge"
	Learning curve for routine use of a unit of knowledge	
	Time to match need with person	Access time for knowledge related to the requested knowledge
Quality	Amount of remedial training	Number of pre-qualified knowledge suppliers
	Individual performance ratings	
	New hires who exceed expectations	Knowledge suppliers who exceed expectations
Functionality	Range of competencies/job level	Accuracy in meeting real customer needs
	Certifiable skills	
	Skills of entry level employees	Number of contributing knowledge suppliers
	Average time to adapt to new job requirements	Scope of accessible knowledge base

examples of quantifiable results from each of the perspectives. One benefit of establishing metrics and a measurement process for the four perspectives is to gain guidance on the weaknesses of the existing knowledge supply chain and on how and where it should be expanded.

5. *Expand the chain into a web including additional tiers of knowledge suppliers.* A simple chain may meet a narrowly defined need, but generally the linked needs for knowledge will expand beyond the capabilities of a single or a few knowledge suppliers. That's the time to expand the knowledge supply chain horizontally and vertically, growing in scope and depth. The scope must be wide enough to include all relevant providers and users that will add to the knowledge's value for the ultimate customer. The depth will include the research centers that generate the new knowledge, the academic and

commercial teaching centers that transform and distribute the knowledge, the customers who apply that knowledge, and the end user.

6. *Institutionalize the supply web to meet future needs.* Knowledge supply chains may exist for only one transaction—once the specific need for knowledge is met, they disband. Alternatively, once a knowledge supply chain or web is developed and the partners gain experience with one another, they may be used for multiple transactions involving families of related knowledge.

■ THE KNOWLEDGE-READY WORKFORCE

The NGM Report says, "Knowledge is about *action*. Knowledge is information put to productive use." It is the workforce who use knowledge for productive use. Nonaka and Takeuchi, in their book, *The Knowledge-Creating Company,* say that,

> *Knowledge creation is anchored in the very important assumption that human knowledge is created and expanded through the social interaction between tacit knowledge and explicit knowledge. The quintessential knowledge-creation process takes place when tacit knowledge is converted into explicit knowledge, i.e., when our hunches, perceptions, mental models, beliefs, and experiences are converted to something that can be communicated and transmitted in formal and systematic language.*[3]

This blending of the explicit knowledge found in books and manuals with the tacit knowledge found in peoples' heads is what leads to decision and action. Your company will thrive if your workforce does this blending better than the competition. Your company needs systems that facilitate the blending. These systems should recognize the intellectual capabilities of the workforce as part of the company's asset base.

The effect is that everyone in the extended enterprise is both a knowledge supplier and a knowledge worker, because all of them use their heads as well as their hands. We will explore this point further in Chapter 16. What people do causes them to integrate their existing base of tacit knowledge with new, explicit knowledge. This "knowledge mixing" creates new tacit knowledge for the individual. If the new tacit knowledge is captured in explicit terms, it can be shared across the extended enterprise and used in the formation of even more new knowledge.

Given that the individual is the key partner in any knowledge process, it is important that the principles of supply chain management apply to him or her as well as to all the organizational partners. Every individual involved should:

➤ Understand how they fit into the larger, integrated knowledge process.

➤ Operate with a set of unifying goals focused on the ultimate customer.

➤ Expect to contribute to, and ultimately benefit from, the success of the integrated enterprise.

➤ Be an integral part of the continuous, free flow of information and knowledge.

➤ Have access to the measured results.

These are classic people-management practices. Unfortunately, all too often the individual gets lost as attention shifts to the mega-process of integrating diverse institutions and organizations. The workforce will need an educational paradigm that prepares them to assimilate and apply knowledge quickly. Their formal education beyond basic skills and knowledge content should emphasize how to acquire and then use knowledge. The culture of lifelong learning should include techniques for problem solving under time pressures and should distinguish between the corporate value of learning for an immediate application and the societal value of learning for learning's sake.

■ CONCURRENT EDUCATION

It is a broad generality that primary school students are filled with knowledge that is no more current than about 30 years. Middle-school students fare a bit better with some knowledge as new as 25 years. High school students are probably five years more current, community college students a bit more so, and undergraduate majors current as of a decade ago. No wonder there is such a need for lifelong learning.

Unfortunately, almost no new knowledge is given students until the very end of their education. Yet, the new knowledge is what can give a company its competitive advantage. Industry's education and training programs should be focused on today's needs and on preparations for tomorrow's work. If, as is typical in the semiconductor industry, almost all the knowledge content of the work is less than 20 years old, most entry-level workers from community colleges don't have a knowledge base to connect with the realities of the workplace.

One way to correct this deficiency is to better link new knowledge with the knowledge delivery system so that it is taught concurrently at all levels. One concrete example of this is in the semiconductor industry where major manufacturers like Intel are teaming with community colleges to provide students with the education they need to become productive quickly.

The output of the knowledge enterprise is the application of knowledge by the entire workforce, at all levels, with the specific purpose of providing the products and services that satisfy society. The entire knowledge enterprise is responsible for the total process that ensures that those entering or reentering the workforce, at whatever level, are properly qualified for needed positions at all levels. But it is also the responsibility of this total process to ensure that those in the workforce are being efficiently and continuously educated and trained, so they will have the skills to meet the changing needs of the workplace.

■ KNOWLEDGE REPOSITORIES AND DELIVERY TECHNOLOGY

Grey-haired Walt retired five years ago, hung out his shingle as a consultant, did a number of projects for other companies, and was asked to come back and look at his old company's operations. "Oh my goodness gracious!" he said as he realized that the company had forgotten a lot of tricks he thought were Operations 101, things that everyone in the company knew. But he had been the last of the old gang. Tom had a heart attack. Sue was a full-time grandmother. Charlie had a boat out on Puget Sound. Jane had been hired away by a competitor. The new folks were smart, they tried hard for sure, but as problems came up, they let go of most of the stuff Walt and his coworkers had learned through hard experience. In fact, as he looked at operations now, he realized the new crew had gotten into trouble, realized it, and re-invented some of the old procedures—they used a different vocabulary, but the same concepts. Walt's consulting job would have been easy if his gang had just written stuff down where you could find it. As it was, he had to reconstruct all their old ideas before he could see if they would help in solving today's problems. It was good for his consulting business, he guessed, because the project would keep the income coming in. However, since he still had stock in the old company, he wondered about the extra costs the company would have to bear in relearning what it had once been so smart about.

Time after time, we reinvent the wheel. Sometimes we forget about the wheel we invented. Chrysler found a variation on this theme when it shifted to platform teams.[4] The good news was that by assembling teams embodying all the expertise needed to carry through the design and development of a new vehicle platform, Chrysler dramatically reduced time-to-market for increasingly more competitive vehicles. The bad news was that the experts assigned to the teams lost contact with others in Chrysler who shared their expertise. Design glitches in the first generation of the Chrysler LH platform were traced back to things that "fell through the cracks." These glitches probably would not have happened if the platform teams had drawn on the collective knowledge of all of Chrysler's experts.

Chrysler took the glitches seriously and decided to build a shared institutional knowledge base, one that would be accessible to any design engineer, that would be a repository for validated best practices. The Engineering Book of Knowledge (EBOK) is a rigorously managed electronic repository for best practices that have been confirmed by a consensus of Chrysler's experts. It is implemented with Lotus Notes® and a Netscape browser interface and is shared by more than 5,000 users. When completed, it will include 3,800 separate chapters, more than 50 percent of which are in place. Although they are in place, the chapters will never be finished. That is because the EBOK is designed to foster interaction and discussion, the kind of discussion that says: "That may work for compact sedans, but there are problems when you do that with full-size SUVs." It's the kind of discussion that, through a series of shared postings, may result in an even better practice.

Chrysler's EBOK repository isn't something that fills up space on a shelf, forgotten because it is static, hard to use, and not an integral part of the design process. The EBOK is a living electronic document that is dynamic and up-to-date, easily accessible, and a reference point in Chrysler design discipline. Success with the EBOK has led Chrysler to build similar electronic repositories for manufacturing, finance, and sales and marketing knowledge.

Boeing is developing product-oriented knowledge repositories that contain all of the knowledge of a product, including solid models, CAD drawings, and other product and process knowledge, all accessible to whomever in their extended enterprise has a need to know.[5] One aspect of this is Boeing's strategy to replace maintenance manuals, typical of old fashioned paper-based thinking, by compact disks. Each CD can contain a complete manual and quick-search index. In conventional paper form, the primary Aircraft Maintenance Manual for the Boeing 777 takes up 24 binders and requires 10 feet of shelf space. The CDs can easily remastered with updates and distributed automatically, significantly reducing the time users need to spend maintaining the manuals. In addition to the basic Aircraft Maintenance Manual, documents available on CDs will include the manuals for fault reporting, fault isolation, structural repair, wiring and systems schematics, plus the illustrated parts catalog and more. Similar documents for all other in-production and most out-of-production Boeing and Douglas-built airplane models will be prepared.

Smaller companies may not need such an elaborate knowledge repository—so long as the knowledge is readily accessible to everyone who needs it and the on-going investment is made to enter new knowledge and to update existing knowledge. Like any repository in a world that changes, a knowledge repository needs continual care and feeding—the decision to set up a knowledge repository carries with it a commitment to a continuing investment in maintenance.

Many vendors provide "portals" that give organized access to their resources—and the resources of those to whom the portal links—on the Internet. Portals help users frame queries for search engines, organize popular web sites in convenient categories, and lead users toward the answers to their needs. Companies are beginning to develop corporate portals with a web browser-based Home Page as the point of entry to all of the company's knowledge assets. Fully populated corporate portals can reach into the company's structured data resident in database systems and its unstructured information resident in electronic document management systems. Chrysler's EBOK is an example the sort of resource that might be accessed via a portal.

■ EXERCISE

Suppose you are leading an integrated product team responsible for a new product program involving materials and processes not now used by your company. The window of opportunity for the product is such that you'll have to get it into production in half the time the company allotted for its last new product program. Develop an acquisition and education plan for the knowledge you will need. Among the questions you should answer are:

➤ How will you determine your knowledge needs?

➤ What knowledge sources do you have available to you that are easy to access?

➤ How will you avoid knowledge-acquisition and education-creating delays in your program?

➤ What should the important elements in your knowledge management plan be?

➤ How will you ensure that your workforce can use the knowledge?

➤ What mechanisms do you have in place to qualify knowledge providers?

➤ What mechanisms do you have in place, or need to put in place, to evaluate the knowledge they provide?

■ NOTES

1. Lester C. Thurow, *The Future of Capitalism: How Today's Economic Forces Shape Tomorrow's World* (New York: William Morrow, 1996).
2. Peter F. Drucker, *Managing in a Time of Great Change* (New York: Truman Talley Books/Dutton, 1995).
3. Ikujiro Nonaka and Hirotaka Takeuchi, *The Knowledge-Creating Company: How Japanese Companies Create the Dynamics of Innovation* (New York: Oxford University Press, 1995).
4. Warren Karlenzeig, "Chrysler's New Know-Mobiles," *Knowledge Management,* vol. 2, no. 5, (May 1999) pp. 58–66.
5. Boeing Company Press Releases, 1999.

Chapter

Working in the
NGM Company

TUESDAY, 1:30 PM: A DIFFERENT WORKFORCE

The stage had been set. You'd spent all day Monday on Rapid Product and Process Realization. You'd spent all this morning on Knowledge Processes. Now you would turn your attention to people.

You are a product of the post-World War II era. You'd had the typical path. You'd finished your education, did a tour of duty in the Air Force, and went to work at BAI. When you joined BAI, you expected to work there the rest of your life. It turned out that way, too. You'd been forced to grow and change, just as BAI has grown and changed. The people around you have been forced to grow and change, too. Some thrived on change. Others couldn't handle it and fell by the wayside.

You are hoping the afternoon's presentations will give you some insights into the ways people will have to grow and change in the future—and tell you what BAI's role should be helping people make the changes.

■ PRESSURES ON THE NGM WORKPLACE

Three needs will dominate the workplace for next generation manufacturing:

304

1. The need to employ the best knowledge for all decisions, whether they are strategic decisions, product decisions, or operational decisions in the manufacturing cell or within business processes.

2. The need for a rapid response once a customer need has been articulated.

3. The need to meet tighter and tighter cost constraints forced by unremitting global competition.

Meeting these needs will lead to new ways to organize the workplace and to new understandings of the nature of work, management, leadership, and employment. In the NGM company, employees will complete the transition from being physical assets to knowledge assets, from subservience to partnership.

The dynamics and uncertainty of the future will continually push the responsiveness, flexibility, and quickness of the company's workforce. Companies will continually adjust the size and skill sets of their workforce to remain competitive. They will be forced to do so by external and internal partnerships, the requirements for structure and control in global-extended enterprises, and the benefits of rapidly changing technologies.

At the same time, the need for speed and innovation requires companies to use and reward the knowledge effort of all its employees.

The market imperative of rapid responses with the right products in the right places at the right times, combined with emerging information technologies, will force the further extrapolation of today's trends toward team-based organizations. Knowledge retrieval and delivery technology will make it possible to form teams combining human and machine intelligence in natural ways, permitting greater fluidity among the enterprise's work units. Responding to these fundamentally new workforce and workplace conditions requires community-based understanding of employment policies—a new social contract—that strengthen individual participation and security, in the firm, in the extended enterprise, or through lifetime employability.

■ IMPACTS ON PEOPLE

Think of the implications of the ways in which people now work. Make no mistake about it. The impact of next generation manufacturing can have very painful and destructive effects on people who are unprepared intellectually or emotionally for the new paradigms.

The Silicon Valley high-tech industry is an *avant garde* for next generation manufacturing, taking many of the trends to the extreme. As a result, it provides excellent examples of best practices likely to become pervasive. But it also provides a laboratory in which to examine some of the challenges for the workforce.

The nucleus of people who formed Netscape took *discretionary effort* to the extreme, driven by the vision of World Wide Web and of the establishment of new ways to do commerce. They worked with passion and commitment, living at work for days at a time. The team was wildly successful, establishing a multibillion dollar business within five years of the first academic version of the web browser—and giving Netscape's employees opportunities to gain significant wealth.

Within a short time, though, Netscape ceased to exist as an independent company. The team and the vision changed. Many of the early employees of Netscape have left with monetary rewards, but exhausted. People who have gone through the Netscape or similar experiences often say that they are going to take six months off to recover before they go to something new. Others have simply taken their wealth and moved to other ways of life, often no longer using their high-tech expertise.

Many Silicon Valley manufacturing companies have used the discretionary efforts of their employees to perform Herculean tasks. The ambitious "can do" spirit of many companies has led them to accept work whenever they could, often with incredibly tight deadlines, even if it led to surges in workload for which they had insufficient capacity. Common ways to meet the surge are to hire contract workers to work within their facilities, to hire contract workers to work outside their facilities, and to use company employees who literally "moonlight" by taking piecework home. It's a model used by many immigrant families to bootstrap themselves into the American dream, but it's not without physical and psychological costs.[1]

An astute observer of attempts to humanize the Silicon Valley workplace writes that "the now-familiar cycle of the company which is 'employee-oriented' typically starts out by placing the ultimate premium on what the employee can give up to the common goal of short-term wealth."[2] Employees engage in fast-paced, long-hour work weeks that are powered mostly by adrenalin, but always working under the threat of "free-and-easy" downsizing when the company has to react to market trends. Employees are forced to become entrepreneurs, not only on behalf of the company's products but also to market their own talents. This observer has studied ways to keep key employees in the high-tech world, finding that often these employees are treated as a commodity by the people who make decisions about human resources. "The workplace has gotten less conducive to feeding the needs for growth and spirit of the individual than it was not too long ago."

And since companies will be less able to meet the needs for workforce preparation or to give people the emotional support they once took for granted in the workplace, the educational system and communities will have to take more activist roles.

People will be faced with continuous change. They will feel the insecurity of continuous uncertainty. Companies that give teams of employees autonomy will also depend on them to "dig deep" out of self-motivation, to exceed their commitments, and to respond with whatever extra efforts are required to overcome new conditions. This is *discretionary effort,* the effort that goes well beyond the minimum needed just to hold on to a job.

Teaming requires the sharing of power. Managers will share power while ensuring the team's commitments are met, even if that means they become followers much of the time. Employees used to being followers may assume unfamiliar leadership roles and the discomfort of added responsibility.

Each change that happens will require some learning by all employees. *Life-long learning* will be required if employees are to overcome rapid obsolescence of skills. The whole knowledge enterprise—individuals, companies, and even communities—will share responsibility for this learning. Individuals will have to take the initiative to acquire for themselves what companies do not provide.

Just as the walls between functions are breaking down, the walls between segments of the workforce are breaking down. Traditionally, we've treated the people as either managers or workers, two very different species, subjected to different laws, rewarded in different reward structures. As with most traditions, there were once good reasons for the separation. Now the hard-line distinction between managers and workers can be an impediment. The distinction is being blurred by the needs for quick, competitive responses. The future workforce will be an integrated body where everyone is both labor and management; everyone provides both knowledge and leadership; everyone is both a leader and a follower; and everyone is responsible for both productivity and innovation. In this new workforce, everyone will "own" responsibility and take risks for providing the products, services, and results that satisfy all the enterprise's stakeholders. Ownership will include sharing in the rewards that result from meeting customer and stakeholder needs.

NGM companies will be inherently less stable than their predecessors because manufacturing enterprises will be tied to transitory market opportunities. Only rarely will companies be able to offer lifetime employment. The burden of workforce preparation for the uncertain workplace inevitably will have to be shared by companies, individual workers, and public institutions.

Among the shared responsibilities are:

➤ *Career management.* Workers (a term which as used here includes everyone in the enterprise, even managers and executives) will have to be entrepreneurs. They will each have to identify, develop, and market their personal core competencies. Their personal security will come from their employability, not their present employment.

➤ *Education and life-long learning.* While companies may continue to educate workers on the company-specific processes and technologies, they will expect a high level of knowledge in the workforce. There is a trend toward requiring certification of skills (individual core competencies). Much of the knowledge that companies will require will have to be gained at the workers' initiative and provided by public institutions (schools and colleges) and through public access (the Internet).

➤ *Lifetime resource planning.* Given instability in employment, workers will have to take control of their long-term financial (and lifestyle) planning. There will have to be greater portability of retirement savings instruments and other benefits.

➤ *Communications and culture.* As the familiar hierarchical model of bosses directing employees shifts to one of teams of specialists working together to meet shared goals, all workers will have to communicate well, with clarity and honesty, and develop a culture of trust-based relationships. Some companies may be strong enough to do this autonomously, but most will need societal institutional support.

■ KEY CONCERNS FOR HUMAN RESOURCE MANAGEMENT

The issues driving the current and future workforce are unclear, imprecise, and subject to rapid change. Companies, through their workforces, must respond by being flexible and creative, adapting innovatively to the obstacles encountered. Few things will remain constant—and much will be ever changing. New obstacles mean new strategies, new processes, and new solutions.

➤ **Responding to Uncertainty**

People who have never had to do much changing often have difficulty with change. If your father worked for Buick City in Flint or at IBM in Poughkeepsie or at Convair in San Diego for 40 years before retiring, and you worked there for 20, you would not be well-prepared for the shocks that came when Buick lost market share, when CMOS technology rendered the Poughkeepsie plant's high-end processor competence irrelevant, or when the Cold War ended and Southern California's

---

THE KALMAR EXPERIENCE

An example of the effects of change on those who are unprepared for it was the experience of UAW workers in Volvo's Kalmar plant in 1980. Kalmar was the first Volvo plant to assemble cars using small teams of people. The teams were cross-trained so that they could assemble cars even if a team member were missing. This early experiment in teaming was a success. Productivity and morale both were higher than in Volvo's traditional plants.

The United Auto Workers sent U.S. workers to gain experience in this different way to assemble cars, placing UAW workers in the Kalmar workforce. The workers chosen to go to Kalmar were experienced workers from Big Three assembly plants. They had worked on prescribed tasks and had little need for complex decision making. One unexpected result of their working in the Kalmar plant was a high incidence of stomach ulcers, attributed to the UAW workers' difficulty in adjusting to the free flow, problem-solving environment. These workers were unprepared for the day-to-day uncertainty in their jobs.

defense industry shriveled up. Change, when you haven't any practice, when you don't have coping skills, is painful, even devastating.

There is a certain skill in responding to the unknown. As the pace of change increases, this type of skill must pervade manufacturing enterprise—at all levels and in all functions—since change impacts all aspects of companies. The dynamics and uncertainty of the future will continually demand, stretch, and test the responsiveness, flexibility, and quickness of the workforce. The need for perpetual speed and innovation compels companies to use and reward the creativity, knowledge, and leadership efforts of *all* its employees.

➤ The Workforce Is Global

Workforces across the world are getting better and better. In many countries, the labor supply's low cost has provided competitive advantage, in spite of low skills and knowledge. In country after country, however, the quality of available skills and knowledge has improved to the point where the quality of the labor supply is competitive with the highly skilled workforce in developed countries.

Growing productivity in global labor pools will continually cause jobs at higher skill levels to shift to developing regions. All economies will try to continually move their general workforces up the skill ladder to obtain growth in individual quality of life and sustained company and community health—with increased security for all. Every nation will seek to leverage their human and technology resource strengths to compete with innovation, high quality, and productivity.

It is inevitable that more opportunities at higher skill levels will be available in developing countries. There will come a time when skill and knowledge will no longer be a discriminator among countries. Currently, developing regions are producing more highly skilled workers than they can employ. These people emigrate to the developed regions that can reward their talents. The demand for them drove the United States' approval for 150,000 additional visas for high-tech workers in 1999—even as the majority of high school students in Silicon Valley turned away from the educational opportunities that would lead to high-tech careers. A reverse "brain drain" can be expected as economic opportunities become more enticing elsewhere.

➤ Core Competencies versus Core Rigidities

Companies striving to eliminate waste and improve profit margins work hard to identify their core competencies. Companies build on the existing competency base and, ideally, each project they undertake extends that base to a higher level. Knowledge begets more knowledge, and skills more skills. As a company becomes known for its particular strengths, it attracts the best people in those disciplines. Eventually, the company's core competencies dominate all its product and process development projects.

If your company, in 1998, took the lead in e-commerce technologies and built its five-year strategic plan around that core competency, it is probably safe. A core competency can be an asset. But a core competency can be dysfunctional if it blocks consideration of potentially disruptive innovation. For example, if in 1988, you put all your energy into developing better processes for making the vinyl disks for music recordings, you would have been unprepared for the phenomenal growth of compact disks. Because new development projects represent a firm's response to market changes, they are the focal point for the tension between innovation and organizational status quo. A competency that is viewed as a strength can result in a weakened company.

Similarly, people will be valued for their core competencies—for their abilities to get things done. People who have a specialized ability take pride in it—to the point that their capability infuses their identity. It is hard to look past your existing core competencies to the time when you can no longer make contributions of value with them. It is even harder to find yourself fully invested in competencies the enterprise can no longer use. People in charge of their own careers must constantly be aware of their core capabilities and emerging core rigidities[3]—and act to improve or renew existing competencies, and to build the foundation for new ones.

➤ **Discretionary Effort**

Most job descriptions and performance plans, even procedure manuals, provide caricatures of real work. They describe the minimum that is needed to get the job done, giving more or less detail on how to do the job. When people are treated as physical assets—"we need a pair of hands in the process, so I guess we have to hire someone"—they tend to do just the minimum. Since they aren't being paid to think, they don't. Since they haven't much ownership in the end product, they don't have much motivation to do more than the minimum. They just do what they are told—well enough to continue getting paid. But, most people can do much more than the minimum. They can add value by finding ways to do their jobs better, faster, cheaper. They can add value by solving problems when they first appear. They can add value with independent, although disciplined, thoughts, decisions, and actions. This extra effort is *discretionary effort,* the effort that a motivated individual contributes beyond the minimum required just to do a job.

About 20 percent of the workforce in the United States are so strongly motivated that they do all that they can. When these people work with like-minded colleagues—as in Johnson Controls' teams—they are excited about their work and out-produce their competitors. But industry surveys show that nearly half the workers in the United States do no more than the minimum they must to keep their jobs. American workers say that they could nearly double their productivity if they did all that they could instead of just the minimum. The difference is a rough measure of the workers' perceptions of the productivity gains—nearly 100 percent—that can come if their discretionary efforts are tapped. Three-quarters of the workforce say they would be willing to give more discretionary effort if their companies provided a stronger vision and better leadership.[4]

There is anecdotal evidence that the gains can be far greater than a doubling of productivity if the workforce takes on the levels of energy, interdependence, and commitment that are characteristic of a Silicon Valley start-up. The new mega-companies—Microsoft, Sun Microsystems, Cisco Systems, Oracle, and so forth—all have cultures that have successfully tapped into discretionary effort. These are not easy places in which to work. There is significant pressure, much of it generated internally by the strong self-motivations of people. The people in these companies succeed when they believe in their work and share in their company's success. This type of discretionary effort will be the norm in successful NGM enterprises.

Motivating increased discretionary effort will require high-quality thinking, understanding, wise actions, and empathy for others. This cannot be done without an unprecedented amount of trust and a sense of personal and professional security—at a time when trust and job and career security among much of the workforce seem very fragile.

➤ Leadership and Followership

A competitive extended NGM enterprise requires great leadership—at all levels, from the smallest temporary team, through foremen, line management and staffs, the corporate executives. Discretionary effort has been characterized in the NGM Report "as a team sport where the team members leverage each other's leadership and extra effort."

The definition of leadership is changing. In traditional companies, *leadership* is often a synonym for *management.* Many NGM companies will be a network of core competencies that are embodied in individuals and small teams. In a knowledge-based competition, these people and teams will be the legitimate leaders for their competencies. Some will contribute leadership only in their narrow specialty or by taking the initiative in accomplishing their particular tasks. Others will assume a broader technical and motivational leadership role within the team. Management may be the particular competence contributed by a few team members, but leadership will be shared by everyone on the team.

At the same time the successful NGM company needs great leadership, it will require just as great followership—informed followership that recognizes and follows the leader for specific competencies. Leadership and followership will flow dynamically within a team, a company, or an enterprise—always seeking the best decisions, the most effective actions, with the smallest overheads. One moment the team leader, the supervisor, the manager, will be a follower of the person or team with the specialized competence that is important. The next moment, leadership will shift to another team member. The entire workforce—including executives and managers—will have to become comfortable with the transitory and reciprocal nature of their power and influence.

The implied change in corporate culture can be devastating for those rooted in tradition. The kind of leadership that will have to be practiced by everyone, from the most junior team member to senior executives, can be complex and conflicting. As leadership is shared, traditional managers may feel threatened. The values and processes of past decades may feel fragile and ineffective. Followers will no longer follow in the way they once did.

The Evolution of Leadership on the Factory Floor

The roles and responsibilities of the effective factory foreman illustrate the evolution of leadership responsibilities for all in management and supervisory positions. It isn't easy to operate a factory efficiently, in control, meeting shipping schedules, all at a profit. It's especially tough when the factory is in a continual state of change. The foreman stands at the balance-point between controlled production and innovation. Foremen simultaneously must be the immediate supervisors of ongoing, profit-making operations and must replace the old with the new.

Foremen must supervise the move from established core competencies (and rigidities) to new, potentially risky ones. The foreman stands where "the rubber meets the road." If he or she does the job right, productivity and profits go up—the company and the workforce benefit. If things don't work, it is the people whom the foreman leads who are penalized—their income, even their jobs, are at risk. Getting innovation right is very personal at this level.

Traditionally, foremen have had unique status. They have known all the competencies needed for the jobs their workers do. They have been directors, telling workers what to do, and coaches, helping less knowledgeable workers to do their jobs better. Foremen have been the crisis solver, expected to know more about the technical problems of the domain—and their solutions—than anyone else. They have been motivators, usually indirectly as transmitters of the company's motivational mix of reward and fear. Occasionally they have been spare laborers, pitching in to help clear bottlenecks.

With change and innovation, many of a foreman's core competencies become core rigidities. Few people can maintain mastery over all the changes and innovations that are likely to hit the NGM factory floor. Tomorrow's foreman will continue as "the balance-point between controlled production and innovation," with the authority and responsibility to direct a group of subordinates. But the foreman will function within the group as a team member. The foreman's role will be interfacing with the company's management and ensuring that everyone else's core competencies are effectively blended so that the teams meet their cost, time, and quality commitments. The new foreman will have to defer to the competence of their team members. Foremen will have to listen, making judgments on when to trust, when to question. Their coaching will be motivational, not instructional. They will have to frame problems so that others find solutions.

Even the foreman's traditional role as disciplinarian will be shared across the team, as team members share ownership for meeting team objectives. Teams will use self-assessment and 360 degree evaluations to understand their group and individual performances. The employee whose work or behavior threatens achievement of the goals will be disciplined by the team, rather than the management chain.

In some cases, team members will assume the roles of the new foremen in self-organized, self-directed teams. The roles of interfacing with the rest of the company and of ensuring the commitments are met won't go away, but they will be shared by team members.

Executive Leadership

Executives, as we discussed in Chapter 5, will always be a special breed of team members, holding the responsibility to set the company's vision, guide its strategies, and shape its progress. Kim Clark, Dean of the Harvard Business School, has outlined six essential attributes of executive leadership:[5]

1. *Global perspective.* A global perspective includes an appreciation of the differences—and the similarities—of the world's cultures. Integration of global enterprises requires respecting important cultural differences, while using commonalities as the basis for enterprise-wide systems. The authors believe this principle just as true of the executive's need to understand the company's diverse workforce and functional cultures.

2. *Entrepreneurial spirit.* Clark is quoted as saying it's "the ability to see value where others can't" and then to put into place the resources—from inside and outside the company—to realize the value.

3. *Technical literacy.* Generic general management isn't enough. Leaders don't need to be experts in all the technical details of their industry and their company. They do need to know the key concepts, the key attributes, and the key issues—so that they can ask the key questions and make the key judgments that will drive their companies ahead.

4. *Enterprise-design capability.* Executives are going to have to design and redesign enterprises, not just their companies, but the extended enterprises in which they work. And then they have to put together the new teams that can manage and execute the new design.

5. *Leader as teacher.* In the press of continual transformation, leaders can't just do—and expect their people to follow. They have to teach their employees today's reality, preparing them for tomorrow's.

6. *Fundamental values.* Leaders of NGM companies need fundamental values: a code of ethical behavior, integrity and trustworthiness, respect for the value and dignity of other people, and a sense of personal responsibility.

➤ Teaming and Partnering

Teams will be the primary building blocks of NGM enterprises. The teams will add more value—competing better, providing higher profits—than the same set of individual contributors would add in an old-style company. Teams will create ideas and products that no individual could achieve. Teams learn faster than individuals do. They solve problems faster. They get results faster.

Well, maybe. Teams fail, too. Typical reasons given for the failure of teams are:[6]

➤ The team's goals were unclear—if you don't know where you are going, it's even harder for a group to get there.

➤ The objectives shifted and the team didn't keep up with the shifts. Some members never got the word at all, so they worked on the wrong things.

➤ There were no mechanisms to hold the team and its members accountable.

➤ The team didn't have management's support—the rest of the enterprise didn't take them seriously.

➤ There wasn't a clarity of role—the team members didn't understand what each was supposed to do.

➤ The leadership was ineffective—nobody led when leadership was needed, or if they did, they led in wrong direction.

➤ The team was a low priority activity—it gave the results that were expected: none!

➤ There were no incentives for teaming—no team-based pay or other rewards.

The NGM company will have to prepare itself and its workforce for successful teaming. Teaming is sharing power and responsibility in a small group. Partnering is teaming among larger groups and organizations. Sharing power is hard. If we have the power, we are confident that we'll do the right things with it. But if we share it, we have to trust that the other person will use the power as effectively as we could. We have no choice, though. Global competition requires better responsiveness and performance than one person can achieve—simply because no one person can master all the minute details quickly enough to make all the decisions in time.

Teaming, partnering, and other group participatory activities are central for next generation manufacturing—but these kinds of activities are generally not well understood. Teaming when all the team members work in the same room requires much. Virtual teaming when team members are spread around the world requires even more. Much is written about global enterprises involving workforces and workplaces from very different cultures and political/legal/economic environments. But the terms—teaming, participation, partnerships—have different and sometimes contradictory meanings in different settings.

Effective teams and partnerships exhibit four qualities:[7]

1. *Purpose.* Each team member or partner will have a clear understanding of his or her own purpose and then will engage in sufficient dialogue with the others to gain a clear understanding of their common objective.

2. *The right to say no.* Each team member is free to assert his or her autonomy by saying "no." They have permission to disagree with prevailing ideas, but they also have the obligation to offer better ones.

3. *Joint accountability.* Each team member or partner assumes responsibility for the team's outcomes and for the current situation. The outcomes and quality of cooperation within a unit are everyone's responsibility.

4. *Honesty and openness.* Each team member or partner will be honest in making their contribution. Each willingly will share all the information each of the others need to achieve the common purpose. Similarly, each partner will be open to the information and suggestions the others provide.

Teaming Skills

Next generation companies must have to have people capable of making little and big decisions all over the world. These people are going to have to know how to work together. Teaming takes skills—communications skills, problem-solving skills, negotiating skills, multicultural skills—and requires throwing away the "not-invented-here" syndrome.

Communications skills will be crucial in the NGM company. Even a company with a single geographic location may include people whose communications are strongly influenced by a dozen or more ethnic and functional cultures. For example, a team in Los Angeles could be made up of people from any of a dozen major cultures, with hundreds of variants. Your company's people will not be able to avoid the complexity of differences in spoken, written, and body language, differences in cultural norms, and so forth. These differences may create confusion and misunderstandings even among those whose nominal first language is American English.

Different cultures understand and implement teams differently. In the United States, there are conflicted attitudes toward teaming.

Traditional education and work appraisal systems have focused on individual accomplishment. So-called *macho* attitudes—"I can do it myself. Real workers don't need help. Besides, I don't have time to work with anyone else."—blossom into "not invented here" rejection of ideas and knowledge from outside the individual.

The company will contain many internal cultural differences besides those their people bring from the outside. There will be the culture of the executive office, the culture of the designers, the culture of the factory floor, the culture of the accountants. To accomplish the company's goals (hopefully their goals, too), all these functional subcultures must act within an overarching company culture.

Organizations and people will have to make the shift from a system of incentives and rewards based only individual contributions to one based on the results achieved by the team. People are going to have to know how they fit into the bigger picture, how their actions contribute to the company's goal, if they are going to make good decisions. Life will pass managers up if they insist on being directive, specifying the work to be done by teams and individuals.

No workforce will embrace teaming unless its most visible leaders demonstrate their own teaming skills. This is clearly a challenge for directive managers whose egos may depend on the power to command and on their place in the hierarchy. Heenan and Bennis[8] write of successful companies—Intel, Microsoft, Yahoo, Cisco Systems, for examples—where the top leadership is team-based, where responsibility is shared. In these companies, successful modeling of teams at the top is a great teacher for everyone in the company.

Trust

In Chapter 11, we wrote of the central role *trust* has in extended enterprises. Trust is absolutely essential for any kind of teaming. The problem is that trust is elusive. It is often visceral. We know it when we feel it, we know it when it isn't there—but we can't say why. Smith and Berg[9] say trust is one of the central dilemmas for modern business: we are continually faced with situations that require us to trust others, but we don't know how to trust them unless we've already developed trust relationships with them.

As individuals, before we make the commitment of trust in others, we want to know how they will respond to us. Will they accept us or will they reject us? Will they accept our weaknesses as well as our strengths, our fears as well as our hopes, our ugliness as well as our beauty? In order to discover how others will respond, however, someone in a group must be willing to expose his or her weak, fearful, and ugly sides.

There are parallels in business. We want to know that our partners will honor their commitments, but not just to the letter of a contractual agreement. We'd like them to act in a spirit of loyalty to achieving common goals. We want partners who will respect our integrity, yet who will help us when we confront unexpected problems. We want partners who will trust us to help them in overcoming their weaknesses. That is, we need partners whom we trust enough to tell them everything that is important about our abilities to perform within the team or the extended enterprise—and we need them to trust us enough to reciprocate.

■ RISK AND REWARD

If the company depends on its teams for speed and innovation, it must use and reward the creativity, knowledge, and leadership effort of all its employees. The company must innovate in all aspects of the business, from developing products and providing services to establishing new business practices, and to managing the complexities of a global enterprise. Leadership, trust, and the discretionary effort are required of everyone if the company is to sustain the needed level of dynamic change.

➤ Innovation, Change, and Risk

Innovation, doing something in a new way, is a leap into the unknown. It usually evokes uncertainty and anxiety. It often brings resistance. Most of us have experienced change efforts that have gone bad—and we don't like the feelings of failure. Yet we must risk failure if we are to change. There are two types of risks involved:

➤ The risks of something really going wrong in the operational world—the objective risks for the company.

➤ The emotional risk of being criticized, feeling foolish, or being responsible for unintended consequences—the personal risks that can threaten one's livelihood.

It is prudent to do an operational risk assessment *before* making any change. The assessment may be implicit—"doesn't look like there are any serious drawbacks—let's do it!"—or it may be a formal, analytical effort. There may not be time to go into great depth. Once the decision is made, especially in the face of an incomplete analysis, it will be up to the team to make it work. Discretionary effort, effort undertaken by the employee and the team on the spot when a problem arises, is essential to mitigate the operational risks during any time of change. No one can foresee all the side effects, all the problems, all the glitches. It is discretionary effort that carries the day, that finds the way around an unexpected obstacle, that provides the creative solution to the incipient problem.

Mitigating personal risk is more subtle. Corporate cultures and management styles in the United States often encourage personification of failure. When something doesn't work, we often look for someone to blame, maybe ourselves, maybe other people. The corporate culture exhibited by the company's visible leadership can go a long way in mitigating personal risk. The goal must be a culture that gives permission to take responsible risks, that honors honest attempts that fail, and that has leadership that intervenes before a person feels that he or she has been hung out to dry.

➤ Rewarding the Workforce

Figure 16.1 shows three dimensions of rewards for the NGM workforce:

1. Team accomplishments
2. Individual accomplishments
3. Intrinsic worth

Every company has its own reward structure, its own way of rewarding its employees. The NGM company needs to include all three

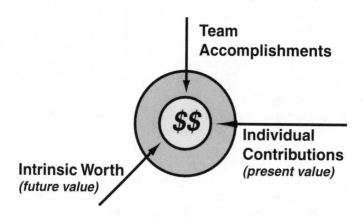

Figure 16.1 Rewarding the NGM Company Employee

of these dimensions in its structure. It's not enough to reward what the team did—what the individual's contribution deserves its reward, too. And it's not enough to reward the immediate past, it's important to recognize the value the employee has in the company's future.

Rewards take many forms, but a central one for all employees is the financial reward—whether they live like hermits giving all the money they earn to the poor, simply try to improve their standard of living, or do in fact measure their self-worth by the income they bring home.

Financial rewards—including the benefits that money buys—are not the only rewards we gain in our work. We may not be able to buy into a company's vision, strategic goals, or operational strategies and choose to leave before our integrity is compromised. We may forgo a higher income in order to work in a team of people whom we value. We may find financial rewards are not enough to compensate for working without trust. The financial rewards of episodic employment may not be adequate to compensate for the loss of security or sense of community.

Other kinds of rewards may be as simple as respect for one's work and one's person, respect given by one's managers, by one's leaders, by one's colleagues, respect conveyed in simple face-to-face communications and in private and public recommendation. Some employees find deep satisfaction in the emotional support, perhaps even spiritual support, that comes from relationships in the workplace.

Companies put a great deal of effort into creating reward structures that blend monetary and nonmonetary rewards. Your company must explain the reward structure to its workforce. You must show the workforce clearly for what they will be rewarded. You must show them that the structure is congruent with what their leaders are telling them. You must show them that the structure has been crafted with respect for their individual interests as well as the company's.

Rewarding Team Accomplishments

If the fundamental unit of the NGM company is the team and if the company counts on the team to take on autonomous responsibilities, then when the team does its job each team member should share in the team's rewards. If the team fails in its responsibilities, then the team will not be rewarded, and there will be no team-based rewards for team members.

Many companies reward accomplishments at the level of business units—still large aggregates of teams. At IBM since the mid-1990s an increasingly greater share—starting at a few percent, now approaching

25 percent or more—of the employees' compensation has come from an annual bonus, sharing in the financial achievements of his or her business unit. As the granularity in a company's organization becomes more apparent, as teams become better defined, it becomes possible to measure and reward contributions made by each of the smaller teams that make up the business units.

As teams become identified with the key idea, or the needed extra effort, or the underlying structure of an identifiable contribution to a company's bottom line, the team will expect a significant piece of that contribution as their reward—whether it is an extra thousand dollars for improving the profit on the company's line of widgets or a few million dollars for providing the guts of a profitable new line of business.

Rewarding Individual Accomplishments

Traditionally, we have tried to tie compensation to the contribution an individual makes. In the days when a worker was a physical commodity, it was easy to assign a value to each job and to pay all the workers doing that job the same amount. Some contracts rewarded loyalty to the company by factoring seniority into the compensation equation.

Companies established pay grades or levels for jobs with varying content. They evaluated each job for its value to the company and assigned it to the appropriate level. Realizing that some people did a given job better than others, they added a merit component so that someone who was really outstanding in a job might make 50 percent more than someone who was doing it in a perfunctory way.

These compensation schemes, even those including merit pay, tended to inhibit creativity, innovation, and discretionary effort. One lesson from the start-up companies has been that people do an enormous amount of discretionary work when individual accomplishment is tightly coupled with reward. Teams are important, but so are individuals. The person who makes the most significant contribution to the team should be appropriately compensated, whether it is the person who worked feverishly alone for weeks to come up with the revolutionary design or the person who held a team together when it looked like it would fail to meet a "make-or-break" deadline.

Rewarding Intrinsic Worth

An individual worker has made a contribution. You pay him or her for that. But you also value that employee for the contributions you think he or she can make in the future. That value is the employee's *intrinsic worth.* You are making an investment in an asset when you pay for intrinsic worth. It's not far-fetched. Increasingly investors value companies not for what last quarter's results were, but for what they can expect the results to be in the future. Your company's future results will depend on your employees' knowledge, creativity, and abilities to make the right discretionary efforts.

Intrinsic worth has been rewarded by seniority pay—presumably the more experience you have, the more valuable you are. Intrinsic worth can be what you know—some companies provide incremental increases each time you take a course or demonstrate another competency.

■ LIFE-LONG LEARNING: A CULTURE OF INQUIRY

One way to think about NGM companies is to consider the transition from a corporate culture based on directive management control to one based on a culture of inquiry and collaborative problem solving. Within hierarchical systems, managers set the goals for themselves and for the entire traditional workforce—and instituted controls to ensure goals were met. A lifetime of setting and achieving goals shaped corporate managers. They came to believe that they were masters of their own destiny—which explains the proliferation of techniques, control systems, and metrics of results rather than processes. Employees were expected to execute management's directives. Together, they represented the *culture of control.*

The *culture of inquiry* encourages a different form of leadership and participation. In this culture, each solved problem is a checkpoint in an on-going process. In this culture, each solved problem creates the next opportunity, the next challenge, the next problem. You may have answered the last question, but now you face a new one. The awareness of living in a never-ending, evolving process shapes leadership and team dynamics. Part of the leadership role is asking the questions that will avoid future difficulties and create larger opportunities.

The NGM culture will nurture perpetual inquiry that questions the status quo, that leads to innovation that borders on the disruptive, that places the company on a different trajectory. This is an ethic that says that dilemmas and paradoxes are symptoms of opportunities. This culture values the process of inquiry as much as it does the finding of specific solutions. This culture also demands the infusion of knowledge at all levels, but especially at the operational ones.

➤ Knowledge Obsolescence

The NGM Report estimates that the combination of new technologies, new customer needs, and changing global economics will result in individual skills obsolescence approaching 20 percent per year. The world's store of knowledge is growing exponentially. The Society of Manufacturing Engineers' Ad Hoc Committee on Life-Long Learning estimates a three-year half-life for engineers.[10] In three years, they will be half as competent as they are today if they don't continue to add to their portfolio of knowledge and skills. The next time your company changes, it will probably use bits and pieces of knowledge that didn't exist when you were in school. So if you are depending only on what you learned in school, you probably won't be in your job for long—the job will move out from under your knowledge base.

A new breed of hybrids is supplanting the manufacturing specialists of the past. Michael J. Termini[11] says that the twenty-first-century manufacturing engineer will be both a business strategist and an operations specialist, able to:

➤ Actively participate in product design and development IPTs.

➤ Advise management on strategic issues as well as technical and process risks.

➤ Design agile material processing, assembly and handling systems.

➤ Specify and obtain capital equipment that will provide competitive advantage.

➤ Develop setup reduction strategies.

➤ Develop preventative and predictive maintenance processes to maximize up time.

➤ Manage hazardous waste disposal.

➤ Administer workplace health and safety processes.

➤ Advise on product liability and other lifecycle issues.

➤ Provide financial and performance data.

➤ Analyze global business and competitive issues.

➤ Act as a mentor, facilitator, and educator of the workforce to encourage cross-training, cross-functional creativity, and teamwork.

➤ Advise on product and process capabilities and limitations.

➤ Advise operations management on logistical considerations as they influence cycle time and product costs.

➤ Oversee production processes and the outside influences that can affect them.

This list speaks to one discipline—manufacturing engineering. But it is typical of the lists that could be written for any functional specialty in the manufacturing enterprise. All are characterized by a need to think strategically as well as tactically, to act as a company owner as well as a technical specialist.

Life-long learning is at the heart of workforce and workplace flexibility. You must be engaged in life-long learning to cope with today's needs and to prepare for tomorrow's. You may find you need to invest as much as a month per year in education and training just to maintain your employability. The NGM company's employees will need the encouragement and support of the teams and of management to take the risks associated with such big investments in learning. New knowledge and new skills allow both the workforce and the workplace to be more flexible. Paradoxically, it is also the flexibility of the workforce and the workplace that facilitates and accelerates the enterprise.

➤ Continuous Individual Learning

The culture of NGM companies will be "learning-focused." The company will be filled with people who are always learning, individually and as groups. The individual, the teams, the companies, and the larger community collectively share the responsibility for continuous learning, but ultimately individuals will have to take the initiative to acquire whatever knowledge they need. That is, individuals will have to carry within themselves the motivation and the ability to learn.

A survey of U.S. manufacturing industry correlated the hours of formal training per plant employee with a number of factors.[12] Productivity per employee, measured by the revenue from products shipped by the plant, increased by a third when employees received more than a week of training. On-time delivery rates increased from 90 percent to 98 percent as training increased. The manufacturing cycle time for companies with more than two weeks of training was half that of companies with a day or less and their annual inventory turn rate was nearly twice that of the companies with the least training. Bottom line: the companies that supported the greater training were better able to meet the time pressures of global competition.

In this age of forced flexibility, an individual's vision must extend beyond his or her current employer. People live now caught between the demands of their current employer for the loyalty that motivates discretionary effort and the realization that changes—often beyond any control of the employer—may put them out of a job. They can't assume that the employer will provide the necessary development and career opportunities that fully satisfy their life-long needs. They must also be loyal to their own development to ensure their employability and ability to contribute beyond one employer and one career. Individuals have to take responsibility for their career development. But that means they need access to affordable education and training—part of the community's infrastructure.

> ### The Learning Environment

Successful life-long learning depends on having a learning environment. A learning environment is one that encourages questions—where "what if we did thus-and-such?" is welcomed and given respectful consideration, where the expenditure of some discretionary effort on the hard work of learning is valued, where experimentation and risk-taking are encouraged.

A learning environment is one in which the leaders take a contagious joy in their own learning and in what their colleagues are learning. A learning environment is one with few preconceptions. Given that real-world problems are usually multidisciplinary, a learning environment encourages learning from any source or discipline that can help. A learning environment is one in which the learner pulls the knowledge that he or she perceives is needed—not a push environment in which others' preconceptions of learning priorities are forced onto the learner.

A learning environment is enhanced when one individual's new learning is transferred to others. But, there is a psychology to transferring knowledge. Attempts to teach the new knowledge may be perceived as an interruption, or as conveying an envied status on the part of the newly minted teacher. Both the newly minted expert and the workplace must be sensitive to how the new learning will be received. The company must internalize and reward shared continual learning as a routine and expected companywide activity. It must give both the new expert and the second-generation learners the support they need.

Leaders in the mainstream of operations often lack the "bandwidth" to consider out-of-the-box alternatives. They are too busy solving the immediate problems to invest time and energy in what might be. But in most companies, there is a cadre of innovators who can establish new business processes. These innovators feel comfortable with change and are generally not afraid to commit offenses against what is considered politically correct in the corporate environment. Successful leaders act as the essential link for balancing of the company's "traditions," on the one hand, and understanding, adapting, and accepting the "new paradigm" on the other. These transitional leaders learn and interpret the "new" for the less visionary population, identify major issues and priorities, create a favorable atmosphere, and propose plausible strategies for reaching common goals. Often, their role diminishes as their innovations are implemented and they turn to the next challenge.

➤ Learning and the Extended Community

Your company won't thrive for long without a healthy extended community. While there are global dimensions to the NGM workplace, your company will build on the resources of its local or regional community. Workers won't thrive for long, either, without a healthy extended community.

Silicon Valley has found that individuals, even companies, can't "go it alone." There needs to be a community infrastructure that supports people who participate in transitory extended enterprises. Leaders from industry, education, and government in Silicon Valley have formed extended community enterprises to create such an infrastructure and institutionalize their community of knowledge.

Sustained regional economic well-being will come from people who are productive and reasonably comfortable with the added responsibilities of being team members and knowledge workers. Education that prepares people to manage their careers and be life-long learners is a primary responsibility of the community infrastructure. In Chapter 15, we discussed the knowledge enterprise, an extended enterprise focused on supplying the knowledge the company needs to thrive. The company, together with other companies in the community, must integrate its resources into the community knowledge enterprise. The community needs to understand the needs of the workforce, and then to deliver on the knowledge needs in a timely, effective, cost-efficient manner. The community will be an essential partner in the process, providing a larger, integrated knowledge process not just for one company, but for all the companies that underpin the community.

It is a reciprocal relationship—no less important or demanding a partnership than the business relationships of an extended manufacturing enterprise. It is a relationship that will demand creative, innovative, and insightful leadership in the community as well as in companies. The community needs the companies for its economic well-being. The companies need the community to build the resources industry needs to be competitive. Chief among those resources is a workforce that has access to knowledge and that can use it.

➤ **The New Partnership for Life-Long Learning**

Communities where manufacturing is an important part of the economy may have to adapt to new models. The consensus model for next generation manufacturing requires a strong societal infrastructure. The model for work in the next generations of industry is one of small teams of knowledgeable people, able to work autonomously with little traditional supervision, able to work together to solve technical, business, and relationship problems, and able to communicate and negotiate with customers and other small teams that may be located anywhere in the world. The model also assumes industry will have access to a continuous supply of new knowledge, delivered in a form that can be put to immediate use. The NGM Project discusses the nature of work in the context of manufacturing. There is consensus, however, that the model is widely applicable in most areas of employment in the public and private sectors.

Education is under great pressure to produce—to provide the skills needed to perform today's jobs. Education is under great pressure to prepare—to provide the skills needed for the future. Often education is stuck with old models of the community that do not meet today's—or the future's—needs. The problem isn't one to be solved just by educators. Industry must play a role in determining the end goals for education. So should government. And so should everyone who benefits from the social and economic activities of the whole community.

Communities should develop an architecture for an agile educational system with feedback loops supporting "near real-time" adaptation to the changing needs of the community. They should also systematize communication throughout the entire community of knowledge, to identify the community's changing knowledge needs, translate them into required competencies, and assess and document worker competencies before and after instruction.

"Near real-time" in this case means that the educational system responds with appropriately educated students when industry needs them. As product and process cycles shrink, "near real-time" means the system may have to respond in weeks or months.

Adaptive Community-Based Educational Systems (ACES)

One model for an integrated partnership among individuals and companies is the Adaptive Community-Based Educational System (ACES) model developed by the Consortium for Advanced Manufacturing—International's Education Advisory Board. (See Figure 16.2.) With the best of intentions, education has focused on partnerships

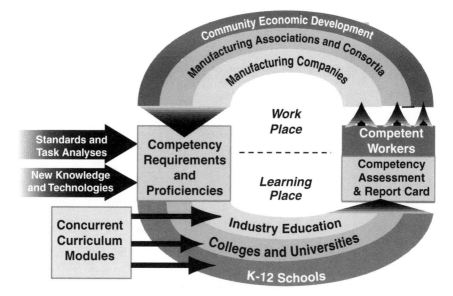

Figure 16.2 ACES

with business using the question, "What can your business give us so we have the resources to do our job better?" and industry's response has been the one-way flow of dollars and other resources. ACES establishes a framework for interdependence and changes the question and response to, "What can we do together today for our community's joint success tomorrow?"

ACES divides the community into two interacting pieces: the *workplace* of employment and the *learning place* of knowledge delivery. For manufacturing, the *workplace* includes:

➤ Large companies that are becoming knowledge-based integrators, the "prime contractors" of extended enterprises.

➤ Small- and medium-sized companies that provide the goods and services used by integrators to build the products that respond to market opportunities.

➤ Increasingly, small- and medium-sized companies that are asked to provide knowledge assets to the extended enterprise. Small companies include entrepreneurial one- or few-person contractors.

➤ The community's leadership for economic development—financial institutions, government and community planners, industry associations, and labor unions.

The *learning place* includes:

➤ K–12 educational systems.

➤ Higher education, including community colleges, baccalaureate colleges, and universities.

➤ Industry education, including in-house proprietary education, educational programs shared across companies, and other forms of life-long learning.

The dotted lines shown in Figure 16.2 within and between the *workplace* and the *learning place* represent the blurring of rigidly defined roles required in a competitive, responsive society. Other important elements of ACES are:

➤ Task analyses and standards that help define the competencies that workers need to be productive.

➤ Sources of new knowledge and new technology that will enhance industrial competitiveness. These include universities (in their research role), technology transfer agencies, and vendors. They also include the many knowledge sources that are electronically accessible.

➤ Curriculum modules to enable learning of the competencies that workers need for employability.

Linking these elements is an iterative process that consists of:

➤ Determining current needs and predicting future needs of the *workplace*.

➤ Mapping the *workplace's* needs to learnable competencies.

➤ Selecting the curriculum modules appropriate for the community's students and workers.

➤ Documenting the student's proficiencies in terms that are applicable and recognized for their value by the *workplace*.

Many communities have implemented elements of ACES. However, there remains a need for well-developed solutions for rapid and systematic identification of *workplace* knowledge needs, mapping the needs to learnable competencies, and assessing and documenting competencies in terms that relate to industry needs. The need is for solutions that can be integrated into a system that accommodates change on a time scale of weeks or months.

CONTINUING EDUCATION IN SILICON VALLEY

An example of some of ACES' features can be found in Silicon Valley's model for continuing education. Much of the continuing education in the high-tech manufacturing environment is conducted by the extension services of neighboring universities. Although the courses are supervised and sometimes taught by academicians, they are more frequently taught by people from industry. This is generally regarded as a successful model, although it might be more successful were there to be more teaming of academics and industry practitioners, not only for the continuing education courses, but also within the universities' core academic courses.

In the Silicon Valley model, the extension courses are taught in off-campus centers conveniently located near the companies where the students are employed. This model is supplemented by distance learning networks—some using public television, some using closed circuit TV, a growing number using the Internet. Integrating technology for knowledge delivery frees students from the constraints of time and space.

ACES is a model that is compatible with the knowledge enterprise and knowledge supply chain introduced in Chapter 15. ACES' integrated view of life-long learning in support of community objectives provides the framework for knowledge supply management.

Alternative Packaging of Education

Many schools are using experiential learning as a way to better prepare students for work. Experiential learning occurs when students learn by solving problems which mimic those seen in the real world. Since real world problems are often multi-disciplinary, experiential training often reinforces learning in several academic disciplines. Because students are more in control of the learning process, they often have a heightened motivation. Experiential learning is often done by teams of students who learn teaming and communications skills in addition to the academic content of the problems they solve.

A needs-based view of education has led many to rethink the packaging and delivery of knowledge. Colleges are exploring developing course modules with fractional course credit. For example, instead of a general three-credit course in electronic circuits, a college might teach the basic circuit theory in a one-credit course, describe a set of general applications of the theory in a second one-credit course, and teach a client company's specific uses of circuits for their products in a third one-credit course.

Distance education technology has proven useful for delivering knowledge in convenient packages to people for whom the overhead of physically congregating in a classroom is a difficult burden. It frees the student from location and synchronicity constraints. The technology need not be sophisticated. One very successful distance learning program—at Mott College in Flint, Michigan—each year graduates more than a thousand students—many of whom live and work hundreds of miles away—with associate's degrees using curricula delivered solely on videotape.

As the Internet becomes even more ubiquitous, its use as an educational medium is growing. Both new and traditional educational institutions are developing curricula for delivery over the Internet. The advantage is that the Internet provides multimedia delivery that can be interactive. Internet education also can facilitate learning on demand. Say you realize that next month you are going to have to design a process for a new class of material—you need to know everything there is to know about those materials and their processing. You may find a materials curriculum module on material properties offered by Penn State, a module on the mechanics of structures made from the materials offered by the University of Leeds, and a module on processes for making structures out of the materials from another company.

The outsourcing of real manufacturing tasks to academic institutions, as at Detroit's FocusHOPE, provides a practical way for students to gain experience with real world applications of knowledge. It may also be a way for companies to gain access to new knowledge quickly and without investment in specialized resources. Such efforts do require close coordination. Inherent differences in motivations and reward systems mean that special efforts must be made to ensure each party receives the value it expects.

College co-op programs are a traditional and effective way of entwining academic and work experience, yielding immediately productive engineers. Similar programs at the community college or even the high school level can yield entry-level employees whose skills fit the current needs of companies. Apprenticeship programs conducted in cooperation with community colleges are another way to marry academic skills and the skills needed for specific tasks.

■ NEW SOCIAL CONTRACTS

We live in communities where there are roles and responsibilities for the individual, the company, and the community. Often these roles and responsibilities are part of the community's tacit knowledge—the set of assumptions that underpin everyone's behavior. They are sometimes codified in law or company policies, but more likely they are implicit. We call the framework established by these assumptions a *social contract*.

Francis Fukuyama writes of *social capital*—the underlying trust that allows businesses, corporations, value chains, and networks to be self-organizing and relatively spontaneous.[13] The NGM enterprise will depend on the leadership and knowledge contribution of every member of its extended workforce. It is much easier for a knowledge worker to learn and innovate continuously if the entire company, the extended enterprise, and the larger community operate with uniform assumptions that enhance its social capital. The NGM report postulates that only enterprises and communities with a high degree of social capital, facilitated by new social contracts, will be able to create and sustain the flexible workforces to compete successfully in the rapidly emerging global economy.

Some argue that the implicit social contract that produced mutual benefits for workers and employers in the past has broken down. They point to the long-term stagnation in employee earnings in the 1990s, corporate re-engineering, downsizing and outsourcing of jobs, increased income inequality, and general worker insecurity and anxiety about the future. In response, some corporate leaders argue that worker expectations and union demands for job security, and calls for corporations taking on increased social responsibility, are incompatible with the realities of today's competition.

A new social contract that meets the needs and expectations of both the workforce and the enterprise of the future is slowly emerging. Efforts by companies, union organizations, communities, and states are beginning to reshape the social support for workers.

➤ The Demise of the Old Social Contract

The implicit social contract in U.S. industry in the three decades following World War II divided the workforce into two distinct groups: production and office workers who were paid on an hourly basis, and professional workers such as managers, engineers, and technical staff who were paid salaries. The former were expected to provide "8 hours' work for 8 hours' pay." They were paid largely for their physical labor and their ability to execute instructions of managers and supervisors. Salaried workers provided the knowledge and information needed to manage the enterprise and design and improve products and processes. Salaried workers—and in some companies like IBM, all workers—were rewarded with long-term job and financial security and protection from cyclical layoffs in return for their loyalty to the goals of the corporation and to the decisions of higher management. This social contract assumed the family unit included two parents of whom the male was the dominant wage earner. The woman's efforts outside of care giving were assumed to be discretionary.

This social contract began to break down in the mid-1970s because of the declining performance of the American economy in international markets, a slowdown in both productivity growth and real wages, a decline in unionization and collective bargaining coverage, a decline in the relative wages of lower level occupations and less educated workers, a more activist investor community, and stricter adherence to free market economics. Global competition, technological innovation, increased pressures from shareholders, and a changing workforce have rendered obsolete many of the principles and practices that guided relationships between employers and employees in prior years. The old assumptions about the family unit have broken down, too, with the rapid rise in single parent households and the growing requirement for two incomes to support the family unit.

During the last two decades, employers, workers, and unions have introduced new practices better suited to contemporary needs. Total quality management, cross-functional product development and work teams, lean and agile manufacturing practices, contingent compensation systems, employee participation and self-managing work teams, labor-management partnerships, and similar programs have significantly improved productivity, quality, and customer service in many organizations. Where a union represents workers, labor-management partnerships have jointly overseen many of these innovations. Where implemented in a systemic fashion, such innovations have paid off in higher productivity and quality.

One of the biggest threats to innovation and sustained commitment to discretionary effort is fear of layoffs or downsizing. Workers don't want to commit their energies to innovations that they think will result in the loss of their jobs. Many workers have seen no increases in real wages even as productivity has improved. International competition and shareholder pressures have diverted the rewards for greater productivity to consumers, as lower prices or increased product/service quality, and to shareholders. The structure of wages has changed so that those with the education and skills demanded by changing technologies and work arrangements are rewarded, while the less educated and those without access to new technologies and work systems are penalized.

➤ Toward a New Social Contract

Global competition is so intense and market forces so dynamic that few honest companies can promise long-term employment security in return for loyalty. Some new arrangement, some new social contract or set of expectations, is needed to replace the old social contract.

Developing a new social contract will require the collective efforts of everyone who influences national policies, organizational policies, and employment practices—workers, employers, labor leaders, business leaders, other labor-market and educational institutions, and government policy-makers. The community must provide the long-term stability that companies no longer can. Innovations in workplace practices in recent years provide a starting point for a new social contract. The NGM Report proposes that such a social contract would include:

1. *Commitment and teamwork in return for a greater voice on the job and greater democracy.* Workers will accept more flexibility in work assignments and the responsibility that comes with teaming. They will expect more opportunities for training, more experience in more jobs, and faster advancement to higher-skilled (and higher-paid) work. Most workplace innovations have been motivated by employer concerns for productivity, quality, and flexibility. While workers value these goals too, they also want concerns such as safety and health, training, benefits, outsourcing, and work/family responsibilities to be addressed, in consultation with them.

2. *Union-management partnerships that oversee and support workplace problem solving in return for union's expanded role in enterprise governance and decision making.* In unionized settings, joint union-management sponsorship and oversight are essential to success of employee participation and related workplace innovations. While these partnerships may take on a variety of forms, their common effects are to broaden union-management discussions to include many issues that in the past were reserved to management. The management process in the future will be one in which power is shared

among different stakeholders. Achieving mutual benefits through negotiations, conflict resolution, and problem solving will therefore become an increasingly important managerial skill.

3. *Open information sharing in return for flexibility to use resources efficiently.* While individual enterprises cannot credibly guarantee long-term employment security, they can be trustworthy. The trust that leads to sustained commitment and discretionary efforts requires open and honest sharing of information on the factors affecting the future of the business, the industry, and the individual's employment prospects. This operates at multiple levels. At the workplace, it may take the form of discussing the relative costs and benefits of outsourcing work versus changing practices to perform the work more competitively within the firm. At the plant level, it may mean discussing ways to organize a new plant or production line to take full advantage of new technologies and work systems. At the corporate level, it may mean sharing information on the competitive position of the firm and market projections that will affect future investments and job opportunities.

4. *Training for employability in return for worker commitment to life-long learning.* If individual firms cannot provide long-term employment, they can help provide training that keeps workers' skills up-to-date and competitive in the external labor market. Since individual firms have little incentive, maybe little ability, to provide this type of training unless they foresee a clear need in the future, they will have to join the entire community of knowledge to make a coordinated effort to offer training for employability. Workers will need to commit to life-long learning.

5. *Pension and benefit portability.* Since individual companies can no longer guarantee long-term employment security, benefits such as pensions and health insurance usually associated with long tenure with a single employer must become more portable. Outside the United States, this is often done at a governmental level, with benefits "banked" through national social programs. In the United States, instruments such as 401(k) plans increasingly substitute for traditional retirement benefits, but there remain significant discontinuities in the portability of health care benefits.

6. *New mediating institutions.* New labor-market institutions are needed that enable firms to find and attract employees with

needed skills and motivation, and provide employees with the ability to enhance their knowledge, earnings, and long-term security as they move to new opportunities within and across organizations. Unions have historically performed this function for American workers, yet they now represent only about 10 percent of the private sector workforce. Educational institutions, staffing agencies, public employment services, professional societies, industry associations, and community-based networks all can play useful roles in meeting the needs of workers and employers.

7. *Employment policies that encourage and support the new contract.* Employment and labor policies must promote adoption and diffusion of innovative policies and partnerships within individual enterprises. They should facilitate labor mobility as companies' needs evolve. In some cases, the required changes are inhibited by current labor and employment laws. The policy and law are still evolving in other cases, for example, that relating to workers who are not permanent employees, but who work directly under contract or are provided to the company under a third-party contract.

The Internet makes it possible to work remotely from home and more and more people are doing so. Early experiments with telecommuting—in the mid-1980s—met with much resistance in large companies worried about management and liability issues. These concerns still exist although there is a growing body of experience in companies that either ignored the concerns or found ways to mitigate them. There still is a need, however, for a better- established set of policies.

In addition, policies must recognize the changing demographics of the workforce. They must consider the needs of cultural and ethnic groups, the needs of single-parent households or—as in Silicon Valley—of households in which both parents must work if the family is to survive, and the specialized needs of the disabled.

8. *National policies and international trade.* Some issues pertaining to governmental protections of workers, the interests of business, and international trade directly affect the development of a new social contract. A number of issues which are in the purview of the federal and local governments, affect the structuring of a social contract. For example, NAFTA has been hailed as a major step forward in improving trade between Canada, the

United States, and Mexico, but also has been criticized for allowing jobs to migrate to Mexico. The December, 1999, meeting of the World Trade Organization (WTO) in Seattle has raised questions on job migration, international labor practices, such as the use of child labor and the exploitation of women, and the balance between economic development and environmental degradation. Great care must be taken that the interests of all parties are addressed openly and in a balanced way.

Comments

There have been several attempts in recent years to find alternatives for the old social contract. One of these is the ESOP or employee stock ownership plan, "a program created to give the worker a feeling of participation in the management and direction of a company."[14] Under this concept employees also can purchase a majority position in a publicly owned company where there are irreconcilable differences between management and the workforce, take the company over, and then hire a new management team. The new team reports to the new board of directors who represent the majority of the current stockholders. The challenge for the new board and the new management is to strike a balance between the objectives of the workforce—the new owners—and business practices, which allow the company to operate profitably in a global environment.

Another alternative has come with the financial leverage of large pension funds. Their very size provides them with the means by which they exert considerable pressure on a sitting board and the CEO for the indirect financial gain of the employees whose funds the pension manage. Pension plans have been able to increase more equitable outside representation on the company board. They have also forced companies to develop more aggressive business plans that would pave the way for greater return on the company's assets. Examples like these and other techniques can have a significant effect on the reshaping of the social order.

Developing a satisfactory new social contract will require truthtelling, acknowledgement of the forces that are destroying the old social contract, and respect for the legitimate interests of the workforce, the company, and the extended community. To do so will require listening, dialogue, and cooperative effort—teamwork—across traditional interest group boundaries.

■ SUMMARY

Workforce flexibility is not something limited to NGM companies. It is required in the companies, to be sure, but the ramifications extend across the community. Innovation and experimentation will continue until the policies and practices are in place to ensure the availability of workers who can participate as active team contributors; who are confident of their abilities to lead and to follow, to learn and to teach; and who are secure in their employability within the extended community.

■ EXERCISE

Think about your job, your career, and your relationship with your company.

1. How well prepared were you for your last assignment? How well prepared do you think you will be for your next one? Who will prepare you for it?
2. How do you learn about new technology, equipment, and processes? Is the process effective? What would you change?
3. How are problems solved in your company? Is the process effective?
4. How would you characterize your relationships with your manager, with the employees in your work unit, with other employees in the company, with suppliers, and with customers. What's good? What's bad? What should change?

Suppose your company is taking globalization seriously and as you advance you'll probably work outside your home country.

1. How would the company you work in now prepare you for the assignments in countries where your home country language is spoken?
2. How would the company you work in now prepare you for the assignments in countries where another language is spoken?
3. How would the company you work in now prepare you for your return to your home country?

4. What changes would you recommend in your company's practices?

■ NOTES

1. Miranda Ewell and K. Oanh Ha, "Why Piecework Won't Go Away," *San Jose Mercury News,* (June 27–28, 1999).

2. Sheldon Hutchinson, Private Communication, (May 1999).

3. Bowen et al., *The Perpetual Enterprise Machine: Seven Keys to Corporate Renewal through Successful Product and Process Development,* (New York: Oxford University Press, 1994) pp. 27–28.

4. Lyle M. Spencer, Jr., *Reengineering Human Resources* (New York: Wiley, 1996), p. 198.

5. As reported in John S. McClenahen, "The Successful Executive," *Industry Week,* (June 7, 1999) p. 101.

6. "Why Teams Fail," *USA Today,* (February 25, 1997).

7. Peter Block, *Stewardship: Choosing Service over Self-Interest* (San Francisco: Berrett-Koehler, 1993), pp. 29–31.

8. David Heenan and Warren Bennis, *Co-Leaders: The Power of Great Partnerships* (New York: Wiley, 1999).

9. Kenwyn K. Smith and David N. Berg, *Paradoxes of Group Life: Understanding Conflict, Paralysis, and Movement in Group Dynamics* (San Francisco: Jossey-Bass, 1987), p. 115.

10. Jean V. Owen, "Have You Learned Something Today?" *Manufacturing Engineering,* (April 1999).

11. Michael J. Termini, *The New Manufacturing Engineer: Coming of Age in an Agile Environment* (Dearborn, MI: Society of Manufacturing Engineers, 1996).

12. Jill Jusko, "Beating the Joneses," *Industry Week,* (December 7, 1998) pp. 27–33.

13. Francis Fukuyama, *Trust: The Social Virtues and the Creation of Prosperity* (New York: Free Press, 1995).

14. Jerry M. Rosenberg, *Dictionary of Finance,* (New York: Wiley, 1993) p. 112.

Chapter 17

Information Systems Integration

WEDNESDAY, 9:00 AM: THE ELECTRONIC INTERSTATE

So, the pieces were beginning to fall into place—people, knowledge, all focused on making Rapid Product and Process Realization work. Each of Monday's and Tuesday's presentations made sense if taken in context—the context of the whole company (and its extended enterprises) working together.

"Working together" meant many different things—but certainly one of the most important things it meant was being sure that everyone with a need to communicate could do so. From a practical point of view, that communication was going to have to be electronic. About three months after BAI was founded—in a converted barn on the edge of a pasture turned into a primitive airstrip—the founders outgrew the ability to shout at each other when they needed to communicate. By the time you had joined BAI, the company had grown to several separate plants at a half dozen locations and you'd watched as the communications difficulties grew, too.

Each plant, each function, had experimented with computers—stand-alone machines with applications that supported the function, and only the function. You had lived with the howls of anguish as functions were asked to give up their separate machines in favor of centralized data processing facilities—and you watched with some awe as the number of terminals attached to them grew. The engineers succeeded in maintaining a separate centralized facility for their work, using more sophisticated terminals. Factory floor automation was a mystery that seemed unconnected to either of the centralized facilities.

Then the workstation created a ripple of discontent as an affordable alternative to centralized mainframes, followed quickly by the PC revolution and the rapid decentralization of computing. Almost without warning all these processors took on a social nature—networking with each other.

The Information Technology functions in BAI struggled to keep up with the changes and there was an uneasy truce among centralized and decentralized facilities, supported by an *ad hoc* communications structure. Clearly BAI was going to have to discipline its information systems infrastructure. You hoped this morning's presentation would shed some light on solutions to the communications challenge.

■ EVOLUTION OF INFORMATION SYSTEMS

In the past two decades, the organization and management of manufacturing enterprises have evolved in ways that closely paralleled advances in information systems. It is little wonder then that when we talk of global competition we draw diagrams of extended enterprises that look like diagrams of information systems. And little wonder that when we speak of the interactions among the teams in an extended enterprise, we use words and images very similar to the ones we use when we describe the interactions among the computers found in the supporting information systems. The one feeds on the other.

Information systems integration is very close to enterprise integration, so close that sometimes we equate the two. But although information systems integration is essential for enterprise integration, it doesn't address the human and business dimensions that have been discussed elsewhere in this book and that are summarized in Chapter 19.

The purposes of information systems are to support the processes of rapid product and process realization (RPPR) described in Chapters 7 to 11, to support the knowledge processes described in Chapters 13 to 15, to support the workforce, the people and teams described in Chapter 16, and to enable the business and manufacturing systems discussed in Chapter 12.

Your company's information systems must be implemented with the understanding that the company is likely to be a part of one or more extended enterprises, and that these enterprises will come and go as opportunities change. The company will not survive if it takes upwards of two years to create the support for a new business system—the lifetime of the business system may be less than two years!

Your company's information systems also must enable *transparency*. Transparency is the presentation of data, information, and knowledge to human users in ways that are clear, intuitive, and unambiguous.

The NGM Report calls the kind of systems that the NGM company needs, *adaptive, responsive, information systems*. These are systems that can adapt quickly to changing business needs. They can provide seamless integration of business and manufacturing processes, equipment, and people. Your company will adapt these systems to today's, and then to tomorrow's, configuration of business, design, and production processes—and adapt the systems again the day after tomorrow.

Your company's information systems can't be the weak link in the responsiveness chain. Dynamic information systems integration is an enterprisewide issue. It requires information systems that can be reshaped dynamically into new systems by reliably adding new elements, replacing others, and changing how modules are connected to redirect data flows through the total system. The NGM Report asserts that adaptive, responsive, seamless, and transparent information systems are achieved by:

➤ Changing the conceptual way we think about for information system design and implementation.

➤ Establishing uniform standards for the data interfaces.

➤ Creating software function modules that can reside anywhere on a global network and that can be readily configured or reconfigured into new systems using standardized data interfaces.

➤ Establishing high-speed communication links using standard protocols.

➤ Developing a framework or infrastructure that allows individual users—through a security shield of authorizations—to easily create, modify, store, access, and execute individual modules and configured systems.

➤ Implementing systems to rigorous standards of integrity and reliability.

Each component in the modular system must be highly specialized to maximize performance and must rely on shared services to reduce complexity.

At its most idealistic, the network model makes all of the data, information, and knowledge of the extended enterprise available, in real-time, to everyone in the enterprise. It makes all this available in ways that fit naturally into each person's cognitive and decision-making processes. In reality, not everyone needs, wants, or should have everything that might be made available. In reality, no one has the time or capacity to use everything that could be available. But in many ways, we are getting close to a practical approximation of the ideal.

➤ Ubiquitous Service Approach

We saw the model for NGM enterprise organization in Figure 5.1, modified here for NGM information systems integration as Figure 17.1. The model is of a global network of computer processors, each directly supporting one or more business or manufacturing processes. The dynamic nature of the enterprise, and hence of the information system is not adequately conveyed by Figure 17.1. Many companies now have more than one workstation/employee and a new one is assigned each time the company hires a new worker. A plant in Tennessee that forms aluminum components may replace one in Pennsylvania that formed them from steel. An electronics plant in Penang may have new fabrication techniques superior to ones used by an older plant in Eindhoven.

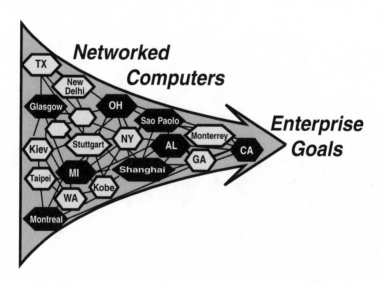

Figure 17.1   Basic Model for NGM Information Systems

So the real picture of the information system is one in which new nodes of the network appear almost without warning at the same time that other nodes disappear almost without a trace.

Your information systems must enable you to communicate quickly and accurately with all your customers, partners, and operations. Your global networks must be more than simple data transport mechanisms. They must support the seamless conveyance of knowledge and information, not just data, in ways that can be used by wide varieties of systems and people, and in a timely manner.

The NGM Report recommends that information systems be built using a *ubiquitous service approach*. In this approach, modules that may reside anywhere in the global network can be reconfigured in moments and act on data resident anywhere in the network. Each module will provide a highly specialized service—a "core competence"—that will be available to any authorized user at any time. Each of these modules will share the underlying communications and computing facilities and services.

It must be easy to incorporate the modules rapidly into reconfigured information systems, no matter what processor they run on. It will be easiest to achieve this if the software components can be "plugged" into the systems. "Plug-and-play" systems recognize the semantics and processes implied by the module interfaces and the modules understand the behavior of the system. Next generation manufacturing must move beyond today's confusion of proprietary formats and competing standards to a suite of standards for data exchange that enables modules to rapidly plug-and-play.

Plug-and-play systems will use object-oriented and functional component software that can be re-used frequently and augmented by agent technologies that will give objects an ability to act autonomously in carefully crafted situations. The technology of the World Wide Web will provide easy access to whatever data and information is needed, from anywhere in the world. This is forcing the rationalization of proprietary formats and competing data exchange standards.

There are two major tribes involved in the development of the ubiquitous service approach. The first is derived from the Unix™ workstation world and is dominated by the traditional mainframe, minicomputer, and workstation hardware and software vendors. The second is derived from the Personal Computer world and is dominated by vendors building up from low-end processors and local area networking. There is crossover as the needs for all kinds of hardware become apparent and as good technical ideas come out of each tribe, but there remain significant differences of approach.

■ GLOBAL MANUFACTURING NETWORKS

Networks for the transport of intellectual assets will be the twenty-first century's analog to the nineteenth-century railroad networks and the twentieth century's autobahns for the transport of physical assets. Whole economies developed along the transportation corridors. Similarly, the global knowledge economy will develop centered on global networks.[1]

As information and information exchange become more valuable to economic performance, countries that develop an effective advanced information infrastructure will gain competitive advantage in global markets. Instead of just chasing low wages, manufacturers increasingly will choose to locate and invest in countries whose infrastructure is able to handle the rapid and efficient dissemination and control of information and the integration of diverse business operations.

To be fully effective, global networks must enable three or more individuals in very different countries and cultures to work together in a virtual workcell. They should be able to work with little advanced warning on a critical, short-term project as if they were long-time team members in a single location and from a single culture. To achieve this, the networks must:

> ➤ Transport high volumes of data at rates that can support real-time interventions on demand and with high integrity and security.

> ➤ Present just enough information to each individual user, just in time, and in a language- and culture-sensitive form that the individual can use transparently.

> ➤ Enable individuals to learn and to innovate.

> ➤ Facilitate cooperative work among geographically and culturally separated individuals.

> ➤ Quickly and seamlessly integrate people and intelligent machines into smoothly functioning systems.

The key to a global network is not in the creation of a system in which electrons can get from one computer to another, nor whether two computers can understand each other's messages. The key lies in the establishment of an environment for manufacturing systems in which real people spread across the world can bring profitable products and services to satisfied customers. If they can, the global networks they are using can be said to be *interoperable*.

➤ Interoperability

Interoperability is the single most important issue in global networking. The essential attribute of interoperability is seamless information transfer in all directions. From a functional point of view, we see a progression of electronically enabled interoperability[2] (see Figure 17.2).

The progression starts with simple e-mail and file transfer—using the network as a substitute for physical mail facilities and telegraphy. When there are protocols for communication within a group, perhaps with access controls and rules for interaction, and a structure for file transfer and word processing, the network begins to enable teaming. The file transfer capabilities often progress to transaction processing using electronic data interchange (EDI) and then to the transfer of data sets describing the technical specifications of a product, or even a process. When there are common computing environments—using the same, or at least interoperable, sets of tools for graphics and product specification—engineering groups separated in time and space can collaborate. As tools are added, the collaboration can expand to all of the people involved in the integrated product and process development (IPPD) effort. Inevitably, the collaboration on IPPD reaches to more and more partners within the extended enterprise. The ultimate in interoperability comes when the network serves as the medium for

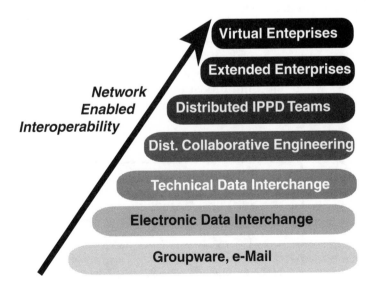

Figure 17.2 The Progression of Interoperability

partners to come together quickly in agile virtual enterprises formed to fulfill a single, transitory, market niche.

Layers of Interoperability

For the NGM company, the challenge is not just interoperability at the factory floor level or among design engineers, but across all the functions of what has been called "Big M" manufacturing. Figure 17.3 shows, very schematically, the layers of interoperability that your company must master.

The *communications systems layer* deals with the transport of signals from one computer system to another across a multiplicity of technologies and service providers. The computer systems layer deals with the ability of computer hardware and software to accept the signals and to present them to the user or to the manufacturing applications. This layer includes the operating systems, the networking systems, and much of the generic application software—often called *middleware*—needed to support specific applications. The manufacturing applications are at the heart of the *product and process layer* in which the results of one application are used in other applications. The applications include solid models, various product and process data bases, and other product- and process-specific applications. The *manufacturing systems layer* provides the interface between the user of one computer system and the user of another as they work collaboratively to make critical decisions and to execute and control manufacturing and business processes.

If we look at interoperability from the bottom layer up, we find that most of the technical problems of the global communications systems layer have been solved—at least in principle. There are still difficulties when telecommunications providers and computer operating systems use incompatible standards. The progression of higher

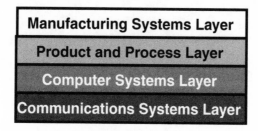

Figure 17.3   Layers of Interoperability

and higher bandwidth capabilities is uneven from region to region and country to country. The available technologies to ensure security sometimes fail, and availability and affordability are issues. However, workable solutions do exist for most companies in most countries.

Similarly, most of the technical difficulties at the computer systems level have been solved and quasi-standards are evolving to ensure that the computer processors and operating systems are transparent in conveying information.

The challenges become more demanding at the product and process level. There remain important semantic issues in naming data items and describing the relationships among data items. STEP and other standards have gone a long way toward solving the difficulties for products, but a standardized vocabulary for processes is still a problem.

Finally, manufacturing systems are still much more of an art than a science, with very little more than empirical methodologies. These systems integrate many specific applications and many people into coherent systems. The difficulties in achieving interoperability at this level can be illustrated by this challenge: think of the art required in interfacing a Malaysian-based manufacturing system with two U.S.-based ones, and then combining the result with a system based in Russia. This is daunting not just because of potential technology mismatches, but because of differences in semantics, in language, in skills and education, and in operating strategies and philosophies.

Time is an important factor in practical interoperability. Time cuts across all four layers. The goal of RPPR is to get a lot of activities done, many of them concurrently and often in many different locations, so that the manufactured good gets to the customer on time and at minimum cost. Your company may need to make a balanced investment at all four levels of interoperability to achieve this goal. For example, you may need to invest in enough bandwidth at the communications level to ensure that slow data transfer doesn't negate your investment in interoperable applications packages.

Global interoperability for integrated enterprises requires a relatively uniform regulatory regimen consistent with international law, with international trade agreements, and with strong international protections for intellectual property.

➤ How to Think about NGM Information Systems

A conceptual model of an information system is a simple picture of the fundamental rules of behavior for the system. A conceptual model is not a fully fleshed-out architecture that identifies system services, interfaces, standards, and their relationships, but instead provides a simple basis for thinking about information systems and their architecture. (The NGM Report calls these conceptual models *basis models.*)

Some Conceptual Models for Information Systems Integration

The traditional conceptual model for integration has been the static model of a shared database with no reflection of the time dependence of the data. This model is often centered on product data. It focuses on the geometric aspects of the product, not on the processes by which the geometry data is created and used.

A more recent conceptual model is that of object-oriented programming. Object-oriented programming views everything as an object that encapsulates data and functions specific to that data. In this approach, you identify all the objects in the overall system, define the data associated with the objects and the methods required to act on that data, and then develop "messages" which request action from other objects. A fundamental premise of this model is that data and function are kept together within the object.

In the late 1990s, there has been much interest in autonomous or responsive agents as a conceptual model. This model is an extension of object-oriented programming and mimics the organizational model of networked autonomous teams. Now the objects have embedded in them rules and methods governing the way they behave, alone and in cooperation with other objects. Again, data and function are kept together. Object and agent models can become very complicated as new objects or agents are created throughout the manufacturing processes. It is difficult to maintain synchronicity and ensure that all the objects used are operating on the most recent data.

The NGM Conceptual Model

The NGM Report describes a new conceptual model. It comes out of the domain of design theory and methodology. The model, proposed for agile manufacturing,[3] asserts that all information processes *transform* data from one type or form into another type or form. The model is generic and applies to all information systems.

In the NGM conceptual model, a *transformation module* is an entity that transforms an input data set into an output data set. *Data sets* can be anything from a single byte of data, to a set of rules encapsulating knowledge, the database of an entire ERP system, or anything in between. The inputs and outputs of transformation modules consist of a command from the Application Programming Interface (API) and one or more data sets[4] (see Figure 17.4).

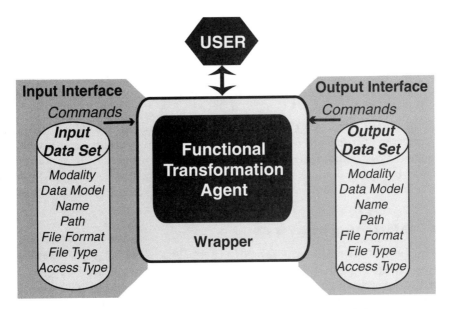

Figure 17.4 The Functional Transformation Module

The Functional Transformation Modules provide services—transformations of engineering or business data. Modules are linked, using the input and output data sets and the commands, into processes. These processes are more complex transformation modules.

The work of the module is done by a piece of software called a *Function Transformation Agent.* The agent may already conform to the interface standards for modules, or it may require a *wrapper* that performs the translation between the native interface of the agent and the module interface standards. Frequently, wrappers are used when the agent is a pre-existing piece of software, a so-called "legacy" system.

The input and output data sets have attributes that provide information about them:[3] the type of data, the data model or the semantics of the data set, the structure of the physical storage, the format of the data in that physical storage structure, the method of access required, the name of the physical storage structure, and the path to it. Other attributes may be necessary in specific instances. This list of data interface attributes is called the data set's "modality."

Within the NGM conceptual model, information systems integration consists of:

➤ Defining transforming modules and their matching data sets.

➤ Providing mechanisms to support linking the modules into higher level transforming modules or processes.

➤ Providing mechanisms to support the execution, monitoring, and control of the modules and processes.

If you did this in a permanent, static way using a shared database, then you would have a traditional information systems solution. If instead, you build an infrastructure in which transforming modules with matching data sets lists can be configured and reconfigured dynamically, then you would have an NGM information system.

➤ Information Systems Architecture

The bottom two interoperability layers of Figure 17.3 are usually treated as part of the enterprise's information technology infrastructure. For NGM, it is essential that the infrastructure have an architecture that is adaptive and responsive to changing needs (see Figure 17.5).

Integration Frameworks

If you try to integrate all the aspects of your company into an enterprise manufacturing system, you will need a structure and a set of rules to guide the linkage of discrete applications. You will need an

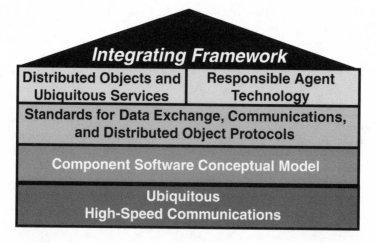

Figure 17.5 The NGM Information Systems Architecture

integration framework. Your applications must use the same semantics, so that the meanings of the data objects do not change as they are passed from application to application. Once you have the framework and the semantics, you can define interfaces. If you expect your systems to interoperate with those of other companies, you and your partners all will have to adhere to standards that are supported by end-users and vendors.

The integration framework (IF) embodies the set of rules by which the pieces of the underlying information system are fit together. The framework design of choice for next generation manufacturing is one that assumes the network of peer-coupled computers shown in Figure 17.1, communicating over links that have as high a bandwidth as is economically feasible. It also incorporates the NGM conceptual model.

The IF is a suite of software modules that provides:

➤ Connectivity and communication at all levels—from physical links up to message passing.

➤ Data, information, object, and knowledge management.

➤ Access, creation, editing, composition, execution, monitoring, and control of all the entities plugged into the system— which might include everything accessible on the Internet.

There are some elements of truth in the myths listed in the box. Certainly an enterprise-wide understanding of the semantics of data and the ability to share the enterprise's data across the entire network are essential. So is the use of standards—many different kinds of standards. So, too, is the use of open systems technologies that permit new function modules to be plugged into the system, and old ones unplugged, transparently. And yes, automating applications is a necessary first step. But integration requires more—a careful analysis and a holistic view.

What Are We Trying to Integrate?

Table 17.1 describes the many ways to think about integration as you develop your integration framework.[5,6,7] Together they present a holistic understanding of integration.

Examples of Integration Frameworks

Most current work on integration frameworks depends heavily on the Object-Oriented Conceptual Model, with an evolution toward the NGM Conceptual Model. We will briefly describe four efforts: the

SOME MYTHS ABOUT INTEGRATION FRAMEWORKS

To achieve integration, put all the data into a single, logically unified database. The problem is that in a dynamic world, static integration isn't practical.

Some particular standard—say, CORBA, OLE, or STEP—will magically solve our integration needs. But these are just enablers and do not, by themselves, provide integration.

"Open systems" are the solution for all integration problems. The problem is that very often one vendor's open system does not adhere to the open systems standards another vendor uses. A true "open system" would provide a framework in which modules built to a robust standard from any vendor could be interconnected with compliant modules supplied by any other vendor.

Automating applications leads to integration. More likely, we'll get islands of automation, at best linked by high impedance causeways. The result often is that you can't combine the best functions of one application with the best functions found in a second application unless some sort of custom interface is developed.

Integration means you own the applications you use. The Internet gives you the ability to link to and launch applications or modules remotely, from anywhere in the world. This means you can buy a module's services for a short period instead of making the outright purchase of the application.

SEMATECH CIM Application Framework Specification, the Department of Defense Common Operating Environment as it might be applied for manufacturing, the National Industrial Information Infrastructure Protocol (NIIIP) Architecture, and the National Advanced Manufacturing Testbed (NAMT) Framework Project. Each of these projects is producing results for large enterprise-wide system integration.

The SEMATECH CIM Application Framework Specification. The SEMATECH CIM Application Framework Specification[8] (see Figure 17.6) addresses some of the needs of next generation manufacturing. It is oriented to the Manufacturing Execution Systems (MES) level between direct equipment control and enterprise systems. The Framework is based on an object-oriented analysis of the semiconductor manufacturing domain. While the specification was developed with semiconductor CIM in mind, it describes the high-level object abstractions common to any manufacturing industry.

Table 17.1	Thinking about Information Systems Integration
Data integration	Services for the storage and management of objects, entities, and their relationships and linkages; version and configuration control; naming services; security services; and transaction control. The ECMA model[5] also provides a metamodel service, a query service, a view service, and data interchange services.
Control integration	Mechanisms so that one module can activate other modules, modules can notify each other of events, and applications can share functions. Mechanisms of control include message passing, triggers, and others.
Presentation integration	User interface services that make the presentations of information consistent in use and easier to learn.
Platform integration	The interoperability of modules and applications across different computing platforms and operating systems.
Process integration	Modules working together with a common understanding of the RPPR process.
Tool integration	Tools sharing data via a common data format, defined for a particular purpose (e.g., STEP/PDES).
Management integration	Facilitation of group work by ensuring effective communication and information dissemination. This includes prevention of corruption of processes by actions of team members.
Team integration	Building an environment that helps the team and managers to control development.
Horizontal integration	Maintenance of the integrity of design information within each life cycle phase across many modeling methods.
Vertical integration	Maintenance of the completeness and consistency of information generated in various stages of the rapid product and product realization (RPPR) process.

MES are characterized by a heterogeneous set of applications. SEMATECH's goal is to simplify integration and interoperability by defining a complete standardized set of messages that can pass between applications. The Framework Specification presents a common object model and an interfacing standard. From the perspective of design and code reuse, the common object model avoids programmers "reinventing the wheel," and allows them to concentrate on those aspects of software that are unique to the application at hand. The Framework Specification also facilitates building a suite of pluggable applications, each of which is object-oriented, and it defines interfaces to the functional layers above and below the MES.

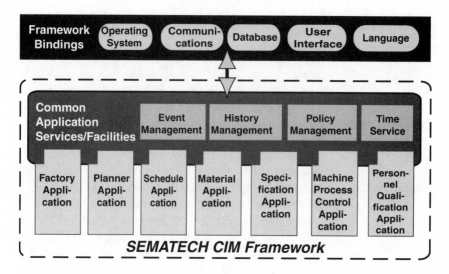

Figure 17.6 SEMATECH's Integration Framework

The Framework Specification also describes the runtime execution environment that will provide the *bindings* for the open system of pluggable applications that make up the MES. For two or more applications to be pluggable, they must share the same binding. The Specification outlines binding considerations between interoperable applications.

An Integration Framework for Next Generation Manufacturing. A large, extended NGM enterprise can be a very complicated enterprise. The most complete description of an integration framework for systems that can support very complicated enterprises is the U.S. Department of Defense (DoD) Common Operating Environment (COE).[9] Figure 17.7 is an adaptation of the COE for NGM companies. The COE describes a system foundation, gives an information architecture, and plots an implementation strategy. The projected benefits of the COE are:

➤ A common core of reusable software for all enterprise systems.
➤ Programmers with more reusable knowledge.
➤ Lower user training costs and higher user productivity.

➤ Adherence to industry standards to reduce development costs.
➤ Increased portability will increase.
➤ Improved systems security.
➤ Reduced testing burdens.

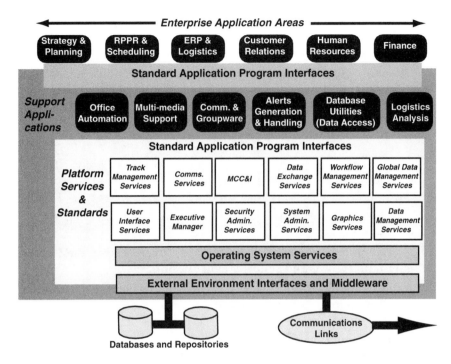

Figure 17.7 Integration Framework for NGM Enterprises, Based on the COE

The COE incorporates an architecture and approach for building interoperable systems, an infrastructure for supporting "functional area" applications, and a rigorous definition of the runtime execution environment. There is a rigorous set of requirements for COE compliance and an automated toolset that enforces COE principles and measures compliance. There also is a collection of reusable software components, a methodology for software reuse, a set of APIs for accessing COE components, and an electronic process for maintaining the COE software library.

The DoD's goal is have any software module loaded into the workstation memory only for as long as it is needed. The DoD system is installed by selectively downloading modules to the user's processor from repositories containing the complete COE.

Under the rules of the COE architecture, all the software except the operating system and basic windowing software would come in *segments*. Precisely defined functions are added to or removed from the integrated system in segments as indicated in Figure 17.7. A segment, implemented in the NGM version of the COE as a function module, is part of the minimum software required to establish an operating environment context, to establish basic data flow through the system, and to ensure interoperability. Other functions included in the COE are of such general utility that there would be a lot of extra effort to rewrite them for each application. Segments are self-contained in that one segment is not allowed to directly modify any resource owned by another segment.

The COE categorizes segments as:

➤ *Infrastructure services* that provide the architectural framework for managing and distributing the flow of data throughout the system.

➤ *Manager services* include network, system, and security administration.

➤ *Communications* provides facilities for receiving data external to the system and sending data out of it.

➤ *Distribution and object management* provides the infrastructure for distributed processing in a networked client/server environment.

➤ *Data management* includes database and file management in a distributed environment.

➤ *Presentation* enables the direct interactions with humans.

➤ *Workflow and global data management* is oriented toward managing logistic data.

➤ *Common support applications* are more specific to a problem domain such as: office automation, real-time signal processing and analysis, and message processing.

Any given NGM enterprise would want to extend this taxonomy to include all of its common functions.

In a perfect world, information systems would be fully compliant to the COE's rules for interoperability:

➤ All segments comply with the COE style guide and their associated data are structured in the COE-specified segment format.

➤ All segments are registered and submitted to the online library.

➤ All segments are validated with the tools provided in the COE.

➤ All segments are loaded and tested in the COE prior to admission.

➤ All segments fully specify dependencies and required resources.

➤ All segments are designed for removability and then tested to confirm that they can be successfully removed.

➤ All segments access COE components only through the published APIs.

➤ No segment duplicates functionality contained within the COE.

➤ No segment modifies the environment or any files it does not own except through files or tools provided by the COE.

In reality, you can have degrees of compliance that range from "peaceful coexistence"—if you add a segment it won't interfere with the other functions, but it also might not talk with them—to segments that are fully integrated. There are four ways to think about compliance: as the user sees it, fit within the system architecture, in the runtime environment, and as a measure of risk in using the software.

The DoD is building the COE incrementally. One of the incremental implementations is the Simulation Assessment Validation Environment (SAVE) described in Chapters 7 and 8.

National Industrial Information Infrastructure Protocol Consortium. The National Industrial Information Infrastructure Protocol (NIIIP) effort[10] is an initiative undertaken by a consortium of manufacturers and vendors under the U.S. Federal Technology Reinvestment Program to enable agile virtual enterprises (AVEs). The vision of NIIIP is to use many of the ideas of information frameworks R&D to build practical systems to enable agile virtual enterprises made up of manufacturers and suppliers throughout the industrial base. The NIIIP effort aims to:

➤ Establish standards-based software infrastructure protocols that integrate a variety of distributed business systems, business processes, data, and computing environments.

➤ Use emerging, existing, and de facto standards and systems technologies to implement NIIIP.

➤ Provide the technical foundation for implementing industrial virtual enterprises by developing software, toolkits, and a resource file documenting the experiences of information systems integration for virtual enterprises.

The key to NIIIP is its heavy utilization of object technology. The NIIIP uses the Object Management Group (OMG) Object Management Architecture as the bus to integrate application objects, common facilities, and basic Object Services (Figure 17.8).

The NIIIP Common Facilities include:

➤ Desktop services to present a common, integrated user interface for managing all application, project, resource, organization, workflow, and system data, tool, and task objects.

➤ Task and session services to manage the user's working environment.

➤ Workflow management to manage the synchronous or asynchronous execution of user tasks.

➤ Application services to manage the registration and execution of application tools.

➤ Agent services to manage the communications between agents—computational proxies for resources (people, machines, teams, software systems) in the manufacturing systems.

➤ Negotiation services to discipline the invocation by one object of the services of another object.

➤ Mediation services to convert names, parameters, or data contents from partners for common use at runtime.

➤ Communications services to provide a common interface for non-ORB communication environments.

➤ Data management services to manage user data objects.

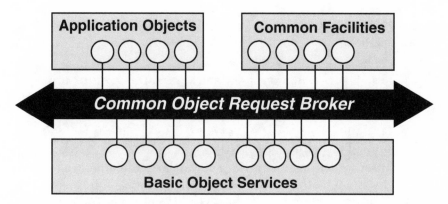

Figure 17.8 The OMG Object Management Architecture Reference Model

➤ Knowledge management services to provide rule, constraint, and trigger management.

➤ Internet tools services that facilitate use of Internet tools (the World Wide Web, Wide Area Information Servers, Web browsers, directories Web-accessible software and knowledge resources, and so forth).

➤ STEP information modeling services to facilitate use of STEP tools.

➤ Virtual enterprise monitor to oversee transactions according to rules imposed by the virtual enterprise.

The NIIIP Communications Layer is implemented using a CORBA-compliant object system with the CORBA 2.0 General Inter-ORB Protocol (GIOP) and TCP/IP as a mandatory transport mechanism. GIOP also provides integration with Netware and OSI-compliant transport mechanisms. The CORBA 2.0 Environment Specific Inter-ORB Protocol (ESIOP) provides integration with DCE as a transport mechanism.

NIIIP demonstration projects include the generic application of NIIIP to manufacturing execution systems (MES) and a more specific application to the shipbuilding industry. The status of the NIIIP development is available at the project's World Wide Web site.

National Advanced Manufacturing Testbed (NAMT) Framework Project. The NIST National Advanced Manufacturing Testbed (NAMT) is a facility for integrating, operating, testing, benchmarking, and refining advanced manufacturing technologies and standards for information-driven design, engineering, and manufacturing operations. The principal objective of the NAMT Framework project is the development of manufacturing systems interoperability standards. The NAMT Framework project is piloting, using proposed standards and protocols, established standards, and de facto standards, an experimental manufacturing system infrastructure that supports distributed engineering and production operations. The standards foundation includes the STEP Standard for the Exchange of Product Model Data, The ISO Concepts and Rules for Enterprise Models, and the Object Management Architecture (OMA). NAMT is a joint effort involving many industry partners. It draws on the SEMATECH CIM Applications Framework Specification, NIIIP's Reference Architecture, and the Technical Architecture Specification developed by the Department of Energy's Technologies Enabling Agile Manufacturing (TEAM) project.

The first manufacturing operation used to test the infrastructure was the automated inspection of mechanical parts. Subsequent operations for testing the NAMT framework will be machining based on NIST's experimental hexapod and precision turning.

➤ Standards

Frameworks are all about component software and software reuse. As with any kind of system, standards development is the key, whether by de facto or formal industry consensus. Either way, given agreement on standards, validation testing (i.e., does a specification do what it intends to do?) and conformance testing (to what degree does an implementation conform to a specification?) will be required.

Before we can build virtual factories, spread across extended enterprises, as dynamically as we will need in the next decade, we need generally accepted information systems standards. The purpose of standards is to facilitate the creation of complex systems out of components such as objects or the transformation modules of the NGM Conceptual Model. Standards are required for all the attributes necessary for data set interfaces and are critical for integration frameworks.

Unless you can use standards that are in general use, you will need to budget for large, time-consuming efforts to translate protocols to achieve information systems integration. Data, information, and knowledge cannot flow seamlessly unless the connections are made in a standard way. Every machine must be able to interpret messages from every other machine. Each application must be able to understand the data from any source in the system. Many successful standards are in place, but there are important areas where accepted standards do not exist, or, even worse, where there are conflicting standards.

The world of information systems is a world where technical developments and vendor self-interests have often led the development of standards. Leading vendors often establish *de facto* standards because the standards organizations have been too slow to act. When the standards bodies do act, the vendors are slow to adopt any sanctioned standards that differ from those already incorporated in their offerings. That was okay 20 years ago when the focus was on integration using centralized, shared databases and on monolithic, often proprietary systems.

Monolithic systems are difficult, and hence expensive, to change. The Unix™ operating system provided a breakthrough, the first generally accepted "open" system. Unix spawned an industry and a set of standards that supported the idea of software and systems that could be easily implemented on many different platforms. Three key results of this movement were: X-windows, a prototypical graphical user interface; TCP/IP, which has become the dominant communications protocol for the Internet; and C++, which propelled object-oriented programming into mainstream computing. Linux carries the Unix ideal of openness into the twenty first century by a vendor-independent process of public enhancement and distribution.

Open systems mimic extended enterprises. One vendor packages its core competence in scheduling in one module, another its core competence in solid modeling, another its core competence in data management. The modules are linked to meet the extended enterprise's particular needs. The interface definition is critical in any modular system. The modules must have clear, standardized interface definitions that allow them to be rapidly integrated. You can call an architecture, or framework, open only if it is freely available and the command interfaces (i.e., the application programming interfaces) and data interfaces (i.e., the standards) are widely published and easily accessible. Linux and the World Wide Web fit this picture.

Your company needs standards for product data including task and production plans, for process data and knowledge, for simulation, and for distributed objects, communications, text, images, video, sound, and modeling. Companies often must choose from conflicting standards (see Table 17.2). For instance, STEP, ICES, and DXF are all used for the exchange of geometry.

Table 17.3 lists additional domains where standards are essential. Companies must be wary when making choices where the standards are immature or do not have consensus acceptance.

A critical aspect in standards of all types is the concept, embodied within STEP and the SAVE Meta Data Format (MDF), of the *data model:* the meaning of the data or information to be exchanged or interfaced. Having a semantic model of the data set eliminates the possibility of two organizations using the same word to describe two different concepts or having two different words to describe the same concept.

State-of-the-Art Standards

Product Geometry Standards

The Initial Graphic Exchange Standard (IGES) is currently used in the design domain to exchange geometric (i.e., computer-aided design) data. Most CAD systems can read in or output an IGES file. The limitations in IGES are that there are various interpretations of some of the entities defined within the standard. This leads to misinterpretation

Table 17.2 Some of the Multiple Current and Emerging Standards That Must Be Rationalized in a Responsive NGM Information System

Topic	Subtopic	Examples of Standards
Communication		CORBA, http, OLE/COM, DCE, ISO/OSI, TCP/IP
Data exchange	Product	STEP, STEP Applications Protocols (APs)
	Geometry	STEP AP2 I, DXF, STL, HPGL
	Text, hypertext	html, SGML, RTF
	Images	JPEG, bitmap, GIF, TIFF, DIB, PCX, MSP
	Simulation data	SAVE MDF/CDF
	Production plans	ALPS, STEP APs
Graphics user interfaces		Windows, X-Windows, Open-GL
Process modeling		IDEF, NIAM
Computer languages		C, C++, ADA, Java, IDL
Sound		WAV, AU, RA, MIDI, ItMI, AIF
Video		MPEG, AVI, MOV
Database query languages		SQL, SDAI

Table 17.3 Areas Where Standards Are Needed

Domain	Subdomain	Status	Examples
Knowledge		De facto	KQML
Information		De facto	None
Text	Formatted	De facto	SQML, Word, RTF
	Tagged, linked	Emerging	SQML, HTML
Design rules		None	
Geometry		STEP—slowly emerging; DXF—pragmatic, vendor-sponsored	
Parametric design Information		None	ProEngineer format

STEP is a series of standards each of which describes an Application Protocol (AP), resources, languages, and models. A number of CAD vendors support STEP AP203, Configuration-Controlled Design, with translators to convert product data from a proprietary structure into the neutral AP203 format. AP203 is oriented to the needs of designers. STEP AP224, Mechanical Product Definition for Process Planning Using Machining Features, is oriented to the needs of manufacturing. AP224, which is nearing acceptance as an international standard after six years of development, provides a complete, unambiguous, neutral, digital data file with all the data necessary for product manufacture.

The effectiveness of AP224 was tested using a conversion system capable of facilitating the capture and translation of legacy data into the STEP format and a Computer-Aided Process Planning system called the Generative Process Planning Environment (GPPE). The GPPE creates macro-process plans—shop floor routings, bills of materials, tooling requirements, and time estimates—in an AP224 STEP-compliant format. Three projects were used as quantitative tests of AP224 as it was developed.

In the first, 50 different orders were processed through STEP conversion, validation, manufacturing, and fabrication—representing 340 parts from a commercial company's production weapons system. All of these were complete and accurate. The total time from receipt of the request to quote to the delivery of the parts was reduced by 31 percent.

The second project involved 20 part orders, some handled in parallel by three manufacturers. Five part orders at each company manufactured using the processes in place before the availability of STEP technology. Again, the AP203 filesets were 100 percent accurate. The time and cost savings achieved using the AP203 input to generate micro-process plans averaged 5 percent to 20 percent and was as great as 30 percent for the more complicated parts.

The third project involved a 17 part sample. The manufacturer saved 30 percent to 42 percent in the time to prepare a bid and 25 percent to 40 percent in the micro-level process planning. Because of the accuracy of the resulting solid models, significant time was saved on the shop floor.

---

*John H. Bradham, *STEP-Driven Manufacturing* (Dearborn, MI: Computer and Automated Systems Association of the Society of Manufacturing Engineers, 1998).

and inaccurate translations. IGES also does not handle text very well, even though the text information in a CAD model is often as important as the graphic information.

Various individual STEP Application Protocols (APs)—the terminology for a standard for exchange in a particular set of design processes—are emerging from the standards process. They are beginning to be accepted and used, more in Europe than in the United States. The groups most interested in STEP are companies that use Unix workstations and mainframes. Vendors are slowly bringing their large design packages into compliance with STEP and many CAD vendors are providing the capability to input or output the STEP APs. The various groups overseeing the further development of the standard have committed to its development as a series of modules. In the personal computer-based market, Autodesk's DXF format is an alternative CAD exchange standard. The NGM Report suggested in 1997 that DXF was more reliable than the STEP Application Protocols, but suffered from the same problems as IGES and does not cover as many subdomains as STEP.

Object Message Passing Standards

There are several emerging protocols for object message passing. Two protocols from the workstation world are the Object Management Group's (OMG's) Common Object Request Broker Architecture (CORBA)[11] and the Open Group's Distributed Computing Environment (DCE).[12] Interoperability for Object Request Brokers (ORBs) from different vendors is uncertain.

The Hyper Text Transmission Protocol (http) and its extensions—think of these as the high-level communications protocols of the PC world—are rapidly becoming low-cost competitors for many of the functions provided by CORBA and DCE. In addition to allowing users easy access to data and information, the World Wide Web is beginning to allow users to access applications running on remote computers. The so-called *Applet,* often written in Java, is one way in which small applications providing limited functions can be downloaded and run in a local machine. An advantage of http is that the client and server software necessary to send and receive the messages is free or low cost.

Microsoft's Object Linking and Embedding (OLE) approach to linking applications has been augmented for distributed computing (distributed OLE). Since OLE uses a different object model, initially none of the three approaches could work with any of the others. The NGM Report predicts that CORBA, OLE, and DCE will merge, with http and Java having a strong influence on the merged result.

Standards for Documents

The Standard Graphical Markup Language (SGML) is a 1986 standard that is very complete in its functionality. DoD uses SGML extensively as part of its CALS initiative. SGML also is at the core of many professional publishing systems.

Word processors such as Microsoft Word do not read in or output SGML files. Special readers and translators are required. Rich Text

XML

An important emerging standard is eXtensible Markup Language (XML). XML defines the content of a "page" rather than its appearance, as does HTML. XML has two important strengths: XML tags separate content from presentation, and XML is extensible—that is, it allows the creation of new tags for new and unforeseen purposes. In this sense, XML is a metalanguage, a language in which the user can create other languages closely matched to the user's business processes.

The XML tags don't specify how to display the information. In the XML world, that is done using a style sheet written in XSL (eXtensible Style Language), an XML language for reformatting and presentation.

Different style sheets can present the same content data in different ways. For instance, a manufacturer might design four different style sheets, one to display product specifications in the print media, one for high-resolution screens of PCs, one for low-resolution screens of TVs, and one for even lower-resolution palmtop computer displays. All four style sheets would work from the same XML "page." So if a specification changes, only the XML tag needs to be changed and the change will show up in all four presentations.

XML enables the manipulation of platform-independent data. The combination of XML with the Internet, which enables platform-independent networking, and Java, which enables the creation of platform-independent programs, is said to provide the three prerequisites for universal computing: global communications, portable software, and portable data.

All this makes XML seem very attractive as a low-cost way to deal with data in global systems. Interoperability, however, will depend on standard semantics for the content data.

Format (RTF) provides a platform-independent word processing format that is convenient as an intermediate among many proprietary word processors.

The Hypertext Markup Language (html) is a fast expanding subset and extension of SGML with extensive use on the World Wide Web. Translations among html implementations are not perfect. There are at least eight formats in general use for images while for movies and video there are five, with at least five more for sound.

Graphical User Interfaces

There are a number of competing standards in graphical user interfaces. In the PC world, Windows is dominant. In the UNIX Workstation, X-Windows appears to be generally accepted except for applications demanding high-performance graphical displays where the Silicon Graphics Open GL windowing system is used. Each UNIX machine vendor (e.g., Sun, Compaq, IBM) does have its own windowing system.

Communications and Networking

The bottom layer for interoperability (Figure 17.3) and the foundation for the information systems architecture (Figure 17.5) is *communications*. Communications includes everything from the physical connection to the protocols used to communicate between applications and objects on separate computers. High-bandwidth communications are becoming like a water or electric utility, enabling people to use them easily just by plugging in a device.

The ISO/OSI seven-layer protocol architecture (Figure 17.9) provides a good overview of the kinds of standards that are required.[13] The ISO/OSI architecture permits diverse standards within a layer as long as the information passed over the layer boundaries adheres to strict standards. One effect of this layer independence is that at the lowest level, the physical level, the nature and speed of the physical connection between two computers can change without affecting the other layers. This means you can replace your 56K modem and telephone line with a 100-megahertz optical fiber connection without seeing any difference except for the dramatic reduction in response times. TCP/IP, the mainstay of the Internet, is another suite of standards. It has been adjusted to adhere to the ISO/OSI architecture. Figure 17.9 compares the functions of TCP/IP to the ISO/OSI architecture.

Transmission speed and bandwidth are interchangeable. An explosion of technologies to increase bandwidth has fed, and been fed by, the explosive growth of the World Wide Web. The 1970's miracle of

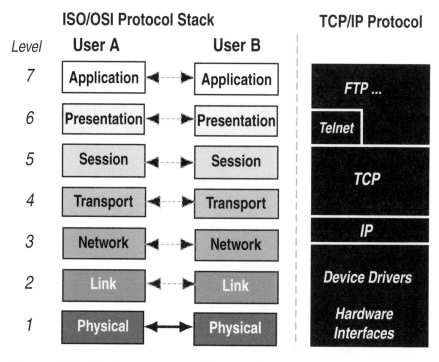

Figure 17.9 The Seven Layers of the ISO/OSI Protocol Stack, Compared with TCP/IP

1200 baud modems has long been forgotten in our impatience with 56 kilobaud and the looming availability of several high bandwidth alternatives: digital telephony, connectivity through Cable TV cables, and more and more optical fiber.

The telecommunications industry is undergoing rapid change with new approaches and technologies appearing almost weekly. Companies are merging and reemerging as they attempt to keep up with and surpass the competition. Telephone companies, telecommunication companies, cable companies, and radio and television companies are collaborating on an unheard of scale. We can be sure that the explosive growth of the World Wide Web will continue, with a gradual increase in functionality and perhaps convergence with conventional telephony. The NGM Report concludes:

> About the only sure bet in this domain is that it (communications) will
> be radically different than it is today. Bandwidths will be much higher

and the average person will be able to communicate and access data and information in a way that is impossible today. Forecasting the future in this domain at this time is just not possible.

Consequently, although the bandwidth requirements for the knowledge-based enterprise are also growing explosively, your company will have many cost-effective options from which to choose. You can choose to use the public Internet, that is, the World Wide Web, through Internet Service Providers (ISPs). You can use private Intranets, incorporating much of Internet technology but over dedicated leased lines. You can use proprietary networks. Or you can use a combination of public and private networking. There has been a proliferation of companies whose core competence is global networking, who can establish and maintain global networks.

➤ Operational Concerns

Security and Privacy

No global electronic network—proprietary or public—will be free of *security* concerns. Today's networks are subject to well-known security exposures, although there are many implementations for which companies have decided that the protections available in common Internet-based products are adequate for routine electronic commerce. Security issues should be evaluated within the spectrum of security exposures a company has—for example, 75 percent of intellectual property losses occur within the company by trusted employees, subcontractors, or joint partners. There are only limited technical protections for these losses. The network security issues must be solved at a level at which they are satisfactory for a broad consensus of the companies likely to participate in extended enterprises.

Another security issue that is not fully resolved is the balance of the real needs of private companies for security and the equally real needs of governments to protect countries against malevolent transactions. One effect is the ongoing dispute over encryption algorithms that can be used worldwide.

Viruses, Trojan horses, and worms—software that propagates itself as it acts to interfere with the operations and data management of processors on a network—pose problems for network-based operations. We think of them in connection with the Internet, but hackers can introduce them into proprietary networks as well.

The interaction of information systems and people raises another concern. This is the concern for *privacy*—think of privacy as the security concerns of the individual. There are two kinds of issues. The first relates to maintaining the privacy of data about an individual—personnel records, for example. This kind of privacy demands strict access controls so that only people authorized to see private data do so. It also demands a culture of respect for private information so that the people with access do not abuse it. The second privacy issue relates to the ethics of company access to the individual's electronic workspaces and to the individual's use of company resources for activities not related to company business. Trust demands that the company respect the employee's decisions relative to his or her use of electronic workspaces and that the employee respects and uses the company's investment in the workspaces as a company asset.

Robustness and Bandwidth

A company's global electronic network must be *robust;* that is, it must be reliably accessible at least at the level, say, of the domestic U.S. telephone network. Transactions across the network must be completed within consistent and guaranteed time limits. The network must have sufficient redundancy to thwart the effects of natural disaster or sabotage.

Robustness is closely coupled with *bandwidth*. If the network has adequate carrying capacity, it is much easier to guarantee service levels. Market forces are driving communications companies to put in place the physical infrastructure to provide much greater levels of bandwidth, especially in the United States. Other countries provide varying levels of capacity; in some cases (e.g., Singapore) the widespread use of fiber optics provides excellent bandwidth; in other cases, the bandwidth may be limited to that available through public telephone circuits or radio-telephony.

Bandwidth requirements are influenced by patterns of use. There are a number of tools that can reduce bandwidth requirements. Broadly speaking, these are *active filters* that are context sensitive in limiting the requests for information that, say, one application makes of another and training and education of users in setting the context for requests of remotely located users and applications.

Accessibility

Accessibility may be a limiting factor for small companies. As companies become more distributed, it will be more important that individual employees have access to the enterprise's integrated systems from wherever they are. In the United States and in many other countries, the Internet provides accessibility at relatively low cost, but access to proprietary networks may be prohibitive.

Intellectual Property

The development of widely accepted international regulatory norms, that are consistent with the model of globally distributed NGM Company and extended enterprise operations, has been slow. On the one hand, countries want to benefit freely from global markets. On the other, especially in developing countries, they want to protect fragile national economies and every economic advantage their people may have.

The negotiation of Intellectual Property Rights (IPR) agreements is a slow and tedious process that must be conducted first by national governments. There remain many differences over the basic IPR. NGM companies must take care when dealing with partners based in countries with widely different understandings or weak protection for IPR.

The International Intelligent Manufacturing Systems (IMS) program of joint R&D projects is being conducted by international consortia with companies from Australia, Canada, the European Union, Japan, Korea, Switzerland, and the United States. The consortia conduct the projects under *Terms of Reference* that include *Intellectual Property Rights* negotiated by the participating governments. The Terms of Reference provide a starting point that companies can use as they form knowledge-rich partnerships. They are available through the IMS program's web site, www.imsorg.org.

► Testing and Reliability

If you are going to live by your global network, you need to be very sure you won't die by it. Your global network is a "you-bet-your-company" proposition. For decades, companies have known that the networks that supported their financial transfers and transaction processing needed to work all the time. People heavily involved in more general e-commerce are learning that Six-Sigma reliability of their systems is necessary, too. In practice, the problems are heavily weighted toward unreliable software.[14] E*Trade's outage in early 1999 and E-Bay's outage later that year demonstrated the negative impact such outages have with the company's relationships with its customers and shareholders. Of course, they also have an impact on the bottom line: E*Trade lost an estimated $6 to $8 million in trading for every hour its network was down. Companies doing business with other companies are just as vulnerable as are the highly visible customer-oriented networks.

Global networks need reliable components. This may require redundant equipment, such as processors, storage units, and communications channels. It may even require redundant sites with one site shadowing another in case of emergency. Software should be developed at the highest standards of software engineering, using tools that minimize bugs.

The components of global networks should be subjected to stress tests before they are introduced into the network, and the network itself should be stress tested to determine the limits at which it breaks down. For example, at what transaction rates will bottleneck occur? Or will the transaction simply be lost in the great bit bucket in the sky?

■ USER INTERFACES AND TOOLS

People—and especially people's intellectual contributions—will provide the competitive advantage for the successful next generation company. Integrated manufacturing systems with people and machines working together seamlessly will bring all those human contributions together. People will communicate with and through the manufacturing systems using a variety of computer systems. It is at the user interface that *transparency* issues dominate. The user interface must not impede the flow of data, information, and knowledge to and from the human decision maker.

Interfaces between people and machines should be intuitively easy to use—easier said than done. Arguments between Mac and Windows adherents show that one person's intuition is counter-intuitive for another. The information presented to humans should be in a form that enables immediate comprehension and action. The system should be refined enough that it can acquire and deliver *knowledge* in ways that reflect the context of its use. Since people differ in their abilities and methods for learning and comprehension,[15] the interfaces need to be multisensory. If the extended enterprise is a global one, its systems will include people from diverse cultures. The need for interfaces that are culturally sensitive will be reinforced by their participation.

Figure 17.10 shows the multiplicity of processors and tools that will be typical of the NGM enterprisewide computing environment. These tools can make music or noise depending on whether they are linked in enterprise models and simulations that allow them to run autonomously.

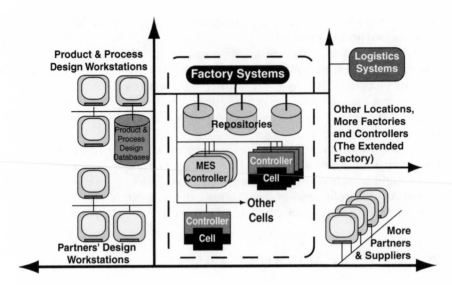

Figure 17.10 Where Are All the Interfaces?

Information technology (IT) was originally built into specific, existing production equipment and processes by developers who often invented the underlying software and interface concepts while focusing on specific markets. The result is a plethora of more-or-less proprietary tools and interfaces embodying incompatible semantics and computing technologies. These incompatibilities are costly:

➤ Incompatibilities lead to uncertainties in data, information, and knowledge as they are transmitted from process to process or from process to human. In turn, the uncertainties lead to slow decision processes and further mistakes in communication.

➤ Data, information, and knowledge are frequently used by only a small subset of the enterprise even though they could be used to advantage elsewhere in the enterprise if they were available in a timely way and in a usable form.

➤ People who move from process to process or from machine to machine must unlearn the old tools and interfaces and learn the new ones.

It's been estimated that these incompatibilities cost U.S. industry many billions of dollars each year. User interfaces and tools that facilitate the seamless integration of human intelligence into systems would reduce these costs. The ideal is:

➤ Transparent interfaces between humans and the NGM company's systems that are consistent across all media and applications, adaptable to cultural and linguistic diversity, use all sensory media appropriately and cost-effectively, and enable transparent programming by all employees. (Transparent programming is programming using nonconventional methods that permit those not trained in explicit programming languages to program new applications in their natural languages and media. Some object-oriented visual programming applications approach being transparent programming languages.)

➤ Support for coupling human and machine intelligence into collaborative, productive, and cost-effective teams.

➤ Aids for manufacturing personnel in quickly finding, analyzing, filtering, and synthesizing vast amounts of data to provide manufacturing decision support.

➤ Real-time modeling and simulation tools to predict product, process, and system failures and provide alternative, perhaps even optimized, solutions to avoid failure and to ensure highest quality.

➤ Real-time tools and applications that are designed to adjust to unanticipated changes to any of the NGM company's systems.

➤ Essential Characteristics of Effective Interfaces

Table 17.4 describes the most important characteristics of an effective interface.

A first essential condition for the near-transparent interface between people and machines that will characterize enterprise integration in NGM companies is *ease-of-use*. There should be minimum impedance between human and machine intelligence. Brain research is beginning to lead to better understanding of the ways human cognitive processes and styles can interact with the computer. This research and other usability R&D is leading to interfaces that are specially designed to meet the needs of individuals participating in collaborative teams.

The common graphical user interfaces (GUIs) found on workstations and PCs provide a starting point for easier to use interfaces; visual languages often provide better ways to convey knowledge; and standard graphical presentations minimize the human effort. There is, however, much more to ease-of-use. For many, the keyboard is a significant impediment. For others, poor ergonomic design can render an interface nearly impossible to use. Ultimately, the human

Table 17.4 Key Characteristics for User Interfaces and Tools

Characteristic	Maturity	Unresolved Issues
Ease of use	PC-based interfaces use common "look and feel" and may incorporate multimedia. Visual programming and object technology reduces the effort in programming for nonprogrammers. There are simple tools that adapt interfaces to specific users (e.g., in word processing programs).	There is a conflict between the idea of interfaces incorporating common "look and feel" and that of adapting the interfaces to the individual cognitive styles of users.
Multisensory input and output	The keyboard and optical character recognition are the most mature I/O. Speech recognition and synthesis are OK for many applications, but may require training overhead. Virtual reality offers the integration sensory I/O. Tactile sensors are available, but not often employed.	Virtual reality still needs to be coupled with product, process, and facilities models to build realistic and affordable simulations that employees can use to learn and to experiment with new processes.
Culturally sensitive systems	More flexible data repositories are allowing discipline-oriented groups to have common sets of data presented in discipline-specific language. Systems for machine translation from language to language systems are beginning to move into practical applications.	Full function machine translation systems are costly and do not vet provide high quality translations for general applications. No tools exist to adapt computer programs and systems easily to specific cultural norms.
Knowledge acquisition, representation, and delivery	Some automated knowledge acquisition systems use learning and other advanced AI algorithms. Methods for data acquisition and for the fusion of data obtained from several sources are improving. Knowledge representation, using rules, concept definition languages, and so on is becoming practical. Search and retrieval algorithms often incorporate learning to develop context sensitivities. Presentation of knowledge is increasingly tailored for use of multimedia.	There is a need for a concept representation able to represent the time-dependent, multidimensional products and processes of manufacturing and for the tools that can articulate the concepts into useful documents in a variety of natural languages.
Missing and uncertain data	There are data acquisition techniques that build redundancy into data sets and analysis techniques that compensate for missing data. Standard statistical methods and stochastic methods can be used to compensate for uncertain data.	There is a need for adaptive, context-sensitive or model-based techniques for identifying and compensating for missing or uncertain data in critical decision-making applications.
Enterprise modeling and simulation	There are existing enterprise modeling tools (e.g., those based on the IDEF modeling protocols).	There are few tools to model time varying manufacturing enterprises.

interface must break away from the keyboard and accommodate *multisensory input/output (I/O)*. There is need for interfaces that include auditory and tactile sensors, as with virtual reality.

An NGM company may have a unifying companywide corporate culture. However, it is also likely to incorporate a wide variety of other cultures—the traditional functional cultures of finance, engineering, production operations, and so forth, and the ethnic and linguistic cultures found within the distributed workforce. Integrated systems will need culturally sensitive interfaces designed to reduce the overhead of learning and using unfamiliar languages couched in foreign cultures.

The user interface ultimately is only as good as the underlying tools for knowledge acquisition, representation, and delivery. Computer science and artificial intelligence have gradually moved beyond the era of database schema and then expert systems to model- and case-based acquisition, representation, and delivery. The presentation to humans of the knowledge needed for complex decisions remains difficult. Note that the knowledge representation should be language- and culture-neutral, but that knowledge acquisition and especially knowledge delivery need to be culturally sensitive. Companies are learning from their web sites about cultural sensitivity. These lessons, often learned through customer reaction, are as valid within global enterprises building portals for their Intranets as they are for interactions with customers. Some of the considerations are:

➤ Symbols don't have the same meaning from country to country. An analogy to the slippery slope of an icy mountain isn't going to have much meaning in Singapore.

➤ Color evokes different responses. A black background that is effective in the United States may have sinister connotations in Latin America. A figure dressed in white may evoke a joyful response in Italy, but be thought to be in mourning in China.

➤ Gestures can evoke even more visceral responses. One country's friendly wave is another's invitation to fight.

➤ Modesty is in the eye of the beholder. Some parts of the body are sacred (the top of a child's head) and others are offensive (the bottom of the foot) in Thailand.

English is not the same in England, Australia, India, and the United States. An English-based system may require interfaces specialized for each country, or alternatively a neutral version understood in all four countries. Similarly, Spanish is not the same in Spain, in

Argentina, and in Mexico. Technical words especially may differ from country to country. And Chinese presents special problems—with very different major dialects (Mandarin, Cantonese, Taiwanese) overlaid on more than 200 regional languages and with at least two important character sets.

The integrated systems of an NGM company will have to support decisions that may be made under extreme time pressures. The humans and the automated systems will need to deal with missing or uncertain data.

Enterprise modeling and simulation tools will be required for strategic and operational decision making. They are required for enterprise investment decisions as well as for business, process, and product modeling. These tools should have provision for inputs of NGM Company metrics in real time and the capability of modeling a mix of real and simulated operations.

■ EXERCISE

Think of the information system in your company that is most important to your work.

➤ What are the strengths of the information system? What are the weaknesses?

➤ Where does the data the system uses come from?

➤ Can you obtain results from the system anytime you need them? Do time delays in the information system inhibit the quality of your work or your productivity?

➤ Does the information system easily communicate with other systems when you need knowledge from them?

➤ Can you use the system to provide the results for which you are responsible to other people using other systems?

➤ What problems do other people have when they use the system?

➤ What would be your major criteria for system design if you were to redesign the information system?

■ NOTES

1. Stan Davis and Christopher Meyer, *Blur: The Speed of Change in the Connected Economy* (Reading, MA: Addison-Wesley, 1998).

2. Richard Bolton, NIIIP Presentation, CTS/AUTOFACT'98. See also the NIIIP web site at www.niiip.org

3. J.J. Mills, "A Basis Model for Agile Computer Integrated Manufacturing," *Proceedings of the Third International Conference on CIM,* (Singapore, 1995).

4. J.J. Mills et al., "The Systems Integration Architecture: An Agile Information Infrastructure," *Information Systems Development for Decentralized Organizations,* (eds.) A. Solveberg, J. Krogstie, and A.H. Selltveit, (Chapman Hall, 1995).

5. "A Reference Model for CASE Frameworks," *ECMA Technical Report TR/55* (European Computer Manufacturers Association, Geneva, 1983).

6. A.I. Wasserman, "Tool Integration in Software Engineering Environments," in *Proc. Int'l Workshop on Environments,* (ed.) F. Long, (Berlin: Springer-Verlag, 1990) pp. 137–149.

7. A.W. Brown and J.A. McDermid, "Learning from IPSE's Mistakes," *IEEE Software,* (March 1992) pp. 23–28.

8. *SEMATECH CIM Application Framework Specification V 1.3* (SEMATECH, Austin, 1994). Available for download from the SEMATECH web site.

9. *Defense Information Infrastructure: Common Operating Environment Introduction and Run Time System Document: REV2.0* (U.S. Department of Defense Department of Information Systems Management, Washington, 1996). Available for download from the Department's web site.

10. *NIIIP Reference Architecture* (NIIIP, Inc., 1998). Available from the NIIIP home page at www.niiip.org

11. *CORBA: Architecture and Specification,* (Boston: Object Management Group, 1996).

12. See the DCE web site at www.opengroup.org/dce/

13. W.A. McCrum and K.G. Beauchamp, "Open System Interconnection," *Information Technology and the Computer Networks* (New York: Springer-Verlag, 1984).

14. "Software Hell," *BusinessWeek,* (December 6, 1999) pp. 104–118.

15. Howard Gardner, *Frames of Mind: The Theory of Multiple Intelligences, Tenth Anniversary Edition* (New York: Basic Books, 1993).

Chapter 18

Measuring the NGM Company

WEDNESDAY, 1:30 PM: HOW GOOD ARE WE?

The professor from the local Business School was here. This was the right time to think again about how BAI could achieve its strategic goals. On Monday, you'd thought about them in terms of a balanced set of perspectives or views of the company. Then you'd spent your time on the resources and processes BAI had available—or would have in the future. Now it was time to tie the resources and the processes back to the goals.

The professor had worked in a major manufacturing company for several years before she'd gotten a Ph.D. and come to the university. When she was in industry, she'd struggled with her company's investment strategies—and continued that as her field of research. There still weren't foolproof ways to make investments. But she had a discipline, based on ideas that had been promoted by Kaplan and Norton,[1] that might tie BAI's operational strategies to its corporate goals. And that might help you make better investment decisions.

■ STRATEGIC GOALS AND METRICS

Why do manufacturing companies exist? While the owners and leaders of companies may have many secondary social or intellectual

380

purposes, the primary purpose of a manufacturing enterprise now and in the future will be to provide solutions, combinations of goods and supporting services, to internal or external customers, generally for a profit.

In Chapter 3, we discussed the needs of Next Generation Manufacturing (NGM) companies for a set of strategic goals balanced from several points of view, or *perspectives*. We used the four perspectives described by Kaplan and Norton, in their popular book, *The Balanced Scorecard*[1] (see Figure 18.1) as a starting point. These perspectives focus management attention on four kinds of goals for the business:

1. The customary financial goals that every company seeks to achieve.
2. Goals related to the way customers see the company.
3. Goals relating to the efficiency and effectiveness of the company's operations.
4. Goals relating to the ways in which the company and its people prepare for the future through learning and growth.

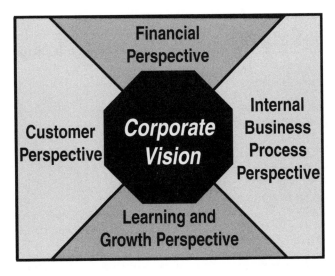

Figure 18.1 Four Perspectives for Strategic Planning

As we have seen, the NGM Report makes two important assertions:

1. Globalization will so fundamentally change the rules of competition that no company can survive unless it sees itself as a player in a tempestuous global sea of competitors and markets.
2. The best defense in the global competition is innovation—being first with the best ideas.

This means that a manufacturing company needs to have goals in two additional perspectives, which we call the *Globalization Perspective* and the *Innovation Perspective*. (Kaplan and Norton consider Innovation within their *Growth and Learning Perspective*.)

Given strategic goals in each of these perspectives, the company can define metrics. Once the metrics are chosen, they can be used to guide investments in operational strategies and implementation substrategies. The objective is prioritizing the many possible actions to achieve a balanced improvement in the company's performance. A specific prioritization strategy, for instance, might give precedence to actions that provide improvement in several perspectives.

Measurements will show whether the company is making progress toward the goals and if the measurements in any set of goals lag behind, the company has warning that it is going out of balance.

➤ Financial Metrics

The twenty-first-century company will need to show sustained profitability and shareholder value. Only rarely will the company enjoy a steady revenue stream from a "cash cow" without continually refreshing the base product family to meet evolving competition. Suggested goals and metrics are:

Return on Investment

The most important financial measure for the NGM company is return on investment (ROI). ROI is the amount of money earned by a business over a predetermined period divided by the amount of capital invested in the business.

Earnings Change per Invested Dollar

A measure for assessing a company's competitiveness in the market place and each incremental investment should result in a growth of earnings. The higher the growth rate, the more effective the corporate business strategy. A reduced growth rate introduces questions about the strategy and could be indicative of a number of factors, such as rising operating costs, price erosion, or shrinking market share.

Turnover Rates

Turnover rate is the number of times that the capital invested in a business is utilized during a 12-month period. Turnover rate is a measure of the efficiency with which a company or the extended enterprise uses its available capital.

Margins

Margin is defined as percentage of sales revenues retained as profit. Margin is important as a companywide metric, as a metric of the extended enterprise, and as a metric of product line and market segment.

Percentage of Revenues from New Products and Markets

In an NGM company, sustained revenue will come from customizing existing product platforms for small batches of discrete, differentiated products; differentiated products for new markets; and the introduction of new product platforms. The percentage of revenues derived from products introduced within the last 12 months and the percentage from markets developed within the last 12 months provide measures of the dynamism of the company.

Supplemental Financial Metrics

Additional important financial metrics include:

> ➤ The average time between the start of an investment and the time when it begins to contribute to earnings.
> ➤ Revenue per full-time equivalent employee.
> ➤ Costs versus competitors' costs.

➤ Customer Metrics

Customers' current and future needs for and acceptance of the NGM company's products and services will drive the company. The goals must relate both to the business results from any customer relationship as well as to making the relationship desirable, from the customer's point of view.

Revenue Growth by Market Segments and Product Lines

The revenue growth over time produced by product lines and within market segments is key to strategic marketing choices. However, in the dynamic NGM era, different market segments and different product lines will be at different levels of maturity. Therefore, it is important to track revenue growth in order to understand the dynamics of any given market segment or product line at any one time.

Net Profit by Customer or Segment

Mass customization is a subtle, two-way street. The NGM company will view customers more as individuals than as members of large groups. The decision to offer, or not offer, products and services often will be based on the actual or potential demand and resulting profitability of the individual customer or small market segment.

Customer Perceptions

Ultimately, in a fiercely competitive industry, customers will buy from the manufacturer whom they perceive will provide the best total package of tangible and intangible value. Measuring the customers' perceptions of the company and its products provides a better insight than do internal measures relating to customers. Typical metrics are degree of customer satisfaction, product preferences, the company's preferred status with the customer, and retention. These metrics are especially valuable if they also compare customer perceptions of the competition.

Supplemental Customer Metrics

Additional important customer metrics include:

➤ Total cost to the customer of product or service solutions (life-cycle cost).

➤ Elapsed time to fulfill a customer need.

➤ Percentage of products not delivered as and when promised.

➤ Mean-time products are out of service for repair.

➤ Operations Metrics

The NGM company's operations will incorporate the lessons of lean and agile manufacturing and optimize time, quality, and cost factors. Every operation will be expected to contribute directly to realization of the company's strategic goals and profitability.

Break-Even Time for Products and Processes

Products and processes that are leading edge today will be obsolete tomorrow. Therefore the investment in a product or process should provide a profit quickly, before it is rejected by a fickle market or replaced by improved technology. Break-even time is the time in which revenues from a product or attributable to a process have returned the original investment and are starting to produce a profit. This assumes that products are priced on the total expected sales and average unit lifecycle costs, not on first cost.

Percentage of Six-Sigma Designs

A Six-Sigma design is one that is executed to minimize the rework at any point in the product or process lifecycle, targeting for a zero reject rate. Any upgrade should be designed to the same standards as the original design and should clearly enhance the functionality or reduce the cost of the product or process.

Rate of Productivity Improvement

In the NGM company, continuous gains in productivity will be a given. The metric is a measure of the rate at which improvement happens.

Accuracy and Completeness of Information-Provided Work Units

The operations of a company whose success is based on its optimal use of its intellectual assets must provide those assets, accurately, where and when they are needed. The metric is the percentage of tasks that fail for lack of accurate and complete information provided to a work unit.

Supplemental Operations Metrics

Additional important operations metrics include:

- ➤ Time to obtain product or project status.
- ➤ Cost of scrap and rework as a percentage of sales.

➤ Globalization Metrics

We depart from Kaplan and Norton by adding the global perspective that is so fundamental to the future of manufacturing. Globalization includes the globalization of markets, products, and production.

Market and Major Account Share by Geographic Region

Market share, the percentage of a given market that the company holds, provides an important basis for competitive position. Major accounts may be thought of as distinct markets. This metric is a measure of universality and effectiveness of the market strategy and product acceptance.

Market Penetration by Geographic Region

Since the markets in the various geographic regions mature at different rates, market penetration will provide a measure of the remaining opportunity and guide regional or country strategies.

Percentage of Employees Engaged in Trans-National Teaming

A responsive NGM company will focus all of the resources it needs, from any of its globally distributed operations, to meet a local market opportunity. This metric is a measure of the utilization of the knowledge and skills of the total personnel resources of the company.

Supplemental Global Metrics

Additional important globalization metrics include:

- ➤ Percentage of systems integrated.
- ➤ Information systems availability.

➤ Innovation Metrics

The NGM company will live by the timely and competitive use of the best available knowledge employed in new and creative ways. The innovation perspective recognizes this all-important quality explicitly.

Percentage of Revenue Invested in R&D and in Market Development

An important measure of the vitality of an NGM company will be its investment in innovation. There are three elements to innovation:

1. R&D of new technologies, products, and processes
2. Pilot implementations
3. Creation of new markets

The metric is the annual investment in innovation as a percentage of annual revenue.

Earnings Attributable to Innovations

It is not enough to have a flow of innovations. Innovations should make visible contributions to earnings commensurate with investments.

Percentage of Compensation Attributed to Innovation Contributions

Employee rewards should be aligned with their innovative contributions to the company. While new ideas should be rewarded, the emphasis should be on their successful implementation. The compensation plan should include rewards based on earnings attributable to innovations.

Supplemental Innovation Metrics

Additional important innovation metrics include:

➤ Average product and process lead (or lag) times relative to competition.

➤ Average time to develop and implement next product or process.

➤ Learning and Growth Metrics

The Kaplan/Norton perspective on learning and growth includes innovation, which we have amplified in a separate perspective. The learning and growth perspective provides a sense of the company's readiness to accept and master change.

Qualification Level and Percentage Qualified for Teaming

The NGM company will function by teaming. Teaming is a learned skill and companies will want a workforce highly skilled in teaming. The metric is the percentage of employees trained to established standards.

Cost of Training and Retraining to Meet Existing Job Standards

In an innovative company, training in new technologies and processes will be an ordinary, expected, expense. A more important measure of workforce readiness is the cost of education and training so that employees have an adequate knowledge and skill base for the current generation of technologies and processes.

Perceptions of Trustworthiness

In NGM enterprises, a good company will be one that its stakeholders—customers, partners, and suppliers, shareholders, and employees—can trust to meet or exceed its commitments and to act reliably and constructively as conditions change.

Supplemental Learning and Growth Metrics

Additional important Learning and Growth metrics include:

➤ Percentage of critical decisions made by work units and individuals.

➤ Information systems literacy rate.

➤ Summary

Table 18.1 summarizes the metrics. Most companies will choose a subset of the suggested metrics, or alternatives, as the guideposts for

Table 18.1   NGM Strategic Metrics

Financial Perspective	Customer Perspective	Operations Perspective
Return on investment (ROI)	Revenue growth by targeted market segment and product lines	Break-even time for products and processes
Change in earnings/ $ invested	Net profit by customer or segment	Percent of Six-Sigma designs
Turnover rate and margins	Customer perceptions of products and fulfillment process	Rate of productivity improvement
Percent of revenues from new products and markets		Accuracy and completeness of information provided to work units
Cash-to-cash cycle (from inception to first cash returns, by expenditure or investment)	Total cost to the customer of product or service solutions (life cycle cost)	Time to obtain product or project status
Revenue/Full-time Equivalent Employee (FTE)	Elapsed time to fulfill a customer need	Cost of scrap and rework
Costs versus competitors' costs	Mean time products are out of service for repair	

Global Perspective	Innovation Perspective	Learning and Growth Perspective
Market and major account share by geographic market	Investment in R&D and market development as percent of revenue	Percent, level of teaming qualifications
Share of total market potential	Earnings attributable to implemented innovations	Cost of training for the skills and knowledge to meet job standards
Percent of employees engaged in transnational teaming	Percent of compensation attributable to innovation	Customers', partners' and suppliers' perceptions of trustworthiness
Percent of systems integrated	Average product/process lead (lag) relative to competition	Percent of critical decisions made by individuals and work units
Information systems availability for all employees	Time to develop and implement next product, next process	Information systems literacy rate

Figure 18.2 A "Quick Look" at Metrics for the NGM Company

their investments and measurements. The important thing is that each of the six perspectives be represented in the chosen subset.

Your company may want to reduce the subset further, to display (see Figure 18.2) a set of summary measures that provide a "quick look" at its position.

■ ACHIEVING STRATEGIC GOALS

Fundamentally, an NGM company's strategic goals will best be achieved if all of the company's activities are designed to help meet them. Assuming the activities are well designed, there remains the need to track them, to ensure that the design is executed and gives the expected results. The way a company goes about doing performance management can support or inhibit the realization of goals.

➤ Performance Management

Your company's performance management systems need both an activity view—is the activity making the contributions it should? and an enterprise focus—is the totality of the extended enterprise's activities achieving the enterprise's goals? You need an enterprise-wide performance management system (see Figure 18.3) to support projects for reducing cost, time, and investment while maximizing enterprise outcomes, all in alignment with the company's vision, mission, and strategic plans.

Figure 18.3 shows two kinds of performance measurement loops. The *tactical loops* provide for the measurement, analysis, and evaluation of individual activities—unit processes, tasks, and so forth. The measurements can be compared with expected measurements, the deviations from expectations analyzed, and appropriate corrective interventions taken. If more than a simple intervention is indicated, the measurements and the underlying processes can be evaluated to see if some sort of change effort is required. The *strategic loop* tracks the achievement of strategic goals, using a balanced set of strategic metrics. These outcomes are the drivers for revisions to strategic goals.

An NGM company's strategies for performance management will have to be *agile,* that is, they should be designed so that they can readily

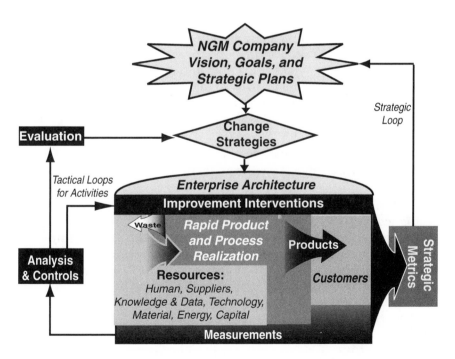

Figure 18.3 Performance Measurement and Management

adapt to unpredicted change. They will also have to be accurate, because NGM companies will have little margin for error.

Performance measures developed for the enterprise—the strategic loop—must include a set of broad metrics that relate to the enterprise processes. For the NGM company, these metrics must place as much emphasis on readiness for future competitions as they do on the financial measurements of today's competition. The NGM Balanced Scorecard and its associated metrics provide a framework for companies that seek to thrive both today and tomorrow.

The performance management system must:

➤ Identify the cost of resources consumed in performing significant activities of the enterprise. NGM companies, in general, will want to account for costs on an activity basis to ensure that each activity is contributing value. The activity-based cost data for product life cycle processes can then be used for a predictive accounting system on which financial analyses of future product offerings can be made. Cost-effective, timely performance measurement feedback of financial and non-financial data is essential to ensure accountability for effective management of implementing operational strategy.

➤ Determine the efficiency and effectiveness of the activities performed and of the utilization of resources. Process improvement requires that all resources (such as material, capital, energy, human, data, technology) be measured so that their utilization is synchronized and controlled to minimize waste and maximize outcomes. This should result in a closed-loop performance feedback process that yields accountability for every process at all levels.

➤ Identify and evaluate new activities that can improve the future performance of the enterprise.

Performance measures for activities—the tactical loops—should be aligned with the strategic goals and metrics. Alignment of tactical change activities—the ones that are more than the routine improvements flowing from continuous improvement programs, but not at the level of pervasive strategic change—is difficult. Of equal importance is prioritization of the activities in order to build an effective investment strategy.

The NGM Report cites a comprehensive pilot study focused on the aerospace industry conducted in 1992–1993 by the U.S. Air Force's Electronic Systems Center with 14 leading aerospace industry companies augmented by management consulting organizations. A comprehensive enterprise integration investment methodology was developed to provide a structured approach to identify the best projects in which to invest. The methodology developed links the strategic business plan of the enterprise to the needs and requirements for process and infrastructure improvements. The methodology also includes a means to form projects with maximal impact on the stated needs and requirements, and to evaluate these projects in terms of investment criteria.

Similar work in the commercial sector led to the definition of *Information Economics*,[2] a methodology for aligning information systems investment strategies with business strategy.

■ EXERCISE

Use the strategic perspectives for the goals of an NGM company, as described in this chapter, to categorize your company's strategic goals and metrics. Build a table using the following template:

Company Goals	Perspective					
	Financial	Customer	Operations	Globalization	Innovation	Learning & Growth

■ NOTES

1. Robert S. Kaplan and David P. Norton, *The Balanced Scorecard: Translating Strategy into Action* (Boston: Harvard Business School Press, 1996).
2. M.M. Parker and R.J. Benson, *Information Economics–Linking Business Performance to Information Technology* (Englewood Cliffs, NJ: Prentice Hall, 1988), and M.M. Parker, H.E. Trainor, and R.J. Benson, *Information Strategy and Economics* (Englewood Cliffs, NJ: Prentice Hall, 1989).

Chapter 19

Integrating the Enterprise for Next Generation Manufacturing

WEDNESDAY, 4:00 PM: THE BOTTOM LINE

After three days you had a lot to digest. There remained the questions: What's the difference between BAI being a collection of smart people with lots of good equipment and BAI being a continuing source of profits and growth? What's fallen through the cracks? Where's the glue that holds BAI together? You knew that you'd heard most—maybe all the answers in the many presentations.

Now your chief strategist is going to talk about enterprise integration. You expect him to review a lot that you've heard, but place it in the context of getting all the smart people and all the good equipment working together to meet BAI's strategic goals.

■ INTEGRATING THE WORKFORCE

A modern manufacturing enterprise, at its best, is a complicated multicomponent, living organism, undergoing constant change with a life force and the coordination to achieve its common purpose. The life force comes from the company's vision and strategic goals, coupled with survival instincts and the will to thrive. Integration provides the coordination of the components as they respond to the goals.

394

Integration is the most important mark of a next generation manufacturing enterprise. Integration is the way the enterprise can respond to the customer quickly and accurately, with no waste of energy or time. It is the prerequisite for globalization. Integration is the facilitator that will bring innovation to the market. It is integration that will keep a company's people, its knowledge, and its equipment, processes, and systems focused on its strategic goals (Figure 19.1). For the NGM company, integration will mean something more, or less, every minute, because the enterprises within which it operates will always be changing.

The *fundamental enabler* for the profitability and survival of the NGM Company of the future will be its integrated human resources—primarily its intellectual resources—as the company's people execute processes. At the most fundamental level, the enterprise is people—the people who are the customers; the people who decide what to build; the designers and developers; the production workers on the shop floor; and those who sell, distribute, service, and recycle its products. At this fundamental level, the integration of the NGM company, of the extended enterprise, is the integration of the activities of people. The central theme of enterprise integration is helping the human resources in NGM enterprises—people and teams of people—to learn, work cooperatively, and communicate. The information technology we discussed in Chapter 17 will make it possible for people to use their intellectual capacities more effectively.

The basic paradigm for the workforce will continue to change from one based on the individual contributor to one based on teams of contributors. Team dynamics will be central to the success of NGM

Figure 19.1 Integration Focuses the Company on Its Goals

companies. Teams will have to form quickly, operate effectively, and dissolve gracefully. There are two aspects of teaming to be considered:

> *Interpersonal teaming.* The workforce of the NGM company will operate in small teams. The small teams will be *empowered,* that is, they will operate semi-autonomously and will make consequential decisions that may affect the success or failure of the company. The teams will take risks for themselves and on behalf of the company. The teams will be transient, operating as teams only for as long as they are needed.

> *Interorganizational teaming.* The work of the NGM company will be accomplished by teams of people, teams that work together to achieve the company's objectives. The interorganizational teams will behave analogously to the interpersonal ones, empowered to make important decisions and take significant actions autonomously on behalf of the entire extended enterprise.

The level of teaming that will be required in the responsive NGM company raises deep issues of trust, culture, and communications. The NGM Report is full of wisdom—but the reason it is so important is not because of any single island of wisdom, important as it might be. The NGM Report is important because it ties the islands of wisdom together and focuses them on dynamic, flexible teaming. The report was written by experts with core competencies, each of which is essential for a successful company, but no one of which is sufficient to ensure success. When you combine all the core competencies found in the NGM Report, you gain a comprehensive view of the successful NGM enterprise.

➤ Defining Enterprise Integration

Enterprise integration (EI) connects and combines people, processes, systems, and technologies so that the right people and processes have the right intellectual and physical resources at the right time. Enterprise integration includes all the activities necessary to ensure that the NGM company does function as a coordinated whole, by itself and within extended enterprises. Enterprise integration is the:

> Pursuit of a set of strategies, concepts, and values that guide the on-going business and product-related processes, implemented through the company's workforce, technology, and management practices, into alignment with the company's specific performance

objectives. The strategic goals for a next generation manufacturing enterprise, which we discussed in Chapters 3 and 18, are the starting point. They are the articulation of purpose on which the whole enterprise should act.

➤ Use of enablers for well-managed physical, financial, people, and information infrastructures that bind the processes together.

➤ Development of enabling practices and technologies required to overcome the barriers and address the drivers and attributes:

—Flexible, responsive organizational structures adapted to twenty-first century needs

—Fully implemented, seamless, global networks

—User interfaces and tools that enable seamless knowledge access and exchange

—Tools to mitigate the negative effects of physical and cultural complexity that will permit effective distributed, global operations across cultures

➤ Use of metrics and tools for operational strategies that will enable the companies to implement and attain NGM attributes.

Enterprise integration has two important characteristics:

1. *It is a discipline,* a way of thinking and an understanding of how—in a given company—people, business processes, and technology are connected and combined so that the right people and processes have the right information and the right resources at the right time. The discipline is needed to establish solid, reliable interfaces—interfaces among people, between people and processes and systems, and among processes and systems—and to ensure that there is coverage of all important issues.

2. *It is the set of activities* a company uses to allow its people, processes, and technology function as a whole, including, for example, information systems integration.

Enterprise integration is an inherently dynamic phenomenon that cannot be solved as a static problem. Enterprise integration requires a *systems* view of the NGM company. One might think of a next generation extended enterprise as a biological organism with neurons firing in parallel, but always focused on satisfying a life-sustaining need. Decisions are guided by a framework or a set of rules leading to decisions and effects that are communicated to all parts of the organism that have the need to know. In the NGM company, that framework is enterprise integration.

There are two related sets of issues in manufacturing enterprise integration:

1. Internally, the decision-making, business, and product-related processes of the NGM company must be integrated to achieve the company's goals. The balanced strategic goals of an NGM company which we discussed in Chapters 3 and 18, or some equivalent, provides an integrated set of goals. Enterprise integration focuses all of the company's resources on meeting the goals.

2. Similarly, the collective decision-making, business, and product-related processes of the extended enterprise must be integrated to achieve the enterprise's goal. The traditional infrastructures that today's manufacturing companies use to enable enterprise integration, infrastructures that are often closed and proprietary, must be opened up to accommodate dynamic participation in extended enterprises.

Enterprise integration is not new—companies have struggled with integration ever since they outgrew what the owner could hold in his mind. What is new for the NGM company is the need to make decisions involving globally distributed partners and operations, much more quickly and accurately—and to do so in the face of rapidly and unpredictably changing conditions. Twenty-first-century enterprise integration will have succeeded if companies can make executive and operational decisions when they need them.

Enterprise integration coordinates the three principle dimensions (see Figure 19.2) that have dominated this book: people as they are organized in the workplace, the processes by which knowledge is transformed for competitive advantage, and the physical systems, processes, and technologies that they use. As any one of the coordinates grows, the resultant point in EI space exhibits greater complexity. Managing the company's response to increased complexity will be essential for the NGM company's success.

In fact, there is a fourth dimension—time. The next generation company will be a dynamic entity. A successful Silicon Valley businessman has the following saying:

It is not the big company that eats the small one, but the fast company that eats the slow one.

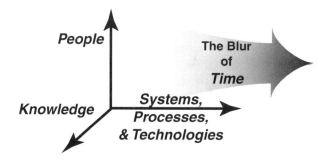

Figure 19.2 The Dimensions of Next Generation Manufacturing Complexity

The world of competitive manufacturing is not standing still. The margins for error are decreasing all the time. An enterprise will be in trouble if it makes mistakes that require rework. Even if the dollar cost is small, a missed delivery schedule can break a product program.

■ KEY ENABLERS OF ENTERPRISE INTEGRATION

The NGM Project identified five essential enablers, which taken together, will position the NGM company for an integrated, competitive response to future opportunities (see Figure 19.3).

The first two—global networks and user interfaces—relate to the information technologies that will enable people and machines to function as integrated systems. We discussed this important aspect of enterprise integration in Chapter 17. As we pointed out, information systems integration is an important part of enterprise integration, but it is certainly not the whole story. If we focus solely on information systems integration, we can overlook the even more important, but less easily defined, challenges of integrating people, cultures, and manual systems.

The remaining three enablers—innovative corporate organization, assists to help people deal with complexity and cultural diversity, and operational strategies driven by metrics—relate to creating a structure and culture that will motivate and enable everyone in the NGM company to work together.

➤ Innovative Organizational Structure and Complexity

A company's organizational structure defines the relationships among people and teams. In the command-and-control world of

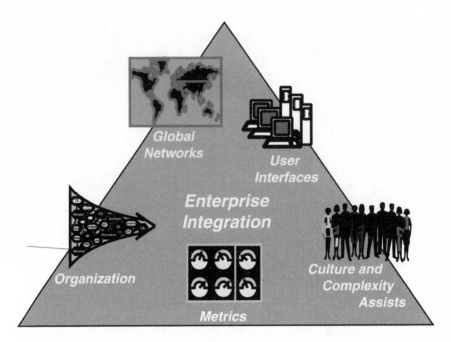

Figure 19.3 Five Enablers for Enterprise Integration

hierarchical organizations, life was pretty simple. You did what your boss told you to do. You told the people who reported to you what to do. Roles were well defined. The company could write procedure manuals for almost all the situations you were likely to see—and there were staff groups who were there to tell you how to handle the things that weren't in the manuals. The company's culture was defined in the manuals and perhaps in its way of dealing with you when you strayed outside the procedure manuals' boundaries.

In Chapter 5, we discussed organization for next generation manufacturing. The trend toward flatter, networked, team-based, globalized organizations introduces much more complexity for everybody. Lines of communication to the corporate office are not prescribed. Procedures are less well defined. Specifications are functional, not prescriptive. Teams or work units have more autonomy, and that means that synchronicity is not dictated by the organizational structure but is created by the responsible activities of the team members. The groups that you are working with may be down the hall, on the other side of the plant, three buildings away, three states away, or on another continent. You may not be able to use the language and cultural clues of the culture in which you grew up. It's almost as if there's a balance of pain principle at work: In return for much more timely and effective responsiveness, you have to figure out how to work without detailed direction and with a bunch of people you don't know and whom you may never see face-to-face. For most workers, this is a level of complexity well beyond what they have experienced in the past and will present a major challenge to them.

There are two broad categories of complexity—physical complexity and cultural complexity. Corporate culture is an integrating force that reduces the complexity by establishing norms for worker expectations and behavior. The complexity of the integrated information systems that bind an enterprise together cuts across both physical and cultural complexity.

Organizational Structure and Process Re-Engineering

Business process re-engineering (BPR), at its best, is a process of simplification. BPR examines processes for their relevance and alignment with what is needed to achieve today's corporate goals and to be ready for tomorrow's. Some of the processes may not have been well thought out. Others may have been corrupted by patches and add-ons. And others may be obsolete or redundant. BPR is grounded in physics—the idea that the best solutions are the ones that are described in the simplest terms and consume the least energy—and popular culture—KISS, or "Keep it Simple. . . ." From either perspective, the goal is to reduce complex problems to the simplest, least costly solutions consistent with their being truthful representations of reality. The BPR question is "What processes are needed to make the system function better—and to add value?" Often the answers result in the elimination of unnecessary work, a sharper specification of the work that is necessary, and a better definition of the interfaces between the tasks with which various groups are charged.

You must conduct BPR with care, however. As we discussed in Chapter 14, the introduction of a change, such as a re-engineered process, should be carefully managed. No process stands alone, so re-engineering will almost certainly will affect upstream, downstream, and peer processes. Some side effects can be predicted, but others will become obvious only after the fact. The NGM company will need to track the effects of BPR and be ready to make adjustments. In the late 1980s, IBM's service division concluded that it was investing too much in reports prepared by branch offices and sent to headquarters. Reporting requirements were chopped from more than a hundred monthly reports to about 10. IBM soon found that they had cut back too much and had to reinstate a half-dozen reports that proved necessary if the business was to run smoothly. The net result of the quick correction was that the business ran smoothly with right-sized information flows and with most of the report writers now free for revenue generating activities.

In your company, you will find a continual tension between imposing processes deemed as "best practices" in all applicable situations and respecting the autonomy of the teams charged with achieving results. That is, any BPR effort must accommodate the local situation and needs. The way to assemble consumer products in a Swedish factory with high labor costs may involve different processes from the way to assemble them in Lithuania where labor costs are much lower.

Physical Complexity

Physical complexity refers to the complexity of modern products, of the international markets where they are sold, and of the globally distributed processes by which they are realized and maintained. Physical complexity refers to the complexity of the transportation and distribution system and information systems. The problems introduced by complexity are exacerbated by the NGM company's need to make decisions very quickly. Time also adds complexity and risk when the NGM company's operations are distributed across many time zones.

One extreme in reducing physical complexity is to replicate one set of processes in every factory. Intel, with its massive fab lines, can do this because they depend on high volumes using the same or similar processes. Companies more tuned to mass customization and requirements for local content, may be unable to adopt this solution.

A goal of the Rapid Product and Process Realization (RPPR) processes we discussed in Chapters 7 to 12 is to mitigate product complexity. They do so by focusing on the customers' needs and on "smart"—that is, knowledge-filled—processes that reduce wastage of time and resources. The integrated product teams deal with complexity by having all of the functional expertise co-located (at least virtually) on the team. The processes are directly targeted to making the best decisions, on time and with the least cost.

The systems discussed in Chapter 12, especially Advanced Planning and Scheduling (APS) and Enterprise Resource Planning (ERP) are the ones being used today to deal with the physical complexity of producing varying products in multiple and geographically separated locations for widely separated markets. In Chapter 17, we discussed the efforts being made to standardize and simplify information systems support.

There are some graphical tools available for representation of complex physical systems. The graphical tools are the most useful for high-level decomposition or for complete representation of less complex subsystems. Given the complexity of the environment in which decisions will be made in NGM companies, and given the complexity of the decisions themselves, there is a need to filter information to that needed for and in a form appropriate to the decision. There's a need to reduce the *decision space* to only those factors that are relevant. The tools should be capable of predicting the effects of local decisions throughout the NGM company in a way that guides the local decision.

Cultural Complexity

Cultural complexity includes issues relating to:

➤ Corporate cultures and work-unit subcultures. Corporate culture is an integrating force that reduces complexity by establishing norms for worker expectations and behavior.

➤ Team-based dynamics and cultures, discussed in Chapters 11 and 16.

➤ The ethnic, religious, and lifestyle cultures found within the NGM Company and among its customers, partners, and suppliers, discussed in Chapter 16.

➤ The cultures embedded in the laws, regulations, and business practices of the various countries in which the NGM Company operates.

➤ Language differences.

➤ Among functional units, and regional ethnic groups within the Company's primary language(s).

➤ Among the several languages the NGM Company may require in the course of its business.

Every culture has its definitions of common sense behavior, behavior that is so ingrained within its culture that "everyone knows. . . . " But not everyone knows. Asian business practices can be baffling to a U.S. NGM Company, but then, U.S. business practices can be equally baffling to an Asian company. The Russian immigrant in Detroit has a different view of common sense than does the Hmong immigrant in Minneapolis, and both differ from the view of the worker in Knoxville who grew up in Appalachia. In Chapter 11, we discussed many of the cultural issues that companies face when they partner in extended enterprises.

In Chapter 16, we discussed cultural complexity within the workforce. While all cultures seem to exhibit some universal behaviors, different cultures have different concerns at different times. For example, the work/life issues that have been much discussed in the United States are not the same as the ones discussed in Japan or South Africa, or in the developing countries where a job is a matter of survival.[1]

Some assists can reduce complexity, in essence by imposing a uniform culture in essential processes. For example, intelligent agents that can conduct simple negotiations are being developed and tested. Typically, relationships between work units within companies or between companies are formalized in standards for business behavior, in agreements and contracts and in the law. The formalities vary from culture to culture and lead to difficulties in the conduct of business and manufacturing operations.

Cultural complexity is dealt with almost exclusively manually, with some augmentation with data collected to satisfy government regulation. Your company's workforce, even if it is contained within a single region of the United States, will be diverse, with little homogeneity of religion, race, or ethnicity, with employees from all sorts of family situations, and with a variety of disabilities. Great cultural variations within the workforce will be the norm. The mix of diversities will vary from work unit to work unit, with each defining a mini-culture within the NGM company.

There is a need for enterprise-level strategies and tools for integrating diversity factors, objectively and constructively, into strategic and operational processes. Companies tend to deal with cultural diversity locally, mostly in the context of relationships within a workforce with diverse ethnic and cultural backgrounds. Few companies do more than train assignees in the cultures of the foreign countries in which they operate.

Aside from the occasional college course that explores issues from a systems perspective, there is very little education about real life complexity in educational institutions or companies. The U.S. educational system is predicated on the decomposition of knowledge into deterministic disciplines. Only rarely are interdisciplinary issues studied, and only more rarely are non-deterministic issues examined. The knowledge enterprise that we introduced in Chapter 15 not only must provide the knowledge that is the content of decisions, it must also provide knowledge that will prepare managers and workers for decision making in the face of complexity and uncertainty. They need to know how to optimize their decisions and actions in synchronization with the whole of the enterprise. The educational systems must improve analytical skills and the ability to synthesize knowledge into practical solutions.

A few companies have established automated (or semi-automated) translation facilities, primarily for internal use, but increasingly as a service offering. The U.S. Department of Commerce has established an English/Japanese translation service and we have begun seeing commercial translation services. The translations are usable by knowledgeable people, although inadequate for literary purists.

■ SUMMARY

Your next generation manufacturing company will be successful *if* you establish a balanced set of goals and shape your effort toward meeting them. Your company will be successful if it is part of an extended enterprise that uses disciplined Rapid Product and Process Realization (RPPR) methodologies:

➤ A systematic integrated product and process development (IPPD) process.

➤ Flexible and modular next generation equipment and processes.

➤ Integrated product teams (IPTs), inclusive of all relevant stakeholders.

➤ Support by an enterprisewide computing environment.

The extended enterprises in which your company participates will be effective *if* they are based on trust and integrity enabled by:

➤ A clear understanding of each partners' core competencies.

➤ Interoperable business and manufacturing systems.

➤ A supportive legal and financial infrastructure.

➤ Honest and ethical behavior.

Your company will be successful *if* you recognize the dynamic nature and value of your knowledge assets, *if* you ensure a reliable supply of new knowledge, *if* you develop processes that nurture and reward learning and innovation, and *if* you actively manage the effects of change and innovation.

Your company will be successful *if* it has a dynamic organization that constantly changes to meet current needs, using the best combinations of traditional and team-based organization. Your company will be successful *if* you employ a well-trained, motivated, empowered, flexible workforce and *if* you contribute to the sustained employability of your people.

But that's not enough. All those things—a well-developed RPPR process, partnering relations across the extended enterprise, knowledge and innovation, and the greatest people on earth aren't enough. They are all necessary, but they aren't sufficient. They aren't sufficient unless you use the five enablers of enterprise integration:

1. Global networks.
2. User interfaces and tools.
3. Innovative organizational structures.
4. Complexity assists.
5. Operational strategies and metrics.

These keep all those resources working effectively to solve the right problems, to make the best decisions, to meet the highest customer expectations, and to optimize the global system that is your company.

■ EXERCISE

Consider your company's newest products:

➤ Who were the people involved with the product lifecycle—from the development of the product concept through to the delivery of maintenance services?

➤ How would you characterize the culture or cultures of the key individuals involved with the product lifecycle?

➤ How effective was communication among these key people? Did anything fall through the cracks? If so, why?

➤ What techniques were used to maintain the product release schedule? Were they effective?

Now, develop a product lifecycle plan for your company's next product (or the product you really want them to market). The design objective is to get the product to market in 60 percent of the time it usually takes your company, and at 40 percent of the cost.

■ NOTE

1. Michael A. Verespej, "Work vs. Life," *Industry Week,* (April 19, 1999) p. 37.

Chapter

Into the Future

■ MANUFACTURING 2010

By 2010, the most successful manufacturing companies will have adopted most of the actions from the NGM Framework for Action. They will focus on the customer. They will be globally competitive. They will be team-based, using human and organizational resources effectively. They will manage intellectual assets as well as they do capital assets. They will apply flexible and adaptive technology. They will be integrated so that there is no wasted time or effort.

A next generation company will be successful if it is part of extended enterprises that use disciplined rapid product and process realization (RPPR) methodologies: a systematic integrated product and process development (IPPD) process, flexible and modular next generation equipment and processes, and integrated product teams (IPTs), inclusive of all relevant stakeholders, all supported by an Enterprise-wide Computing Environment and connected with the global industrial base.

The extended enterprise will be effective if it is based on trust and integrity enabled by a clear understanding of each partners' core competencies, interoperable business and manufacturing systems, and a supportive legal and financial infrastructure.

The next generation company will be organized into empowered teams, employing a well-trained, flexible, and knowledgeable work force. It will contribute to the sustained employability of its work force.

NGM companies will recognize the dynamic nature and value of their knowledge assets, will ensure a reliable supply of new knowledge,

408

and will have processes that reward innovation. They will also actively manage the effects of change and innovation.

The extended enterprise will use global networks, user interfaces and tools, innovative organizational structures, complexity assists, operational strategies and metrics to integrate its activities and support the RPPR methodology.

NGM companies will develop and execute balanced strategies, with financial, customer, internal operations, globalization, innovation, and learning goals and metrics.

Something else: the most successful companies will be continually changing. They will not be static. They will not assume that by employing the best practices of NGM they have reached nirvana. They will understand that their success comes from matching their corporate strategies to the needs of the times, building on a history of change. They won't think of themselves as being far advanced—they'll just be doing what they have to do. One of the things they'll have to do is continually plan for a next generation that looks different from the current one.

➤ Smart and Intelligent Everything

Soon we'll have technology to fabricate even the smallest manufactured goods so they contain "machine intelligence." We'll be at a point where every manufactured good can communicate with every other manufactured good in the world. We'll be close to realizing the science fiction descriptions of "Gaia," a world in which all Creation is interconnected as a single living system. Crazy? No, the technologies are coming fast. Inevitable? Yes, although we can't predict details yet. Scary? Maybe, if we mess up how we use the power of intelligent goods.

There is a convergence of the technologies for micro- and nano-fabrication of electronic and electro-mechanical devices, the technologies for molecular manipulation, and the technologies of genetic and bioengineering. This convergence will lead to deep philosophical pondering of the meaning of life. It will also lead to the incorporation of simple nano-processors in dynamic structures that are constructed at a molecular level, using molecular manipulation and manufacturing or biomanufacturing. The nano-processors may contain a simple set of rules on how to interact with neighboring structures. They may also include the rules for self-replication—analogous to biological DNA. It would seem inevitable that the machine intelligence of the nano-processor will be coupled to the DNA of biologically engineered structures.

While convergence is happening on a molecular level, a more familiar kind of convergence is rapidly happening on a global scale.

That is the convergence of worldwide communication networks using easily transportable and accessible microprocessors and Internet technologies.

In theory at least, there will be no impediment to linking molecular-level nano-processors to the Internet. For example, a molecular manufacturing process going on in Venezuela might be monitored in a control center in Zurich. Or molecular level instrumentation monitoring engine wear in a high performance Cadillac might communicate with a central maintenance facility using GM's OnStar networking links triggering corrective instructions to other "smart" parts in the engine.

■ BEYOND NGM: COMPETING IN A TIGHTLY-COUPLED WORLD

Studies that look toward the middle of the twenty-first century see the extension of the trends described in the NGM Report. Today's trends in manufacturing will slowly evolve as companies adopt NGM policies and procedures. Additional changes will occur as new products, processes, and technologies become available and as new markets and external forces emerge.

Because of the trends identified in the NGM Report, manufacturing across the world will merge into a global network of geographically dispersed extended enterprises and companies. All their operations teams, be they factory, marketing, logistics, legal, organizational, engineering, testing or product services groups, are likely to be drawn from several partners in the enterprise and are just as likely to be geographically dispersed. And that's true, too, of their customer base and their supplier web.

Driven by rapid changes in the business, technology or market, this global network will be constantly changing. New partners and suppliers will replace old ones during the life of the enterprise. Since customers, suppliers, and manufacturers will all be dealing with other suppliers, manufacturers, and customers—each possibly using different communication mechanisms, systems and applications software, and languages, the global networks will have to be standards-based and hardware and software independent. Everyone will be able to communicate data and information in a variety of forms (voice, video, text, data streams, images, etc.) with everyone else, seamlessly, in a manner similar to today's voice telephone systems.

Organizational structure, which will still consist of workers and supervisors, managers and individual contributors, will have to change dramatically. Self-directed teams will become more prevalent and team rewards will become more common.

Many skills and much expertise will be transient. Permanent headcount will be reserved for those few who are judged able to make a sustained contribution to the company's competitiveness. The rest of the skills that are needed will come from shorter term employees, independent contractors, or skill–based guilds that will organize a twenty-first century equivalent of a hiring hall (that will probably be conducted electronically). The skill-based guilds will provide stable pools of expertise, people with certifiable competencies.

➤ A Look at Manufacturing in 2020

The National Research Council's Visionary Manufacturing Challenges (VMC) Study,[1] looking at manufacturing in 2020 and beyond, described the major forces for change:

➤ The competitive climate, enhanced by communication and knowledge sharing, will require rapid responses to market forces.

➤ Sophisticated customers, many in newly developed countries, will demand products customized to meet their needs.

➤ The basis for competition will be creativity and innovation in all aspects of the manufacturing enterprise.

➤ The development of innovative process technologies will change both the scope and the scale of manufacturing.

➤ Environmental protection will be essential as the global ecosystem is strained by growing populations and the emergence of new high-technology economies.

➤ Information and knowledge on all aspects of manufacturing enterprises and the marketplace will be instantly available in a form that can be used for decision making.

➤ The global distribution of highly competitive production resources, including skilled resources, will be a critical factor in the organization of manufacturing enterprises.

Not surprisingly, the list of major forces looks like it could have come out of the NGM Report (see Chapter 2). They continue the trends identified by the NGM Project. But there are three important differences.

First, each of the VMC forces that build on the NGM drivers (see Chapter 2) will be more intense in 2020 than in the first decade of the twenty-first century. If a company is slow to respond to customers, does little to customize its products, lags in innovation, isn't pro-active in using all available knowledge, and has paid little attention to global organization, it may still survive to 2010. The VMC study can be interpreted as saying that that company will be sure to wither away before 2020.

Second, molecular manufacturing and nano-fabrication tech-nologies will radically change the size of a viable factory, even the size of the viable manufacturing enterprise. A self-contained, energy-efficient, low-waste, neighborhood factory, say the size of an enclosed local shopping mall, that can meet most of a community's needs for manufactured goods is a realistic prospect.

Third, sustaining a livable global environment will become an ex-plicit part of every manufacturing company's strategies. Self-interest and government regulation will force companies to adopt environ-mentally friendly policies, practices, and technologies.

The VMC study summarized what is ahead for manufacturing companies. The study described six so-called Grand Challenges that manufacturing enterprises must surmount by 2020:

1. Achieve concurrency in all operations.
2. Integrate human and technical resources to enhance work force performance and satisfaction.
3. "Instantaneously" transform information gathered from a vast array of diverse sources into useful knowledge for effec-tive decisions.
4. Reduce production waste and product environmental impact to "near zero."
5. Reconfigure manufacturing enterprises rapidly in response to changing needs and opportunities.
6. Develop innovative manufacturing processes with a focus on decreasing dimensional scale.

■ TRANSFORMING TECHNOLOGIES FOR MANUFACTURING

➤ Submicron Manufacturing

The seductive attraction of submicron manufacturing lies in the possibility of building dynamic structures molecule by molecule. The vision is of structures that meet all the dimensional and wear attributes specified for a product, and that are built cheaply with little waste or energy overhead costs.

The trends in submicron manufacturing blend four strains of effort:

1. The feature size of integrated circuits is getting smaller and smaller while the production volumes get bigger and bigger. The lower cost of microprocessors is stimulating their use in discretionary applications which, in turn, stimulates investment in processes for even lower cost processors. For example, in 1999, Intel ramped up its production volume for circuits with a feature size of 0.18 microns. At the same time, it began work on a plant to produce circuits with a feature size of 0.13 microns in 2001. (For reference, 0.13 microns is about a quarter of the wavelength of blue light and the size of a small polymer). Intel's plan is that in 2001 the new chips will be fabricated on 200 mm diameter wafers. A year later they will be fabricated on 300 mm diameter ones, for a projected 30 percent per chip cost savings. One result is that microprocessors can be found in increasing numbers of consumer products.

2. Micro-ectromechanical systems (MEMS) are mechanical systems—sensors, motors, nozzles, valves, and others—which fit onto the surface of computer chips. They are built using the same technologies that the semiconductor technology uses for fabricating integrated circuits. At least one MEMS manufacturer has converted an obsolete 2-micron CMOS fabrication line for building MEMS. For example, to create a MEMS pressure transducer, most of the surface material in a defined area of a silicon wafer is etched away. The result is a transparent diaphragm that can be as thin as a single micron. Resistors are then embedded into the surface of this diaphragm and used to translate the slightest movement of the membrane into a voltage.[2]

    MEMS already is a multibillion dollar business with expanding applicability in consumer products, so there is strong motivation to advance the technology by developing better design tools and automating the integrated design and fabrication processes. One thrust in MEMS development is toward submicron-sized electromechanical devices.

    A variant on this is microstereolithography, in which the rapid prototyping technology of stereolithography is applied to build structures with submicron features.

3. The ultimate in submicron manufacturing is molecular nanotechnology (MNT), in which individual atoms and molecules are manipulated to form materials and structures. MNT could enable the production of new materials, whose properties could be tailored for specific applications and whose properties might be varied as structures are built up. Futurists have forecast that intelligent processors would be mated with MNT structures by 2010 and MNT researchers have suggested that the cost of self-replicating materials manufactured by MNT could be reduced to competitive levels by 2020.

4. Molecular self-replication occurs in nature, most notably in life processes involving DNA. Genes are manipulated routinely to grow new organic products. In addition to gene therapies, large-scale applications include the manufacture of tomatoes that last longer with more flavor and the growing of antibiotics in genetically altered alfalfa. The VMC study says, "By 2020, a substantial technology will have been developed for the production of biological materials, the replication of biological materials, and the formation of structures from biological materials."[3]

   Recently, techniques for inexpensive genetic screening have been developed based on the technologies for integrated circuit fabrication. It appears inevitable that the interrelationships between bioprocessing, MEMS, and MNT will lead to the production of hybrid structures that combine DNA and machine intelligence with biological and nonbiological materials. This combination will have profound and perhaps explosive effects on industry and society.

Universities are developing techniques for micromechanical machining processes—microdrilling, micromilling, laser ablation, photo-polymerization, and more. Similarly, there is research on practical applications of micromolding.

■ THE ENVIRONMENTAL IMPERATIVE

While the NGM Project recognized the long-term significance of environmental concerns, it focused on the actions imperative for corporate survival in the first decade of the twenty-first century. The VMC study, in contrast, views environmental compatibility of one of the six greatest challenges to mid-century manufacturing. The world population is projected to grow to 8 billion by 2020.[4] As a viable socioeconomic system, globalization will raise the standard of living in many of the poorer regions of the world, containing billions of people, closer to that in the richer regions. This combination of population growth and increased consumption of manufactured goods will severely strain the global ecosystem.

The VMC study states:

> *The goal of manufacturing enterprises will be to develop cost-effective, competitive products and processes that do not harm the environment, use as much recycled material for feed stock as possible, and create no significant waste, in terms of energy, material, or human resources.*[5]

In the latter third of the twentieth century, efforts for environmental compatibility were often driven by adversarial relationships between special interest groups, governmental agencies, and manufacturing enterprises. The manufacturers' goal became that of achieving compliance with imposed constraints at minimum cost. Current thinking has turned toward a more cooperative understanding of environmental concerns in which *industrial ecology* and *sustainable industry* are expected to lead to a situation in which the consumer, industry, and the environment all win. There are several trends:

➤ The view that products should be designed for minimum environmental impact across the whole of their life cycles is being institutionalized, for example, in the ISO 14000 standard. (See box on page 416.)

➤ Customers are becoming more aware of environmental concerns—especially related to energy production and use, to the scarcity of water, and to landfills for waste management—and are responding with demands for so-called *green* products.

➤ The cost of environmental impacts frequently is being recognized as a component of the product's cost structure or as a contingent liability.

➤ Industry is taking greater responsibility for a product's end-of-life by providing controlled low-cost or no-cost disposal of spent manufactured goods, and recycling them.

In response, successful manufacturers will:

➤ Build environmental knowledge—accurate models of the environmental effects of processes and materials; characterization,

THE ISO 14000 STANDARDS

ISO/TC 207 SPS	Strategic Policy Statement
ISO/TC 207 OM	Operational Manual
ISO/TC 207	Media Implementation of the ISO Media Policy
ISO Guide 64	Guide for the Inclusion of Environmental Aspects of Product Standards
ISO/TC 207/WG 2 TR	Reference Material for Forestry Organizations

Environmental Management Systems

ISO 14001	Specification with Guidance for Use
ISO 14002	Guidelines on ISO 14001 for Small- and Medium-sized Enterprises
ISO 14004	Guidelines on Principles, Systems, and supporting Techniques

Guidelines for Environmental Auditing

ISO 14010	General Principles
ISO 14011	Audit Procedures
ISO 14012	Qualification Criteria for Environmental Auditors

Environmental Assessment

ISO 14015	Environmental Assessments of Sites and Entities

Environmental Labels and Declarations

ISO 14020	Basic Principles
ISO 14021	Self-Declaration Environmental Claims—Terms and Definitions
ISO 14024	Environmental Labeling Type I— Guiding Principles and Procedures
ISO 14025	Environmental Labeling Type III— Guiding Principles and Procedures

416

THE ISO 14000 STANDARDS (CONTINUED)	
Environmental Management	
ISO 14031	Environmental Performance Evaluation—Guidelines
ISO 14040	Lifecycle Assessment—Principles and Framework
ISO 14041	Lifecycle Assessment—Inventory Analysis
ISO 14042	Lifecycle Assessment—Impact Assessment
ISO 14043	Lifecycle Assessment—Interpretation
ISO 14050	Vocabulary

quantification and comparisons of environmental risks; and cost/benefit analyses of environmental choices—into the essential repositories that support RPPR.

➤ View the waste from each step of the manufacturing process as feed stock for another, so that waste production and recycling are internalized as part of the integrated RPPR process.

➤ Use innovative process technologies—net-shape processing, bioprocessing, and molecular self-assembly—to produce customized products with little waste generation.

➤ Seek energy-efficient processes and recover waste heat energy for productive applications.

➤ Form cooperative alliances with consumers, environmentalists, and regulators for environmentally sustainable community-based or regionally-based industry.

By the decade 2011-2020, companies will want to add an *Environmental Perspective* to their balanced scorecard of strategic goals, with metrics of net resources consumed/product, long-term environmental impact liabilities, and environmental operating costs.

There is already a major international effort to put focus on environmental issues. The ISO 14000 family of international standards includes ISO 14001, a standard for Environmental Management Systems (EMS).[6] It covers a broad spectrum of activities that span the product life cycle: waste generation, energy utilization, noise, depletion of natural resources.

As with the ISO 9000 quality standards, you can qualify and register your company as being ISO 14000 compliant. And as with ISO 9000, manufacturers can expect some countries to demand ISO 14000 registration of the manufacturers and their supply chains as the price of doing business in that country.

The EMS provides a structure by which a company can promulgate a clear environmental policy, objectives, and policy, written procedures that reinforce compliance with the rest of the ISO 14000 suite of standards.

EMS AT MILAN SCREW PRODUCTS

Milan Screw Products is a small (30 person) manufacturer of precision fittings that participated in a National Science Foundation (NSF)-funded EMS demonstration project in the mid-1990s and continues to use ISO 14001 to manage environmental concerns. It started by using the NSF's self-assessment tool, then establishing an environmental task group (ETG). The ETG has members from production, support, and management. The ETG is responsible for assuring Milan Screw Product's regulatory compliance and for improving its environmental performance. As with quality initiatives, the ETG found that the EMS required employee "ownership." Employees needed to internalize the mitigation of environmental impacts the way they had internalized the elimination of product defects. The ETG had wide-ranging sessions to identify all the possible processes where environmental concerns might be raised. They came up with 36. These were grouped and prioritized. They put their initial focus on oil recovery. They installed better electrostatic air cleaners that have brought the company to better air quality than required by today's standards and into near-compliance with proposed ones. Implementing a better oil recovery system had the happy side effect of a $20,000 savings. Milan Screw Products has had the luxury of time, with little pressure yet, to implement all the details of ISO 14000, so it is implementing them incrementally as resources permit.

■ MODELING THE EXTENDED ENTERPRISE

In Chapter 7, we introduced the idea of Product and Process Lifecycle Management (PPLM) as a superset of Rapid Product and Process Realization (RPPR) (see Figure 20.1). By 2020, the extended enterprise will take responsibility for the conception, development, production, safe operation and maintenance, upgrading, and recycling or disposal of the product. Similarly, the extended enterprise will take responsibility for the processes used to produce the product and to manage it through its life cycle.

PPLM will supplant RPPR as the defining set of processes that the extended enterprise must support. PPLM will be a complicated, dynamic blend of human and machine intelligence, massive self-consistent knowledge bases, designer materials, flexible multi-purpose equipment, and plug-and-play modular processes. The Virtual Enterprise (Figure 20.2) is the integrated set of models and simulations that describe all of the activities of PPLM. The Virtual Enterprise's models and simulations will have to accurately reflect the complications of PPLM, including the effects of rapid change during the lifetimes of products and processes.

By 2020, companies will need to make very rapid decisions that affect all elements of the extended enterprise and that have implications that reach across the entirety of the product's lifecycle. Because of the complexity of those decisions, they will need tools that can accurately predict the results of alternative courses of action. The best tools will provide prioritization of the alternatives or even optimization to select the best course of action.

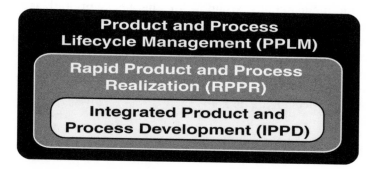

Figure 20.1   Product and Process Lifecycle Management

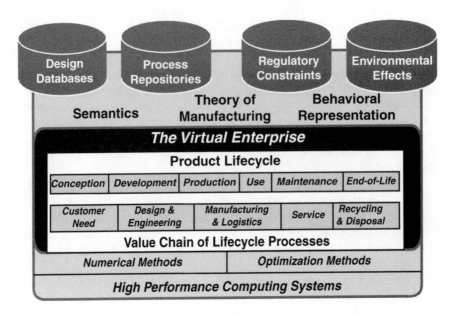

Figure 20.2 Modeling and Simulation of Manufacturing in 2020

The modeling and simulation tools that are the building blocks of the virtual enterprise will have to be self-consistent, incorporating semantics that encompass all the operations and functions, at all levels, of a globally distributed, extended manufacturing enterprise. The semantics and the consolidated knowledge base may be rich enough to yield a comprehensive and systematic theory of manufacturing.

Enterprisewide models and simulations must include human behavior—the most complicated aspect of a complex manufacturing system. The models must account for the behavior and actions of individuals and teams as they relate to each other, to automated or manual processes, and to equipment. The results of the models and simulations must be communicated in a form that will facilitate human decision making. Including all the important aspects of human behavior is a formidable challenge, but one that is required if they are to provide realistic help.

■ THE NEIGHBORHOOD FACTORY

One model for mid-twenty-first century manufacturing that responds to many of the trends is the *neighborhood factory*. Consider the space enclosed in 1970s-sized enclosed malls. Think of one department store sized space, equipped with agile near net-shape and rapid prototyping equipment capable of producing parts as large as a cubic meter with micron precision. It will be driven by a manufacturing execution system integrated with a rich repository of process plans. Most of the materials used by the facility will be relatively common metals, plastics, and composites. A high proportion of the materials will be recycled from used or defective products brought by customers or from recyclables purchased from local waste management companies.

Think of similar sized spaces enclosing an electronic parts facility, a textile manufacturing facility, a biological products facility, and a materials recycling facility. The electronics facility will stock common microelectronic components, but have the capability of building custom microchips for customers' prototypes or special-purpose applications. The facility will assemble most of the consumer electronics used in its service area and assemble common board-level subsystems and finished electronic products for local industry, with most assembly done on demand.

The textile facility, working with the fashion design boutiques, will produce *made-to-fit* outerwear for the residents of its neighborhood. Design boutiques, with their sophisticated tactile VR, will offer custom fabrics with customer specified *look-and-feel*. With body scans for fit and *one-of-a-kind* fabrics, customers generally will have new clothes within 24 hours, the major delay being the time needed to grow or make the fabric. The textile facility will also produce industrial textiles, even composites, with an incredible array of properties.

The biomanufacturing facility will be an ultra-clean facility that will produce designer pharmaceuticals for nearby medical clinics and hospitals. By mid-century, medicine will develop a much greater understanding of individual needs so that most drugs will be designed to meet a very specific need in one individual. The facility will make blood indistinguishable from the normal blood of the person for whom it was intended, similarly matched tissue, and other life-giving substances. Some of the production will be *live-growth* production; for example, of cloned tissue. Live-growth production will include growing the designer fibers for use in the textile facility's fabrics.

The small shops in the connecting corridors of the mall will be replaced by design boutiques for all manner of consumer products. The backbone of neighborhood factory will be a high performance computing and communications system connecting the design boutiques with real-time multi-sensory VR simulators; with product, process, and materials libraries; and with the fabrication and assembly machines.

A substantial fraction of the neighborhood factory's energy needs will be supplied by high-efficiency solar panels on the roof and water usage will be minimized through reclamation and choice of processes.

■ THE END OF THE WEEK AT BAI

As you finish your week, filled with the enthusiasm that comes with a mastery of BAI's vision for the future, and your strategies for getting to it, you delight in the challenges. You think of the many rewarding challenges you have. You have the big picture and enough detail to chart BAI's next generation.

In the strategy meeting, your job was to prepare BAI's leaders for the thrills and joys of mastering the challenges. It's not going to be easy, but it will be deeply satisfying.

You mull over the grand challenges that will face your successors, the people who will lead BAI in the century's second decade. The people with leadership responsibilities for manufacturing will live with change and transformation.

And 50 years from now, manufacturing will be unrecognizable—but it will always be fun. It will always be fun to be the creative force in the economy, to see your products used, to make your contribution to society.

■ NOTES

1. Committee on Visionary Manufacturing Challenges, *Visionary Manufacturing Challenges for 2020* (Washington, DC: National Academy Press, 1998), pp. 9–10.
2. Jean-Michel Karam, "Electronic Design Automation Mainstreams MEMS Design," *Electronic Design,* vol. 46, (July 6, 1998) p. 67.
3. Committee on Visionary Manufacturing Challenges, *Visionary Manufacturing Challenges for 2020* (Washington, DC: National Academy Press, 1998), p. 59.
4. National Research Council, *Linking Science and Technology to Society's Environmental Goals* (Washington, DC: National Academy Press, 1996).
5. Committee on Visionary Manufacturing Challenges, *Visionary Manufacturing Challenges for 2020* (Washington, DC: National Academy Press, 1998), p. 27.
6. Sharon Hogarth, "On the Horizon: ISO 14000," *Manufacturing Engineering,* (March 1999).

Index